T0304674

Maritime Metropolis

Nineteenth-century London was not only the greatest city of its time, but it had an equally immense port. Although the relationship between London and its port shaped development and profoundly affected the lives and livelihoods of its inhabitants, historians have always told their stories separately. Sarah Palmer's authoritative work instead paints a picture of London as a maritime hub driven by trade, shipping, marine insurance, shipbuilding and meeting the needs of seafarers ashore. Drawing on disparate archival materials from dock company records, the National Archives, the London Metropolitan Archives and more, she reveals both the economic importance of international and domestic seaborne trade and the unique urban geography it created. In creating this more interconnected understanding of Britain's capital, Palmer argues that the nineteenth-century transition from sail to steam did not just affect London's port but transformed the metropolis and its economy with an impact comparable to that of the railways.

Sarah Palmer is Emeritus Professor of Maritime History, University of Greenwich. She specialises in nineteenth- and twentieth-century national and international maritime economic history, maritime labour, maritime policy and port development.

Cambridge Studies in Economic History

Editorial Board

Gareth Austin: *University of Cambridge*
Stephen Broadberry: *University of Oxford*
Naomi R. Lamoreaux: *Yale University*
Sheilagh Ogilvie: *University of Oxford*
Şevket Pamuk: *Bogaziçi University*

Cambridge Studies in Economic History comprises stimulating and accessible economic history which actively builds bridges to other disciplines. Books in the series will illuminate why the issues they address are important and interesting, place their findings in a comparative context, and relate their research to wider debates and controversies. The series will combine innovative and exciting new research by younger researchers with new approaches to major issues by senior scholars. It will publish distinguished work regardless of chronological period or geographical location.

A complete list of titles in the series can be found at:
www.cambridge.org/economichistory

Maritime Metropolis

London and its Port, 1780–1914

Sarah Palmer

University of Greenwich

 CAMBRIDGE
UNIVERSITY PRESS

CAMBRIDGE
UNIVERSITY PRESS

Shaftesbury Road, Cambridge CB2 8EA, United Kingdom

One Liberty Plaza, 20th Floor, New York, NY 10006, USA

477 Williamstown Road, Port Melbourne, VIC 3207, Australia

314–321, 3rd Floor, Plot 3, Splendor Forum, Jasola District Centre,
New Delhi – 110025, India

103 Penang Road, #05–06/07, Visioncrest Commercial, Singapore 238467

Cambridge University Press is part of Cambridge University Press & Assessment,
a department of the University of Cambridge.

We share the University's mission to contribute to society through the pursuit of
education, learning and research at the highest international levels of excellence.

www.cambridge.org
Information on this title: www.cambridge.org/9781108426534

DOI: 10.1017/9781108699365

First published 2025

A catalogue record for this publication is available from the British Library

Library of Congress Cataloging-in-Publication Data
Names: Palmer, Sarah, 1943– author.
Title: Maritime metropolis : London and its Port, 1780–1914 / Sarah Palmer, University
of Greenwich.
Description: Cambridge, United Kingdom ; New York, NY :
Cambridge University Press, 2025. | Series: Cambridge studies in
economic history | Includes bibliographical references and index.
Identifiers: LCCN 2024019521 (print) | LCCN 2024019522 (ebook) |
ISBN 9781108426534 (hardback) | ISBN 9781108699365 (ebook)
Subjects: LCSH: Port of London Authority. | Harbours – England – London – History. |
Shipping – England – London – History. | London (England) – Economic conditions.
Classification: LCC HE558.L8 P185 2025 (print) | LCC HE558.L8 (ebook) |
DDC 387.109421–dc23/eng/20240719
LC record available at https://lccn.loc.gov/2024019521
LC ebook record available at https://lccn.loc.gov/2024019522

ISBN 978-1-108-42653-4 Hardback

In memory of Glyn Williams

Contents

Illustrations

Figures, Table and Maps

Maps

Preface

This book has had a lengthy genesis. Its origin is an Economic and Social Research Council-supported investigation in the 1980s into the history of the nineteenth-century Port of London undertaken by Tony Henderson and me. Enticed by the voluminous dock company records in the Museum of London/Port of London Archive, we collected and analysed a large amount of material on these firms, which was subsequently reflected in publications. However, I came to recognise that what we had produced was an extremely limited, even misleading, interpretation of London's port history, so this was 'unfinished business'. Nevertheless, in the period that followed, the focus of my research and writing switched to other aspects of the maritime sphere, including public policy, shipping, trade and shipbuilding.

In 1998, I moved from Queen Mary University of London to the University of Greenwich to take up a new post as the director of the then Greenwich Maritime Institute. The interest in the Port of London shown by its postgraduate students, many with a professional background in the maritime sector, persuaded me to return to the subject, taking advantage of the greater historical breadth I had acquired over the intervening years. Involvement in a Greenwich Maritime Institute investigation by Vanessa Taylor into the governance of the River Thames in the late twentieth century further convinced me that the history of the port should not be separated from the metropolitan context, hence 'London and its Port'.[1]

The intellectual and personal debts underpinning this book are many. They start with Tony Henderson, my assistant on the Port of London Project, and the Museum of London's late Bob Aspinall, Chris Ellmers and Alex Werner who enthusiastically shared their immense knowledge of the Port of London Authority (PLA) archive. Chris, in particular, has continued to support and inspire my research ever since we

---

[1] ESRC RES-062-23-3137. Running the River Thames: London, Stakeholders and the Environmental Governance of the Thames, 1960–2010. 1 August 2011–31 July 2013.

first met. Much more recently, Steven Smith assisted me by tirelessly endeavouring to unearth records relating to the creation of the PLA in the National Archives. I have also gained considerably from discussions with Greenwich Maritime Institute postgraduate students. Subsequent research by two of them, Ken Cozens and Dr Robert Forrester, is cited in this study. I have benefited too from the interest and encouragement of colleagues in the Institute and the University of Greenwich, in particular from Roger Knight (who challenged me to write another book), Suzanne Louail, Mary Clare Martin, Vanessa Taylor, Chris Ware and Martin Wilcox.

London has a thriving community of professional and non-professional maritime historians, as shown fortnightly by the British Commission for Maritime History seminar series hosted by King's College London, the events organised by the Royal Museum Greenwich, and the regular meetings and annual conference of the Docklands History Group. These provided an excellent informed local forum for the discussion of aspects of my research. What I owe more generally to other historians, metropolitan and maritime, past and present, based in the UK and overseas, will be obvious from my sources. However, in addition to those already mentioned, I particularly want to acknowledge the stimulus provided by the work of the late John Armstrong, the late Frank Broeze, Roy Fenton, David R. Green, Gelina Harlaftis, Alston Kennerley, Michael B. Miller, David J. Starkey, Malcolm Tull and the late David M. Williams.

Finally, I want to thank my 'merged' family, Jessica, Matthew, Sonia and Jan, as well as my late husband, Glyn, for their love and support of what at times may have appeared to be a baffling commitment.

Abbreviations

GSNC	General Steam Navigation Company
HLRO	House of Lords Record Office
IMEHA	International Maritime Economic History Association
LCC	London County Council
LSE	London School of Economics
MLD	Museum of London Docklands
MP	Member of Parliament
ODNB	Oxford History of National Biography
P&O	Peninsular & Orient Steamship Company
PP	Parliamentary Papers
RC	Royal Commission
SC	Select Committee
TNA	The National Archives

Introduction
London and its Port

Illustration 1 The Pool of London in the mid-eighteenth century. The Legal Quays are to the right of London Bridge. Image: General Views of London, 1766, © London Metropolitan Archives (City of London).

Until its docks closed in the later twentieth century, London remained what it had been since Roman times: a port city. It owed its existence to its role as a gateway, and in the late eighteenth century, port-related activity was central to economic prosperity. London was a port: the port was London. Over the following century, it ceased to be the focus of an increasingly diverse London economy, though no less essential. London's nineteenth-century growth would have been impossible without its port. By the late nineteenth century, its prime function was serving the burgeoning local market for overseas produce created by the capital's population growth. By then, 14 million tons of shipping with cargoes entered each year. A hundred years earlier, the figure had been 2 million.[1]

Geographically, the port continued to shape London. As activity expanded eastwards beyond its historic heart, industrialisation and settlement followed, as in the case of downriver West Ham. There was more to the port than handling shipping and cargoes, though this employed large numbers of skilled and unskilled workers as well as the owners of facilities and their managers. The industries generated included victualling, shipbuilding and repairing, rope and sailmaking, sugar refining, milling and serving the needs of seamen ashore. In the City, as well as elsewhere in London, there were many merchants, shipowners, shipbrokers, insurers and bankers. In short, as well as being much else, London was a maritime metropolis.

The capital has never lacked historians. Jerry White's magisterial three-volume study spanning the eighteenth century to the twentieth century, Roy Porter's *London. A Social History* and Schneer's *London 1900. The Imperial Metropolis* are three outstanding examples of the fascination its past continues to exert.[2] To a varying degree, political, social, economic and cultural facets have separately received attention, and continue to do so. Few general London histories, academic or popular, pay much attention to its port, although publicly momentous events like the 1800s dock building boom, the decline of shipbuilding and the 1889 Great Dock Strike usually feature. Even where there is a narrower focus, such as economic history or mercantile activity, mentions are few.[3] This is not to suggest that there are not studies that throw valuable informed light on elements of London's port history. Indeed, as will be clear from its chapters, without their assistance, this book would have been impossible to write. But it is fair to say that you could read a lot of London history without gaining much awareness of the maritime dimension.

London's port itself has had relatively few historians. Until the appearance of Rodwell Jones, *The Geography of London River* (1931) and James Bird's *The Geography of the Port of London* (1957), the only work that traced it from early origins was Joseph Broodbank's two-volume history

---

[1] PP 1902 XLIV.1 [Cd. 1153], RC on the Port of London, Appendices, 232–9. See Appendix A.

[2] Jerry White, *London in the 18th Century, A Great and Monstrous Thing* (Vintage Books, London, 2012); *London in the 19th Century, A Human Awful Wonder of God* (Vintage Books, London, 2008); *London in the 20th Century, A City and Its People* (Bodley Head, London, 2001); Roy Porter, *London, A Social History* (Penguin, London, 1994); Jonathan Schneer, *London 1900. The Imperial Metropolis* (Yale University Press, New Haven & London, 1999).

[3] For example, see Michael Ball and David Sunderland, *An Economic History of London 1800–1914* (Routledge, Oxford, 2001); David Kynaston, *The City of London. Volume I: A World of Its Own 1815–1890* (Pimlico, London, 1995).

published in 1921. As a senior dock company officer, he was a partici-
pant in the most recent developments he covered and was far from neu-
tral. However, by separately considering interests such as wharfingers,
lightermen and the Thames Conservancy, Broodbank highlighted the
port's complexity. As geographers, Rodwell Jones and Bird emphasised
physical and industrial aspects, avoiding the impression that docks were
the most significant aspect of operations. More recently, there is Peter
Stone's admirably comprehensive narrative *History of the Port of London.
A Vast Emporium of All Nations* (2017). However, neither Stone nor
Broodbank approach their subject from an analytical perspective or set
developments within a broader context.[4]

Individual aspects of London's maritime past have attracted far more
attention. For the 'long nineteenth century' between 1780 and 1914,
there is a considerable body of specialist work dealing with port architecture, marine engineering, shipping, shipbuilding and port labour, from
which I have benefited. But what both the general port histories and
more specific investigations have in common is a separation of the port
from London's wider history. It is as if these spheres existed in isolation
from the metropolitan environment. Yet it was this that made it unique.

I pointed out some years ago that port historians had rarely treated
their subjects as urban entities.[5] This criticism no longer applies to the
same extent, as Michael B. Miller's *Europe and the Maritime World* (2012)
and John Darwin's *Unlocking the World. Port Cities and Globalisation in the
Age of Steam 1830–1930* (2020) testify.[6] There is also a greater willingness to recognise that the basic functional characteristics of all commercial ports – trade gateways handling cargoes and shipping – provide a
basis for the comparative analysis of port cities themselves.[7] But as a port
city in the long nineteenth century London defied comparison. It was a
world city before others followed. As a great national and European marketplace, financial and political capital and an imperial power, already

---

[4] Joseph G. Broodbank, *History of the Port of London, Volumes 1 and II* (Daniel O'Connor,
London, 1921); L. L. Rodwell Jones, *The Geography of London River* (Methuen & Co.,
London, 1931); James Bird, *The Geography of the Port of London* (Hutchinson, London,
1957); Peter Stone, *The History of the Port of London. A Vast Emporium of Nations* (Pen &
Sword, Barnsley, 2017).
[5] Sarah Palmer, 'Ports', in Martin Daunton (ed.), *The Cambridge Urban History of Britain*
(Cambridge University Press, Cambridge, 2000), 133–50.
[6] Sarah Palmer, 'History of the Ports', *International Journal of Maritime History*, 32 (2020),
426–33: Michael B. Miller, *Europe and the Maritime World. A Twentieth-Century History*
(Cambridge University Press, Cambridge, 2012); John Darwin, *Unlocking the World. Port
Cities and Globalization in the Age of Steam, 1830–1930* (Allen Lane, London, 2020).
[7] Robert E. Lee and W. R. Lee, 'The Socio-Economic and Demographic Characteristics of
Port Cities: A Typology for Comparative Analysis?', *Urban History*, 25 (1998), 147–72.

by the early nineteenth century, it brought together 'all treasures that the four quarters of the globe possess' and, as we shall see, then continued to do so as a new world economy forged by steam power emerged.[8] Underpinning these developments was a physical and human infrastructure of facilities and working lives.

My study is not a conventional port economic history. Measures of efficiency, comparisons of performance with other ports and detailed investigation of trade flows, costs and earnings are largely irrelevant to its core purpose. As the title indicates, it is about the relationship between London and its port. By describing this great city as a 'Maritime Metropolis' I am not suggesting that this is the only, or even prime, historical description London merits. It might fit the late eighteenth-century city to some extent, but certainly not the diversity and scale of the metropolitan economy as it developed thereafter. London was far less a maritime city in 1900 than in 1800, not because port activity had diminished but because this was dwarfed by so many other aspects. Even so, the description highlights what for some will be an unfamiliar aspect of London's history and accords it the prominence it deserves.

The period covered was one of major technological transformation – the transition from sail to steam shipping – so the impact of this on port facilities, management and labour is a central theme. The fact that there was a real difference between how the Port of London functioned before and after steam technology took hold is the justification for the book's division, not intended to be exact, into the first and second halves of the nineteenth century. As a long-established port city, with trade global before much of the rest of the world, it did not suffer the extreme economic and social traumas experienced by some new or remodelled port cities. But like these it had to adapt to the consequences of the triumph of liner trades, with its effect on the balance of power and influence in the capital's maritime communities.

As well as new material, the book brings together a range of sources, primary and secondary, antiquarian and scholarly, generated independently and rarely considered together. From the maritime history perspective, sail to steam was an obvious theme. Other themes, of possibly greater importance for the historical record, emerge from what is a wide-ranging investigation covering at least 130 years of London's past. If the concept of *laissez-faire*, for example, were not already almost entirely

---

[8] See Martin Daunton, 'London and the World', in Celina Fox (ed.), *London – World City 1800–1840* (Yale University Press, London and New Haven, 1992), 21–41; the quotation is from *Letters from Albion Gale* (Curtis and Fenner, London, 1814), cited in Celina Fox, 'Introduction. A Visitor's Guide To London World City' in Celina Fox, (ed.), *London – World City* (Yale University Press, London & New Haven, 1992), 11–20.

excised from the lexicon of reputable discussion of the mid-Victorian State, it would be seriously undermined by the evidence here. For government the Port of London had unique status: its success was a measure of national prosperity. It could not be entirely left to its own devices. There was an enduring sensitivity to the performance of London's great port. In 1799, radical government action, with financial commitment, led to the introduction of docks and other reforms. In 1909 came creation of the Port of London Authority, close to nationalisation. The years between these two benchmarks were marked at first by protectionist policies, which influenced the way the port functioned. When free trade brought these to an end and customs officers were a less dominant government presence, there came Board of Trade shipping offices and active suppression of crimping on the Thames.

The London Thames was both a public highway and a sewer. These functions have garnered scholarly attention from transport and environmental historians, but the river's role in serving wharves and docks has generally been overlooked.[9] Yet for Londoners the shipping and lighters that crowded the water, attracting the attention of artists, were daily reminders of London's trade and commerce. Major changes to the capital's riverscape – the replacement of Old London Bridge by the New, along with the construction of the Thames Embankment and Tower Bridge – were issues for its port. So too was the role of the Corporation of London and subsequently the Thames Conservancy Board in river management. Conflicts between port and river users, between urban improvers and waterfront businesses, as also between shipowners and those responsible for dredging, were endemic and rarely resolved. Indeed, the fundamental question 'To whom does the Thames belong?' has continued to resonate.[10]

The maritime metropolis I portray, which includes shipbuilding and other maritime industries, was more than facilities, trade and business. For this reason, the book also deals with the Londoners who worked there as well as their waterfront communities, which gave parts of London a distinctive, sometimes misunderstood, identity. London has been well served by historians of labour. Anyone familiar with the work of Gareth Stedman Jones or David R. Green, among others, will not be unaware of the impact of casual employment and the pressures faced by skilled and unskilled workers and John Lovell has provided an unparalleled

---

[9] T. C. Barker and Michael Robbins, *A History of London Transport. Volume One – The Nineteenth Century* (George Allen & Unwin, London, 1975); Bill Luckin, *Pollution and Control. A Social History of the Thames in the Nineteenth* Century (Adam Hilger, Bristol, 1986).

[10] See Vanessa Taylor, 'London's River? The Thames as Contested Environmental Space', *The London Journal*, 40 (2015), 183–95.

analysis of late-nineteenth-century port trade unionism.[11] My longer perspective builds on such foundations. It is clear from this that, as far as the maritime sector was concerned, the industrial action of the seventies and eighties, culminating in the 1889 Great Dock Strike (re-examined here), was not as exceptional as it might seem and that involvement in earlier labour disputes was not entirely restricted to skilled workers. Indeed, when considering the nineteenth-century London labour force as a whole, the maritime sector, although occupationally divided, stands out as exceptionally unionised. Where militancy was muted, this was sometimes because union strength allowed achievement of objectives by other means. Theirs was 'an economically strategic location'.[12] Time imperatives, swift voyage turn-around in the case of cargo handling and payment on completion in shipbuilding, could make the threat, and reality, of labour stoppage a powerful weapon.

Eighteenth-century London was a fusion of neighbourhoods, which remained the case even as the city spread well beyond its ancient core in the nineteenth century. Sea-related occupations dominated water-front parishes on both sides of the river, so I have paid some attention to the Surrey shore, as well as the better-known maritime quarter of Wapping. Exotic 'Sailortown' dominated contemporary perceptions of East London until obscured by an immiserated 'Outcast London' image. It is the latter that has attracted most critical scrutiny but both were distortions. As I seek to show, meeting the needs of a transient seafarer population was just one element of a local economy that included docks and maritime industries and was not totally based on casual, unskilled labour.

The book is in two sections. Part I – The Sail Era looks at the relationship between London and its port before the introduction of steamers carrying cargoes from distant parts of the globe, which transformed the Port of London, along with the shipping industry. Until mid-century, most of the shipping it handled were sailing vessels powered by wind. Despite the apparent modernity of docks, the port operated much as it had done over past centuries. Chapter 1 deals with the character of the Port of London in the late eighteenth century and the background to subsequent reform. Chapter 2 considers dock financing and construction

---

[11] Gareth Stedman Jones, *Outcast London. A Study in the Relationship Between Classes in Victorian Society* (First Published 1971. Reprinted with a new preface, Penguin, London, 1984); David R. Green, *From Artisans to Paupers, Economic Change and Poverty in London, 1790–1870* (Scolar Press, Aldershot, 1995); John Lovell, *Stevedore and Dockers. A Study of Trade Unionism in the Port of London, 1870–1914* (Macmillan, London, 1969).

[12] Frank Broeze, 'Militancy and Pragmatism: An International Perspective on Maritime Labour, 1870–1914', *International Review of Social History*, 36 (1991), 179.

and Chapter 3 their trade, business operations and workforce management. The focus shifts to the London and the river port in a lengthier Chapter 4. This considers other elements of port reform, including compensation to injured parties, replacement of London Bridge and the Corporation of London's role in river management. It also looks at the introduction of steam shipping into wharf trades and the cargoes these handled. Chapter 5 moves beyond the port, first to maritime industries and their workforce, particularly timber shipbuilding, then to economic activity in London's maritime districts and the experiences of those who worked and lived there, temporarily in the case of seamen.

Part II – The Steam Era deals with the impact of steam shipping from the 1850s when steamers began carrying cargoes from distant parts of the globe. This was more than a technological phenomenon. The movement from sail to steam transformed the character of the shipping industry and required the Port of London to accommodate ever larger vessels, running to regular timetables and handling hitherto unprecedented quantities of produce. Chapter 6 examines the phases of the transition to steam shipping, the effect on London's trade and the dock building response. Wharf investment and conflict with public authorities over the Thames Embankment and Tower Bridge are also considered. Chapter 7 initially deals with the economic problems faced by the dock companies and the eventual outcome. It then turns to port labour and industrial conflict, notably the 1889 port-wide strike. Chapter 8 further pursues the themes of Chapter 5, looking at iron shipbuilding, sugar refining and flour milling. It focuses again on the maritime districts, including the myth of 'Outcast London' and developments affecting the sailor economy. As well as labour issues, Chapter 9 takes up again the question of river and port governance. It examines the role of the Thames Conservancy, the background to the 1902 Royal Commission on the Port of London, conflicting proposals for reform, and eventual establishment of the Port of London Authority in 1909, which ushered in a new phase of London's relationship with its port.

In conclusion, it is impossible in a single volume to provide a comprehensive explanation of all that was involved in serving as the capital's port and how the two interreacted. Omissions, some intended, others not, are certainly many. Nevertheless, my hope is that the scope of this account metaphorically succeeds in relocating London's maritime sector to where historically it properly belongs, within the broader economic, social, cultural and political history of London.

Part I

The Sail Era

1   'This Immense Maritime Forest'
London River in the Late Eighteenth Century

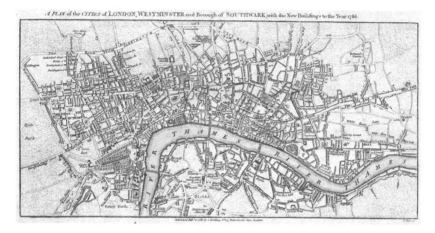

Map 1.1 Central London in 1786. Image: John Carey, A Plan of the Cities of London, Westminster and Borough of Southwark, 1786. © London Metropolitan Archives (City of London).

> Through this immense maritime forest, we have a comparative view at once of the wealth of every port in Europe; each vessel here displaying its variegated colours, to denote from whence it bears that produce which adds to our wants, and even luxuries of our capital.[1]

An idea of the scale of London's maritime trading activity in the later eighteenth century can be gained from the number and tonnage of sea-going craft recorded as entering the port every year. Figure 1.1 shows the number of vessels in the coastal and foreign trades arriving, with some making repeated voyages. Routine communication with the rest

[1] Samuel Ireland, *Picturesque Views on the River Thames from Its Source in Gloucestershire to the Nore; with Observations on the Public Buildings and Other Works of Art in Its Vicinity. In Two Volumes, Volume 2* (T. Egerton, London, 1802), 234–5.

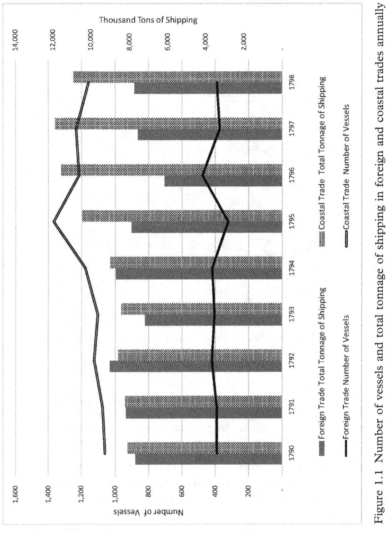

Figure 1.1 Number of vessels and total tonnage of shipping in foreign and coastal trades annually entering the Port of London, 1790–1798. Source: House of Commons Sessional Papers, 1798–1799, 124, SC Improvement of the Port of London, Second Report, Appendix D.2, 73, D.9, 86.

of the country dominated the day-to-day business of the port, in terms of both numbers and tonnage.

In the 1790s, there were almost 1,700 individual vessels serving London's domestic trade, with about a quarter of voyages made by colliers bringing coal from North East England to meet the demand from London's households and industries.[2] But the extensive geographical range of contacts between London and the rest of the country reflected not only the capital's huge and diverse market for fuel, foodstuffs and raw materials but also its pivotal position as the country's leading foreign trade port. More of England's foreign trade passed through London than all its other ports combined, and it was to this that it owed its national and international commercial dominance.[3] As the merchant and port reformer William Vaughan explained in 1796: 'London forms, as it were the great focus for foreign trade from its capital and its relation to foreign markets and circulates its commerce to all parts of England by means of its coasting traders, the country making its returns in corn, coal, salt, provisions, fish, stone and manufactures'.[4]

For London, geography was key. Its commercial strength lay in part in its situation, which gave access to northern and continental Europe, and in part in the City's association with the East and West Indies. Overseas trade increased impressively over the eighteenth century, when London's long-established trade with the rest of Europe, though still growing, became relatively less important than its oceanic business. The capital was at the heart of a booming Atlantic economy as well as commerce with the East, in which London had a monopoly through the East India Company. Deeply immersed directly and indirectly in slavery, sugar was its leading trade.[5] In 1799, London handled 72 per cent of England's sugar imports, Bristol and Liverpool just 8 per cent and 11 per cent, respectively.[6] Such connections

[2] House of Commons Sessional Papers, 1795–1796, Vol. 102, Committee Appointed to Enquire into the Best Mode of Providing Sufficient Accommodation for the Increased Trade and Shipping of the Port of London, iv–v, Appendix G, H, 272–3, Qq., 401, 1798–1799, Vol. 124, SC Improvement of the Port of London, Second Report, Appendix D.7, 84.
[3] Jacob M. Price, 'Competition between Ports in British Long Distance Trade, c. 1660–1800', in Agustin Guimera and Dolores Romero (eds.), *Puertos y Systemas Portuarios (Siglos XVI–XX): Actas del Coloquio Internacional, Madrid 19–21 Octubre, 1995* (Madrid, 1996), 22.
[4] William Vaughan, *Reasons in Favour of the London Docks* (London, 1795), 2.
[5] James A. Rawley, *London, Metropolis of the Slave Trade* (University of Missouri Press, Columbia and London, 2003), 15–17, 18–39, 123–48; Maxine Berg and Pat Hudson, *Slavery, Capitalism and the Industrial Revolution* (Polity Press, Cambridge, 2023), 97–100.
[6] House of Commons Papers 1808, 337, Account of Quantities of Articles Imported and Exported for England, 1790–1792 and 1799–1802. Unusually, this return provides a quantitative profile of the trade of individual major ports.

fostered an expanding re-export sector that made London 'the greatest emporium of trade in the world'.[7]

The structure of London's trade affected its port in many ways. High value and volume coincided in the case of colonial and East Indies cargoes. These bulky valuable capital investments required secure warehouse space and timely access to markets and consumers. In the oceanic business, there was a bias towards vessels of above average size. During the peak months from July to October, the West India trade accounted for over a third of ships but two-thirds of total tonnage in the Pool of London, the stretch of the Thames between London Bridge and the Tower of London.

Vessels moored in the deeper central section of the tidal river, where they could escape frequent tidal grounding on the river bed, and then lighters transhipped their cargo to the shore.[8] The timber, coal and other cargoes carried by vessels making repeated voyages into London were far less valuable, but certainly made up for this in terms of their volume and the river space such shipping occupied. The seasonality of distant trades, as well as the timing of the home harvest, affected the availability of work on the river and economic activity in the wider London economy. Late spring was marked by a peak in port business when ships from America began arriving. Vessels from the West Indies came in from May onwards, but most in September or October, and departed in the New Year, about when the East Indies fleet arrived. Ice closed off the Baltic trades in the winter months, when collier voyages from the north were also fewer. The river was therefore at its most busy in late summer. Indeed, it was reported in 1796 that sometimes as many as 775 vessels could be found at one time in the Pool, riskily moored together in tiers.[9]

A River Port

London was a tidal river port. Seagoing vessels, having made their way the sixty or so miles from the Thames estuary, found moorings in a variety of natural or man-made waterfront inlets but most commonly in the

---

[7] Ralph Davis, *The Industrial Revolution and British Overseas Trade* (Leicester University Press, Leicester, 1979), 43–6; Christopher J. French, '"Crowded with Traders and a Great Commerce": London's Domination of Overseas Trade, 1700–1775', *London Journal*, 17 (1992), 28–35, 29; House of Commons Sessional Papers, 1798–1799, Vol. 102, SC Improvement of the Port of London, Second Report, Appendix E3, 114.

[8] Walter M. Stern, 'The First London Dock Boom and the Growth of the West India Docks', *Economica*, New Series, 19 (1952), 59–60.

[9] L. D. Schwarz, *London in the Age of Industrialisation: Entrepreneurs, Labour Force and Living Conditions 1700–1850* (Cambridge University Press, Cambridge, 1991), 107–9; SC Port of London (1795–1796), Young, 268.

river itself. Liverpool and Hull had enclosed wet docks where trading vessels were loaded and discharged, but London's two enclosed wet docks (the Howland Dock at Rotherhithe and that originally built for the East India Company at Blackwall) were used for laying up ships, not handling commercial cargo.[10] The legal limits of the Port of London extended down to the Thames estuary, but customs regulations meant that dutiable goods from overseas had to be landed where they could be checked by the Customs. This was along limited stretches on the north and south banks immediately between London Bridge and the Tower of London. Income from duties was of great importance to the public finances; in the early 1790s, two-thirds of total Customs revenue came from duties on ten to twelve articles (out of over a thousand items) in which London particularly specialised.[11]

Maritime-related activity extended beyond the Pool of London. Private shipyards in which mercantile vessels were constructed, repaired and broken up were to be found on both banks of the river, as far down as Blackwall, while above London Bridge at Lambeth, there was a thriving boat-building industry.[12] On the north bank beyond the Tower, riverside settlements, Wapping, Shadwell, Ratcliffe and Limehouse, 'along a long narrow street, well paved and handsomely flagged on both sides, winding along the banks of the Thames', provided lodgings and services for the itinerant seafarer population and were hubs of other sea-related endeavours, including victualling, outfitting and scientific instrument-making.[13] Security and cartage considerations meant that warehouses in the City that stored high-value dutiable goods were no great distance apart from the landing places, forming part of the port's facilities as did more rough-and-ready buildings and yards for cargo storage across the river in Southwark and Bermondsey. Secure warehouses included those belonging to the East India Company whose cargoes, carried in vessels moored downriver because they were too large for the Pool, were transferred to its wharves and transit depots near London Bridge by specially

[10] See Stuart Rankin, *Shipbuilding in Rotherhithe: Greenland Dock and Barnard's Wharf*. Rotherhithe Local History Paper No. 3 (Dockside Studio, London, 1997); Hermione Hobhouse (ed.), 'Blackwall Yard: Development, to c. 1819', in Survey of London: Volumes 43 and 44, Poplar, Blackwall and Isle of Dogs (Athlone Press, London, 1994), 553–65.

[11] SC Port of London (1798–1799), Second Report, 463.

[12] Philip Banbury, *Shipbuilders of the Thames and Medway* (David & Charles, Newton Abbot, 1971), 111–44; John E. Barnard, *Building Britain's Wooden Walls, The Barnard Dynasty c. 1697–1851* (Anthony Nelson, Oswestry, 1997), 55–6.

[13] Thomas Pennant, *Of London* (Robert Faulder, London, 1790), 281; Derek Morris and Ken Cozens, *London's Sailortown 1600–1800: A Social History of Shadwell and Ratcliffe, An Early Modern Riverside Suburb* (East London History Society, London, 2014).

constructed 50–100 ton hoys and then moved by closely guarded carts to the Company's City premises.[14] Colliers also tended to moor down-river, serving as floating warehouses until their cargoes were sold, while in the timber trade, the wood itself sometimes floated in the tideway, transported in the form of great rafts, creating problems for other craft.[15] In fact, the river served as both a harbour and a highway, with large num-bers of barges and lighters needed for the transportation of cargoes within the port vying for space with watermens' wherries carrying passengers.[16]

As will be seen, campaigners for improvement, many closely con-nected with West Indian interests, made much of the limited extent of permitted landing places, but it is important not to let the views of mer-chants connected with a narrow range of overseas trades shape percep-tions of the port in this period. There was a greater spread of waterfront cargo handling than a concentration on sugar, cotton, wines or tobacco suggests. A passage downriver from Westminster in the late 1790s would take the traveller first past open coal yards on the north bank up to and beyond Blackfriars Bridge and then past wharves, including that of the Carron Company that handled iron. On the opposite bank were wharves devoted to unloading of tallow and logwood, for making dyes, and mahogany. Approaching London Bridge, to the north there was Queenhithe, where corn, malt and fruits were landed, and also pub-lic wharves such as at Three Cranes below Upper Thames Street that handled some foreign cargoes, including 'Irish produce' as well as coast-ing business. Below London Bridge, with its twelve narrow arches, there was Billingsgate Dock for coal, salt and fish; the Custom House and the twenty-one so-called 'Legal Quays', with accompanying warehouses and fifty-seven cranes, which were the core of the foreign trade port. Facing these on the Southwark shore was a group of wharves, most backing on to the Tooley Street. Also on the south bank was St. Saviour's Dock, and further down towards Rotherhithe, the above-bridge pattern of water-front use reasserted itself, with a number of landing places dealing with coal, timber, dyestuffs, pitch and tar.[17]

---

[14] Huw Bowen, 'So Alarming an Evil': Smuggling, Pilfering and the English East India Company, 1750–1810', *International Journal of Maritime History*, 14 (2002) 10–11; Margaret Makepeace, *The East India Company's London Workers: Management of the Warehouse Labourers, 1800–1858* (Boydell & Brewer, Woodbridge, 2010), 18–20.

[15] SC Port of London (1795–1796), Mills, 192.

[16] SC Port of London (1795–1796), xi; Humpherus, Henry, *History of the Origin and Progress of the Company of Watermen and Lightermen of The River Thames, Volume III 1800–1849, Volume IV 1850–1883* (S. Prentice, London, 1887).

[17] MLD, Vaughan Papers, *A Correct List of Sufferance Wharfs Now in Use ... from a List of Accounts Called for by Customs*, 2, 62; SC Port of London (1798–1799), Fellows, Meriton, French, 235–41.

The Customs Quays

This pattern of waterfront specialisation was, to a great extent, an artificial creation: the product of restrictions imposed in the interests of the Customs. The space was devoted to London's lawful 'Legal Quays' for the landing of foreign dutiable goods. As shown in Illustration 1 they covered just 1,464 feet of waterfront between London Bridge and the Tower of London.[18] First authorised in the reign of Elizabeth I, there had been no extension of privileges since the Great Fire. In the 1790s, the Legal Quays were being operated as ten separate concerns. Customs and Wool quays were held by the Crown, Lyons and Somers by the East India Company. The rest were private wharfinger businesses benefiting from long leases granted by wealthy landowners strongly represented in Parliament.[19]

Sugar, cotton and some dried fruits landed at these quays could be stored on site, but a great range of overseas imports were carried away. Tobacco was placed under King's Lock in Crown premises, but other cargoes were either housed in the importer's own premises or in public warehouses; some connected with the Legal Quays.[20] Only St. Dunstan's Hill and Fish Street Hill offered a passageway of reasonable width between the waterfront and the City. Some of the remaining steep and narrow streets giving access to the quays and warehouses were blocked off or impassible for carts, but the amount of business was such that there was no choice but to move the goods further into the City.

Apart from the Legal Quays, the port had 112 active working wharves. Known as 'Sufferance Wharves', sixty-four were authorised to handle foreign cargoes.[21] Most were private, used by merchants for their own goods or for the unloading of raw materials for local manufacturing concerns. At first, the majority of those with 'sufferance' licenses dealt with foreign cargoes such as timber or foodstuffs where the levels of duty were low, so security was not a prime consideration. But with the eighteenth-century expansion of trade, the situation changed. Increasingly, permits were granted for cargoes that would previously have been handled only by the Legal Quays, including on occasion even sugar, the most valuable dutiable cargo. In the main set of Sufferance Wharves on the south

---

[18] Chester's, Custom House, Dice and Smart's quay also handled domestic produce. SC Port of London (1795–1796), 79.

[19] Patrick Colquhoun, *A Treatise on the Commerce and Police of the River Thames* (J. Mawman, London, 1800), 29–30; MLD, Vaughan Papers, Vol. 2, 79; Henry Roseveare, 'The Eighteenth-Century Port of London Reconsidered', in Agustin Guimera and Dolores Romero (eds.), *Puertos y Systemas Portuarios (Siglos XVI–XX): Actas del Coloquio Internacional, Madrid 19–21 Octubre, 1995* (Ministerio De Fomento, Madrid, 1996), 39, 45.

[20] Port of London (1795–1796), Appendix Bbb, Gossett, 106–9, Stoyles, 109–12.

[21] MLD, Vaughan Papers, *Hints & c on the State of the Legal Quays*. Vol. 2, 73.

bank, just below London Bridge, Davis's dealt exclusively with foreign produce, but Chamberlain's, Hay's, Beal's and Griffin's to a varying extent also handled home produce. Further downriver, at Bankside, Scott's wharf was equipped with 'a very powerful crane' for mahogany.[22]

In 1789, the Customs Commissioners, concerned at what they saw as a costly and inefficient proliferation of permissions 'increased beyond what is necessary', decided to designate all twenty-one wharves between the Bridge and Hermitage on the north bank and down to St. Saviour's Dock on the South as Public Foreign Sufferance Wharfs. With a few exceptions, they would then automatically reject further applications.[23] Rather than a recognition that these premises had become an integral feature of London's foreign trade facilities, this decision at a time of great port congestion was possibly an attempt to encourage them to handle foreign produce. Vaughan, writing in 1794, thought that up to two-thirds of all imports into London were being handled by such wharves, but a detailed report produced by Customs about the same time on the type of goods these handled suggests that in most cases, home produce predominated. Even so, the Customs' description of Davis's 511-foot premises as 'the most extensive and commodious wharf upon the banks of the Thames, where nothing but foreign business is done', of Chamberlain's and Cotton's as 'spacious, convenient', and of Scott's as providing 'peculiar dispatch' suggests that in quality some of these wharves were certainly not inferior, and may indeed have been superior, to the Legal Quays. Not all the sufferances, however, applied to such impressive facilities. At Churchyard Alley, near to the Tower of London, mats and lampblack were carried up steps from the river with Customs officers 'obliged to stand in the public open passage to take a cursory account thereof, as they are conveying on porters' back [sic] to different places'.[24]

Workforce and Employers

In a 1795 pamphlet, Vaughan identified 'the principal leading interests' in the Port of London. Distinguishing between private and public (by which he meant wider) interests, he placed the owners and operators

---

[22] TNA T1/4133/17047, *Petition from Foreign Sufferance Wharves* ..., 20 August 1824.

[23] Port of London (1795–1796), Appendix Uu; MLD, Vaughan Papers, *Hints & c on the State of the Legal Quays*, Vol. 2, 73; Regulations of the Commissioners of Customs respecting Sufferance Wharves, 13 May 1789, reprinted in Henry Longlands, *A Review of the Warehousing System as Connected with the Port of London* (John Richardson et al., London, 1824), 3–7.

[24] SC Port of London (1795–1796), *A Plan Shewing the Situation of the Public Foreign Sufferance Wharves*; MLD, Vaughan Papers, *A List of Sufferance Wharfs* ... 2, 62.

Illustration 1.1 Working on the river. Image: Tower of London Engraving, unknown date. © Patstock/Getty Images.

of Legal Quays, gangsmen (managers of operations), porters, labourers, carmen and watermen in the first category and 'City and Commercial interests', shipping and the Revenue in the second. Vaughan commented that in relation to plans for improvement, 'the parties immediately affected are comparatively few, either in classes or numbers', but even on his own terms, it must be questioned whether this judgement was correct, and if we include omitted groups including lightermen and pilots, the scale and complexity of the late eighteenth-century port as an economic and political entity become apparent.[25]

Legal monopoly and political connection at Guildhall and Westminster made the Legal Quay wharfingers the port's strongest vested interest. In the 1790s, their public face was the Committee of Proprietors, Lessees and Wharfingers of the Legal Quays, but in the past, these had a more clandestine identity. From 1674 they worked as a cartel, with rates and terms of business determined by secret agreement rather than competition, and it is probable that similar arrangements persisted in the late eighteenth century.[26] Some of these wharfingers were

---

[25] Vaughan, *Reasons in Favour*, 7.
[26] Henry Roseveare, 'Wiggins' Key' Revisited: Trade and Shipping in the Later Seventeenth-Century Port of London', *The Journal of Transport History*, 16 (1995), 1–20; Roseveare, 'The Eighteenth-Century Port of London Reconsidered', 37–52; 'Extracts

also involved in warehousing on site and elsewhere in the City, so were part of another significant port interest, the warehouse keepers.[27] The Sufferance Wharfingers were yet another group with a stake in existing arrangements, though without the long-term legal security enjoyed by the lessees of the Legal Quays. There is no direct evidence but the tendency, once the docks were built, of former Sufferance Wharf operators to collaborate in petitions to Ministers and Customs suggests that they too may have arrived at mutually beneficial arrangements for cargo handling and storage rates.

Corporation regulations were responsible for the creation and maintenance of a number of port-related interests. Licensed porters included men concerned as managers or labourers with loading and unloading cargoes into lighters, on to the quays and then with the carrying of goods onwards as individual burdens to their destination. There were four porterage fellowships, each with a claim over a particular sphere of work. The picture is complex, but broadly Billingsgate Porters (also known as Fellowship Porters) dealt with dry goods such as corn, coal, salt and fruit, whereas Ticket Porters were concerned with American produce. The other two porterage brotherhoods, the Tacklehouse Porters and Alien Porters, had rights over the weighing and measurement of a wide range of commodities and acted as contractors and employers. All these 'City Porters' were authorised by the Corporation as was another group of workers, the Carmen, whose employment was similarly regulated by a licensing system. The equally privileged members of the Company of Watermen and Lightermen exercised their monopoly of water carriage under the security of sixteenth-century legislation, whereas a chartered body, Trinity House, controlled pilotage and the supply of ballast to ships.[28]

The Corporation itself had a direct financial stake in the port. It derived income from waterfront property, including Billingsgate fish market, and profited from dues on certain types of cargo. It also possessed, though it apparently infrequently exercised, some Thames powers and duties; the Lord Mayor as conservator of the river had authority to remove obstructions and to license piers and landing places. There was nothing, however, that gave the Corporation, or indeed any other body at this time, the status of a harbour authority. It could, and did, resist change

---

of a Petition of the Merchants and Traders in London to the House of Commons', in Vaughan, *Reasons in Favour*, 25. The inclusion of this document is a strong hint that the cartel persisted.

[27] Port of London (1795–1796), 298.

[28] Walter M. Stern, *The Porters of London* (Longmans, London, 1960); SC Port of London (1798–1799), Day, 30 May 1797; Humpherus, *Watermen and Lightermen*, III, 99–107; PP 1824 VI.1, SC Foreign Trade, First Report (Pilotage), 3–6.

but its influence over the port was less than that of the Commissioners of Customs, whose decisions on what should be landed where, or how many officers should be available, affected not only the course of day-to-day business but also shaped waterfront use over the longer term.

One reason why the Customs was such a significant player is that, with the exception of the East India Company, there was no other single port organisation to match it in terms of scale of operation. The Customs permanent establishment, at busy times augmented by temporary officers or 'glutmen', in the 1790s stood at about 1600.[29] By contrast, the port's cargo-handling businesses were typically owned and operated as separate units. With nine firms running sixteen quays, there was some concentration in the Legal Quay sector and a few Sufferance Wharfingers with interests in more than one property, but the leasehold nature of most of these premises discouraged expansion.[30] In warehousing, there were some large enterprises – Hanson, Pearson and Company had twelve warehouses – but these were probably the exception. Where integration occurred, it was vertical rather than horizontal. Edward Ogle, the most publicly prominent Legal Quay wharfinger, with premises at Wiggins', Young's and Ralph's, used his own lighters to discharge West Indian produce that he stored in his warehouses off Bishopsgate. Similarly, Thomas Bolt, lessee of Fresh, Smart's and Dice, was 'wharfinger, warehouseman, lighterman and bargemaster' and John Dutton of Chester and Brewer's undertook his lighterage, though he also employed independent workers. According to Matthias Lucas, who had extensive lighterage interests, before 1792 'a company of wharfingers', presumably the Legal Quay cartel, had charged low rates in an attempt to exclude independent operators, but this arrangement did not survive the breakup of this combination.[31]

Large operators though Bolt and Ogle were, their commercial freedom was limited by dependence on others because the process of loading and discharge, landing and warehousing and packaging and sampling entailed a sequence of activities, each of which was a source of income for other port workers. Even within their most immediate sphere, wharfingers and warehouse keepers found their control over labour severely curtailed, not only by the rights of licensed porters and carmen but also by the traditionally independent status of other port workers.

[29] Makepeace, *East India Company's London Workers*, 5; William Vaughan, *Memoir of William Vaughan, Esq. F.R.S: With Miscellaneous Pieces Relative to Docks, Commerce, Etc* (Smith, Elder & Co., London, 1839), 14.
[30] MLD, Vaughan Papers, *Sufferance Wharves*, 2, 62.
[31] SC Port of London (1798–1799), Appendix A, 124–5; TNA T76, Port of London Compensation Commission, 4, Memorials 180, 239: TNA T76, Memorials 129, 64; SC Port of London (1795–1796), Lucas, 147.

Most cargo handling required teamwork and the grouping together of labourers was typically handled within the workforce itself on a sub-contract basis. Foreign-owned vessels coming into London invariably used their crews to unload the cargo, but the majority of Masters of British vessels paid off the crew once in port and recruited the men to do this from the port workforce. They either gave the job to a set of men working together, 'the team', or more commonly employed an individual known as a 'lumper' who would then recruit the rest.[32] Under the 'lumper' arrangement in the river, the employer's relationship with the group and their formal relationship with each other ended once the task was completed.

In other areas of port work, greater consistency in employment led to the emergence of permanent partnerships of workers. On the Legal Quays, as also in some uptown warehouses, business was sub-contracted to partnerships of 'gangsmen' who were responsible for the hiring and firing of labourers. These also developed and maintained contacts with ancillary workers, in particular coopers, who were skilled men with a strong craft tradition employed on a similar semi-independent basis. The permanently employed gangsmen were an elite among port workers, enjoying 'places of trust and confidence, and mostly for life'.[33] But if such status was exceptional, the system of sub-contract which they represented was not.

As Schwarz has noted, 'by the standards of its time, the Port was enormous', but it is not easy to establish either the total number of people who worked there or the size of particular occupational groups. Patrick Colquhoun, magistrate and founder of the marine police force, in 1800 published a detailed breakdown of employers and employed, providing numbers for each category.[34] At first sight, the precision of this listing encourages the impression that this is an authoritative source, but the difficulty he must have faced in obtaining such information throws doubt on its accuracy. When set against the evidence of the 1801 Census, itself open to criticism, Colquhoun's totals of 10,250 employers and 122,320 workers would imply the participation in port business of almost half the

---

[32] Stern, 'Porters of London', 60–6; SC Port of London (1798–1799), Ogle, 308.

[33] For six who worked as partners at Cox's and Hammond's quay, the costs of setting up in business included acquiring the Freedom of the City of London, becoming Ticket Porters plus an initial investment of £100 each for tackle and other expenses; TNA T76, Port of London Compensation Commission 4, 314; 10, 422; Peter D'Sena, 'Perquisites and Casual Labour on the London Wharfside in the Eighteenth Century', London Journal, 14 (1989), 132; Vaughan, Reasons in Favour, 7.

[34] Patrick Colquhoun, A Treatise on the Commerce and Police of the River Thames (J. Mawson, London, 1800), xxx–xxxii; ODNB, Patrick Colquhoun (1745–1820).

capital's males. The Census statistics for the riverside parishes below the Tower and Southwark, giving a total population, female and male, of 89,733, further undermine his credibility. The inescapable conclusion is that Colquhoun's keenness to demonstrate the importance of the port within the London economy led him to grossly exaggerate the numbers involved. The more sober approach of Peter D'Sena suggests a river and wharf workforce of about 10,000 in 1800.[35]

Those with an occupational interest in the port were not limited to those with identifiable legal claims. A number of those employed had professional, skilled or semi-skilled status, but the heavy manual nature of much port work leaves no doubt that labourers were the largest single group of workers. Both Colquhoun and Vaughan, who refers to 'a fluctuating class of men employed by the job or half-hour', distinguish between ticket porters and labourers. In practice, despite the legal position, many of those who worked as porters were not members of 'the Brotherhood', though those with a ticket may have had a more permanent, less casual rank and a stronger claim in the contest for work. Recruitment of men outside the ranks of the more regular workforce was routine when the port was busy, with 'soldiers from the Tower' the main source for the Legal Quays.[36]

On the river, transporting cargoes was in the hands of lightermen, skilled men who had served an apprenticeship, while, as already noted, discharge of West India vessels was in the hands of lumpers employed by Master Lumpers, many of whom were publicans with no direct involvement in the business and so worked through foremen. The unloading of East Indiamen was also subcontracted but operated under the supervision of Company officers. Lumping was a distinct type of port work; ordinary labourers were only employed as a last resort.[37] The same rule applied elsewhere. In the coal trade, coal heavers, who were much at the mercy of the publican 'undertakers' employing them, formed a distinct group of workers with such appalling working conditions even by contemporary standards that they had attracted the attention of Parliament and the Corporation.[38]

Port labourers then cannot be considered as an undifferentiated mass and, even in the case of the most intermittently employed 'extra' men, the importance of personal contact in getting work no doubt in many instances encouraged men to maintain connections with particular trades

[35] Schwarz, *London in the Age of Industrialisation*, 8–9, Appendix 1, 247–8; 144 ftn. 10.
[36] D'Sena, 'Perquisites and Casual Labour', 132; Vaughan, *Reasons in Favour*, 7.
[37] MLD, Minutes of the West India Merchants Committee, 28 June 1799, 2 July 1799.
[38] Jerry White, *London in the Eighteenth Century, A Great and Monstrous Thing* (Vintage Books, London, 2012) 242–5; Peter Linebaugh, *The London Hanged, Crime and Civil Society in the Eighteenth Century*, 2nd ed. (Verso, London, 2003) 306–8; 311–8.

and wharves. However, although there were differences in the handling
of cargoes, the underlying pattern was consistent. It was predominantly
task-based, with labour itself measured 'by the cask, bale or piece, as
lumpage, lighterage, landing, wharfage, housing' and team systems had
evolved in all types of port work.[39] Gangs were permanent partnerships,
but the services they offered involved the employment of others to per-
form a specific finite job priced as a lump sum, with payment to the
labourers by the hour or on a piecework basis. Given the impact of seasons and weather on the work available, the majority of port workers,
in common with Londoners more generally, worked on a casual basis
in response to the state of demand. But the frequency of their employment, within a fairly predictable annual framework, was not a lottery; it
depended on a man's status in terms of his skills and connections.[40]

That status also played a part in their remuneration, but assessment of
port workers' earnings presents difficulties not only because of the casual,
intermittent nature of employment but also because a piece rate or money
wage cannot be taken as a measure of their reward. Perquisites and payments in kind were an established feature at all levels of waterfront work
and seen in some circumstances as 'the legitimate payment of workers in
return for services rendered', even to the extent of being the entire reward.[41]
The casual labourers told by a ship's captain 'to be sharp and I would
give them some short pieces [of rope] which lay on the deck' were part of
the same system that allowed gangsmen on Cox's and Hammond's Quay
'ready money called Good Money and certain perquisites in the scraping of
the floors'. The sums paid by merchants to Master Coopers for cooperage
and to Master Lumpers for loading and discharging cargo were frequently
not sufficient to meet the labour costs, so it was understood by employers
and workers alike that some of the cargo would go towards the reward.

Unsurprisingly, the dividing line between legitimate and illegitimate
reward, between perquisites and pilferage, could prove difficult to establish, hence prosecutions where the defence was that goods had been taken
but no theft had taken place. Nevertheless, non-monetary rewards, permitted by those who directly hired the men, rather than the merchants who
owned the cargo, were not exacted under duress. They had a managerial
function, serving as 'bait to mobilise labour'. From a different perspective,
the practice of mixed reward, which amounted to an individual contract,
fostered an identity of interest between regular and casual workers.[42]

---

[39] SC Port of London (1798–1799), Ogle, 313; Vaughan, *Reasons in* Favour, 7.
[40] Schwarz, *London in the Age of Industrialisation*, 117–23.
[41] D'Sena, 'Perquisites', 130; Linebaugh, *London Hanged*, 307.
[42] D'Sena, Ibid. 141; SC Port of London (1798–1799), Ogle, 318; PP 1823 IV.489 [411],
SC Foreign Trade, Third Report (West India Docks), Drinkald, 224–5.

Port Reform Proposals

In 1780, London handled more than half of the foreign trade shipping entering England's ports, and Liverpool, its closest rival, handled just 9 per cent.[43] Impressive although this measure of activity appears, over the century, the value of the capital's trade had grown relatively more slowly than that of the outports. London had opened the country's first wet dock, the private Great Howland, at Rotherhithe in 1700, but it lagged in public dock construction. Liverpool gained four docks between 1709 and 1788, Bristol opened one in 1712 and Hull in 1778.[44] Meanwhile, London struggled to cope with greater volumes of cargo within the physical confines of the Legal Quays and Sufferance Wharves. Yet, not until the 1790s were the inadequacies of the Port of London effectively addressed. This was not due to a lack of effort on the part of merchants, frustrated by the cartel monopoly, still less any satisfaction with the state of things as they were. From the early 1700s, the Commissioners of Customs had received proposals for improvements, including a practical suggestion in 1764 for a new Legal Quay at St. Katharine's, but all attempts foundered in the face of opposition from the Legal Quay owners and wharfingers. The 'landed interests of the wharfs', wrote Vaughan, 'overcame the interests of commerce'.[45]

In September 1793, the Committee of West India Merchants set up a special sub-committee to look into the question of landing and delivery of their produce at the Legal Quays. The immediate context was the arrival of 100,000 hogsheads of sugar in just two months as a result of the British acquisition of French West Indian islands. With storage only for 32,000 hogsheads, the port could barely cope with this sudden increase in business, though as usual the Customs responded by authorising Sufferance Wharves to handle sugar. Lack of space delayed the handling of cargoes, so lighters were effectively being used as warehouses. The result was a dispute between the wharfingers and lightermen over the rates to be charged and the committee's immediate brief was to consider how to resolve this issue. But it was also asked to 'concert, if possible, some means of preventing in future those numerous inconveniences under which the West India trade at present labours', and when the

---

[43] Price, 'Competition', 22, ftn. 12.

[44] D. Swann, 'The Pace and Progress of Port Investment in England, 1660–1830', *Yorkshire Bulletin of Economic and Social Research*, 12 (1960), 39, 33, 36.

[45] MLD, Vaughan Papers, *Reports for the Improvements of the Port of London*, Vol. 2, 26; Vaughan, *Treatise on Wet Docks, Quays and Warehouses for the Port of London* (J. Johnson and W. Richardson, London, 1793), 25–6; Roseveare, 'Port of London Reconsidered', 41–4.

report was published three months later, it berated London for its lack of dynamism, contrasting this with other English ports:

While several of the Out-Ports have made a rapid progress in the construction wet docks, erection of commodious warehouses and other means of facilitating the discharge of trade and discharge of shipping, thereby greatly advancing their trade and prosperity, the metropolis of Great Britain has, in these material respects remained torpid: its improvements checked or suspended, and its abuses gradually gaining head.[46]

Instead of concentrating on how to improve existing arrangements, the committee argued that London should follow the lead of Liverpool, Hull and Bristol by adopting the far more radical solution of extending waterspace and warehouse storage through the introduction of dock accommodation. Its report set in train a period of intense campaigning, planning, debate and compromise that ended with the decision to build no fewer than three docks, each serving different elements of London's foreign trade, as well as cutting a canal across the Isle of Dogs.

A number of studies have traced in some detail the series of events that culminated in the 1799 Act 'For rendering more commodious, and better regulating, the Port of London', giving the go-ahead for the West India Dock, and this work provides the starting point for discussion here.[47] In brief, following the support for the idea of docks given by a 1794 meeting, a forty-one-member committee was appointed to produce more detailed proposals. This was reported the following year with a £800,000 scheme for wet docks at Wapping, to be financed by a tonnage duty on all shipping using the port. In 1796, a bill was submitted to Parliament in connection with this plan for 'the Merchants Dock'.

The Corporation petitioned against the Wapping proposal, as predictably did many of those whose established interests were threatened, including the Legal Quay and Sufferance Wharves, watermen, lightermen, carmen and porters. Even those who favoured a dock solution were not all convinced that the Wapping site was the right one. Among doubters was the leading West India merchant Robert Milligan who preferred a downriver location – the uninhabited Isle of Dogs.

The Corporation was not acting purely obstructively. It was already developing its own Isle of Dogs project, encouraged by an assurance by William Pitt, who was Chancellor of the Exchequer as well as Prime Minister, 'that they had a fair claim to a preference in the execution and

[46] MLD, Vaughan Papers, Vol. 2, Report of West India Merchants, 20 December 1793.
[47] Sir Joseph Broodbank, *History of the Port of London, I* (Daniel O'Connor, London, 1921); Rupert C. Jarvis, 'The Metamorphosis of the Port of London', *The London Journal*, 3 (1977), 55–71; Stern, 'First London Dock Boom', 59–77.

superintendence of the Plans'. Neither its Bill nor the earlier Merchant's Bill got a second reading, but the outcome of these submissions was the appointment in March 1796 of a Parliamentary Select Committee charged with examining the various proposals under discussion. The Committee investigated the state of the port very thoroughly, decided that London's resources were 'incompetent to the great purposes of its intended commerce' and signified support for a dock scheme, rather than a plan for Legal Quay improvement proposed by the wharfinger Edward Ogle.

In November, the Merchants' Bill was resubmitted, followed in the spring of 1797 by one from the Corporation involving two docks and a canal on the Isle of Dogs. This was drawn up in collaboration with a breakaway group of West India merchants led by Alderman George Hibbert, supported by Robert Milligan.[48] Both the group of Wapping supporters and those now favouring the Isle of Dogs initially saw these proposals as rivals, but the government refused to back either one or the other, preferring that both should go ahead. Fresh bills for these schemes were then put before Parliament, handled by the same Select Committee. Both included a twenty-one-year monopoly clause. West India cargoes were reserved to the West India Dock's premises; tobacco, wines, brandy and rice (except from the East and West Indies) to the 'London Dock' at Wapping. The act creating the West India Dock Company passed into law in 1799 and that for the London Dock the following year. In 1803, an act with a similar reservation of trade established the East India Dock Company.[49]

Motives for Port Reform

A number of questions arise from this sequence of events, not all of which have been adequately explored by historians. The first is why the campaign for reform emerged when it did. Most interpretations suggest a mounting crisis that finally propelled merchants into taking action.[50] These place emphasis on growth in port activity leading to congestion, delays and encouragement of theft, but such problems were by no means new. It was certainly the case that war increased the pressure – entries in 1793 were at record level – but, as already noted, these exceptional

---

[48] For detailed analysis of investors, see N. Draper, 'The City of London and Slavery: Evidence from the First Two Dock Companies, 1795–1800', *Economic History Review*, 61 (2008), 432–66.

[49] 39 Geo. III. c. 69; 39 & 40 Geo. III. c. 47; 43 Geo. III. c. 126.

[50] See, for example, Stern, 'First London Dock Boom' and John Marriott, *Beyond the Tower. A History of East London* (Yale, New Haven & London, 2011), 96–8.

conditions were not initially seen by merchants as necessitating fundamental reform. Furthermore, the Commissioners of Customs had shown
themselves in 1787 to be much more willing to concede the need to land
goods under sufferance permits.

If indeed Legal Quay interests had for over twenty years successfully
deterred their opponents from even attempting to extend facilities, some
explanation is needed as to why this was no longer such an issue. One
factor may have been a change in the Legal Quay proprietors. A com-
ment by West India merchant John Inglis is relevant here: 'I have in all
my time considered the Legal Quays as a species of monopoly, degrading
and injurious to the merchants, though I think they are [less so?] under
the present proprietors than in former times'.[51] This may also explain
Vaughan's claim in one of his earliest publications that Legal Quay interests would be satisfied with compensation for the loss of their privileges.

A more important factor in the history of London's dock development
was the contribution of Vaughan himself. Without his commitment and
willingness to engage in detailed exploration of the issues, as also his commercial contacts, the campaign for port reform could not have got underway as rapidly or effectively as it did. In contrast to the vehement crusader
for Thames policing, Patrick Colquhoun, Vaughan was not an outsider but
an established City figure, with commercial experience in West Indies and
American trades. He was also a director of the Royal Exchange Assurance,
a chartered company with interests in the insurance of port properties.
His enthusiasm for port reform does not, however, seem to have derived
from his career, or even from what was, by his own account, a lifelong fascination with canal and dock projects.[52] Though Vaughan has long been
recognised as a free-trader, a 2014 research study by Spike Sweeting has
revealed the full extent of Vaughan's association with the acolytes of Adam
Smith in the Bowood Set, of which he was a member. Sweeting argues
for an ideological basis for Vaughan's overtly practical approach; it was
'unflinching faith in the enlightened economy' that underpinned his support for a port solution which he believed would challenge those monopolistic interests which fatally impeded economic progress, with docks
serving as 'a new wheel in the great machine of commerce'.[53]

Vaughan's first pamphlet was in fact privately circulated in advance
of the 1794 investigations by the Committee of West India Merchants.

---

[51] SC Port of London (1795–1796), Inglis, 295.
[52] ODNB, William Vaughan (1752–1850)'; William Vaughan, *Memoir*, 4–9.
[53] Spike Sweeting, 'Capitalism, The State and Things: The Port of London, circa 1730–
1800' (Unpublished Doctoral Thesis, University of Warwick, 2014); Vaughan, *London
Docks*, 7.

Once supported by 1796 Select Committee Report, Vaughan's basic case – that the port's facilities did not meet the needs of commerce – appears within a few years to have become generally accepted as correct in mercantile and government circles. Few witnesses suggested that a solution could be found by improving existing arrangements, so the argument that the docks were the way to achieve 'accommodation, security and dispatch' became accepted as the alternative. Given their introduction in other ports and the London examples of wet docks at Rotherhithe and Blackwall, this is unsurprising. What does require further explanation is how what started as a plan to build one dock came to be transformed into the massive project approved by Parliament between 1799 and 1803.

Part of the answer lies in the determination of the Corporation to benefit from any change and its identification of an Isle of Dogs canal as the way to achieve this. By linking this with a scheme for docks, it found allies in the group of West India merchants who from early on argued for this location against the Wapping site favoured by Vaughan and his associates. Even so, since the West India interests had initially petitioned Parliament in favour of the Wapping scheme, Robert Milligan did well to persuade them at a meeting in April 1797 to change direction and back his proposal instead.

The advantages, explained to the General Meeting of Planters and Merchants the following November, were that this would:

Provide for the general accommodation and dispatch of trade at the Port of London; the better protection of private property; and the increase of the public revenue; with the least intrusion upon individual and corporate rights; at the least expense; and with the least delay; guarding at the same time, against all unnecessary sacrifices of interests to be in any manner ultimately affected.

Furthermore, the Isle of Dogs plan would not arouse the 'spirit and perseverance' of the opposition to Wapping, and, because the area was virtually uninhabited, the land would cost much less.[54]

The support of the West India Committee was not based solely on such considerations. What was also important to them was that the Isle of Dogs scheme promised a complete system for the handling of West India shipping and cargo. The Wapping proposal was for a dock open to all trades with no provision for on-site storage. As was noted in the report, this would leave 'the business of working out the ship, and the immediate and subsequent disposal of all goods imported, in precisely the same hands as are at present concerned therein'. In contrast, on the

[54] MLD, West India Committee Archives, Minute Book IV, 2 March 1796, 25 April 1797.

Isle of Dogs, West India vessels would discharge directly on to the quayside, with cargo stored in an adjacent warehouse, so all stages of cargo handling would be in the hands of the dock company. The result, it was claimed, would be the destruction of the 'whole system' of plunder, to the benefit both of merchants and the public purse.

Belief that adoption of the Isle of Dogs scheme would put an end to 'embezzlement and plunderage' indeed proved influential in shaping government attitudes to reform, but we need to be wary of seeing the issue primarily in terms of professional criminality, despite the writings of Patrick Colquhoun and his role in establishing a force to police the London Thames. His much-quoted *A Treatise on the Commerce and Police of the River Thames*, with its colourful names and descriptions of those preying on mercantile property – 'river pirates', 'night plunderers', 'scuffle hunters', 'light horsemen', 'heavy horsemen' – conjures up a dramatic image of a port under siege from felons.[55] Among these were the 'Light Horsemen' who, Colquhoun said:

> ... went on board completely prepared with *Iron Crows*, *Adzes*, and other utensils, to open and again head-up the casks – with shovels to take out the Sugar, and a number of Bags made to contain 100 lb. each. These bags were denominated *Black Strap*; having been previously dyed black, to prevent their being seen in the night, when stowed in the bottom of a wherry.[56]

There is no reason to doubt Colquhoun's account, although it was not in his interest to minimise the problems he hoped to solve. Elsewhere he was forced to admit that what he also counted as criminal behaviour, such as over-sampling by coopers, was not seen in that light by everyone. Some merchants were prepared to overlook some loss through theft as the necessary price of quick unloading of cargo. Others were not, hence two West India Committee attempts in the 1790s to regulate discharge procedures.[57] Both foundered because in a competitive system not all merchants were prepared to abide by the rules. For some leading merchants, experience of the difficulty of tackling the problem within the existing framework no doubt increased the attraction of a scheme that guaranteed compliance by the entire trade.

Estimates of the loss from plunder of cargo varied. Wharfinger Hibbert, admittedly hardly a disinterested witness, put the annual loss on West India produce at £200,000–£300,000.[58] From the merchants' point of view, there was much to be gained from stemming this drain of

---

[55] Colquhoun, *Treatise*, 58–71.
[56] Colquhoun, Ibid., 59.
[57] Sweeting, 'Capitalism, the State and Things', 134–44.
[58] SC Port of London (1798–1799), Hibbert.

profit, but becoming direct employers of labour promised other rewards as well – the chance to introduce new ways of organising cargo handling. As Colquhoun pointed out in 1800, by taking upon themselves 'the responsibility of the whole labour which is at present performed by Lumpers, Coopers, Lightermen, Wharfingers, Tackle-house Porters, Ticket Porters, Warehousemen, Gangsmen and Labourers', in their role as stock holders, the proprietors of the West India Dock Company would benefit from reduced labour costs and, in their role as merchants or shipowners, from greater speed in working out vessels.[59]

For Linebaugh, the docks in general, as also the policing of the river, were primarily conceived as a means of subjugating independent port workers to the oppressive demands of capitalist interests.[60] In fact controlling labour did not feature in Vaughan's Wapping proposal – his ire was directed at the Legal Quay privileges. But while it is clear that the emergence of a separate proposal for the West India trade cannot be regarded simply as a matter of preference for one site over another, equally there was more to this initiative than an intention to manage the workforce. Rather than dissolving the monopolistic influences over the Port of London represented by the Legal Quays, as the free-trader Vaughan wished, the Hibbert plan effectively transferred these to the powerful West India interest, enhancing its position. In short, there were a number of rationalities in play.[61]

For the supporters of Wapping, as also those identified with the newer Isle of Dogs proposal, these schemes were rivals, alternatives; it appeared impossible that both projects could be implemented. That both these docks did in due course come to be built, along with a third dock for the East India trade, is not satisfactorily explained within the free enterprise context in which these developments are conventionally set. Establishing companies to raise capital and the extinction of property rights required parliamentary authorisation, but in the case of London's dock enterprises, the involvement of the State was not similar to its role in turnpike or canal development; the Pitt administration played a defining role in the refashioning of the Port of London.

The Role of Government

The starting point for understanding government interest in the Port of London is public finance. In 1793, Customs and Excise receipts

---

[59] Colquhoun, *Treatise*, 380–83.
[60] Linebaugh, *London Hanged*, 417–36; Anthony R. Henderson and Sarah Palmer, 'The Early Nineteenth-Century Port of London: Management and Labour in Three Dock Companies, *Research in Maritime History*, 6 (1994), 31–50.
[61] Sweeting, *Capitalism, the State and Things*, 19–20.

at London were two-thirds of the total national income of £5.2 million.[62] War demands pressed heavily on the Exchequer in the 1790s, leading to the eventual expedient of income tax.[63] The tariff structure differentiated between the 'necessities' (basic foodstuffs such as grain, butter, meat and cheese) and luxuries (sugar, tobacco, tea, wines and spirits), hence the greater security needed for these and their value in the eyes of Customs officers, smugglers and thieves alike. Between 1799 and 1801, 'loss sustained by plunderage' of West India produce cost importers an estimated £803,000 but also deprived the public purse of £411,000.[64]

Reconstruction of the country's leading port on lines that would improve revenue collection was therefore a matter of considerable interest to Pitt's government, which had already embraced financial reform as a matter of urgency.[65] Evidence of Pitt's personal attention to the issue is provided by three large volumes of maps and documents relating to the Port of London among the Chatham Papers, by Sir William Young's request for Pitt's approval of his draft report as Chairman of the 1796 Select Committee, and by a surviving letter to a friend by the engineer Thomas Telford suggesting that the government intervened when it seemed no progress was being made by those pressing for reform: 'I have twice attended the [1796] Select Committee on the Port of London, Lord Hawkesbury is Chairman – The subject has been agitated for four years and might have been so for many more had not Mr Pitt taken the business out of the hands of the General Committee and committed it to a Select Committee'.[66]

Government involvement was nurtured by the promoters of the West India Dock, who took 'some of His Majesty's ministers and persons connected with the Board of Trade and different public bodies' down to the Isle of Dogs to show them the location and took every opportunity to stress the benefits to the public purse from a more secure system. But the government's vision for the future of the Port of London went beyond the schemes promoted by its merchants. In 1797, the Select Committee on Finance heard evidence in favour of the introduction of a Free Port

---

[62] MLD, Vaughan Papers, Volume 5, *An Account of the Gross Produce of the Revenue of Great Britain*. London revenue from duties totalled £3,536,911.

[63] Martin Daunton, *Trusting Leviathan. The Politics of Taxation in Britain, 1799–1914* (Cambridge University Press, Cambridge, 2001), 43–5.

[64] SC Foreign Trade, *Appendix VI*, 175–6.

[65] See William J. Ashworth, *Customs and Excise: Trade, Production and Consumption in England, 1650–1845* (Oxford University Press, Oxford, 2003).

[66] TNA 30/256; Thomas Telford letter quoted in John Pudney, *London's Docks* (Thames & Hudson, London, 1975), 25–6.

system from Irving, the Inspector General of Imports and Exports. As a witness to the 1799 Select Committee on the Improvement of the Port of London, he subsequently argued that the introduction of docks would provide an opportunity to implement such a scheme. Allocation of goods to secure warehouses in particular docks would allow these to remain there until re-exported, or on payment of duty, released for the home market. He pointed out that such a system, already in operation for East India Company produce, would need compulsory warehousing, similar to those planned for the West India Dock, at the London Dock at Wapping.[67]

Since warehouses and monopoly over the handling and storage of certain cargoes had not been part of the original proposal for Wapping, but featured in the final Act, government influence is evident. In a private letter, Vaughan wrote regretfully that his original plan for the port as a whole was for 'encouraging commerce on the broadest basis & leaving our Revenue Laws to support themselves by their own regulation'.[68] But the government had other ideas.

Under the 1799 Act, the Legal Quays were to be purchased by the Crown, compensation paid to those adversely affected by the new system and the Corporation given a loan to assist with the cost of construction of its canal. These measures were to be funded by an unlimited-term Treasury loan to be repaid with the revenue from a special tax, the 'tonnage duty', imposed on foreign trade shipping using the port, with assessment and award of compensation determined by a Compensation Commission.[69] With this strategy, the State provided the means of buying off those vested interests which in the past had succeeded in preventing change, so effectively subsidising the dock companies by relieving them of a potential financial burden. Pitt may have taken some persuading over the grant of a monopoly to each dock company in the handling and storage of certain regional cargoes. Certainly, the privilege was hedged about with precautions. After twenty-one years, the monopoly itself had to be renewed; companies were limited to dividends of 10 per cent; maximum charges were laid down, and annual accounts had to be presented to Parliament. Private enterprises though they were, the dock companies that opened for business in the early 1800s were far from free agents.[70]

---

[67] PP 1796–1797, Vol. 12, SC on Finance, Fourth Report, Appendix L.3, Irving, 139–41; SC Port of London (1798–1799), Second Report, Appendix E3, 515–6.
[68] MOLD, Vaughan Papers, Vol. 2, Draft Letter to Lord Gwydir, 18 April 1800.
[69] Walter M. Stern, 'The Isle of Dogs Canal. A Study in Early Public Investment' *The Economic History Review*, New Series 4 (1952), 359–61.
[70] Geo. III. c. 69.

Government engagement in the reform of the capital's port went beyond docks and warehouses. The preamble of the 1799 Act identified four evils: the circuitous course of the Thames, the crowding of shipping, the absence of regulations for mooring vessels and the inadequacy of accommodation for goods. 'Great delays, accidents, damages, losses and extraordinary expense' were said to be the result, leading to 'hindrance of commerce and great injury of public revenue'. A key feature of the legislation was the central role given to the Corporation not only as builder and operator of the City Canal but also as the employer of new officials, 'Harbour Masters', to be responsible for traffic in the river and supervision of moorings. The owners of privately owned mooring chains were to be bought out. These provisions reflected the determination of the Corporation to be associated with the changes in the port but equally defined a role for Parliament as the ultimate authority over the river. If the Corporation failed to exercise its powers adequately, it was frustrating the wishes of the legislature, hence the recourse to Parliament in the 1830s and later in the century by critics of its performance.

On Saturday 12 July 1800, the 'concurring hands' of Prime Minister William Pitt, Lord Chancellor Lord Loughborough and West India merchants George Hibbert and Robert Milligan laid the foundation stone of the West India Dock. This was the first of the wet docks that were to become the dominant feature of London's port in the nineteenth and twentieth centuries.[71] However, magnificent docks and impressive buildings added to the port's physical fabric but were not a replacement for the existing river wharves, quays and warehouses. Such resources remained, some being put to new uses, others continuing to meet the same needs as before; for London's coasting and coal trades, the new century brought no sharp break with the past comparable with that experienced by certain foreign trades when the docks opened.

Even so, the ways in which cargoes were handled by docks in their early years cannot be properly understood without taking into account the situation before they existed. A number of developments were a reaction against the previous system, but equally, expectations and constraints created by past practices continued to shape the way the port worked. By mid-century, the impact of steam on both sea and land transport – ship and railway – in London as elsewhere altered the terms in which ports conducted their business and increasingly distanced them from the pre-industrial past. But until this stage, while the introduction of

[71] MLD, WID 301, 287, WID 304, 75; MLD, Cuttings Collection, 2.2, Sheets 21, 24; EID 278, 26 July 1806.

its first docks must certainly be seen as a revolution affecting more than facilities, the Port of London retained many of its traditional features. Finally, if a defining organisational characteristic of the port throughout the nineteenth century was the role of private enterprise in the provision of facilities and services, then the terms and limitations of the late-eighteenth-century settlement of 'the Port of London question' exerted a profound and lasting influence.

2 'Carrying the Plan into Effect'
Building and Systems

Illustration 2.1 The West India Docks, 1802. Image: William Daniell, An elevated view of the docks and warehouses now constructing on the Isle of Dogs, 1802. © Historical Picture Archive/Getty Images.

> The dock itself appearing like a great lake, was an object of beauty and astonishment. The warehouses are the grandest, the most commodious and spacious we have ever seen.[1]

The 1799 Act ended years of debate and lobbying. Now it was time to put the exceptionally ambitious plans into effect. The successful establishment of the two companies encouraged others. Within barely a decade, London not only had a dock close to the City at Wapping and another spanning the Isle of Dogs, but also one further downriver at Blackwall. Across the river at Rotherhithe, there existed a dock complex around the site of the old Greenland Dock. Apart from the rebuilding after the Great Fire, nothing on such a physical scale was attempted

---

[1] *Times*, 28 August 1802, on the opening of the West India Docks.

before in the capital or elsewhere. In 1800 dock accommodation in the whole country had totalled seventy-eight acres, with the largest system being Liverpool's twenty-eight. London's West India and London docks alone totalled fifty-four.[2]

London's dock enterprises were also unique in terms of scale of operations. The Navy's victualling yard at Deptford, its dockyards and some of the private shipyards were substantial enterprises, but not in the same league as the largest of the new dock companies. It was an extraordinary engineering and industrial achievement.

The East India Dock Company

Those specialising in the trades monopolised by the East India Company had not been part of the strident movement for port reform. The East India Company effectively had its own port at Blackwall, which handled shipping and cargoes with military efficiency. Facilities for outfitting, masting and repair were close by in the Brunswick Dock and Blackwall Yard. However, with dock investment the current fashion, East India merchants, shipowners and shipbuilders were among the subscribers to the new companies and some saw an additional investment opportunity. These included shipbuilders John and William Wells, owners of the Brunswick Dock who stood to gain from its sale, wealthy shipowners Robert Wigram and John Woolmore and Joseph Cotton, Deputy Master of Trinity House.[3] It has been suggested that, following the opening of the West India and London Dock, thieving gangs had moved downriver to prey on the hoys and ships of the East India Company, which spurred on proposals for an East India Dock.[4] Since in 1803, the West India had been functioning for little over one season and the London had yet to open, this is implausible.

By March 1803, the Wells brothers had East India Company approval for a dock. The Company did not itself own ships – it hired them from a small group of wealthy shipowners – but its control of the trade made the agreement essential. The Wells brothers disingenuously argued that

[2] A. W. Skempton, 'Engineering in the Port of London, 1789–1808', *Transactions of the Newcomen Society*, 50 (1978–90), 100, 106; D. Swann, 'The Pace and Progress of Port Investment in England, 1660–1830', *Yorkshire Bulletin of Economic and Social Research*, 12 (1960), 32–44.

[3] On the East India Dock, see George Pattison, 'The East India Dock Company 1803–1838', *East London Papers*, 7 (1964), 31–40; *Survey of London, 43*, 575–92. The author's research on primary sources relating to dock companies in the Port of London archives was undertaken prior to the publication of Volumes 43 and 44 of the *Survey of London*, so in this chapter and elsewhere, there is some overlap with references in that magisterial work.

[4] Pattison, 'East India Dock Company', 31; *Survey of London XLIV*, 575.

'the real motive is the public good, and the surplus profit going to the reduction of the further duties [for cargo-handling] cannot but be a striking beneficial feature of this undertaking'. They also made a well-judged reference to the prevention of theft.[5]

Despite its reputation for security and efficiency, the company had for years encountered serious problems with smuggling and theft in home waters as well as elsewhere.[6] Over 200 chests of tea were said to be stolen in the Port of London every year, a loss of £2,100. The attraction of secure accommodation for East Indiamen and hoys in a non-tidal environment, saving a day and a half (three tides) of time unloading in the river, was obvious.[7] As early as July 1803, the creation of the East India Dock Company and the construction of docks at Blackwall 'for the accommodation of the East India shipping' were in the statute book. Like the other two north bank companies, the East India Dock Company gained a twenty-one-year monopoly, with all vessels trading to China and the East Indies compelled to unload, refit and load stores in its facilities alone.[8]

In contrast to the novelty of the other dock projects, promoters saw the East India Docks as essentially a modification of existing arrangements. 'They remained far too strongly attached to traditional practices and procedures ever to embrace the notion of developing a full-integrated commercial docking and warehousing operation on its Blackwall site'.[9] There was no provision in the 1803 Act for rentable facilities and quayside services, nor were the docks designated as Legal Quays, so cargoes could not be landed. The new Commercial Road, with a branch to the East India Dock, opened up the possibility of transporting merchandise by land to the City, so in 1806, it gained Legal Quay status.[10] Even so, the focus of the East India Dock Company continued to be shipping rather than cargoes and it 'retained the maritime and East India character which the founders gave it in the early days' throughout its existence.[11]

The Rotherhithe Docks

Although different in ambition and management to the East India system, the development of dock facilities on the Rotherhithe peninsular

[5] MLD, EIDC 276A, 19 March 1803.
[6] H. V. Bowen, '"So Alarming an Evil:" Smuggling, Pilfering and the East India Dock Company, 1750–1810', *International Journal of Maritime History*, 14 (2002), 1–31.
[7] MLD, EIDC 276A, 19 March 1803, 20 April 1803.
[8] 43 Geo. III. c. 126; MLD, EIDC 277B, 22 November 1805.
[9] Bowen, 'Smuggling, Pilfering', 31.
[10] *Survey of London*, *44*, 120; 46 Geo. III. c. 113.
[11] Pattison, 'East India Dock Company', 32.

similarly owed much to established maritime connections. These included the Greenland Dock (with whaling in decline used primarily for laying-up vessels) as well as waterfront shipbuilding and repair premises which imported timber.[12] In 1806 the Greenland Dock was sold by its owners, again the Wells shipbuilding family, to one William Ritchie. After some improvements, in 1807 Ritchie sold it on to a consortium that included City magnates Sir Charles Price MP, a banker, and Alderman Thomas Rowcroft, an oil merchant and naval contractor.[13] The opening of the West India and London docks had affected Rowcroft's Sufferance Wharf business, giving him a motive for involvement. Charles Enderby, a member of the Enderby whaling dynasty, William Tooke Robinson, a timber merchant, and John Saint Barbe, a whaler owner, were among others involved.[14]

The Greenland Dock, renamed the Commercial Dock, continued to function under its new owners. They bought out a group of local land-owners, led by 'Joseph Moore of Dorking', who threatened to establish a rival dock on the basis of a Treasury promise of an exclusive preference for bonding timber by the Treasury.[15] The promise proved a fantasy, but the enlarged Commercial Dock estate permitted the development of a string of ponds for floating bonded timber. By 1815 these extended over forty-seven acres.[16] Other contestants for Baltic shipping and cargoes embarked in 1807 on building the East Country Dock, a narrow strip of water running parallel to the Commercial Dock site. Negotiations for a merger having failed, in 1810 the Commercial Dock Company was finally incorporated as a joint stock enterprise for the 'discharge of ships and vessels laden with Timber, Wood, and other Merchandize ... and securing such cargoes of Timber and Wood' as

[12] See Reginald Heaton Page, 'The Dock Companies of London 1796–1864' (MA thesis, University of Sheffield, 1959); Nathaniel Gould, *Historical Notice of the Commercial Docks 1844* (London 1844, reprinted *Rotherhithe Local History Paper No. 5*, Stuart Rankin (ed.), Dockside Studio, London, 1998); Stuart Rankin, *A Short History of the Surrey Commercial Docks, Rotherhithe Local History Paper No. 6* (Dockside Studio, London, 1999); Josiah Griffin, *History of the Surrey Commercial Docks* (Smith and Ebbs, London, 1877).
[13] *Public Ledger and Daily Advertiser*, 8 April 1807.
[14] Roger Knight and Martin Wilcox, *Sustaining the Fleet 1793–1815. War, the British Navy and the Contractor State* (Boydell Press, Woodbridge, 2010), 108; Alan Frost, 'Thomas Rowcroft's Testimony and the "Botany Bay" Debate', *Labour History*, 37 (1979), 101–7; TNA, T76, Port of London Compensation Commission, Report 496, Memorial Thomas Rowcroft; PP VI.1 [186], SC Foreign Trade (Timber Trade), 81, Appendix No. 14.
[15] MLD, CDC 558, 12 May 1809; 50 Geo. III. c. 207 s. 41; Heaton Page, *London Dock Companies*, 130 ftn. 1.
[16] Swann, 'Port Investment', 39.

well as landing hemp, pitch, tar and tallow, fish oil, blubber and whale fins.[17] The following year, the rival East Country Dock Company was established.[18]

The two dock companies were not the only Rotherhithe enterprises providing facilities for shipping and cargoes. The 1801 Grand Surrey Canal Act promised little benefit for the locality except an encouragement to market gardening along its route.[19] Others saw greater potential. Early in 1802, civil engineer John Hall persuaded the Grand Surrey's directors to include a basin and lock entrance from the Thames suitable for shipping.[20] By 1811, the three-acre Grand Surrey Canal Company basin had proved so attractive for berthing vessels that the company obtained parliamentary authorisation to charge for dockage, rent and wharfage. The range and type of Baltic produce set out in the schedule of charges mirrored those handled by the docks.[21]

Dock Company Investors

There were 353 West India Dock Company subscribers for the first half £million stock, with half holding £500. Eighteen individuals invested £5,000 each, enough to qualify for a directorship, and a few even more than this.[22] A joint investment by twenty-nine Common Councillors of £1,000 each made the Corporation of the City of London the largest single shareholder. Eight also invested individually. In all, a third of the West India Dock Company's initial capital was contributed by twenty-four people.[23] Subscribers included those with West Indian trade interests but also others involved more generally with shipping and port industries. Only a third have been identified as overseas merchants, but this group was well represented on the Court of Directors. George Hibbert was Chairman, Robert Milligan his Deputy and Milligan's bankers, Smith, Payne and Smith, subsequently the company's bankers, were among financial investors. The West India Dock Company was very much a metropolitan venture. Most stockholders had addresses in

---

[17] Rankin, *Short History*, 10; MLD, CDC 558, 18 September 1807; 50 Geo. III. c. 207.

[18] 51 Geo. III. c. 171.

[19] 41 Geo. III. c. 31. 1801.

[20] Heaton Page, *London Dock Companies*, 137–8; *Times*, 12 October 1803.

[21] 51 Geo. III. c. 170. Second and Third Schedule; Joseph Priestley, *Historical Account of the Navigable Rivers, Canals and Railways of Great Britain* (Longman, Rees, Orme, Brown & Green, London, 1831), 312–16.

[22] MLD, 'Alphabetical List of Subscribers to the West India Docks', 8 August 1799.

[23] On dock company slave trade connections in general, see Nicholas Draper, 'The City of London and Slavery: Evidence from the First Dock Companies, 1795–1800', *Economic History Review*, 61 (2008), 432–66.

the capital or surrounding area.[24] Buoyed up by its monopoly status, subscribers were confident of profits. They rejected an 1802 proposal by directors for a further issue of stock, voting to raise additional capital from existing 'proprietors'. Although this has been largely forgotten, the West India Dock was itself the lasting physical embodiment of London's long-standing role in Britain's slave trade.

It is less clear who was responsible for the £800,000 originally raised for the London Dock. The 1800 Act names subscribers, but not the sum contributed. However, by linking a 1795 register of subscribers with 583 appearing in 1800, Nicholas Draper has produced an indicative list. Twenty-one individuals provided £5,000 or more, 16 per cent of the total. Investment in the London Dock Company was therefore more widely spread than in the West India Dock Company. This pattern reflects the broader range of foreign trades, and greater variety of commercial interests, which the London Dock was to serve. A third of stockholders were merchants in overseas trades, but banking, ship and insurance broking and cordage manufacturing were also represented.[25] Hibbert's breakaway group which created the West India Dock Company failed to entice all those with West Indian connections. The London Dock Company Chairman, Sir Richard Neave, and his Deputy, Edward Forster, were both active in the West India Merchants Committee. Its Treasurer was Beeston Long, another prominent West India merchant and a Director of the Bank of England. Indeed, London Dock Company investors included most of the major slave traders, some with stock in both companies.[26]

Just over a hundred individuals financed the East India Dock, responding by invitation rather than public advertisement. With investment restricted to managing owners of East India shipping, despite joint-stock status, the company was in practice a private concern. The eleven promoters, five shipbuilders and the owner of part of the site contributed £61,000 of the initial £200,000 stock. The remaining amount was raised *pro rata* from shipowners based on their tonnage. Compared with the great wealth of most concerned, the cost of the East India Dock was modest, so there was little difficulty in raising the £375,000 eventually spent or dealing with short-term cash flow problems by loans from directors.[27]

---

[24] MLD, 'Alphabetical List'; Derek Morris and Ken Cozens, *Wapping 1600–1800. A Social History of an Early Modern London Maritime Suburb* (East London History Society, London, 2009), 44–5.
[25] Draper, 'City of London and Slavery', 436, 438, 440.
[26] MLD, LDC 137/1, 9 July 1800.
[27] MLD, EID 291, *List of Subscribers;* EID 278, 7 November 1806, 13 January 1807; *Survey of London, 44,* 576.

The Commercial Dock had an authorised capital of £260,000. Information is scarce, but since its promoters had a whaling or Baltic trade background, it seems probable that many of the ninety-five proprietors named in its 1810 Act had similar connections. The Commercial Dock Company's ten directors qualified by holding at least £2,000 in stock.[28] The East Country's authorised capital was £40,000 in £100 shares, and its act names 116 investors. The history of the creation of both companies suggests a role for speculative investment, something confirmed by a surviving 1808 certificate testifying 'that John Cotton, Bride Street, Fleet Street, City, Musical Instrument Maker' had two East Country Dock shares.[29]

Dock Design

Engineering and architectural historians stress the scale and, in some respects, technical novelty of London's dock construction, completed in a remarkably short period of time.[30] All three on the north bank were in working order by 1806 and those on the south bank following shortly after. The companies were able to draw on expertise honed in the previous century's canal, bridge and harbour building boom when recognisable functional roles emerged. In major projects, the preparatory and construction phases often involved a senior advisory and planning engineer, responsible for the overall design, and a resident engineer, responsible for the progress of the work.[31] Unsurprisingly, given the magnitude and complexity of the work, this was also the system adopted by the north bank companies, although as it transpired not without problems.

Several eminent civil engineers were involved. Ralph Walker, who devised the plan for the West India Dock despite no experience, was the exception. The companies were not in competition, so their engineers faced no problem with allegiances. At various stages, the West India Dock Company employed William Jessop, builder of the Grand Junction Canal, Thomas Morris, former engineer of the Liverpool Docks, and the canal and bridge builder, John Rennie the Elder. Jessop also worked on the City's Isle of Dogs canal. Rennie had a hand in the design and construction of almost all of London's early docks. He led a small group that produced the final outline of the plan for the London Dock and

[28] 50 Geo. III. c. 207. s. IV–V; Gould, *Historical Notice*.
[29] 51 Geo. III. c. 171; LMA, 0/339/006.
[30] For more extensive, detailed general histories of both the West India and East India docks, see the *Survey of London*, Chapters X (Volume 43, 247–81) and XX (Volume 44, 575–92).
[31] D. Swann, 'The Engineers of English Port Improvements, 1660–1830 Part 1', *Transport History*, 1 (1968), 153–68, 153.

subsequently became the company's engineer. He also worked on the design of the East India Docks. Daniel Alexander was the author of the original proposal for the London Docks submitted to the 1795–6 Select Committee. As its 'Surveyor', he then devised the final detailed plan for Wapping and designed its warehouses.[32] For these men, the national status of London's dock building programme must have added to the attraction of involvement, but no doubt so did the remuneration. Rennie received from the London Dock Company £500 for ninety days work annually and was paid the same on similar terms when acting as joint engineer with Ralph Walker for the East India Dock Company. The West India Dock Company paid Jessop £500 a year, then five guineas a day plus expenses, with a gratuity of £1,000 on completion of construction.[33]

There were several iterations of design for the West India Dock system, but by 1800, it was settled as two parallel docks. 'The Great Dock for unloading inwards' offered thirty acres of water for imports. 'The dock for light ships and loading outwards' was twenty-four acres. Both were twenty-three feet deep. Such separation of import and export facilities, insisted on by Customs and Excise for all the north bank docks, was unprecedented. With locked entrance basins connecting with the Thames, the docks straddled the entire width of the otherwise unoccupied Isle of Dogs.

Ralph Walker was the originator of this straightforward, though immense, scheme. Walker had a Thames seafaring background. His West Indies connections included a stint in the trade as a commander and then as a Jamaica planter.[34] The design of warehouses was more complex and here the West India Dock Company sought external advice. A competition for a single warehouse 'stack' attracted an impressive sixteen proposals. Even so, none proved suitable, perhaps because the authors lacked practical knowledge of cargo handling. The company turned to some leading wharfingers and armed with their specifications approached the architectural partnership of George Gwilt and Son. The Gwilt scheme, approved in March 1800, was for nine standard warehouse 'stacks' of a functional design on the north quay of the Import Dock, with additional warehouses at each end.[35]

[32] *The Gentleman's Magazine*, 26, 1846.
[33] MLD, LDC 137/1, 21 May 1801; EIDC 276A, 3 February 1804; *Survey of London, 43*, 253.
[34] Sessional Paper, 1795–6, 102, Committee Appointed to Enquire into the Best Mode of Providing Sufficient Accommodation for the Increased Trade and Shipping of the Port of London, 107, 153, Appendix Bb; PP 1798–9, 124, SC Improvement of the Port of London, 192.
[35] *Survey of London, 43*, 284–5.

Although certainly imposing, these were not ostentatious buildings. Indeed, one architectural historian has lamented the failure, given the spectacular water vistas, to seize the opportunity to create impressive edifices in the contemporary neoclassical style.[36] But their number, scale and position made them unique. 'Quayside warehouses were not a typical feature in docks elsewhere. They were an innovation particularly suited to high-value imports and the re-export trade, to provide security and minimal handing'.[37] Inclusion in the plans for the West India Docks, as also subsequently for the London Dock, was in preparation for the granting of bonding privileges for their monopoly trades, due to follow once the docks were open. Three warehouses were already constructed in time for the inauguration of the Import Dock in August 1802 and three more followed in January. By July 1806, with the Export Dock and additional warehouses now open, the company declared its works complete.[38]

The London Dock Company faced a greater challenge than the West India Dock Company. In contrast to the open pasture of the Isle of Dogs, its eight-acre location between Ratcliffe Highway and Wapping High Street was dense with housing, workshops, factories and public houses, all needing demolition.[39] Alexander, more visionary than practical, proposed two connected docks, one of twenty-five acres for imports with an eleven-sided irregular shape, and the other ten and a half acres for exports.[40] A team led by Rennie, which reviewed Alexander's scheme, judged it insufficiently 'compact or effective in active capacity' and, with the ink barely dry on the London Dock's Act, warned that access problems meant that parliamentary authorisation for more land would be needed. Their no-nonsense alternative, approved by the Directors in March 1801, was for 'a parallelogram pure and simple, of 20 acres of water; the length being 1260 feet, and breadth 690 feet'. Rennie recognised that there was more to dock operations than water space:

Due reference having been had for the Wharfs and Quays; and leaving space sufficient round the whole, for the utmost extent which may be considered necessary for Warehouses of different kinds; for yards; for offices and counting houses;

[36] Edward Sargent, 'The Planning and Early Buildings of the West India Docks', *Mariner's Mirror*, 77 (1991), 119–41.

[37] Peter Guillery, 'Warehouses and Sheds: Buildings and Goods Handling in London's Nineteenth Century Docks', in Adrian Jarvis and Kenneth Smith (eds.), *Albert Dock, Trade and Technology* (National Museums & Galleries on Merseyside, Liverpool, 1999), 78.

[38] Sargent, 'Planning and Early Buildings of the West India Docks', 122–3: *Survey of London, 43, 253.*

[39] 40 Geo. III. c. 47.

[40] Sessional Paper 1795–6, 102, Port of London, Alexander, 22 March 1796, 25.

for a bason [sic] of adequate size proportioned to the number and frequency of entering and leaving the dock; for the lock of communication between both and the Entrance lock from the River; and lastly for the large wharf next the River, to which all vessels are to approach for entrance.[41]

Not everyone was happy with the final plan for the London Dock. In June 1802, Vaughan, to whom the whole enterprise owed so much, declined re-election as a director. His precise reasons are now obscure, but it seems that he felt excluded from decisions and was frustrated by what he perceived as a lack of ambition for this 'great undertaking'. Vaughan was a staunch supporter of Alexander, so he may have been troubled by his treatment.[42] In fact, Alexander's warehouse designs fared better, apparently being approved by directors without substantial modification. Stretching along the dock's north quay were five separate four-storey buildings with cellars, each containing six warehouses. At its eastern end were two bonded warehouses for tobacco, with specifications agreed with the Treasury and Customs and Excise (Illustration 2.2).[43]

Developing a design for the East India Docks was rather more straightforward. Even so, there was an element of trial and error. The plan devised by Rennie and Ralph Walker involved the adaptation of the former Brunswick Dock to serve as an Export Dock and a new twelve and three-quarters-acre Import Dock. In the winter of 1804, when progress in digging out the Import Dock was already well underway, doubts about whether this would be large enough to accommodate the number and tonnage of vessels then involved in the East Indies trade resulted in an expansion to eighteen acres.[44] As Daniell's view shows, with no warehouses, the facilities were more basic than the other two docks (Illustration 2.3).

On the south bank, where again warehouses were not needed, re-fashioning the Greenland dock into the Commercial Dock under the direction of Ralph Walker, assisted by his nephew James, later the company's resident engineer, proved uncomplicated. The same seems to have applied to docks and timber ponds added between 1810 and 1812. Little is known about the planning of the East Country Dock, but it is unlikely that its long, thin design presented problems. In contrast, the Grand Surrey Canal Company, plagued by financial uncertainty, did not arrive easily at a scheme for its ship lock and basin. Engineer John Hall continued to influence developments. His major contribution was

---

[41] MLD LDC 137/1, 17 March 1801, 94.
[42] MLD LDC 137/1, 25 June 1802, 6 July 1802; Vaughan, *Memoir*, 28–9.
[43] MLD LDC 137/1, 3 November 1801, 11 May 1802.
[44] *Survey of London, 43*, 578; Skempton, 'Engineering, 1789–1808'. 98.

Illustration 2.2 The mid-nineteenth-century London Dock in its urban setting, surrounded by housing and industry. Image: Docks de Londres c. 1850. © Universal History Archive/Getty Images.

Illustration 2.3 The East India Docks, 1808. Image: William Daniell, A view of the East India Docks, 1808, © Heritage Images/Getty Images.

the distinctive island in the centre of the basin. After the original engineer left, Hall also temporarily managed on-going construction until the ubiquitous Ralph Walker took over.[45]

[45] Skempton, 'Engineering, 1789–1808', 100–102.

Managing Construction

London's north bank companies found dock construction as demanding as arriving at a design. As the London Dock Company directors were reminded:

... a great many objects present themselves for consideration. The quality of the soil to be worked; the comparative resources in this Metropolis and distant parts, so as to keep down the expense of the whole; the machinery to be conceived, and reduced into figure, from former example or invention .... The expense of the whole undertaking depends as much on these several points, as on the design itself, and the extent of each portion of the plan.[46]

The choice of those to supervise the building work was also vital. Assiduous Robert Milligan visited the West India Dock Company works almost daily, but there was no substitute for good employees on the ground. These could be costly, but as Rennie observed, 'one or two hundred pounds per annum is ill saved in the purchase of Abilities, Honesty and Economy – for such a sum or even more may soon be expended in these works by mismanagement'.[47] In the case of the West India Docks, when it became apparent that their designer lacked competence in agreeing contracts and overseeing the building, the directors brought in the more experienced William Jessop as lead engineer, appointed Walker as subordinate resident engineer, and took over the award of contracts themselves.

Under pressure to complete the work in time for the arrival of the West India fleet, the relationship between the two men deteriorated. Things came to head in October 1802 with 'improper language' used in a dispute over the failure of a wall. The Directors were convinced by Jessop's account of the incident, so Walker was asked to resign and Jessop given full charge.[48] Walker then moved to the East India Dock Company, where, having assisted Rennie with preparing its plan, he became resident engineer.[49]

In Rennie, the London Dock Company had not only an outstanding technical engineer but also someone with insight into managing large projects. Rennie recommended that the departments of surveyor and engineer should be separate, 'so no jarring or unpleasant interference may take place'. He set out the respective roles: the principal engineer (himself) was to devise all plans and specifications; the resident engineer,

---

[46] MLD, LDC 137/1, 17 May 1801.
[47] MLD, LDC 137/1, Report of John Rennie, 2 June 1801.
[48] Sargent, 'Planning and Early Buildings', 122; *Survey of London*, 43, 254.
[49] MLD, EID 276A, 3 February 1804.

aided by an assistant, was to see that the work complied with these, supervise the construction of 'coffer dams, locks, quay walls, earthwork and the steam engine, mortar mill and pipes' and keep an account of the work done by contractors. Surveyor Daniel Alexander was to deal with the building of the warehouses, sewers, dock wall and paving. Mindful that his part in the rejection of Alexander's original dock plan might appear to be a problem, Rennie assured the directors that he was satisfied that he could work with him.[50]

Building the Docks: Labour

In theory, the introduction of docks on the London Thames was not an engineering challenge. As a leading Victorian civil engineer subsequently observed, 'the thick gravel beds on the sites of the docks are readily excavated [and] offer excellent foundations'.[51] But there was more to the first stage of construction than digging a pit. This included the need for steam engines and piping, keeping docks and their locks free of water while the bottom was puddled with clay and the sides lined with bricks. Cofferdams to protect the worksites from the Thames were indispensable. It was a demanding operation which the companies tackled with a combination of traditional heavy manual labour using spades and shovels and the latest in technology that the industrial revolution could offer.

Excavation resulted in an immense quantity of spoil, about 1.5 million cubic yards of material for the West India Dock system alone. Some gravel was used for backfill or ground levelling, but much had to be removed. Wagons, which in the London Dock works ran on iron rails (something previously unknown in construction work), carried away spoil to open ground or to river jetties for onward transport. These wagons, which also moved building material brought in by water, were mainly hauled by horses, but a six-horsepower steam engine was used on a steep slope in the London Dock works and subsequently sold to the West India Dock Company for the same purpose. However, in the East India Docks, the combination of 100 horses and 400 men alone achieved a weekly average excavation of 8,000 cubic yards in the summers of 1805 and 1806.[52]

A group of firms already experienced in canal work handled this work, moving on from one dock company contract to the next as each project was completed. The five firms handling the massive West India Dock

---

[50] MLD, LDC 137/1, 132.

[51] Leveson Francis Vernon-Harcourt, *Harbours and Docks. Their Physical Features, History, Construction Equipment and Maintenance* (Clarendon Press, Oxford, 1885), 490.

[52] Skempton, 'Engineering, 1789–1808', 100.

excavations were Holmes & Bough, Clark & Thatcher, Bolton & Pixton, Millar & Smith and Samuel Jones.[53] Holmes & Bough was also the main contractor for the London Dock. Clark & Thatcher dug out the gravel levels of the City Canal and Samuel Jones was involved with the construction of the Surrey Canal basin before being dismissed on grounds of poor workmanship.[54] Excavation of the East India Dock was undertaken by Hugh McIntosh, a former canal navvy who had worked with Rennie. McIntosh became a permanent Poplar resident and went on to be one of the country's leading civil engineers, with contracts 'too numerous to detail', accumulating significant wealth.[55]

Excavation firms sub-contracted some of the groundwork to experienced gangs of labourers, paying them weekly or fortnightly according to the amount of spoil.[56] Pedlington, one of five West India Dock labourers killed in July 1802 when a coffer dam collapsed, was said by another contractor to have worked for him for many years. When the bodies that had been retrieved from the river were released by the Coroner, *The Times* reported that they were taken away for burial by 'their friends', presumably workmates.[57] References to recruiting in Kent for labourers to work on the West India Dock, as also the employment of 'men from the country' on the East India Dock excavation, indicate that others normally worked as agricultural or small-town labourers in nearby counties. Such workers were paid by the day.[58]

Maintaining a large workforce could be difficult. In August 1800 about 700 were reported working on the West India Docks, a figure said to be lower than usual in part due to the harvest. In October when contractors Holmes & Bough threatened to stop work until Spring, the West India Dock Company was forced to pay more. Even so, by January 1801 'holidays and wet weather' had reduced numbers to 'only' 450.[59] Some years later, the East India Dock Company encountered similar problems. In February 1806, a bank across the entrance lock was not demolished when planned, 'owing to the workmen having absented themselves in drinking parties, to wet days & to the steam engine having got out of order'.[60]

Disruption by weather and absence were to be expected, but war also had an impact. In autumn 1802, delays in Wapping excavations

[53] PLA, WID 301/1, 220, 21 April 1800.
[54] Skempton, 'Engineering, 1789–1808', 94, 96.
[55] Ibid., 100–101; ODNB, Hugh McIntosh (1768–1840).
[56] Charles Hadfield, *The Canal Age* (David and Charles, London, 1969), 56–7; MLD, WID 301/1, 21 April 1800.
[57] MLD, WID 304, 30 July 1802, 10 August 1802; *Times*, 26 July 1802.
[58] MLD, WID 301/1, 9 September 1800; MLD, EID 276A, 2 November 1803.
[59] MLD, WID 302/1, 10 October 1800; WID 302/2, 2 January 1801.
[60] MLD, EIDC 277B, 21 February 1806.

were blamed on 'laborers [sic] being called away on national services'.[61] Impressment threatened recruitment for early work on the East India Dock. Contractor McIntosh reported in October 1803:

I have within these few days perceiv'd some Alarm amongst the Men employ'd on account of the Danger of being impress'd, a Report being circulated of a number of Hands being taken from the London Docks, and as I have drawn (and shall be obliged to do) many of my Men from the Country where the dread of such an event is perhaps greater than here.[62]

Once work progressed beyond excavation to construction, labourers were joined by skilled men. In December 1804 the London Dock Company complained of 'the impossibility of obtaining and keeping together a sufficient number of workmen, many of whom have been called off to National Works'.[63] Even so, the impact of scarcity should not be overstated. A housebuilding boom meant a tight labour market. In autumn 1802, for example, delays in completing the West India warehouses and boundary wall were blamed by the contractors in part on difficulty in finding carpenters, masons and stone sawyers.[64] However, except for the occasional problems identified, the large numbers of labourers and skilled artisans working on dock building do not suggest persistent supply problems. This is consistent with the lack of evidence that military demand for manpower caused shortage in the wartime economy.[65]

Not all difficulties in keeping the work going resulted from harvest, weather or war. There was at least one instance of a formal labour dispute. In May 1805, the strongly unionised London journeymen millwrights struck for an increase in wages. Millwrights were 'all-rounders' who possessed a range of skills, including large-scale carpentry and metalworking, but were particularly engaged in the application of mechanical power to water and wind, including steam engineering.[66] Most worked under Master Millwrights (a category that included Rennie himself), and it was these who dealt with the dock companies. The strike brought work to a halt in a range of industries and projects across the capital, including

[61] MLD, LDC 137, 18 November 1803.
[62] MLD, EIDC 276A, 21 October 1803.
[63] MLD, EIDC 277B, 27 July 1804; LDC 137/1, 11 December 1804.
[64] MLD, WID 304, 19 October 1802, 177a.
[65] Patrick O'Brien, 'The Contributions of Warfare with Revolutionary and Napoleonic France to the Consolidation and Progress of the British Industrial Revolution', Revised Version of Working Paper 150, *Economic History Working Papers* No. 264 (2017), 16–17.
[66] James Gerard Moher, 'The London Millwrights and Engineers 1775–1825' (Doctoral thesis, Royal Holloway and New Bedford College, 1988), 27; Iowerth Prothero, *Artisans & Politics in Early Nineteenth Century London: John Gast and His Times* (William Dawson & Sons Ltd., Folkestone, 1979), 59.

construction at the East India Docks.[67] The north bank dock companies were among a group of London employers, mostly manufacturers, pressing the masters to resist the 'most unreasonable imposition' of a rise in wages. However, these skilled men were in a strong bargaining position and not all employers were prepared to hold out. After about a month, the dispute was settled on terms that favoured the journeymen.[68]

One reason why millwrights were involved in dock construction was the use of steam engines.[69] In 1805, there were at least six at work. Excavations needed pumping engines to remove water, a well-established application of steam power, but the massive scale and urgency of dock construction encouraged innovation. Boulton and Watt's Birmingham factory supplied a twenty-horsepower engine for the West India Dock to grind and mix limestone for mortar on site. A similar substantial machine was used at the London Dock and, in a smaller model, at the East India Dock Company works.[70] A steam engine hoisted the ram to drive piles for the cofferdam at the entrance of the London Dock, 'the first recorded example of its kind'.[71]

Canal precedents meant that the dock companies had no difficulty in sub-contracting excavation. Handling the construction of docks, locks, basins, quayside, warehouses and offices was potentially a greater problem. Although not everything went smoothly, the London Dock Company benefited from Rennie's experience and used a combination of directly employed labour and contracts with specialist firms or tradesmen. Instead, the less-blessed West India Dock Company initially handed over the entire operation to Adam and Robertson, a partnership of Master Builders, 'employing between 2,000 and 3,000 men, with its own timber wharf, brickyards and quarrying interests'. Their contract included five warehouses and lining the dock and lock walls with 40 million bricks made by themselves using the Isle of Dogs excavation clay.[72]

---

[67] MLD, EIDC 277B, 31 May 1805.

[68] Moher, *London Millwrights*, 205–8.

[69] MLD, WID 301/1, 27 June 1800, 31 July 1800.

[70] John Farey, *A Treatise on the Steam Engine, Historical, Practical and Descriptive* (Longman, Rees, Orme, Brown and Green, London, 1827), 654, 499–500; A. E. Musson, 'Industrial Motive Power in the United Kingdom, 1800–70', *Economic History Review*, New Series, 9 (1976), 413–39.

[71] Sir John Rennie, 'Address to the Annual Meeting January 30, 1846', *Minutes of the Proceedings of the Institution of Civil Engineers*, 5 (1846), 41; Skempton, 'Engineering, 1789–1808', 96.

[72] *Survey of London*, 43, 254–255; Alistair J. Rowan, 'After the Adelphi: Forgotten Years in the Adam Brothers' Practice', *Journal of the Royal Society of Arts*, 122 (1974), 659–70, 667–8; David Barnett, *London, Hub of the Industrial Revolution: A Revisionary History 1775–1825* (Taurus, London, 1998), 118–9; E. W. Cooney, 'The Organisation of Building in England in the 19th Century', *Architectural Research and Teaching*, 1 (1970), 46–52.

Adam and Robertson had overextended themselves. The Adam side of the partnership was already indebted before taking on the work (their historian describes the financial records as 'a Pandora's Box of monetary horror'), and in November 1801, the firm announced that it was unable to complete the contract. It had failed to manufacture enough bricks, was being pressed for payment by suppliers and owed the Excise brick duty. This was a fraught moment for the West India Dock Company, which could not afford the delay of finding a fresh contractor. Rather than let Adam and Robertson go under, it took charge of construction, assumed responsibility for the partnership's sub-contracts and expropriated its stock. Adam and Robertson continued to supervise the labour force and in fact were subsequently awarded more building contracts.[73] However, lessons were learned. Thereafter, directors kept central control of the building, avoided large-scale agreements and restricted the award of contracts to particular trades.

Large quantities of building material were needed for dock and warehouse construction. Quarries in Portland, Aberdeen, Dundee and Cornwall were among the stone sources. As well as limestone and sand, ingredients for cement mortar included volcanic ash, 'pozzulana', from Sicily. Welsh and West Country forests supplied timber for the London and Germany and Quebec provided some of the oak for the East India.[74] Wartime shipbuilding demand meant that oak timber in particular was costly and scarce.[75] The completion of the lock gates for the West India Dock relied on the goodwill of shipbuilders Perry & Wells in passing on stocks of Hastings timber, and when told in April 1802, that 'the supply comes in but slowly but time presses' the Admiralty agreed to loan the West India Dock Company timber from the navy's Thames dockyards.[76]

Construction of the docks required millions of bricks, made from London Clay, and deposits of brick earth along the Thames and its tributaries.[77] Initially the West India Dock promoters were confident that London Clay in the digging spoil could be used. However, bricks

---

[73] MLD, WID 303/3, 13 November 1801, 52–54b; *Survey of London, 43*, 254.
[74] *Survey of London, 43*, 290, *44*, 582–3; Skempton, 'Engineering, 1789–1808', 96; Sargent, 'West India Dock', 124.
[75] See Roger Morris, *The Foundations of British Maritime Ascendancy: Resources, Logistics and the State, 1755–1815* (Cambridge University Press, Cambridge, 2011), 175–8.
[76] MLD, WID 303/3, 16 February 1802, 9 April 1802, 13 April 1802, 23 April 1802.
[77] Peter Hounsell, *Bricks of Victorian London. A Social and Economic History, Studies in Regional and Local History, Volume 22* (University of Hertford Press, Hatfield, 2022), 18–28; Alan Cox, 'Bricks to Build a Capital', in Hermione Hobhouse and Ann Saunders (eds.), *Good and Proper Materials: The Fabric of London Since the Great Fire* (London Topographical Society, London, 1989), 13–15; Alan Cox, 'A Vital Component: Stock Bricks in Georgian London', *Construction History*, 13 (1997), 57–66.

produced from this were of poor quality and unsuitable for facing, so additional supplies of earth had to be brought in.[78] Some excavated material was also used for the East India Dock, although again external clay had to be found.[79] Forty million bricks were used to line the West India Import Dock walls and the Gwilt warehouses took about 20 million; the London Dock Company purchased at least 47 million and a further 2 million came from demolished properties; the East India Dock boundary walls alone took 5 million. Since the total output of bricks in England and Wales at the time averaged 782 million bricks a year, this scale of demand was nationally significant.[80]

Brick making involved considerable skill and there were several specialist brickmaking firms, most operating either in yards west of London or in temporary works close to clay deposits.[81] Brentwood and Chiswick brickmaker William Trimmer was the main supplier to both the West India and East India companies, and one of the London Dock Company contractors.[82] The companies competed for supplies and the cost to brickmakers of transport downriver to the Isle of Dogs put West India Dock Company at a disadvantage as customers. In 1801 they reported an agreement between a cartel of brickmakers and the London Dock Company 'Wapping Gentlemen' to take all these manufacturers could spare at the same price as would be offered by the West India Dock Company.[83] At times, dock construction outpaced the stream of bricks. In May 1804, notwithstanding its rules barring such involvement, the London Dock Company turned to director Sir Christopher Baynes for 1 million bricks from his yard.[84]

Despite the difficulties, the West India Dock Company's Import Dock opened in 1802 for the summer arrival of the West India fleet in 1802, but the Export Dock was not completed until 1806. The East India Dock project was more straightforward. Since vessels could continue to discharge in the river until the new facilities were ready, directors were under less pressure. It began operating in August 1806, having encountered few problems once the design was settled. In contrast, the London Dock Company failed entirely to keep to its timetable. No construction

---

[78] MLD, WID 301/1, 8 November 1799, 75–7.
[79] *Survey of London, 44,* 577.
[80] *Survey of London 43,* 254, *XLIV, 581*; MLD, LDC 154, 27 May 1804; H. A. Shannon, 'Bricks-A Trade Index, 1785–1849', *Economica, New Series,* 1 (1934), 316.
[81] Hounsell, *Bricks of Victorian London,* 62–3, 79.
[82] MLD, WID 301/1, 7 February 1800; LDC 137, 28 April 1801; *Survey of London 44,* 591.
[83] MLD, WID 303/3, 1 December 1801.
[84] MLD, LDC 137/1, 8 May 1804; MLD, LDC 154, 27 May 1804; Susan Reynolds (ed.), *A History of the County of Middlesex: Volume 3* (London, 1962), 247–251, *British History Online,* www.british-history.ac.uk/vch/mddx/vol3/247-251, accessed 20 December 2022.

work took place in the first year, given over to the preparation of plans, agreeing contracts, and purchasing houses and other premises on the site. Unlike the Isle of Dogs, this was not 'an open marsh unencumbered with covered property' as Alexander reminded his dissatisfied employers.[85] Problems with the supply of labour and materials then brought further delays. Far more complex a project than the other north bank docks, the London Dock eventually opened in January 1805, followed by five north quay warehouses in July and a large warehouse to the south in December 1806. Not until at least 1815, however, was all the work completed.[86] On the Rotherhithe peninsular dock, development proceeded on an incremental basis. With no warehouses or surrounding walls needed, construction seemingly presented few problems.

Costs

Costs escalated for all north bank companies, exceeding the original estimates and necessitating further parliamentary authorisation.[87] The West India Dock, with a water area of about sixty-four acres, cost £1.2 million, the twenty-four-acre London Dock £3.25 million, the thirty-acre East India Dock £375,000 and the Commercial and East Country dock systems £490,000.[88] General wartime inflation had been exacerbated by competition for bricks and timber. Engineer Alexander told a Lords Select Committee in 1810 that building, labour and material prices had generally doubled over the previous decade but quadrupled in the case of timber.[89] Furthermore, under the 1803 Warehousing Act allowing imported goods to be stored for fifteen months before payment of duties, stringent standards were set by the Customs and Excise. The warehouses and high surrounding walls of the West India and the London were exceptionally massive and solidly built. 'The security was far beyond that which the risk required' commented Board of Trade official, James Deacon Hume, some years later.[90]

[85] MLD, LDC 137/1, 3 November 1801, 11 December 1804.

[86] Skempton, 'Engineering, 1789–1808', 97.

[87] LCC, *Royal Commission on the Port of London, 1900. Statement of Evidence by the Clerk of the London County Council* (LCC, London, 1900), Table 1, 2–31.

[88] Swann, 'Pace and Progress', 39; PP 1821 XXI.115 [57] Accounts of West India Dock Company 1799–1820; PP 1818 VI.329 [430], SC Petitions Relating to the East India Company, Appendix A, 68–78; Swann, 'Pace and Progress'.

[89] Roger Knight, *Britain Against Napoleon. The Organisation of Victory 1793–1815* (Allen Lane, London, 2013), 357–70; MLD, WID 303/3, 9 April 1802, 13 April 1802; Parliamentary Archives, House of Lords Committee, London Docks Bill, Alexander, 21 May 1810.

[90] TNA T1/4385, J. D. Hume, 'Memorandum on the Warehousing System', 5 February 1835.

Disparities in cost per acre reflected individual circumstances. Use of existing facilities and minimal need for storage explain the relatively modest figures for both the East India Dock and Rotherhithe systems. The West India Dock Company had the advantage of the almost uninhabited Isle of Dogs site, whereas the London Dock Company had to compensate owners of dock site property in Wapping. Unanticipated costs included the £50,000 purchase of Shadwell Water Works and land to allow future expansion to the East.[91] Engineering historian Skempton considered that 'London Docks show Rennie at the height of his powers, as an innovator, designer and director of great undertaking in which excellence ranked as the main criterion'. But such excellence came at a price, as did the fine classical architecture of Daniel Alexander's warehouses.[92]

In the early months of 1804, building work on the London Dock could only continue with the aid of advances from the Bank of England, personally guaranteed by certain directors. Legislation then increased its authorised stock of £1.5 million by a further million and empowered the company to assign dock rates as security for loans.[93] The London Dock Company's financing arrangements in its first decades are obscure, but the Bank of England was among its creditors, and there is no doubt that the initial costs of the enterprise created a dividend and loan repayment burden that affected longer term financial prospects.[94]

How large a sum by contemporary standards was approximately £5.3 million spent in total on building the docks? Given the short time involved, it seems immense when compared with an estimated £6.5 million in fixed capital investment by the entire cotton industry between 1795 and 1817.[95] A more relevant comparison, given the role of mercantile and shipowning interests in financing port reform, is with the cost of shipping. A fully equipped 1,200-ton East Indiaman cost about £42,000 in 1796 and £64,000 in 1810.[96] There were thirty-five vessels of similar or greater tonnage launched in the Thames for the East India Company between 1796 and 1810.[97] The East India business was certainly exceptional

---

[91] PP 1802–3 VII.15 [122], Account of Receipts and Disbursements of the London Dock Company.

[92] Skempton, 'Engineering, 1789–1808', 97; Pudney, *London's Docks*, 44.

[93] 44 Geo. III. Cap. 2 1804; 45 Geo. III. Cap. 58 1805; MLD, LDC 137/1, 3 January 1804, 28 February 1804, 6 March 1804, 27 March 1804.

[94] MLD, LDC 137/1, 18 November 1803, 3 January 1904, 6 March 1804, 27 March 1804, 19 June 1804, 26 February 1805, LDC 138/2, 14 November 1809.

[95] Stanley D. Chapman, 'Fixed Capital Formation in the British Cotton Industry, 1770–1815', *Economic History Review*, 23 (1970), 252.

[96] PP 1812 VI.117 [151, 182] SC Affairs of the East India Company, Fourth Report, Appendices 43, 44.

[97] PP 1812–13 VIII.59 [84], Return of Ships Launched in the River Thames for the East India Company, 1770–1812.

within the shipping industry in its high capital requirements, but these figures help us to appreciate that London's mercantile class was used to costly capital-intensive projects.

Even so, financing these major infrastructural works in wartime might be supposed to have presented a problem, yet clearly this was not the case. With the project for reform of the Port of London underwritten by government and future business guaranteed by their monopolies, investment in the docks was less risky than many commercial projects, but while this may account for a willingness to invest, it does not explain the ability to do so.

During the French Wars, 'prices for shipping, insuring, financing and organizing the carriage of freight overseas all rose to very high levels', generating substantial financial benefits for many of those concerned. The conflicts dislocated foreign trade, but the years 1792–1802 were marked by strong growth, particularly in the volume and value of imports and re-exports.[98] This rise highlighted the inadequacy of the traditional Port of London to cope with the increase in business, so it is no coincidence that this period was marked by the campaign for port reform.

As we have seen, funds for the north bank schemes came predominantly from the City's commercial elite of merchants, bankers and shipowners, many of whom combined several of these roles. There is little sign that these suffered the wartime hardships that undoubtedly afflicted many others.[99] The heavy national burden of taxation, with an emphasis on indirect rather than direct taxes, was broadly regressive, falling most heavily on those with lower incomes. In a break from traditional public finance, taxes rather than government borrowing provided almost two-thirds of the funds for military spending. Private savings were not diverted into the purchase of government bonds on a sufficient scale to seriously affect the available pool of investment capital, as London's dock boom confirms.[100]

Preparing for Shipping and Cargoes[101]

Design and construction were not the only issues confronting dock company directors. How the work of handling ships and cargoes was to be organised, who was to be employed, and on what terms, had to be

---

[98] O'Brien, 'Contributions of Warfare', 71, 75–6; François Crouzet, 'The Impact of the French Wars on the British Economy', in H. T. Dickinson (ed.), *Britain and the French Revolution* (Macmillan, London, 1989), 191.

[99] Clive Emsley, *British Society and the French Wars 1793–1815* (Macmillan, London and Basingstoke, 1979).

[100] Patrick K. O'Brien, 'The Political Economy of British Taxation, 1660–1815', *Economic History Review*, 41 (1988), 1–32; H. V. Bowen, *War and British Society 1688–1815* (Cambridge University Press, Cambridge, 1998), 64–5.

[101] This section is based on Antony R. Henderson and Sarah Palmer, 'The Early Nineteenth-Century Port of London: Management and Labour in Three Dock

decided. In the case of the London and West India docks, tasks associated with warehousing, such as stripping leaves from tobacco stems and garbling (sifting) pepper, had previously been carried out within the Legal Quay and Sufferance Wharf systems. In design and function, the dock warehouses mirrored the best of those in the traditional port.[102] However, the process of handling dutiable goods *before* they reached the warehouse was very different. Entry, berthing and departure of vessels needed direction and supervision. Instead of the customary laborious river transfer from ship to lighter, to quay, to cart or porter, and finally onwards to warehouse, cargoes would be unloaded directly from the ship on to the quayside before transfer to warehouse.[103]

There was not the same range of waterfront activities requiring organisation at the East India Dock, although the new Commercial Road provided an opportunity for land carriage of produce to the East India Company's City warehouses. Across the river in the Commercial Docks, the extent of activity was similarly limited. Later, there would be granaries, but at this stage, the business was primarily timber, where quayside and water space itself provided storage.

In July 1802, with the first vessels expected the following month, the West India Dock Company agreed to the preliminary establishment of permanent staff. Record-keeping and clear lines of responsibility were set out, with reporting upwards via defined routes of communication. At the apex of the hierarchy pyramid was the Court of Directors. Below was a Principal Storekeeper and Dockmaster 'to be supreme' over all other departments. Under him were the Blackwall Dockmaster, responsible for vessels entering the dock, and the Limehouse Dockmaster, for those leaving. Each warehouse 'stack' was run by a 'captain' assisted by a deputy who managed the labourers. On the quayside, there were to be 'Clerks of the Cheque', responsible for checking the weights and measures of cargoes landed. In the office was the Accountant and the 'Collector of Dock Dues'. Coopering, the repair and making of barrels, was treated differently. Though still under the overall supervision of the Principal Storekeeper, this skilled craft department was effectively sub-contracted to a Master Cooper who employed journeymen-coopers and provided hoops and nails. A Watch Department to handle security was added later.[104]

Companies, 1800–1825', in Simon Ville and David M. Williams (eds.), *Management, Finance and Industrial Relations in Maritime Industries: Essays in International Maritime and Business History, Research in Maritime History, 6* (IMEHA, St. John's Newfoundland, 1991), 31–50.

[102] *Capitalism, the State and Things*, 194–206.
[103] Guillery, 'Warehouses and Sheds', 79.
[104] MLD, WID 304/4, 9 July 18028b-17b; 26 October 1802, 191a-194a.

The London Dock Company records reveal a broadly similar hierarchical structure.[105] Their docks handled more disparate cargoes than the other two systems, which necessitated much sorting on the quayside before allocation to specific warehouses. The quay department, where the men employed were known by the traditional title of 'gangsmen', was managed independently of the warehouses. There were two cooperages, each run by a Master Cooper, one for dry goods and tobacco and the other for wine and spirits. Again, coopering was a largely independent service, but throughout the London Dock, departments operated with considerable autonomy and less external supervision than occurred in the West India Docks. Essentially, the London Dock Company replicated the old Legal Quay regime in its docks. Unlike the West India Dock Company directors, it had no ambition to revolutionise cargo handling.[106]

With the East India Dock focussed on the shipping role, its minimal establishment consisted of the Dock Master, his deputy and one assistant, all 'to be on active Inspection everywhere', six ship superintending foremen, six subordinate 'foremen of the Hold', twenty-four labourers, six watchmen and a gatekeeper.[107] Because of the seasonality of the East India trade, not all were contracted to work for a full 365 days in a year. The Commercial Dock Company similarly appointed few permanent staff. As well as a Dock Master, whose considerable duties included keeping records of cargoes and employing labourers, they engaged a Lock Master, a Principal Accountant, an Assistant Accountant, a Warehouseman and a Timber Rafter. The accountants were based at the Commercial Dock Company's counting house in the City.[108]

All companies selected men with maritime experience for shipping roles and the East India Dock Company generally preferred those with experience in the East India trades. Little is known of the earlier careers of those chosen by the West India Dock Company and London Dock Company to run the cargo side of their businesses. However, it is reasonable to assume that they had previously undertaken similar work in the traditional port. The salaries of the most senior officers were impressive but commensurate with their significant responsibilities. The London Dock Company Superintendent received an impressive £500 annual salary with a house, warehousemen 200 guineas.[109]

[105] See MLD, LDC 137/1 for scattered references to appointments from August 1804 to May 1805.
[106] MLD, LDC 138/2, 243–55, Report of the Special Dock Committee, 1808.
[107] MLD, EIDC 278C, 25 July 1806, 53–64; Pattison, 'East India Dock Company', 34–5.
[108] Rankin, Short History, 6–7; MLD, CDC 558, 3 November 1809, 2 March 1810, 19 July 1811.
[109] Henderson and Palmer, 'Port of London'; LDC 137/1, 25 August 1804.

The Opening of the Docks

The official opening of the West India Docks on 27 August 1802 was an impressive affair. Attended by Prime Minister Addington and other members of the government, a highlight was the entry of a recently launched West Indiaman, *Henry Addington*. Large numbers of Londoners made their way downriver to witness the spectacle.[110] The West India Docks, with its attractive rural downriver setting, soon became one of the sights of London, with the Prince of Wales among the first to make the 'aquatic trip'.[111]

Two years later, on a bitter, snowy day in late January, the London Dock Company directors, along with a small group of government ministers, representatives of the Corporation and 'a small party of fashionables', were among those who watched, 'with a total absence of every comfort, but that of curiosity satisfied', the filling with water of the London Dock.[112] This event, presumably designed to reassure those frustrated by its slow construction, was 'exceeding unpleasant for any kind of public show', so not an auspicious beginning. A return visit in May by the same dignitaries proved more successful. As the *Morning Chronicle* reported, 'the day was exceedingly fine, and the whole of the spectacle was such an exhibition of the wealth and the genius of the nation, that it could not fail of exciting a degree of honest pride in the breast of every Englishman'.[113] The East India docks were more obviously a private affair, but again, the government was well represented at the opening in August 1806. This time the *Admiral Gardner* and three other East Indiamen and the Trinity House Yacht processed into the dock.[114]

There was no similar fanfare for the smaller-scale developments on the Rotherhithe peninsular. These did not benefit from government support or capture the imagination of the wider public. The March 1807 opening of the Grand Surrey Canal basin, marked by the entry of John Hall's brig *Argo*, was witnessed by 'a numerous assemblage of spectators composed principally of the proprietors and their friends'. In July 1809, the Lord Mayor's barge, 'followed by three vessels laden with timber, iron and tar, under Swedish colours', inaugurated the Commercial Dock and a dinner for a hundred proprietors at the London Tavern marked the opening of its East Country Dock.[115]

---

[110] *Morning Chronicle*, 28 August 1802.
[111] *The Morning Post*, 16 July 1803.
[112] *Morning Post*, 1 February 1805; *Morning Chronicle*, 1 February 1805.
[113] *Morning Chronicle*, 27 May 1805.
[114] *Times*, 5 August 1806; *Morning Chronicle*, 5 August 1806.
[115] *Morning Post*, 12 March 1807; *Kentish Gazette*, 4 July 1809; *Saunders Newsletter*, 27 March 1811; *Public Ledger and Daily Advertiser*, 26 March 1811.

The presence of prominent politicians at the north bank dock celebrations testified to these as great national public works, something that both companies and the government were keen to emphasise. Their creation was seen as evidence of resilience in the face of war. In contrast to France, with 'no trade but of murder and rapine', commented the *Kentish Gazette* in 1804, 'in England, the confidence and the wealth of the people are such that, after every sacrifice which the safety of the empire demands, we find millions embarked in commercial speculation'.[116]

However, not everyone had a reason for celebration. Many whose livelihoods had previously depended on the Legal Quays and Sufferance Wharves now faced the unfamiliar work environment of docks, with their restrictions, discipline and lack of traditional perks. Legal Quay porters and carmen needed to find new customers, as did others. In February 1801, two lightermen alerted the West India Dock Company to a possible attempt to flood the works. Their letter concluded with a veiled threat:

Finally we beg leave to add respecting the most material calamity to be guarded against taking a retrospective view of the present Calamity of the Times which is so materially felt by every Rank in Life whose pressure in particular falls so heavy on the middle and lower Orders of Society we may expect the worst of Consequences when the Plea is pretended to arise from the want of the common necessaries of Life owing from being prevented from following their Employments by stating such services are no longer of use.[117]

A warning the following year of a bid to burn down the West India warehouses was seen as credible 'considering the dread with which the Works at the Isle of Docks [sic] are regarded by those numerous Classes at present engaged in a System of Plunderage upon the River', and the government supplied a military guard.[118]

The docks decimated much of the ancient hamlet of Wapping. The destruction of 'about 300 houses constituting the worst part of Wapping and in no wise contributing to its wants, being either filled with Paupers or such in perspective' was advertised by the London Dock Company as a benefit. Those forced to find new lodgings in already overcrowded parishes would have been less enthusiastic. In his autobiography, the cooper William Hart recalled that rents rose because 'apartments were

---

[116] *Kentish Gazette*, 13 January 1804.
[117] MLD, WID 302, 20 February 1801.
[118] MLD, WID, 16 March 1802.

much wanted at that time for whole streets were pulled down to make the London Docks'.[119]

The West and East India systems did not require similar demolition, and the population of the small hamlet of Poplar increased from 4,493 in 1801 to 7,708 in 1811. But the self-contained nature of dock business meant that so far their local impact was chiefly 'as a market for traders supplying them and their employees'.[120] The effect of the docks and basin on Rotherhithe was similarly muted. With small demand for labour and services, they added little to a waterfront economy already dominated by wharves, shipyards and maritime industries.[121]

---

[119] Pat Hudson and Lynette Hunter, 'The Autobiography of William Hart, Cooper, 1776–1857: A Respectable Artisan in the Industrial Revolution', *The London Journal*, 7 (1981), 144–60.

[120] Stephen Porter, 'All Saints', Poplar: the Making of a Parish, 1650–1817', *The London Journal*, 17 (1992), 103–14.

[121] Rankin, *Short History*, 8.

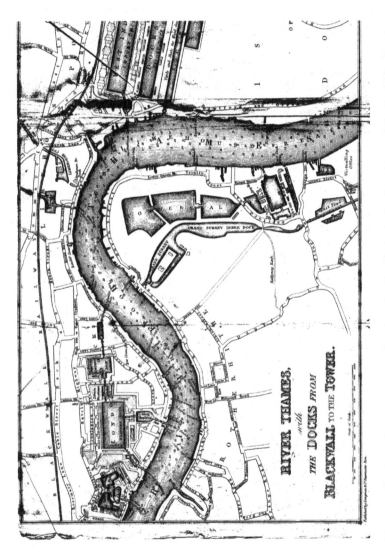

Map 3.1 Section of an 1844 map showing the St. Katharine's, London and Rotherhithe Docks. Source: J. R. McCulloch, *A Dictionary of Commerce and Commercial Navigation* (Longman, Brown, Green and Longmans, London, 1844).

In what manner are from two to three thousand labourers, who must be frequently employed at one time in these docks, and those of a class that have been accustomed to plunder, and are not refrained by any sense of the turpitude of their actions, to be overawed and controlled?[1]

Gaining parliamentary authorisation, raising capital and then designing and building the docks was a considerable achievement for promoters. Now they had to realise the vaunted claims of their greater efficiency and economy than the cargo-handling systems they replaced. The scale of commercial operations on individual sites was greater than anything previously seen in the Port of London, with the recruitment and control of large numbers of workers being a particular challenge.

For the West India Dock Company, generating income was less of an issue than controlling costs. They had a captive market, and the problem was coping with demand, not finding customers.[2] Not forced to raise additional funds for construction, it was able to both pay 10 per cent dividends and accumulate a reserve fund of almost £400,000. In contrast, burdened with interest payments on debenture shares and loans by the Bank of England and other lenders 'for completing and perfecting the works', the London Dock Company was barely profitable. Between 1815 and 1823, dividends varying from 3 to 5 per cent absorbed any operating surplus.[3] However, both companies benefited from the fact that, although their costs were lower due to scale of operations, the rates they were legally allowed to charge had been set at the former customary legal quay levels. In the final monopoly years, both companies were forced to rebut claims of excessive profits by reducing these 'Prime Rates'.[4]

The 1823 Select Committee on Foreign Trade recommended non-renewal of dock company monopolies, which would allow cargoes to be handled and stored in any dock, irrespective of where in the world they originated. Trade liberalisation was already well on course, so there was nothing unexpected about this verdict or its acceptance by government.[5] The only protection left to a dock company was that foreign produce permitted to be re-exported free of duty had to be kept in suitably secure warehouses licensed by the Customs, which initially gave them an advantage over waterfront wharf premises.[6]

---

[1] MLD, West India Merchants Committee, Minutes, Patrick Colquhoun.
[2] MLD, WID 322, 3 January 1809; SC Foreign Trade (West India Docks), Inglis, 292–3.
[3] MLD, LDC 137/1, 6 March 1804, 338, 5 March 1805, 413–4, LDC 138, 14 November 1809, 326, 23 January 1810, 342–4; RC Port of London, Appendix, 424, 427.
[4] SC Foreign Trade (West India Docks), Report, 9, Longlands, Qq. 75–6.
[5] Ibid., 14.
[6] Barry Gordon, *Economic Doctrine and Tory Liberalism 1824–1830* (Macmillan, London and Basingstoke, 1979), 14–16.

With the prospect of an open market for cargo handling came a new venture, the St. Katharine's Dock Company.[7] Promoters included the prominent economist and Russia merchant Thomas Tooke and another free trade advocate, Sir John Hall, a ship and insurance broker whose honorary title had been awarded by Hanover in recognition of service as consul.[8] Hall was a long-standing critic of the West India and London companies, and the project was his brainchild, although perhaps because he became the company's well-paid secretary and manager, he always denied this.[9]

Debates on the St. Katharine's Dock Bill centred on the need or otherwise for additional warehousing accommodation in London, but for the London Dock Company the issue was the potential impact on its profits of a well-connected new neighbour. The chosen site was the medieval church and buildings of the Hospital of St. Katharine (a community of lay brethren) right next to the London Dock, close to the Tower of London. The company opposed the bill when it came before Parliament in 1824, engaged in a pamphlet war and went so far as to secretly offer Hall the vacant post of London Dock Company superintendent.[10] Eventually, government support for the project, in which some Members of Parliament had a financial interest, convinced directors that continuing the fight was pointless. The St. Katharine's Dock Bill became law in June 1825.[11]

---

[7] *London Courier and Evening Gazette*, 27 October 1828; Walter Thornbury, *Old and New London, Vol. II* (Cassell, London, 1878); Malcolm Tucker, 'St. Katharine Dock', *The Arup Journal*, 5 (1970), 10–19; Thomas Telford, *Life of Thomas Telford Written By Himself* (James and Luke G. Hansard and Sons, London, 1838), 152–9.

[8] ODNB, Thomas Tooke (1774–1858); MLD, SKD 001, 5 July 1825; *Public Ledger and Daily Advertiser*, 11 April 1825; *Post Office London Directory*, 1817, 144; PP 1823 IV.265 [452], SC on Law Relating to Merchants, Agents and Factors, Hall, 128; Francis Townsend, *Calendar of Knights* (W. Pickering, London, 1828), 222; Skempton, 'Engineering 1789–1808', 100; A. W. Skempton et al. (eds.), *A Biographical Dictionary of Civil Engineers in Great Britain and Ireland Volume 1. 1500–1830* (Thomas Telford, London, 2002), 293. Skempton identifies Sir John Hall with the promoter of the Surrey Canal basin. However, the Surrey Dock and Canal Company's John Hall may have been the civil engineer who also briefly worked as the St. Katharine's DC Resident Engineer; *London Courier and Evening Gazette*, 27 October 1828.

[9] John Hall, *Observations Upon the Warehousing System and Navigation Laws* (Richardson, London, 1821); MLD, SKD 003, 9 January 1838, 189.

[10] John Hall, *Plain Statement of Facts Connected with the Proposed St. Katharine Dock in the Port of London to be Established Upon the Principle of Open and General Competition* (Richardson, London, 1824); Anon, *Facts Plainly Stated: In Answer to a Pamphlet Entitled 'Plain Statement of Facts Connected with the Proposed St. Katharine's Dock'* (J. M. Richardson, London, 1824); S. Cock, *Case of the London Dock Company* (J. M. Richardson, London, 1824); Parliamentary Debates, 2nd Series, 11, 2 April 1824, cc. 96–101; MLD, SKD 003, 9 January 1838.

[11] Parliamentary Debates, 2nd Series, 12, 11 March 1825, cc. 990–2; 6 Geo. IV. c. 105.

Construction work started immediately. Outline plans had already been drafted by Thomas Telford and Philip Hardwick who, as architect and engineer, received annual salaries of £500.[12] Eighteen of the nineteen original promoters put up £50,000 and another contributed £30,000. A further call in 1825 brought the amount up to the £1,352,752 needed to cover the cost of acquiring and clearing the site and initial construction. The 392 subscribers included major merchants and shipowners like Joseph Somes and George Lyall, but also speculative investors such as clergymen. Most subscribers had London addresses; seven from Yarmouth were the largest from elsewhere.[13]

Before construction the area was cleared of the Hospital, seventy or so streets and courtyards, a distillery, a brewery, cow houses, workshops, warehouses and twenty-three public houses. The demolition of 1,250 houses and tenements caused over 11,000 impoverished tenants and their families to lose their homes.[14] In contrast, the St. Katharine's Hospital did well out of eviction from its ancient site. The freehold was sold to the company for £125,000, individual officers gained compensation and £36,000 was paid towards relocation to a new, certainly more salubrious, site in Regents Park, 'a very eligible domain in one of the best situations in town'. Income from the invested funds made the Hospital considerably wealthier than before.[15]

The twenty-seven-acre constricted site of a 'very irregular figure' allowed just ten acres of waterspace for two docks. As Telford explained, 'it being obvious that the accommodation required could not be obtained by the simple forms of squares and parallelograms, I was, from necessity, led to adapt the shape of the docks to that of the ground'.[16] The result was a novel butterfly-shaped configuration. Unusually, warehouse blocks were positioned against the quayside, supported on the first floor by giant columns. Underneath were wine vaults. Other buildings included the administrative Dock House and dock master's residence.[17] Construction began in May 1826, sometimes employing 2,500 men. Bennett & Hunt

---

[12] Telford, *Life*, 152–9; Skempton, 'Engineering, 1808–1834', 82–7; Tucker, 'St. Katharine Docks', 11.

[13] *Parliamentary Debates*, 2nd Series, 11, 2 April 1824, cc. 96–101; MLD, SKD 001, 16 June 1825, 20 February 1827, *List of the Subscribers to the St. Katharine Docks* (1825).

[14] 6 Geo. IV. c. 105; Frederic Simcox Lea, *The Royal Hospital and Collegiate Church of Saint Katharine near the Tower in its Relation to the East of London* (Private Publication, London, 1865); *London Courier and Evening Gazette*, 27 October 1828.

[15] Ibid., 34–6; C. F. Lowder, *St. Katharine's Hospital: its History and Revenues, and their Application to Missionary Purposes in the East of London* (Rivingtons, London, 1867), 7–10.

[16] Telford, *Life*, 153.

[17] Tucker, 'St. Katharine Docks', 11.

Illustration 3.1 View from the East of St. Katharine's Docks, c. 1830. © Mary Evans/Peter & Dawn Cope Collection.

built the warehouses and Bramah & Sons built the dock and lock gates. By October 1828 the West Dock, basin and associated buildings were open for business. Two years later so too were the East Dock, additional warehouses and a steam packet wharf.[18]

Remarkably, the entire project had taken just four years. Telford considered the haste urged by directors had involved too many risks but recognised what had been achieved. In his opinion such swift progress would have been impossible anywhere except London, 'where materials and labour to any extent are always to be procured, as likewise the command of capital in the power of intelligent directors, accustomed to transactions on a large scale'.[19] It all cost £2 million, £332,000 more than estimated. Covered by a debentures issue, the overspend was due mostly to the steam wharf addition, extra spending on fire safety demanded by insurers, warehouse fittings and higher labour costs arising from the pace of work.[20]

[18] Skempton, 'Engineering, 1808–1834', 82–7; *London Courier and Evening Gazette*, 27 October 1828.
[19] Telford, *Life*, 154–5.
[20] MLD, SKD 001, 19 January 1830.

In October 1828, a crowd of about 20,000, including Prussian Minister Baron Bulow and the Swedish ambassador, watched the entry of vessels representing the St. Katharine's Dock Company's trade ambitions. These included an East Indiaman, a Baltic trader, one from the Cape of Good Hope, and another loading for New South Wales. Guests, partaking of 'a plain but plentiful cold collation', heard Chairman Thomas Tooke contrast the present with the recent past. Conveniently ignoring the St. Katharine's church and hospital, he told his listeners that previously the space 'was covered with heaps of filth, and by a mass of wretched hovels, the resort of the profligate and abandoned characters'. In its place was now 'one of the ornaments of a great commercial city'.[21]

The East and West India Dock Company

When the East India Dock Company's monopoly ended in 1828, it protected its connection by annual payments for exclusive use of the docks and caravan service to the City, an arrangement that collapsed in 1833 with the East India Company's loss of trade privileges. Having until then handled almost exclusively Indian and Chinese produce, the docks faced competition. Prospects looked bleak and permanent staff, salaries and shareholder dividends were cut.[22] Even so, two years later, having purchased the company's City warehouses, it handled much of London's tea trade.[23] However, this was not sufficient to secure its future and just seventy-two vessels used the East India Docks in 1835, fewer than half bringing cargo. In comparison, entries into the West India Docks approached a thousand.[24]

The East India Dock Company needed capital to widen dock entrances to cater for steam vessels and lacked storage capacity, whereas the West India Dock Company had surplus warehousing. Mutual interests included the projected railway linking Blackwall and the City, with a station at the East India's Brunswick Steam wharf where General Steam Navigation Company's vessels docked. Merger was therefore attractive to both parties, but particularly so to the East India Dock Company. Under an agreement that united the two companies in 1838, £100 of East India Dock Company stock was exchanged for £110 of the West India's.[25]

---

[21] *London Courier and Evening Gazette*, 27 October 1828.
[22] MLD, EID 286, 27 September 1833; PP 1831 V.225 [320A], SC Affairs of the East India Company, Hall, Q.2521.
[23] MLD, EID 290, 17 February 1838, 40–53.
[24] PP 1836. XIV.1 [557], SC Port of London, Appendices 16 and 19, 231–2.
[25] MLD, EID 290, 17 February 1838, 46–53, EWID 515, 7 January 1842, LDC 102.

Ships and Cargoes

The united East and West India Dock system was physically London's largest. However, since other docks benefited from the repeated voyages in the European trades, its lead in handling most shipping tonnage was narrow. In 1844, three-quarters of vessels recorded in the London Customs Bills of Entry arrived in the Port of London from Europe, but many ran to the Thames wharves, including passenger and cargo steamers.[26] Overall, foreign trade shipping activity reflected the vagaries of the trade cycle. Between 1816 and 1850, there were three main cycles; a peak in 1818, followed by a fall to 1821, then an upturn to 1825, fair constancy to 1832, then rapid growth to 1839, after which the rate of growth slowed, with a marked downturn in 1843, before a sharp recovery to mid-century (Figure 3.1).

The total tonnage of foreign trade shipping arriving in London provides a reasonable indication of import volumes. However, due to the inclusion of shipping in ballast or transferring to other British ports, records of shipping leaving the port are a poor guide to its exports, although these were certainly much less significant for the Port of London than were imports.[27] Re-exports were a different matter. Warehousing produce for re-export was a source of income for the north bank docks, particularly the East and West India systems. But exactly how significant re-exports were for the Port of London in the first half of the century is difficult to determine.

Dock company specialisation in handling particular types of cargo from certain parts of the world did not survive the end of monopoly. As Figure 3.2 shows, within fifteen years of competition, all companies were attracting shipping and merchandise entering London from a range of overseas regions.

Sugar, rum, coffee and mahogany dominated West India Dock activity in the monopoly years, but it then faced stagnation in sugar imports and competition from other docks.[28] Colonial trade remained important, but

---

[26] Only cargo-carrying vessel entries were recorded by the customs, but passenger vessels usually carried some cargo. PP 1847–8 [340], House of Lords SC on the Policy and Operation of the Navigation Laws, First Report, Porter, Q. 138; Sarah Palmer, 'The Character and Organisation of the Shipping Industry of the Port of London 1815–1849', Doctoral Thesis, London School of Economics and Political Science, 1979, 11–12.

[27] Arthur D. Gayer, W. W. Rostow and Anna Jacobson Schwartz, *The Growth and Fluctuations of the British Economy 1790–1815. An Historical, Statistical and Theoretical Study of Britain's Economic Development 1790–1850*. Volume II (Clarendon Press, Oxford, 1953), 799–801.

[28] PP 1847–48, LVIII.527 [400], Account Sugars Imported into the United Kingdom, 1793–1847; PP 1862 XIII.1 [390], SC on Sugar Duties, Appendix 1, 305–6.

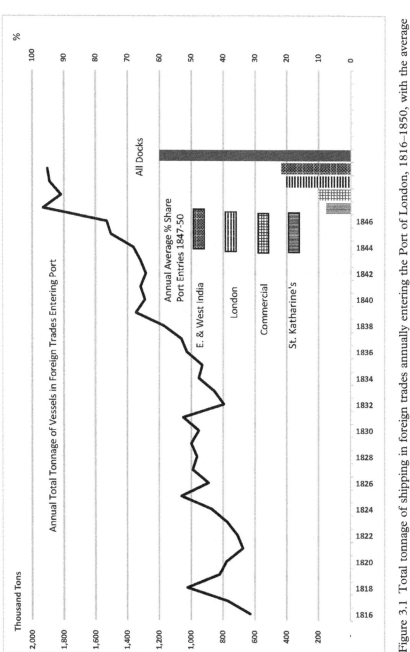

Figure 3.1 Total tonnage of shipping in foreign trades annually entering the Port of London, 1816–1850, with the average annual percentage share entering the docks, 1847–1850. Sources: PP 1902 XLIV.1 [Cd.1153], RC on the Port of London, Appendix, 42–3; MLD, LDC 102; MLD, 'Ships and Tonnage Entered 1809–1844', in Nathaniel Gould, *Historical Notice of the Commercial Docks in the Parish of Rotherhithe, County of Surrey* (London, 1844, Reprinted, Rotherhithe Local History Paper No.5), Stuart Rankin (ed.) (Dockside Studio, London, 1998); MLD, CDC 575.

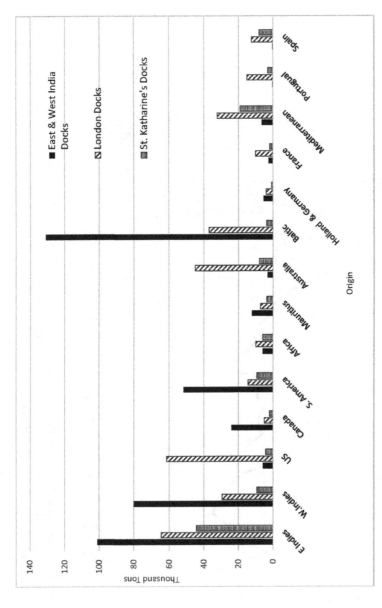

Figure 3.2 Tonnage of north bank dock vessel entries by the region of origin, 1850. Source: MLD, LDC 102, Half-Yearly Accounts of Tonnage of Vessels Entering London, St. Katharine, East and West India Docks.

East and West India Dock Company business became more regionally diverse and ample space enabled it to seize opportunities, such as accommodating cargoes in the new guano trade and benefiting from the 1846 abolition of the Corn Laws. With the Rotherhithe system overwhelmed by large numbers of grain-laden vessels arriving in response, in 1850, their docks handled more shipping from the Baltic than from either the West or East Indies.[29]

The company operated a strict system for handling ships and cargoes.[30] Once berthed, officers and crews had to leave their ship, and the cargo was discharged by the company's own workers. Apprentices were housed in the 'Naval School', an accommodation vessel moored in the Export Dock.[31] Once cleared, the vessel was moved to the Export Dock, where stevedores employed by the shipowner dealt with loading. No craft or individual was allowed to remain anywhere after dark. With the gates locked overnight, guards patrolled outside the walls of the silent deserted site.

Casks and chests containing sugar, coffee and rum were checked for damage on the quayside and if necessary repaired by coopers. Once sugar was sampled and rum gauged, goods were pushed in trucks over iron-plated pavements to warehouses and sheds, where they were weighed and quantities recorded. Cranes hoisted goods into the upper floors and shoots carried rum down to the vaults. All this was supervised by the company's servants in the presence of Revenue officials.[32] Produce for immediate delivery was transferred by lighter or cart. Owing to their bulk, mahogany and other timber were sold directly from the wood wharf to merchants and furniture makers. Except for this, no commercial transactions took place on the dock premises and 'no stragglers or strangers' were allowed entry.[33]

The West India Docks achieved a high degree of proficiency and security, but its system was best suited to the limited types of cargo handled in the monopoly years.[34] In 1838, a deputation from Liverpool

---

[29] MLD, EWID 008, 14 January 1848, 5 October 1849; LDC 102, Half-Yearly Accounts for 1850.

[30] SC Foreign Trade (West India Docks), Appendix 1, 404–8.

[31] MLD, WID 333, 17 February 1815; WID 350, 8 August 1823; EWID 009, 8 March 1850; SC Foreign Trade (West India Docks), Mitchell, 130, Inglis, 290.

[32] PP 1813–14 IV.1 [343], SC Gauging in the Port of London, Colville, 191.

[33] SC Foreign Trade (West India Docks), Mitchell, 96; Charles Dupin, *The Commercial Power of Great Britain*, Vol. I (Charles Knight, London, 1825), 34–66; PP 1840 V.475 [464], SC Inland Warehousing, Longlands, Q. 2383.

[34] Dupin, *Commercial Power*, 34–66; SC Foreign Trade (West India Docks), Report, 5; SC Inland Warehousing, Longlands, Qq. 2379–80.

noted that 'for general trade an Export Dock ought to be larger than the Import Dock', but the West India Docks were the opposite.[35] Similarly, when most vessels were British-registered, excluding crews created few difficulties. Once there was more non-colonial business, this became a problem. Barring foreign crews from staying on board increased the risk of desertion, so was unpopular with Masters and, since no other company demanded this, put the West and East India Dock Company at a competitive disadvantage. The rules were partially relaxed in 1842, but opposition from some influential customers ensured that the survival of an earlier commercial environment continued into the 1850s.[36]

About 800 ships in foreign and colonial trades came into the London Dock each year in the 1820s. By the 1840s the number had risen to about 1,200. Most of these were relatively small, less than 300 registered tons.[37] The London Dock Company always dealt with a wide range of cargoes.[38] Benefiting from the opening up of West and East Indies business, in the later 1840s its warehouses contained half as much sugar as those in the West India Docks. It also did well out of the East India Company's decline. In 1839 one warehouse was devoted entirely to tea, one to indigo, another to silk and other types of valuable dutiable produce and more tea warehouses were added in 1844. (Most of the men first recruited to work in these were former East India Company warehouse labourers.)[39] By 1847, 15 per cent of shipping tonnage entering the London Dock came from the East Indies and wine trade vessels from France, Spain and Portugal accounted for just 9 per cent of tonnage entries.[40]

The London Dock, where discharge and loading could be undertaken either by the crew or by the company's labourers, was seldom filled with ships.[41] Its problem was sufficient quay space to sort an extraordinary range of cargoes.[42] In the first two weeks of March 1837, for example,

[35] MDHB, Report to the Finance Committee of the Council of Liverpool, January 1839.
[36] Anon, *East and West India Docks, Regulations and Rates on Shipping* (Charles Skipper and East, London, 1839); MLD, EWID 009, 8 March 1850.
[37] SC Port of London, Appendix 13, 232; MLD, LDC 140, 1 April 1828, LDC 150.
[38] SC Foreign Trade (West India Docks), Inglis, 283.
[39] PP 1851 [604], SC Customs, Second Report, Appendix 30; MDHB, Report 1839, 58; MLD, LDC 142, 31 March 1835; Anon, *London as It Is Today: Where To Go and What To See* (H. G. Clarke & Co., London, 1851).
[40] MLD, LDC 102, Half Yearly Account of Tonnage of Vessels, 1847; George Dodd, *The Food of London* (Longman, Brown, Green and Longmans, London, 1856), 486–7.
[41] Anon, *Rates and Charges of the London Dock Company* (J. Metcalfe, London, 1832): PP 1825 XX.207 [119], Account of the Progress of the Works of the London Dock Company; Skempton, 'Engineering, 1808–1834', 37–88.
[42] SC Foreign Trade (West India Docks), Tilstone, 27, Chapman, 308.

Illustration 3.2 Wine tasting at the London Dock in the presence of coopers, 1821. Image: Social Life, George Cruickshank (1792–1878). © London Metropolitan Archives (City of London).

hides, barilla, wool, wine, grain, rags, linseed, black lead, pork, beef, tin, cassia and sugar were simultaneously being discharged from thirteen ships.[43] To improve loading, a wide internal jetty with sheds was added to the Export Dock in 1838.[44]

The atmosphere in the London Dock was very different to that in its orderly Isle of Dogs rival. Private carts and wagons crowded the quays and, far from being excluded from the premises, in daylight hours, members of the public were free to come and go, though they might be searched at the gate.[45] For many merchants, the London's quays served as a marketplace. In the wine and spirit trades, tasting by customers was usual, so public access to the vaults was essential. Tours of the wine vaults, with tastings, were also a popular entertainment.[46]

As the latecomer, St. Katharine's learned from the organisational experience of the other dock companies. With its layout and buildings designed specifically for a wide range of commodities, it claimed to

---

[43] PP 1837–38, XLV.317 [88], Return of Vessels with Cargoes from Foreign Ports.
[44] MDHB, Report 1839, 59.
[45] SC Foreign Trade (West India Docks) 1823, Gibson, 312.
[46] Pierce Egan, *Life in London* (Sherwood, Ely and Jones, London, 1821), 328–9.

provide a more efficient service than its Wapping neighbour. The dock's modest scale was promoted as an advantage. In implied criticism of the more remote management of other companies, the St. Katharine's Dock Company emphasised the personal attention merchants and shipowners could expect from a secretary who lived on the premises, 'ready at every moment to attend to any matter'.[47] However, by mid-century, managers considered the small site and limited water space to be a handicap, encouraging 'offensive comparisons' with the considerably greater capacity of the London Dock.[48]

Like the London Dock, although on a smaller scale, St. Katharine's handled a variety of foreign cargoes. Thanks to purchasing the East India Company's Cutler Street warehouses, it specialised in East Indies produce to a greater extent than its rival.[49] There were vaults for wine and spirits, and allocation to dock warehouses was according to the type of produce.[50] Such storage specialisation and the novel positioning of warehouses directly above the waterfront were not without problems. A vessel carrying mixed cargo might have to move berth several times.[51] In the early 1830s, around 800 ships, averaging 250 tons each, arrived in St. Katharine's every year.[52] Occasionally, there were larger vessels, such as the 720-ton *Duke of Bedford*, which arrived from Calcutta with indigo, sugar, rice and silk in April 1837. Apart from allowing vessels to be docked and undocked by night as well as day, something not offered by any other company, regulations were similar to those for the London Dock.[53]

Rotherhithe's Commercial Dock Company had the advantage of an unrestricted sixty-acre site, with plenty of space for docks, ponds, sheds and warehouses, though access to the further ponds was complex.[54] It was popular as a place to lay up vessels for the winter or offer them for sale. Besides timber, in its early years, the Commercial Docks handled tallow, whale oils, hemp, pitch and tar. Most ships entering the docks with cargo after 1815 were carrying timber or, less

---

[47] *Times*, 20 January 1830.
[48] MLD, SKD 125, Report of the Special Committee, 21 June 1852.
[49] *Morning Post*, 17 January 1838; MLD, LDC 102, Half-Yearly Reports.
[50] MDHB, Report 1839, 58.
[51] Tucker, 'St. Katharine Dock', 11.
[52] Return of Vessels with Cargoes, 25.
[53] J. R. McCulloch, *A Dictionary, Practical, Theoretical and Historical, of Commerce and Commercial Navigation* (Longman, Brown, Green and Longman, London, 1844), 486–7.
[54] Stuart Rankin, *A Short History of the Surrey Commercial Docks. Rotherhithe Local History Paper No.6* (Dockside Studio, London, 1999), 9–12.

commonly, foreign grain. Arrivals of other types of Baltic produce had virtually ceased by 1835.[55]

In the mid-1830s, most of the timber ships coming into docks chose the Commercial Docks, though many more still used the river, and it also received timber lightered or rafted in.[56] Logs floated in the timber dock, and deals and other sawn wood were piled high on the quays. It took about ten barges to discharge a full cargo, so the water space could be filled with these. To the chagrin of directors, some barges stayed for several weeks, using the docks for storage or even as a marketplace, earning the company no income.[57]

Until the 1840s, only a minority of ships using the Commercial Docks carried grain, but storage of home and foreign produce discharged in the river was an important element of its business. Some arrived in the company's own barges, originally purchased as a marketing ploy to 'create interest among importers of corn in small vessels'.[58] Corn Law suspension, followed by abolition, had a major impact. In the three years 1840–1842, there were almost twice as many grain vessels coming into the docks as those loaded with timber and they made up about 40 per cent of entries for the rest of the decade.[59]

Income and Expenditure

Dock companies had three main income sources: shipping, goods landed or loaded, warehouse space and services.[60] Warehousing was what made money. Shipping and to some extent dock dues were 'loss leaders', ways of attracting business. A buoyant market for foodstuffs might mean more shipping, but little warehousing.[61] Conversely, sluggish

[55] MLD, CDC 563, 5 August 1831, 14 October 1831; SC Port of London, Appendix 24, 542; Nathaniel Gould, *Historical Notice of the Commercial Docks in the Parish of Rotherhithe, County of Surrey* (London, 1844, Reprinted, Rotherhithe Local History Paper No. 5. Ed. Stuart Rankin, 1998). An original edition in the Museum of Docklands Library also contains 'Ships and Tonnage Entered 1809–1844'; MLD, CDC 561, 21 June 1822. SC Port of London, Appendices 11, 15.
[56] PP 1835 XIX.1 [519], SC Timber Duties, Carter, 1835.
[57] MLD, CDC 563, 13 January 1832; CDC 585, 10 May 1837.
[58] MLD, CDC 574, 8 June 1821, 1 November 1824, 9 January 1829, 13 June 1834, 12 January 1838; CDC 575, 13 January 1843; CDC 577, 3 May 1815; CDC 579, 10 October 1820; CDC 719, 11 January 1822.
[59] Gould, *Historical Notice*, 'Ships and Tonnage Entered 1809–1844'; Josiah Griffin, *History of the Surrey Commercial Docks* (Smith and Ebbs, London, 1877), 29.
[60] See Sarah Palmer, 'Port Economics in an Historical Context: The Nineteenth-Century Port of London', *International Journal of Maritime History*, 15 (2003), 27–67.
[61] *Morning Post*, 21 January 1846; MLD, CDC 575, 14 June 1850.

market conditions could lengthen storage times.[62] There was income
from produce maintenance and sale preparation. The West India Dock
Company undertook the 'taring, lotting, rummaging, pitching and turning of sugar'. The Commercial not only 'turned' grain, as was routine in
granaries, but could also 'peel' (de-husk). The London Dock Company
offered bottling, packing and 'fining' of wine and spirits.[63]

The arrival of the St. Katharine Docks initially spurred a rate war,
but collusion followed. By 1833, there was 'general harmony and
friendly understanding' and by 1841, charges were agreed by a 'United
Committee of Rates'.[64] However, even when competition on charges
was muted, war between companies continued by other means. Masters
of vessels arriving in the Port of London were not always set on using
a particular dock, so company agents boarded vessels at Gravesend to
solicit custom. Both the London Dock Company and St. Katharine's
provided free steam towage services and, despite being lower downriver, the West India Dock Company was forced to emulate its rivals.[65]
An inducement offered by St. Katharine's to 'Gentlemen, Brokers,
Captains and other persons visiting' was a dining room where, in 1847,
'an excellent dinner of the best meat, bread and vegetables is supplied
for 8d'.[66]

Companies looked to directors to bring in business. In 1851, the
London Dock Company chairman told a Select Committee that its directors were selected 'generally for their importance as merchants, and in
order, on the one hand, that we may have their influence as to getting
goods, and also that they may have a motive in going there to look after
their goods'.[67] Contacts with London's trade associations were fostered.
For decades, the St. Katharine's Dock Company's John Hall served
as secretary of the Society of Merchants Trading to the Continent, 'as
many of the members give the Docks a turn in consideration of my gra-
tuitous services to the Society'.[68] Connections between the West India
Dock Company and the Society of West India Merchants were still
strong enough in the 1820s for society subscriptions to be collected at

[62] MLD, CDC 574, 14 June 1822.
[63] SC on Foreign Trade (West India Docks), Longhurst, 363; MLD, LDC 141, 1 June
1830, CDC 585, Minute Book 7, 1 March 1838, LDC 148, 10 July 1823.
[64] MLD, SKD 117, 27 May 1830; SKD 002, 19 December 1833; SKD 119, 11 March
1841.
[65] MLD, EWID 515, 7 January 1831, 6 January 1832, 11 January 1833.
[66] Shipping and Mercantile Gazette, 24 July 1847.
[67] SC on Customs (1851) Second Report, Cattley, Q. 2597, Tooke, Q. 3671.
[68] LMA B15/168, Society of Continental Merchants, Minutes, 10 February 1825; MLD,
SKD 003, 9 January 1838.

the dock.[69] Formal contacts faded with the diversification of its trade, but the original trading links remained important. Even though by 1840, East and West India Dock Company handled more cargo originating in the East Indies and elsewhere, over half of the directors attending a Court meeting that year had West India interests.[70]

Growing the share of port business was difficult. Efforts to drum up custom had limited impact and rivals soon matched any lowering of charges.[71] The immediate response of directors to pressure on earnings was therefore to identify and implement cost savings. Costs not directly connected with current operations included insurance, pensions and rates, a significant expense because of the value of dock property. For the London Dock Company, for example, in the 1830s they amounted sometimes to 15 per cent of total expenditure. Highway, sewage and poor rate assessments therefore rarely went unchallenged. Legal fees, historic loan repayments, construction and property purchases also had a bearing on the overall financial position. The burden of interest payments, resulting from high construction costs and delays in reaching full commercial operation, bore particularly heavily on the London Dock Company. Its dividends were always lower than those of the East and West India Dock Company, which was not burdened to the same extent by historic capital costs and had accumulated reserves during its profitable monopoly period. However, wages and salaries were by far dock companies' largest expenditure category. In the 1840s, these were 75 per cent of the costs for the London Dock Company, slightly more for the East and West India.[72]

Managers

Most of those who worked at the docks were casual labourers, but every company had a core of permanent employees.[73] In the East India Dock, since there was little shipping activity except when the fleet was in the port and no warehousing, before amalgamation with the West

---

[69] Alexandra Franklin, 'Enterprise and Advantage: The West India Interest in Britain 1774–1840' (Doctoral Thesis, University of Pennsylvania, 1992), 246.

[70] MLD, EWID 003, 25 June 1840; University College London, Legacies of British Slave-ownership database, www.ucl.ac.uk/lbs/, accessed 12 June 2019.

[71] Palmer, 'Port Economics', 27–67; David R. Green. *From Artisans to Paupers. Economic Change and Poverty in London 1790–1870* (Scolar Press, Aldershot, 1995), 51; L. D. Schwartz, *London in the Age of Industrialisation. Entrepreneurs, Labour Force and Living Conditions, 1700–1850* (Cambridge University Press, Cambridge, 1992), 85–9.

[72] Palmer, 'Port Economics', 53–4.

[73] Ibid., Appendix, Tables 2 and 3, 61–7.

India Dock Company, those officers holding permanent posts might be contracted for only part of year. The situation on the south bank was different. The Commercial Dock Company relied predominantly on a small core of officers and gang-based sub-contracted labour. As an almost entirely indirect employer, it was not much involved with the day-to-day management of its workforce, firmly divided into timber and grain sides.[74]

In 1828, the West India Dock Company had about 300 salaried permanent employees, and the London and the St. Katharine's Dock perhaps 200 each. By mid-century, all had an establishment of approximately 350. Such employees ranged in status from a company secretary with an annual salary of £500 to a junior clerk earning perhaps 50.[75] Added to these were appointed waged permanent labourers. In 1832, the St. Katharine's Dock Company had 150, and in 1851 the London Dock Company at least 400. In fact, at mid-century more than a quarter of all employees, salaried and waged, were permanent.[76]

With bureaucratic controls resembling those of the East India Company, the West India Dock Company's warehouse superintendents had the title 'Captain', presumably to signify military efficiency. In theory, there were consistent procedures throughout its system, but in practice, in all the north bank companies, the sheer scale of dock operations meant conceding a high degree of autonomy to senior officers, particularly in hiring labourers.[77] Much depended on the recruitment and retention of suitable officers. In the words of the East India Dock Company secretary in 1818, 'dispatch and efficiency arises more from having active, intelligent persons to direct, inspect & controul [sic] than from an additional number of labourers, or the subordinate Officers attending and working with them'.[78]

Senior staff were paid impressive salaries. In 1804, the London Dock Company Superintendent received £500 a year, plus a house, and its warehousemen £200 a year. The East India dockmaster, appointed in 1834, had £400. Rent-free housing, salary increases based on length

[74] Mayhew, Henry, *The Morning Chronicle Survey of London Labour and the Poor, The Metropolitan Districts, Volumes 1–6, Routledge, Library Editions: The History of Social Welfare*, Vol. 22 (Routledge, London, 1982), Volume 5, 52–5; Geoffrey Crossick, *An Artisan Elite in Victorian Society, Kentish London 1840–1880* (Croom Helm, London, 1978), 64–5.

[75] MLD, SKD 001, 8 August 1828.

[76] MLD, SKD 125, 21 June 1852; SC Customs Second Report (1851), Cattley, Q. 2726; Chandler, Q. 7072.

[77] MLD, WID 310; 12 December 1803, LDC 138, Report of Special Dock Committee, 243–55.

[78] MLD, EID, 25 July 1818.

of service and occasional gratuities were used to attract and retain suitably qualified men.[79] The companies did not take the trustworthiness of such officers for granted. On appointment they had to provide security, forfeited in the event of wrongdoing. In 1805 the guarantee required of a London Dock Company deputy warehouse keeper, paid £120 a year, was £500.[80]

When appointing senior officers, the East India Dock Company asked for experience in East India trade and other companies also looked for those who had previously undertaken similar work. Dennis Chapman, a London Dock Company warehouseman, had previously worked for twenty-four years at the Legal Quays,[81] When the St. Katharine's Dock Company recruited its first officers in 1828, it was able to draw on a cohort already with dock experience; almost all those initially appointed to supervisory posts came from the other companies, predominantly from the West India Docks.[82] However, choosing a new Secretary in 1840, the East and West India Dock Company looked for someone with wider administrative experience. George Collins, appointed with a salary of £1,000, had previously worked at the War Office and came with glowing testimonials, including one from the Duke of Wellington.[83]

Not all staff enjoyed high salaries. In the 1840s permanent junior clerks employed by the St. Katharine's Dock Company received 20 shillings a week, quite close to the wage of a permanent foreman, but longer-term prospects were attractive. In 1828, for example, its good starting salary for St. Katharine's Dock Company copying clerk Jonathan Tabor, 'acquainted with the French, Dutch, German and English languages, writes a good hand', was £70, but annual increments increased this to £100 within four years.[84] There were age limits for appointment. The West India Dock Company barred anyone over forty years old; at St. Katharine's, it was over thirty-five. But once appointed, sometimes through the patronage of a director, it was usually a job for life.[85] Promotion was generally according to seniority and even when positions were advertised externally, they often went to an internal candidate. When the St. Katharine's Deputy Dock Master was promoted in 1846, a warehouse manager 'esteemed

---

[79] Henderson and Palmer, 'Early Nineteenth Century Port of London', 42; MLD, LDC 137/1, 28 August 1804, EWID 003, 8 May 1840.
[80] MLD, LDC 137/1, 8 January 1805.
[81] SC Foreign Trade (West India Docks), Chapman, 302–3.
[82] MLD, SKD 001, 30 September 1828.
[83] MLD, EWID 003, 25 June 1840.
[84] MLD, SKD 005, 11 March 1845, SKD 001, 14 October 1828.
[85] MLD, WID 308, 24 April 1804, SKD 001, 1 February 1831.

for his urbanity of manner by many of the commanders of ships who frequent the docks' defeated twelve outside applicants for his vacant post.[86]

By mid-century, many permanent staff had begun their service before steam shipping and wharf competition became serious issues for companies. This had implications for the quality of management. As an 1852 confidential report to St. Katharine's directors commented, 'seniority, which while it should not be neglected but should be allowed to have its due weight, ought not to be allowed to ride over merit'. The company had a particular problem with seniority. Sir John Hall was then seventy years old, with a £1,500 salary. He retired in 1852, possibly blamed for the inattention to management revealed in a dispute with the Customs, to be discussed later.[87]

Labour

Companies categorised workers according to the consistency of their employment: 'permanent', 'preferable' – guaranteed work if there was work to be done – and 'extra', those taken on when there was more work than the preferables could cover. In the early 1820s, the number of West India Dock labourers could reach 2,600 a day; in the late 1840s, as many as 4,000. By this time, there could also be as many as 3,000 men at work in the London Dock and those employed in the smaller St. Katharine's could approach 2,000. Only a minority of these were constantly or regularly employed.[88]

In answer to the question posed in the quotation at the start of this chapter, the companies aimed to create a labouring workforce composed of respectable, hard-working and competent men, loyal only to themselves. In 1831, the St. Katharine's Dock Company gave this direction to officers:

Judgement must be used in the selection of labourers according to the description of work to be performed, due regard being had to the muscular power and capabilities of the labourers respectively as the Board is determined upon preserving a just distinction between those labourers who shall distinguish themselves by their good conduct from such who from idle habits and inefficiency shall be undeserving of consideration.

---

[86] MLD, SKD 005, 7 July 1846.
[87] MLD, SKD 125, Special Committee, 21 June 1852, 69, Appendix E, Half Year General Meeting Report, 19 July 1853.
[88] Dupin, *Commercial Power*, 48; Mayhew, Reprint, Volume 1, 70, 86–8; SC Affairs of the East India Company, Hall, Qq. 2502, 2528.

Promotion to permanents was normally from preferable, and to preferable from extra.[89] In practice, there was not much difference between permanent and preferable. A company could seldom rely entirely on its permanent labourers. In the busy late 1840s, the London Dock Company abandoned the distinction entirely.[90] The line between preferable and extra labourers was also blurred. Companies issued 'tickets' to trusted extras regularly employed if work was available. An Irishman interviewed by journalist Henry Mayhew in 1850 explained that 'I got my name on at the West India Dock as an extra cooper and have worked there in succession every year since. I got a number and have kept at it all along'.[91]

From the start, the north bank companies rejected the traditional river-port system of sub-contracted, task-based labour. Instead, they chose direct employment, selecting and managing their own and paying them by time.[92] As competitive pressures mounted from the 1830s and productivity began to be an issue, payment by results had attractions. The St. Katharine's Dock Company moved to piecework for all wine and spirit coopers. Imitating the rival Commercial Dock Company system, the East and West India Dock Company sub-contracted the discharge of guano, wood, mahogany to gangs of its own workers and, following the lead of the London Dock Company, grain.[93] In 1846, it put its entire engineering department out to tender.[94] Although judged successful in reducing labour costs, such cases of piecework and sub-contract were exceptional. At mid-century, companies remained committed to an employment and payment system established in the early 1800s.[95]

Information on wage rates is fragmentary. Highest in wartime, in 1807 at the London Dock, permanent and preferable labourers were paid 24 and 21 shillings respectively for a six-day week. By 1825 rates had fallen to 18 shillings a week for permanents, 16s 6d for preferables and 15 shillings for extras. They appear then to have broadly stayed at

[89] MLD, SKD 001, 1 February 1831, 436; SKD 002, 24 September 1833.
[90] MLD, LDC 143, 30 April 1839, 215–6.
[91] MLD, WID 345, 4 May 1821, 186; MLD, PLA, SKD St. Katharine Docks, Printed document '15 December 1831'; Mayhew, *Morning Chronicle* Reprint, Volume 6, 18.
[92] Sarah Palmer, 'The Labour Process in the 19th Century Port of London: Some New Perspectives', in Anne-Lise Piétri-Lévy et al. (eds.), *Environnements Portuaires, Port Environments* (Universités de Rouen et du Havre, Havre, 2003), 318–28.
[93] MLD, SKD 119, 20 December 1838; MLD, EWID 002, 10 May 1839; MLD, EWID 003, 29 May 1840; MLD, EWID 004, 30 July 1841; MLD, EWID 005, 29 July 1843.
[94] MLD, EWID 007, 25 April 1825, 20 February 1846.
[95] MLD, EWID 011, 28 January 1853.

this peacetime level for all companies, until at least mid-century.[96] As a skilled unionised craft, coopers commanded higher wages. The lowest rate for London Dock Company coopers in wartime was 30 shillings a week. In the 1840s, if not on piecework, East and West India pay varied from 18 shillings a week for dry coopers and 33 shillings a week for oil coopers.[97] It must be remembered that, except for those permanently employed, actual weekly earnings entirely depended on the availability of work.

Daily Routine

Initially all the north bank docks were open from 6 am to 6 pm in the summer, 7 am to 5 pm in winter, with an hour and half allowed for meals. However, Customs and Revenue officers worked from 8 am in summer, 9 am in winter and finished at 4 pm. Little work could be done in their absence, so in 1808 the London Dock Company adopted Customs hours, cutting labourers' break times. 'It was thought that when shorter hours were taken, there would be no excuse for their going out to get meals' explained the London Dock Company chairman in 1851. In the London and St. Katharine's, 'Summer' ran from March to the end of October. Until 1847, the conservative East and West India Dock Company still had the shorter hours and summer period laid down in 1800. 'Both the upper dock companies get forty-eight hours more labour per year from all their employees than we get from our dock labourers', noted its chairman.[98]

The effective working day was longer. Permanent and preferable labourers were expected to be at the dock gates at least thirty minutes before opening. Those competing for casual employment also had to arrive early. In 1848, bold extra labourer George Austin unsuccessfully applied to the East and West India Dock Company 'for pay for extra time extending over the last seven years; this extra time resulting from the Dock practice of calling the men half an hour or more [before] the legal hours commence'.[99] The 1838 Liverpool delegation described the London hiring process:

---

[96] MLD, LDC 154, 14 April 1807; MLD, LDC 153, 2 December 1824; MLD, SKD 117, 3 June 1830; Mayhew, Reprint, Volume 1, 70; PP 1835 XLIX.1 [52], Tables of Revenue, Population and Commerce of the United Kingdom and Dependencies, 410.

[97] MLD, LDC 138, 25 April 1809; Pattison, 'Coopers' Strike', *Mariner's Mirror*, 55, 1969, 165.

[98] 42 Geo. III. c. 113; LDC 138, 13 September 1808; SC Customs Second Report (1851), Cattley, Qq. 2579–94; McCulloch, *Dictionary of Commerce*, 471; MLD, EWID 07, 26 April 1847.

[99] MLD, EWID 008, 31 March 1848.

The warehouse keeper, besides his permanent coopers and assistants, hires daily such additional labourers as he requires. These people wait for hire outside the gates. Each warehouse keeper has a list, containing the names of such of them as have recommendations, or are known as able and honest labourers, who are called ticket men, and receive three shillings per day, and have almost permanent employ; and he hires each day the number of labourers wanted, giving these men the preference. If more men are required, extra labourers are hired by the day or hour, at 2s 6d per day; but their employ is precarious and there is therefore great inducement to industry and honesty, in order to get on the ticket lists. For the convenience of these labourers, a notice-board outside is marked each night with the probable numbers required next day; and thus, if little is going on, they can look out for employ elsewhere.[100]

The daily reality was more chaotic than this suggests. In a vivid much quoted passage, journalist Henry Mayhew described 'a sight to sadden the most callous', of a large crowd of men in the early 1850s 'struggling for a day's hire' at the London Dock. The throng outside the gate was not, however, an undifferentiated mass, as Mayhew seems to suggest. Many would have been known to company officers.[101] Nor was it the case, as he claimed, that 'this class of labour is as unskilled as the power of a hurricane. Mere muscle is all that is needed; hence every human "locomotive" is capable of working there'.[102] As George Pattison points out, 'the business of the docks could not possibly have been carried on if the only labour available was the starving and inefficient horde fighting for work at the dock gates'.[103] The work was casual, but experience counted, so many taken on were not anonymous unknowns to those who hired them.

Mayhew's account is not entirely misleading. When the amount of cargo to be handled produced acute labour shortage, the docks were a source of employment for unqualified men. Moreover, apart from the relative few in permanent positions, all those seeking dock work, experienced or otherwise, faced the prospect of disappointment. 'We live half the year, and starve t'other', an East and West India Dock Company mahogany labourer told Mayhew.[104] Demand for labour fluctuated from season to season and even from day to day, so wage rates were little indication of longer-term earnings. Dock labourers, in common with the capital's other casual workers, could be miserably poor.

---

[100] MDHB, Report 1839, 64.
[101] SC Foreign Trade (West India Docks), Mitchell, 127; Hibbert, 147.
[102] Mayhew, Reprint, Volume I, 66–7; Stedman Jones, *Outcast London*, 73–4.
[103] Pattison, 'Dock Labour' 265, Palmer, 'Labour Process'.
[104] Mayhew, *Morning Chronicle*, Reprint, Volume 5, 51.

Control and Resistance

Laziness, incompetence and flouting regulations were punished. In 1832, the St. Katharine's Dock Company sacked twenty-nine preferables 'for skulking, pilferage, and inebriation and other breaches of the regulations and also inefficiency during the last twelve months'. Foreman cooper William Hart came close to losing his job in 1817 for failing to curb drinking in the West India Dock warehouses. But drunkenness was common, to some extent tolerated and in isolation seldom led to dismissal.[105] When in 1828 the St. Katharine's Dock Company suspended one of its constables without pay for a week, it was as much his 'unsightly' appearance as his drinking that caused concern.[106]

Theft could lead to criminal prosecution.[107] Penalties varied between fines, imprisonment or transportation. In the early 1840s, a London Dock labourer found with four ounces of liquorice hidden in his boots could choose between five shillings fine or four days in prison, but a man who stole clothing from a sailor was imprisoned for four months. Those more senior were punished severely. Transportation awaited the long-serving manager of London Dock indigo warehouses for stealing indigo worth 30 shillings on impulse when drunk, which was also the fate of an East and West India Dock Company foreman convicted of premeditated organised theft of 2,000 lbs of cotton.[108] Although dishonesty must have gone undiscovered, strong security appears to have largely succeeded in eliminating the endemic thievery that characterised the unreformed port.[109] However, the distinction between a legitimate customary perk and stealing remained contentious. In 1843, a preferable labourer was 'severely admonished' by East and West India Dock Company for attempting to take home the binding around a cask to use for apron strings, a practice said to be commonplace at the Rum Quay.[110]

This company tried to control worker behaviour beyond the dock walls. Publicans supplying beer risked this privilege if they allowed its labourers to 'congregate in their houses in the evenings and be there encouraged to spend their wages perhaps in drunkenness'. The revelation that some uptown warehouse workers were moonlighting in local

[105] Pat Hudson and Lynette Hunter, 'The Autobiography of William Hart, Cooper, 1776–1857: A Respectable Artisan in the Industrial Revolution, Part II', *The London Journal*, 8 (1981), 70; MLD, LDC Staff Box 3, Discipline Book 1833–1845.
[106] MLD, SKD 117, 18 December 1828.
[107] MLD, WID 337, 24 June 1817.
[108] *Old Bailey Proceedings Online*, www.oldbaileyonline.org, accessed 19 August 2019. Trial of James Goddard, February 1843; Trial of John Sharratt, July 1844.
[109] SC Customs Second Report (1851), iv.
[110] MLD, EWID 005. 12 May 1843.

theatres prompted prohibition of after-hours employment, including by those casually employed. Permanent and preferable workers were banned from keeping grocery shops – a potential outlet for stolen produce.[111] It might seem unlikely that such rules would be obeyed, but in the local world of the dock labourer, word could get back to managers. Those with permanent or preferential status risked losing their job or guarantee of regular employment and an extra labourer would not welcome blacklisting.

Not all dock workers were compliant employees. London Dock Company labourers who struck in 1809 were dismissed, but the balance of power was less firmly weighted in favour of the companies when it came to coopers.[112] At mid-century about 400 of these skilled men, who had served a seven-year apprenticeship, were employed in the docks, most repairing casks. Less demanding than manufacturing, such coopering was not without challenges; a stormy voyage could crush a cask containing sugar into 'every shape except their original rotundity'.[113] Much of the work went on in the Master Cooper's own little kingdom, out of the view of dock company managers.

Coopering was a strongly unionised London trade. There were at least nine industrial disputes in London over the period 1808–1834, some affecting the docks.[114] Action in 1812 achieved a substantial wage increase for West India Dock Company coopers, but not those of the London Dock Company. Some sacked were later reinstated on the advice of the Master Cooper that 'the service will feel considerable difficulties without some of these men'.[115] In August 1821, when over seventy vessels were waiting to discharge, West India sugar-quay coopers struck for fifteen days. To break the strike, directors unsuccessfully attempted to persuade private cooperage firms to lend men, then brought in thirty-two 'country' coopers from Bristol and Liverpool. All but twelve were induced by the union to return home with fares paid.[116] Even so, the West India Dock Company held firm and when rum coopers failed to join the action, the men returned to work. The four strike leaders were

[111] MLD, EWID 002, 12 April 1839, EWID 005, 1 September 1843, EWID 002, 17 May 1839, EWID 003, 1 November 1839, 11 November 1839.
[112] See Bob Gilding, *The Journeymen Coopers of East London, Workers' Control in an Old London Trade, with Historical Documents and Personal Reminiscences by One Who Has Worked at the block* (History Workshop Pamphlets, History Workshop, 1971).
[113] Mayhew, Reprint, Volume 6, 2–10.
[114] Green, *Artisans to Paupers*, 257–60; PP 1825 IV.565 [417], SC on the Combination Laws, Chappell, 39–41, Raven, 46–53; Mayhew, Reprint, Volume 6, 13–14.
[115] Pattison, 'Coopers' Strike', 164.
[116] MLD, WID 345, 10 August 1821, 14 August 1821.

charged with conspiracy, but the Old Bailey Grand Jury acquitted. The jurors may have been impressed by the impassioned defence lawyer who asked whether the accused 'ought to be thrust into prison, while their prosecutors are lolling in the lap of luxury, which perhaps the half-paid labour of poor men, like my client, has produced to them'.[117]

Shaken by the strike, to fend off further trouble, directors proceeded cautiously. There were sackings, but some coopers escaped punishment. These included cooper William Hart, who had briefly stored '£20 in gold wrapped up in a small parcel' intended for strike pay and acted as a character witness at the trial.[118] Half of those originally dismissed were reappointed. Reform of cooperage arrangements included an increase in permanent men. The last strike-breaking 'country' cooper was still working for the company in 1873.[119]

Paternalism and Self-Help

The dock companies paid *ex-gratia* pensions both to officers and permanent labourers. Such provision by employers had a long history and was by no means unique.[120] However, unusually among early nineteenth-century businesses, in 1825 the London Dock Company set up formal pension arrangements. With a rival dock at St. Katharine's in the offing, it was anxious to retain key workers. Under the London Dock Company system, a pension of half the final wage would be paid to a man 'of good character, who have been at least 20 years in the service, or become incompetent to labor (sic) through accident or illness incurred in the Company's employ'.[121] The St. Katharine's Dock Company seems to have followed suit. The East and West India Dock Company continued to award retirement gratuities and annual payments to 'meritorious servants' on an individual basis. In 1852 it established a contributory pension fund for newly appointed officers and clerks, but this did not extend to employees at lower levels.[122]

[117] *Report of the Trial*, 195; *Old Bailey Proceedings Online*, 5 December 1821, www.oldbaileyonline.org, version 8.0, accessed 21 September 2019).
[118] Hudson and Hunter, 'William Hart, Part II', 71–2.
[119] Pattison, 'Coopers' Strike', 172.
[120] Pat Thane, *Old Age in English History. Past Experiences, Present Issues* (Oxford University Press, Oxford, 2000), 243. See also Kathleen Francis McIlvenna, 'From the Civil List to Deferred Pay: the British Government, Superannuation and Pensions 1810–1909' (Doctoral Thesis, Institute of Historical Research, University of London, 2019).
[121] MLD, LDC 153, 2 December 1824.
[122] MLD, EWID 010, 7 June 1851, EWID 013, 8 February 1856.

There was no automatic entitlement to any of these dock company pensions. They were discretionary, given only to those deemed deserving. In the West India docks, age or infirmity meant progressively more menial tasks, such as extracting nails, for lower pay. In June 1845, the East and West India Dock Company directors, shedding 'worn out and inefficient Foremen and Labourers', granted pensions or one-off gratuities to ten men.[123] The sums involved were not large. In 1833, cooper Hart was one of seventeen West India Dock Company employees dismissed in a cost-cutting exercise. He recalled that 'it was no small trial to me, to be reduced from £105 per year to £30 – now near fifty-seven years of age and my family not provided for, and being in their service near 30 years', but conceded that he had done better than many others.[124] For extra labourers, there was no such expectation of income in old age. Faced with the prospect of destitution, with reliance on charity or the Poor Law, they continued to toil as long as they possibly could.

Dock work was dangerous. According to an 1851 report, accidents in the London and St. Katharine's systems alone averaged one a day.[125] All companies routinely made subsistence payments, typically half-pay, to injured permanent and preference labourers. They also took some responsibility for extra labourers. In 1817, for example, the West India Dock Company agreed to pay six shillings a week to support the children of a labourer in an infirmary and in the late 1830s, the London Dock Company authorised a similar sum to be paid routinely to hospitalised married extra labourers, half this for unmarried men. A donation of £5 was usually given to the wives of those killed at work, but there could be resistance to giving more. In 1823, the West India Dock Company refused a widow's paltry request for additional help to enable her to buy a mangle, which would allow her to support herself with laundry work.[126]

Companies contributed to some extent to the cost of treatment. 'Infirmary expenses', averaging £453 a year in the 1840s, always featured in the London Dock Company accounts.[127] All were regular subscribers to London Hospital in Whitechapel, 'founded for the express

[123] MLD, LDC 153, 20 December 1825, EWID 006, 15 April 1845.
[124] Hudson and Hunter, 'William Hart. Part II'. 72–3.
[125] Cormack and Semple, 'The Hospitals of London. No. 5', *London Journal of Medicine*, 3 (1851), 480.
[126] Henderson and Palmer, 'Early Nineteenth-Century Port of London', 47; MLD, SKD 117, 2 January 1829; LDC 141, 6 April 1830; WID 337, 8 July 1819; LDC 143, 19 November 1839; WID 350, 6 June 1823.
[127] MLD, LDC 150.

purpose of affording adequate relief in the various contingencies arising from the hazardous occupations carried on in a district containing
shipping, docks, shipyards, warehouses, & c. & c.'.[128] However, their
contributions were modest. The West India Dock Company gave £100
annually from 1816, but the London Dock Company only raised its
twenty-guinea donation to this level in 1846 when confronted by the
cash-strapped hospital with evidence of the large number of its workers
admitted.[129]

Unable to rely on assistance from their employers but with the
income security to afford contributions, permanent workers joined
friendly societies providing sickness and sometimes other benefits.[130]
In the early 1840s, most of the East and West India Dock Company's
foremen, coopers and engineers and two-thirds of appointed labourers
were members.[131] The dock companies were ambivalent about such
self-help. For them, friendly societies were a vehicle for trade unionism.[132] They also distrusted the conviviality and opportunities for
social mixing associated with friendly society activity.[133] In 1823, the
West India Dock Company directors were outraged by the discovery
that a Rum Quay sickness benefit society operated by some labourers
held an annual dinner, funded by forbidden tips received from merchants, which senior officers also attended. 'This kind of association',
the directors complained, 'must break down the pale of distinction,
and be subversive of all proper discipline'.[134] Even so, faced with a regular stream of appeals from employees to continue to receive pay when
absent through illness, they also approved of workers who saved the
company money by insuring themselves against misfortune.[135]

The London Dock Company solved this dilemma by establishing its
own contributory Friendly Institution for the Labourers at the Dock in
1838. The East and West India Dock Company's Provident Society,

---

[128] PP 1844, IX.93 [531], SC on Medical Relief to Sick Poor under Poor Law Act,
Appendix 1, 828.
[129] SC Foreign Trade (West India Docks), Longlands, 80, Inglis, 284–5, Appendices 2
and 3. MLD, LDC 144, 31 March 1846; EID 287, 11 July 1834; SKD 004, 2 March
1841; LDC 144, 31 April 1844.
[130] Mayhew, Reprint, Volume 6, 13–14; P. H. J. H. Gosden, *The Friendly Societies in
England, 1815–1875* (Manchester University Press, Manchester, 1961); Simon
Cordery, *British Friendly Societies* 1850–1914 (Palgrave Macmillan, Basingstoke,
2003).
[131] MLD, EWID 005, 12 August 1842.
[132] Pattison, 'Coopers' Strike', 169.
[133] Gosden, *Friendly Societies*, 115–27.
[134] MLD, WID 350, 22 August 1823.
[135] MLD, WID 341, 3 August 1819.

open to all grades, from warehousemen to messengers, followed two years later.[136] For some years, the Provident Society had difficulty attracting members but did better once the company followed the London Dock Company in making this a condition of employment for those promoted or newly appointed.[137] By 1858, three-quarters of those eligible had joined.[138]

Self-interest was also behind the East and West India Dock Company's decision to build cottages for labourers on its estate. The 1848 Chartist demonstrations alerted directors to the vulnerability of 'its remote and isolated position'. Having trusted men available nearby solved the problem of securing the site if under attack. Designed by the company's engineer and influenced by the model homes promoted by the Society for Improving the Condition of the Labouring Classes, its seventy dwellings were let at modest rents to trusted permanent and preferable workers.[139]

Rented housing, sick pay and pensions were relevant only to such appointed workers, not to those precariously employed as extra labourers who in hard times relied on charity or the Poor Law to survive. The companies only very occasionally supported philanthropic initiatives.[140] If engaged at all with the dock parishes, the context was usually a dispute over rate assessments. Even where docks caused pressure on amenities such as the sewage system, they accepted little liability and frequently challenged rate demands, sometimes resorting to litigation.[141] As major ratepayers, the London Dock Company and East and West India Dock Company saw to it that they were represented on the local Poor Law Guardians, where they attempted to curb expenditure. Yet demands on Poor Law funds reflected not only the vagaries of casual employment but also decisions by dock directors. 'The competition of the dock companies has reduced profits; they have reduced the wages of labourers and the number of labourers', explained Wapping's

[136] MLD, LDC 143, 17 August 1838; EWID 003, 4 September 1840; PP 1842 XXVI.275 [73], Return Related to Friendly Societies.
[137] PP 1849, XIV.1 [458], SC on Friendly Societies, Finlaison, Qq. 645–648; MLD, EWID 009, 6 July 1849; EWID 007, 4 July 1845.
[138] MLD, EWID 011, 30 July 1852, 12 August 1853; EWID 014, 30 July 1858.
[139] *Survey of London*, 43, 21–22; MLD, EWID 008, 14 April 1848; EWID 009, 28 September 1849, 5 April 1850, 435–7; EWID 515, 11 January 1850, Report to the United Court of Proprietors.
[140] MLD, CDC 002, 6 April 1821, LDC 145, 5 February 1850.
[141] Stephen Porter, 'All Saints' Poplar: the Making of a Parish, 1650–1817', *The London Journal*, 17:2, 111–2; MLD, WID 350, 18 July 1823; EID 278, 20 February 1807, EID 287, 12 December 1834, LDC 155, 7 April 1812, 3 May 1812, LDC 156, 29 April 1817, LDC 158, 20 January 1824, LDC 142, 1 October 1833; PP 1834, XVI.1 [600], SC on Metropolis Sewers, Baker Jnr, Qq. 397–409; *Times*, 30 May 1837.

St. George-in-the-East parish officials to the 1834 Royal Commission on the Poor Laws.[142]

Customs and Excise Officers

Not everyone at work in the docks was a company employee. In the early 1820s, there were over a hundred Customs officers at the West India Docks, double at the London Dock, with a further hundred Excise men collecting taxes on tobacco, coffee, sugar, tea, wine and spirits, as well as many watchmen.[143] Revenue service reform, including transfer of collection roles to the Customs or companies themselves, meant that the number of officials was much the same in the 1840s, despite increasing trade.[144] Even so, the Customs remained a significant presence on dock company premises until final free trade measures in the 1860s.

The relationship between companies and Customs was uneasy. Custom officer absence could hold up work, extension of normal working hours to deal with a glut of business required their agreement and there were clashes over whether dock company rules, such as banning the bringing-in of refreshments, applied to Customs employees.[145] The landing waiters, searchers and gaugers who examined cargoes had remunerative pensionable posts and dock company employees working alongside them resented differences in pay and job security.[146] Furthermore, a dock company had a greater interest than the Customs in preventing theft, being responsible for reimbursing the merchant for the value of stolen goods and the Crown for lost duty.[147] Company employees were searched at the dock gates, but the Customs refused to allow its officers to be examined. A proposal to include them caused 'such a ferment amongst the Custom-house officers, who considered

---

[142] PP 1834 XXVII–XXXI.1 [44], RC on the Poor Laws, Appendix B2, 83–4, 153; *Survey of London, 43*, 78–83.

[143] SC Foreign Trade (West India Docks), Appendices 4–11, 442–8; PP 1820 VI.559 [46] Commission of Inquiry into the Customs and Excise, First, Second, Third, Fourth and Fifth Reports, 33–35.

[144] Edward Carson, *The Ancient and Rightful Customs* (Faber and Faber, London, 1972), 135; PP 1851 Cd.209, SC on Customs, First Report; SC Customs, Second Report (1851), iv; PP 1843 XXIX.133 [481], Commissioners of Customs on Customs Frauds; SC Customs, Second Report (1851), Cattley, Q. 256, Appendix 8, 1511–13.

[145] MLD, WID 319, 11 December 1807.

[146] SC Foreign Trade (West India Docks), Appendices 4–11, 442–8; 1851 SC Customs, Second Report (1851), Appendix 34, 2171–2221; Customs on Customs Frauds (1843), 8–9; Pat Thane, *Old Age*, 237–40.

[147] SC Customs, Second Report (1851), Cattley, Qq. 2515–6.

themselves of a grade much superior to the dock officers' that it was abandoned.[148] Company belief that the Customs was responsible for some theft was not unfounded. Over the years, a number of cases reached trial and in 1843, an official report identified many 'frauds and malpractices' by officers.[149]

Attempting to repair its reputation, the Board of Customs embarked in 1848 on an extraordinary investigation into alleged company fraud by both the London Dock Company and St. Katharine's.[150] Both were raided without warning by Customs officials, who seized casks and packages. They had in their sight sticky sugar waste, known as 'black stuff', and coffee, cocoa and other refuse found on warehouse floors, which the companies were allowed to dispose of, paying notional duty. It was alleged that both companies fraudulently added unspoiled produce to such 'scrapings and sweepings', so evading duty.[151] In what the press named 'the treacle case', nineteen labourers were detained for theft. The London Dock Superintendent, along with seven senior officers, were arrested, charged with defrauding the Revenue'.[152] There followed months of disruptive stock-taking.

Such attacks on two of the largest and most influential London businesses were unprecedented, and the St. Katharine's Dock Company directors complained to the government of harassment. An interview that Chairman Tooke secured with the Prime Minister and Chancellor proved a debacle. Prime Minister Sir John Russell remained silent throughout and the Chancellor told the deputation that he had been assured that 'great frauds had been discovered in the docks'.[153] Faced with this crisis, the companies, supported by leading merchants and some MPs, embarked on an aggressive press campaign. They turned the tables by securing the appointment of a Select Committee to investigate the Customs Department itself. Members included the Deputy Chairman of the St. Katharine's Dock Company ironmaster Alderman Thompson, and leading wharfinger Alderman Humphery (sometimes

---

[148] MLD, LDC 138, 9 January 1810; SC Customs, Second Report (1851), Dawson, Q. 1698, Cattley, Q. 2508.

[149] PP 1843 XXIX.157 [502], Commissioners of Customs, General Report on Commissioners of Revenue Inquiry; 1851 SC on Customs, Second Report (1851); *Times*, 26 September 1843.

[150] SC on Customs. Second Report (1851), Fremantle, Q. 5144, Tooke and Hall, Qq. 6863–94; MLD, SKD 121, 25 July 1850.

[151] Ibid., Cattley, Q. 3044, Fremantle, Q. 4907, Appendix 28, 2034.

[152] Ibid., Fremantle, Q. 4794. Tooke and Hall, Q. 3769, 543–5, Chandler, Qq. 6850, 6868.

[153] Ibid., Tooke and Hall, Qq. 3691–3743.

'Humphrey').[154] Meanwhile, the Customs' prosecutions continued, with the civil court returning a mixed verdict in the one case it considered. The eventual settlement was a compromise. In exchange for dock company acknowledgement of 'irregularities' and a £100 fine, the Customs dropped all charges and returned seized goods. Criminal charges, which had hung over several unfortunate labourers for many months, were dropped.[155]

By attracting unwelcome public attention, censure by the Select Committee and forcing some reforms, arguably the Customs lost most from this fiasco.[156] However, the companies were far from unscathed. The admission of guilt irked them and had its critics, but they could not risk prolonging the dispute. Investors were taking fright (the value of London Dock Company stock fell by 7 per cent in a year) and the legal costs were significant, affecting the St. Katharine's Dock Company's dividend. Reputational damage was also considerable.[157] The 'irregularities' in measurement and record-keeping revealed by the Customs investigations suggested management slackness. 'There was not that supervision of labour that there might be', observed a disgruntled St. Katharine's Dock Company proprietor.[158] It was clear, too, that the two companies could rely neither on the competence of their employees, nor their loyalty. The Customs' case had been founded on evidence provided by sixty-four dock workers.[159]

London's Docks at Mid-Century

By mid-century, London's docks were no longer a novelty, but they continued to attract popular attention. 'Should you feel disposed to visit the East and West India Docks, dine at Lovegrove's [the Brunswick Hotel], at Blackwall, and return by steam-boat, visiting the Thames Tunnel on the way: the Blackwall Railway will take you into the immediate locality of the Docks', wrote the author *of Limbird's Guide to London* (1851). This was one of several publications aimed at visitors to the Great Exhibition

---

[154] https://HistoryofParliamentonline.org/volume/1820-1832/member/thompson-williams-1792-1854, accessed 14 October 2019.

[155] PP1852 [498], SC Customs, Report, vi, viii, xi–xiii, Appendices 1 and 2, 1122–6; *Shipping and Mercantile Gazette*, 22 July 1851.

[156] Joseph Hume MP, Parliamentary Debates, 3rd Series, 126, 12 February 1852, c. 472; SC Customs (1852), Crawford, Q. 981, Travers, 271–3; Parliamentary Debates, 3rd Series, 126, 12 April 1853, cc. 165–218.

[157] SC Customs, Second Report (1851), Cattley, Q. 2868, Tooke and Hall, Qq. 3883–8.

[158] *Morning Chronicle*, 21 January 1852, 3 July 1852.

[159] SC Customs, Second Report (1851), Appendix 27, 2030.

that included the docks among the sights of London and explained how entry tickets could be obtained.[160]

The companies had long since lost the status of their early years as partners with the government. As the dispute with the Custom's highlighted, however important dock performance was to national interests, their managers could not expect for that reason to be treated with greater respect or favour than any other businesses. Influence had also waned at a more local level. There were fewer connections with the Corporation of London than in the early years. The two aldermen most active in representing port interests were both wharfingers. Continued representation of the Corporation on the East and West India Dock Company Court remained a vestige of its original connection, but the public campaign on river management waged by Sir John Hall in the 1830s had damaged relations.

Internally, the dock companies faced problems. Built and operated to fit conditions earlier in the century, the growing importance of steam shipping and railway connections, together with the effects of trade liberalisation, had already to some extent reduced their competitive advantage over the waterfront wharves. In addition, the greater quantity of cargo being handled each year and, in the case of the East and West India Dock Company, the sheer physical extent of the combined enterprise, posed greater problems of management than in the past. Superficially, the north bank dock companies appeared to be doing well. Dividends in the late 1840s were healthy, but, as their directors appreciated, the longer-term outlook for profits was less promising. In the 1850s, all three north bank companies embarked on major investigations into their systems and productivity.

---

[160] John Limbird, *Limbird's Handbook, Guide to London: Or What to Observe and Remember* (John Limbird, London, 1851), 47; *London As It Is Today*, 177–82; Anon, *The British Metropolis in 1851* (Arthur Hall, Virtue & Co., London, 1851).

4   The Commerce of the Kingdom
The River Port

Illustration 4.1 The Pool of London in 1839. Image: Thomas Allom (1804–1872). © Adoc-photos/Getty Images.

... there are scarcely two interests in the Port of London that are the same; for instance, the docks below the Pool have an interest opposed to those above, and vice versa; the wharfingers and warehouse-keepers on the water-side have an interest opposed to the docks altogether; the lightermen have an interest also opposed to the docks, and they are strongly opposed to steam navigation; and I can scarcely find any two interests upon the river but what are strongly in collision with each other.[1]

Docks were the first phase of port reform. Next came dealing with compensation and improving management of the still busy London Thames. Central government and the Corporation of London had previously had a role, but this became much greater. Before drawn into debates

---

[1] SC Port of London, Tickner, Q. 567.

on reform, beyond Customs and Excise, the government had had little direct engagement with the country's greatest port. However, Pitt's administration had identified – and acted on – a connection between London's port and national prosperity, so from this point no distancing was possible. Reform left both an economic and political legacy for government. Not only was the Consolidated Fund the port's creditor, but its management was now the State's concern, hence a number of parliamentary committees and commissions over the rest of the century.

Under the 1799 Act, the Corporation gained a central role in port improvement. In 1796, as 'conservators of the Thames, and natural and legal guardians of trade and commerce' they had declared themselves 'willing and desirous to take on themselves the care, management and superintendence' of a range of reforms.[2] Both the Isle of Dogs canal venture and enlarged responsibility for the management of river navigation and moorings proved challenges. Conceived in the conditions of the unreformed port, the canal was soon revealed to be a solution to a problem that no longer existed once steamers could tow vessels upriver. In addition, thanks to the continued growth of trade in foodstuffs, corn and coal and the impact of steam propulsion on river traffic, the Corporation's governance of the river proved more demanding than anyone had anticipated.

In the early 1800s such developments were far from the thoughts of those whose income had depended on handling cargoes now destined for the docks. As it turned out, after a period of transition, reform was not such a disaster for waterfront wharf and warehouse capitalist interests as predicted. Since docks had no effect on London's busy coasting trade or on imports of corn, timber and food, they supplemented rather than replaced the older facilities. Moreover, under the 1803 Warehousing Act, some dutiable articles 'of coarse and bulky description' were permitted to be stored in less secure warehouses away from the docks.[3]

For most outside London's charmed mercantile circles, there were no such advantages. Waterfront porters were excluded from the docks and the business of carmen was effectively destroyed by the closure of the Legal Quays.[4] Some were awarded compensation, but this was only a short-term benefit to those with little expectation of finding new employment. Those in the 'alternative economy' who depended for income on

---

[2] Frederick Clifford, *A History of Private Bill Legislation Vol II* (Butterworths, London, 1887), 646.

[3] 43 Geo. III. c. 132.

[4] PP 1837 XXV.1 [239], RC Municipal Corporations, Second Report (London and Southwark, London Companies), 344–6; Stern, *Porters of London*, 136–41.

pilfering or stealing on the river and quays were also affected.[5] But for others, little was changed. Thanks to the Free Water Clause, watermen and lightermen were able to treat the dock water space as an extension of the river, which increasingly irked the dock companies as time went by. Much river employment remained much as in the past, although the dire working conditions of coal heavers and ballast heavers attracted parliamentary intervention in the 1840s.

Compensation

The Treasury paid £486,087 for the eight Legal Quays. It also loaned the Corporation the sums needed to build the Isle of Dogs Canal and purchase moorings from the Crown and private owners.[6] A Commission of Compensation, not wound up until 1825, looked into approaching a thousand claims for 'loss, injury and damage', which totalled £3,705,419. This eye-watering sum owed much to 'the power of imagination possessed by the mercantile classes', observed *The Times*.[7] Many of the sixty-four Compensation Commissioners had interests in port business, some were even claimants, but they proved parsimonious. Even so, the £677,382 paid out from the Consolidated Fund by 1825 was an immense sum, roughly equivalent to £48 million today. The loan was repaid by the tonnage tax on shipping using the Port of London. Much complained of by shipowners, a parliamentary investigation concluded in 1824 that the 'excess of compensations awarded to particular interests' offered little hope of early abolition.[8] Altogether, the State made a significant direct and indirect financial contribution to reform of the Port of London.

Legislative expropriation of property was nothing new. Construction of most canals would have been impossible without compulsory land purchase. But with London's new docks, justification for compensation went beyond property confiscation, or reduced capital value, to loss of prospective income. Not only were the administrative scale and potential financial commitment exceptional, but the principle was novel. When West India slavery interests unsuccessfully argued for government compensation in

---

[5] William J. Ashworth, 'Labour and the Alternative Economy in Britain, 1660–1842', in Thomas Max Saffley (ed.), *Labor Before the Industrial Revolution. Work, Technology and Their Ecologies in the Age of Early Capitalism* (Routledge, London, 2020), 238–41.

[6] Parliamentary Debates, 2nd Series, 21, 16 April 1829, c. 887.

[7] *Times*, 18 October 1828.

[8] PP 1824 VI.287 [431], SC on Foreign Trade (London Port Duty), 9, Appendix Y; Parliamentary Debates, 2nd Series, 21, 16 April 1829, c. 887. The tonnage tax was also known as 'Port Duty'.

debates over the abolition of the slave trade in 1807, owner of enslaved people George Hibbert cited recent port reform as a precedent.[9]

Claims, based on three years' financial records before a dock opened, ranged from many thousands to under a hundred pounds. Thomas Bolt requested £185,000 for lost profits on his warehousing and lighterage business caused by the West India docks. As a Legal Quay wharfinger, Bolt had already benefited from the sale to the Crown of Smarts and Dice Quays. At the other extreme were Harriet Frampton, Ann Groves and Elizabeth White, owners of licensed cart stands, who each claimed £80.[10] These were not the only female claimants. Some may have been applying on behalf of male relatives, but it would be unwise to assume that there were no women acting for themselves. Several porterage gangsmen cited both loss of income and the value of now useless cargo-handling equipment. There were also references to wasted occupational investment such as apprenticeship as a lighterman or the cost of becoming a City Freeman in order to qualify for a porter's 'ticket'. In a particularly blatant example of special pleading, Hibbert claimed £21,686 for lost income on his sugar warehouses: '... we were among the first promoters of the plan for constructing docks at this Port, fully relying that the loss we would thereby substance would under a just legislature, receive from the public liberal compensation'.[11]

Hibbert did not convince the Commission, which awarded £4,600. On appeal it was cut by £385. Bolt hoped for £185,000 but received £15,300.[12] Most claimants got about a fifth of what they asked for. The Commission rejected many submissions as tenuous, as subsequently did the appeal court. Lord Chief Justice Ellenborough expressed his frustration: 'We shall have the taylors who make cloathes for persons employed on the Legal Quays apply next for compensation. There is no knowing where such compensation is to end. I do not see why every hackney coachman who had taken a fare from the Legal Quays should not come for compensation'.[13]

Although most awards fell well short, the sums received were not inconsiderable. As dock investors or customers (in many cases both), the already wealthy stood to gain from the very same facilities that

---

[9] Parliamentary Debates, 1st Series, 8, 23 February 1807, c. 991; Katie Donington, 'Transforming Capital: Slavery, Family, Commerce and the Making of the Hibbert Family', in Catherine Hall et al., *Legacies of British Slave-ownership. Colonial Slavery and the Formation of Victorian Britain* (Cambridge University Press, Cambridge, 2014), 203–249; Nicholas Draper, *The Price of Emancipation. Slave-ownership, Compensation and British Society at the End of Slavery* (Cambridge University Press, Cambridge, 2010), 85–7.

[10] TNA T76, 4, Memorials 5, 23, 38, 40, 84, 129.

[11] TNA T76, 4, Memorials, 1, 63, 346; 6, Memorial 414.

[12] SC Foreign Trade (London Port Duty), Appendix Y.

[13] *Morning Advertiser*, 6 February 1808.

were said to have caused them financial damage. For more than a few, the lump sum must have been a windfall. The case of Matthias Prime Lucas, Master Lighterman, Alderman and Lord Mayor, is suggestive. A subscriber to both the West India Dock Company and London Dock Company, Lucas shared a £6,100 award with partner John Barnard, and in 1820 purchased the Wateringbury Place estate in Kent, becoming a fruit farmer and prominent local dignitary.[14]

The City Canal

The Corporation's City Canal across the Isle of Dogs cost £168,812. Opened in December 1805, its traffic was always insufficient to cover quite moderate operating costs, and it began to be used for laying up vessels, not profitable but picturesque. 'They are ranged on a line of about a mile in length, and present a magnificent sight', wrote French visitor Charles Dupin in 1825. By then, annual losses were amounting to well over a thousand pounds. At first, the new docks freed the river of shipping, undermining the attraction of a short cut across the peninsular. River congestion returned with increasing port traffic, but the canal remained unpopular with ship Masters.[15] Using small steamers or steam tugs to tow vessels upriver lessened dependence on the tide and saving just two hours of passage time was hardly worth the cost. For a 500-ton vessel, this was more than £4 – to be met out of the Master's own pocket.[16]

By 1809, the Corporation already wanted to dispose of its loss-making investment but sale was a matter for the government, so it was not a free agent. The Treasury came under pressure from the coal trade, which was concerned that the canal might become a collier dock, rivalling the waterfront coal wharves.[17] When the Treasury eventually called for bids in 1829, it shrewdly took advantage of the confidential process to convince the West India Dock Company, long keen to buy this close neighbour, that it faced strong competition. Only after the dock company's £120,000 offer was accepted did its directors discover that theirs had been the only tender.[18] Sale of the City Canal and waiver of the

---

[14] I am grateful to Mr. Terence Bird for drawing my attention to the Wateringbury connection.

[15] *Survey of London, XLIII*, 275–6; Stern, 'Isle of Dogs Canal', 363; Charles Dupin, *The Commercial Power of Great Britain, II* (Charles Knight, London, 1825), 47; Parliamentary Debates, 2nd Series, 21, 16 April 1829, c. 887.

[16] SC Foreign Trade (Port Duty), Montague, 30.

[17] *Survey of London XLIII*, 276.

[18] Stern, 'Isle of Dogs Canal', 364–70; Parliamentary Debates, 2nd Series, 21, 16 April 1829, c. 887; 10 William IV C.XXX.

Corporation's outstanding canal loan interest went a long way towards reducing what was owed for compensation payments to the Consolidated Fund, so in response to shipowner lobbying, tonnage duty was considerably lowered. In 1849, fifty years after Parliament had approved reform, the Port of London debt to the State was finally paid off.[19]

London Bridge

After completion of docks and canals, one element of the original port reform proposals remained outstanding. Much had been heard in 1799 about the problems caused by the ancient London Bridge, which effectively dammed the Thames. Beneath the central arch, introduced in 1762, at high tide there was only a fifteen-and-a-half-foot gap between bridge and river, with the almost six-foot tidal drop creating a dangerous rapid. 'Shooting' under when the tide ebbed risked damage to vessels as well as injury or death to those on board, while waiting until the tide was lower risked grounding on shoals beneath the bridge.[20]

Responsibility rested with the Corporation, but arguments over whether to reconstruct or completely replace the bridge hampered progress. With an 1820 Select Committee favouring a new bridge, it decided to act.[21] By now change was urgent. The twenty-one-foot bridge had become both a river and a road traffic bottleneck. On a single day in July 1811, 90,000 pedestrians, 5,500 vehicles and 764 horse riders crossed over.[22] Debates over design and access route negotiations brought further delays, but in August 1831, the new bridge was opened with great pomp by William IV and Queen Adelaide. Its designer was John Rennie and construction was done by Jolliffe and Banks under the direction of Rennie's sons, John and George.[23] The government had been anxious that the replacement of the bridge would not be held up by cost

---

[19] 39 & 40 Geo. III; 4 & 5 Will. IV. c. 32; PP 1833, XXXIII.117, Account of Payments out of the Consolidated Fund; TNA, T1 3924 Part 1, 1 October 1831; 12 & 13 Vict. C. 90, ss. 41–2.

[20] PP 1821 V.281 [609], SC Present State of London Bridge, Appendix 2, 88; PP 1799–1800 CXXXII [260], SC Improvement of the Port of London, Third Report, 260, Appendix A.1, 290–1; L. L. Rodwell Jones, *The Geography of London River* (Methuen & Co. Ltd., London, 1931), 62–9.

[21] Bruce Watson, 'The Last Days of Old London Bridge', in Bruce Watson, Trevor Brigham and Tony Dyson (eds.), *London Bridge: 2000 Years of a River Crossing, Museum of London Archaeology Service, Monograph* 8 (Museum of London, London, 2001), 156–66.

[22] Peter Matthews, *London's Bridges* (Shire Publications, Oxford, 2008), 155–7; SC London Bridge; Jerry White, *London in the Nineteenth Century. A Human Awful Wonder of God* (Vintage, London, 2008), 15.

[23] *Times*, 2 August 1831.

Illustration 4.2 The Old and New London Bridges, 1831. Image: George Scharf (1788–1860). © Heritage Images/Getty Images.

concerns. In yet another example of State support for port reform, under the 1823 London Bridge Act, the project received a government grant of £150,000, justified on the grounds that 'the building of London Bridge was not so much a local as a national object'.[24]

While the wide arches of the new London Bridge eliminated the most serious physical problem for the port, they exacerbated the endemic problem of shoals. With the tide no longer stemmed, it ebbed lower upstream, revealing mud banks and shallows that threatened to ground vessels.[25] Remnants of the ancient piers were left in the river and, according to one critic, the unsaleable building rubble 'went overboard with the shovel', increasing the long-standing challenge that 'hills' in the waterway posed to navigation. Difficulties with arranging removal of these obstructions by the dredging authority, Trinity House, highlighted the more fundamental practical problem of maintaining the tideway depth and argued for narrowing the river by embankment.[26] Such issues remained outstanding at mid-century.

[24] *Parliamentary Debates*, 2nd Series, 9, 16 June 1823, cc. 988–9.
[25] PP 1840 XII.271 [554], SC on Thames Embankment, Walker, Q. 174, Winter, Q. 1137.
[26] SC Port of London, Blenkarn, Qq. 240–2; SC Thames Embankment (1840), 3.

Legal Quays

In Crown hands, the eight former Legal Quays fell into a 'dilapidated and insecure state'. With short-term leases, wharfinger tenants had little incentive to maintain them well, although this changed with the award of twenty-one-year contracts in March 1820, at annual rents varying between £3,580 and £2,295.[27] Such high sums reflected the potential value of their remaining privileges. Even so, the Legal Quay interests successfully lobbied for substantial reductions on grounds of competition with the London Dock Company after relaxation of warehousing regulations.[28] Wearied by continued demands from tenants and anticipating more to come once the St. Katharine's Dock opened, the Treasury decided to sell.[29] Fresh Wharf was disposed of in 1827 and other freeholds were auctioned in 1832, netting a total of £160,400 for the Exchequer.[30] Current occupiers were the Treasury's preferred purchasers, but, given the specialised nature of the quay business, even without this favour, it is unlikely that there would have been much competition. All except two of the eight quays appear to have been purchased by existing tenants or close associates. Considerable improvements followed.[31]

By selling the Legal Quays, the government did more than rid itself of a troublesome commitment. For a small group of London capitalists, the decision cemented a significant financial stake in the river port. The claim when the quays were sold that they 'at all times will command the chief portion of the wharfing, warehousing and stowage connected with the coasting and European trades' proved little exaggeration.[32] Although warehousing privileges would diminish, City location and established commercial presence ensured long-term survival of several original wharfinger and warehousing partnerships. In 1902, Fresh Wharf, Cox and Hammond's Quay were owned and managed by John Knill & Co., while Brewer's, Chester's and Galley were in the hands of Joseph Barber & Co. John Knill had been manager of Fresh Wharf before purchasing it in 1827, and his son, Sir Stuart Knill, Lord Mayor of London in 1892–3,

---

[27] TNA T92, 18, Half-Yearly Report, 29 December 1820; TNA T1 4134, 15 March 1823.

[28] TNA T1 4134, Memorial Proprietors of Legal Quays, 6 November 1822, 7 June 1823; 4 March 1824, 9 September 1824, 10 January 1825, 6 April 1825.

[29] TNA 4134, 6 April 1825.

[30] TNA T1 4133, 5 September 1834, Customs Report to Treasury; *Morning Chronicle*, 1 November 1832, 12 April 1839.

[31] TNA T1 4133, 12 April 1839, Memorial Proprietors of Legal Quays; PP1902 XLIV.1. [Cd.1153], RC on the Port of London, Appendices, Appendix No. 7, 752.

[32] *Times*, 18 October 1832.

succeeded him. The Barber connection went even further back. Joseph Barber was one of the original 1806 tenants of Brewer's and Chester's.[33]

London's Warehousing System

Following the 1803 Warehousing Act, storage of high-duty articles was monopolised by the north bank dock companies, but with Customs approval, lower-duty produce could be warehoused elsewhere.[34] Grant or refusal therefore not only affected the economic prospects of individual enterprise but also significantly shaped the way in which the Port of London operated. In 1816, the former Legal Quays, fifty wharves, sixteen up-town warehouses and the Commercial and East Country docks were judged sufficiently secure to house certain types of dutiable produce.[35]

With their substantial warehouses designated 'Special Security', the docks still had a right to store high duty cargoes denied to almost all other interests.[36] The Customs came under pressure from occupants of the former Sufferance Wharves and the Commercial Dock Company to be given similar warehousing privileges to those enjoyed by the north bank docks.[37] It turned down all such requests, explaining in 1836:

Since the establishment of wet docks we have felt it our duty, as far as justice to old established sufferance wharves would allow, to restrict the sufferance wharfs privileges, with the view of concentrating the Foreign Trade in the Port of London to the Great Dock Establishments which in point of accommodation, security and economy are so peculiarly adapted for the Trade and Revenue of the country.[38]

Concentrated warehousing required fewer officers, so expense was one reason for this policy.[39] Whatever its practical justification, the Customs approach took no account of the shift in commercial policy towards freer trade begun in the 1820s, which continued in a modest fashion in the 1830s with reduction of duties on a miscellaneous group of articles. Most had little impact on Customs revenue, but equalisation of duties undermined the basis of the warehousing system – categorisation of

---

[33] PP 1884–85 VIII.47 [228], SC Corporation of London Tower Bridge Bill, Wight Qq. 6911–25; RC Port of London, Appendices, Appendix No. 1, Table of Sufferance Wharves and Legal Quays; TNA T1 4134, 6 November 1822; TNA CUST 29/6, 25 March 1805.

[34] 43 Geo. 3. c. 132. 1802–3; Guillery, 'Warehouses and Sheds', 80.

[35] TNA, T92, 21, 7 November 1816.

[36] PP 1834 XLIX.705, Return of Warehouses of Special Security in Port of London.

[37] TNA, T1 4133, 17 May 1824; 28 July 1825; 29 July 1831; 31 December 1835.

[38] TNA T1 4133, 20 April 1836.

[39] PP 1851 [209] SC on Customs, First Report, Fremantle, Qq. 605–7.

articles according to value.[40] At the Board of Trade, the Joint Secretary, James Deacon Hume, was a committed free-trader with no love of a warehousing system, which he regarded as largely unnecessary.[41] Under Hume's influence, in 1839 the Treasury overturned Customs policy by extending limited bonding privileges to south bank wharves.[42] Similar concessions were granted to warehouses and granaries on the waterfront and elsewhere. By 1845, the Port of London had at least seventy places licensed for Ordinary Security bonded storage. In 1820, there had been just twenty-six.[43]

Ongoing trade liberalisation shrank the number of dutiable articles from 1,046 in 1840 to 543 in 1850 and 143 by 1860. Sugar, tea, tobacco, wine and spirits became the principal types of dutiable produce. With imports of these increasing in response to the growth of London's population, depending solely on docks for high-security warehousing was unrealistic. In 1851, the Customs finally abandoned any attempt to restrict licensing.[44]

River Governance

The 1799 West India Dock Act added responsibility for shipping regulation and moorings to the Corporation's existing conservancy duties.[45] Creation of a Harbour Service and a coordinated approach to the port's berthing arrangements were considerable advances on the previous free-for-all system. But nothing was done to address the fundamental problem of governance: the conflicting jurisdictions and claims of the Admiralty, Crown, Trinity House, Corporation and the Company of Watermen and Lightermen.[46] Admiralty byelaws forbade the mooring of non-naval vessels close to Royal Docks. On grounds of potential obstruction to naval vessel movement, the Admiralty also routinely

---

[40] See Lucy Brown, *The Board of Trade and the Free Trade Movement 1830–42* (Oxford University Press, Oxford, 1958); Boyd Hilton, *Corn, Cash, Commerce. The Economic Policies of Tory Governments 1815–1830* (Oxford University Press, Oxford, 1977); Barry Gordon, *Economic Doctrine and Tory Liberalism 1824–1830* (Macmillan, London and Basingstoke, 1979); Anthony Howe, *Free Trade and Liberal England 1846–1946* (Clarendon Press, Oxford, 1997).

[41] Brown, *Board of Trade*, 51–2, 23–5; TNA T1 4385, Warehousing System, 2 May 1835; PP 1840 V.99 [601], SC Import Duties, Hume, Qq. 1094–1239.

[42] TNA T1 4133, 12 April 1839, 25 April 1839.

[43] PP 1845 XLVI.483 [214], Articles ... Permitted to be Bonded in the Port of London; TNA T92, 7 November 1820.

[44] PP 1863 VI.303 [424], SC on Inland Revenue and Customs Establishments, viii; PP 1870 LXI.329, Articles subject to Import Duties 1840–69; PP 1857 Session 1 III.301 [2186], Commissioners of Customs, First Report, 28–9.

[45] 39 George 3, c. 69; SC Port of London, Q. 3694.

[46] Ibid., iii; PP 1846, 692, RC on Tidal Harbours, Second Report, xvi.

opposed pier construction. This caused disputes with the Corporation, but a more serious source of conflict with the State was ownership of the 'soil and bed' of the Thames itself. The Corporation claimed this as part of its 'immemorial rights and usages', but according to Whitehall, the foreshore was State property, with the Corporation 'merely the officer of the Crown, constituted to preserve its navigation'.[47] The Crown's insistence on its title set off a protracted and expensive legal battle, not resolved until 1857, when the Corporation lost its authority over the river to a new body, the Thames Conservancy.

The Corporation had no jurisdiction over the riverbed, but shoals that caused problems for navigation were often left untouched by Trinity House, the holders of dredging rights. For Trinity House the provision of ballast for shipping was 'an affair of profit', using the income to support its charities.[48] In any case, the problem was not only natural shoals, potentially suitable for ballast, but also how Londoners treated their river. It was reported in 1842 that in addition to 'thousands of tons of coals and ashes thrown over by steam vessels', its bed was raised by the dumping of 'large quantities of bricks, rubbish, foundations, excavations, sweepings and refuse from factories, warehouses and dwellings on the banks of the river; sweepings from ships, straw and rubbish'.[49]

For thirty years, a Port Committee dealt with the Corporation's role as harbour authority. A separate Navigation Committee licensed encroachments, but in 1830, the two amalgamated. Thirty City ward 'commoners' and eighteen Aldermen (who seldom attended) served on the new body. There was much conservancy business, so the full committee met at least monthly, sub-committees more frequently, sometimes twice a week. Site visits were undertaken in the Committee barge, the *Maria Wood*.[50]

The Harbour Master and three subordinates, all with a maritime background, handled the day-to-day business of controlling shipping. From 1837 there were Harbour Master's offices at Limehouse, Greenwich and Gravesend, with each deputy responsible for a corresponding section of

[47] Ibid., Q. 3616. Jones, Newman, Q. 3695.

[48] Ibid., Q. 3346, Beaufort; Parliamentary Archives, Minutes of the House of Lords SC on Lastage and Ballastage Bill, 1843; PP 1863 XII.1 [454], SC Thames Conservancy, vii; Sarah Palmer, 'The Character and Organisation of the Shipping Industry of the Port of London 1815–1848' (Doctoral Thesis, London School of Economics & Political Science, University of London 1979), 262.

[49] MLD, COL/CC/TNC, Navigation Committee, 40/PP, 1 January 1842.

[50] SC Port of London, Qq. 220–3; Blenkarn, Qq. 516, 524; Tickner, Q. 3; SC Thames Embankment, Robinson, Qq. 905–6; RC Municipal Corporations (1837), Section 237; Fred S. Thacker, *The Thames Highway. Volume I: General History* (1914, Reprinted 1968, David & Charles, Newton Abbot), 210–12.

the river. These were demanding posts, not least because of the need to be on the river in all seasons and all types of weather and were well rewarded (annual salaries ranged from £500 for the senior post to £300 for the most junior). Considerable expertise was needed, as an 1849 report makes clear:[51]

No officer unacquainted with the Thames can possibly know the details of the several orders and instructions of your committee, of the laws, rules, order and regulations for the Harbour Service, on the three distinct stations the nature and competency of the moorings, sets of the tides, formation of existing shoals, depths of water or the requirements of shipping and classification of trades coming to the Port and City of London.[52]

In the 1820s, the Harbour Masters increasingly struggled to meet the conflicting needs of the various trades and at the same time ensure a clear route for shipping. Obstruction by colliers was a particular bugbear of St. Katharine's secretary Hall, concerned about steam wharf access. In 1829, Hall successfully persuaded the Corporation to introduce bye-laws to maintain a 300-foot passageway through the Pool.[53] The Harbour Masters considered this unrealistic, so they took no notice. Hall then used his role as a witness to the unrelated 1831 Select Committee on Calamities by Steam Navigation to attack the Harbour Service which concluded that regulations 'are not duly attended or enforced'.[54]

In response, the Corporation's Navigation Committee heard evidence from a wide range of interested parties. Hall suggested clearing water-space by moving collier moorings to the south bank. A nine-yard petition he organised had 5,700 signatories, including some leading shipowners and merchants, but, as critics pointed out, a large number were St. Katharine's labourers and passengers embarking and disembarking at its wharf. Against Hall's proposal were coal traders, wharfingers and others concerned about blocking their entrances, as well as the London Dock Company and Commercial Dock Company. After almost two years of investigation, the Navigation Committee opted for a 250-yard passage, much as it already existed. It had been impressed most by the views of its own Harbour Masters, who had borne the brunt of Hall's attack. Hall then turned to central government, persuading the Home Secretary to support a Select Committee investigation.[55]

[51] SC Port of London, Fisher; Q. 1396, Q. 530, Tickner.
[52] LMA, COL/CC/TNC, Navigation Committee, 49/XX, 2 March 1849.
[53] 10 Geo. IV. 1829; SC Port of London, Appendix 1, 214.
[54] PP 1831 VIII.1 [335], SC Calamities by Steam, 6.
[55] SC Port of London, Hall, Q. 903–4; Qq. 1328, 1580–7, Fisher; Qq. 219, 1908, Rowland, Q. 1908, Appendix 1, 131–137, 157–9.

The 1836 Select Committee on the State of the Port of London was quite an expert body. Many members had mercantile or shipping connections. Witnesses rehearsed their arguments on the passage breadth once more, but the five-month investigation covered other issues.[56] The committee's final recommendations, subsequently incorporated in new bye-laws, were a victory for Hall, but included concessions to his opponents: a 300-foot clear passage up to St. Katharine's, then 200 to London Bridge, and restrictions on steamboat speed.[57] Responding to evidence of conflicting river interests it called for river governance by a single body. However, almost two decades elapsed before any government responded even in part, and a further half century before the Port of London Authority was established.[58]

The question of river management was now on the table, as was the fitness of the Corporation for this role. Some witnesses suggested that lack of relevant expertise gave the Harbour Masters too much influence over Navigation Committee decisions. John Blenkarn, a Legal Quay wharfinger with steamship trade interests, one of the few Common Councillors with a port background, described it as 'a body of general citizens, shopkeepers and persons in the mediocrity of life'.[59] A former chairman saw an advantage in its impartiality, 'in selecting practical men there would be a danger of a majority predominating for a particular interest'.[60] Even so, the committee subsequently benefited from the experience of Master Lighterman, Joseph Robinson. As Chairman in 1838, he was responsible for new collier arrangements that increased the number of tiers while maintaining a clear waterway.[61]

The ideal balance between interested and disinterested parties continued to feature in discussions on how the river and port should be governed throughout the century. However, there was little that could be done to make membership of the Corporation's Navigation Committee a better reflection of London's maritime sector. The City of London was changing in character. Depopulation and redevelopment were underway, with railways and new roads intruding.[62] 'Thames Street, Queenhithe and the

---

[56] Ibid., iii.

[57] *Times*, 2 December 1836, 3.

[58] SC Port of London, i–iv.

[59] Ibid., Blenkarn, Q. 212,

[60] Ibid., Tickner, Q. 567.

[61] SC Thames Embankment, Robinson, Qq, 890–2, 899–909; PP 1854 XXVI.1, RC State of the Corporation of London, Turnley, Qq. 7707–15, Woodthorpe, Qq. 6185–6.

[62] See David Kynaston, 'A Changing Workscape: The City of London Since the 1840s', *The London Journal*, 13 (1987–88) 99–105; Peter Claus, 'Languages of Citizenship in the City of London, 1848–1867', *The London Journal*, 24 (1999), 23–37; Roland Quinault, 'From National to World Metropolis: Governing London, 1750–1850',

thoroughfares to the warehouses at the waterside, some twenty or thirty years ago, were respectably inhabited by parties connected with mercantile life. They are now all left to more humble tenants', noted journalist Morier Evans in 1852.[63] Many of the Common Councillors were retail trade, 'middling sort', occupants, and few had relevant knowledge of the river. In the early 1850s, only two serving on the Navigation Committee had any direct connection with the port, and again these were senior lightermen.[64] The merchants who had dominated both port and Corporation in the early nineteenth century and played so active a part in reform had no successors. Neither Alderman John Humphery proprietor of the extensive Hay's Wharf, nor ironmaster Alderman William Thompson, Deputy Chairman of the St. Katharine's Dock Company, had any similar involvement.[65] By mid-century, serving the Corporation was too time-consuming, burdened with ceremony and poorly regarded by the public to appeal to a new generation of busy leading merchants, most of whom now lived in the country, distant from their London workplaces. 'They have no longer the attachment to the City they formerly evinced', William Cotton, shipowner and Director of the Bank of England, told the 1854 Commission on the Corporation of London.[66]

The River Port

By 1806, London effectively had two ports: the corporate dock sector devoted to high-value dutiable cargo and the port of privately owned landing places, warehouses and granaries, which served the rest of London's trade. In the 1820s, Frenchman Dupin, immensely impressed by the architecture and operations of the docks, was struck by the physical contrast between these and the rest of the port, 'confined by ungainly walls and palings and clumsy piles; the whole surmounted by smoky and irregular sheds and houses'.[67] As port historian Gordon Jackson noted, there was nothing romantic about the great

---

The London Journal, 26 (2001), 38–46; John Davis, *Reforming London: The London Government Problem 1855–1900* (Oxford University Press, Oxford, 1988), 51–3.

[63] David Morier-Evans, *City Men and City Manners. The City; or the Physiology of London Business, with Sketches on 'Change ad at the Coffee Houses* (Groombridge and Sons, London, 1852), 165.

[64] SC Thames Embankment (1840), Robinson, Qq. 890–2, 899–909; RC Corporation of London (1840), Turnley, Qq. 7707–15, Woodthorpe, Qq. 6185–6.

[65] SC Thames Embankment (1840), Robinson, Qq. 1019–3; RC Corporation of London (1854), Leach, Qq. 6450–51.

[66] RC Corporation of London (1854), Cattle, Qq. 1266–72, Cotton, Qq. 1797–1801, Hankey, Qq. 1693–5.

[67] Charles Dupin, *Commercial Power*, 28–9.

nineteenth-century ports.[68] They were dirty, industrial places, and London's river port was no exception. Although by mid-century some of the worst of the ancient waterfront buildings were being replaced, it remained the untidy, busy harbour it had always been.

London's domestic sea trade was unaffected by dock company monopolies. Except for some home-grown grain and timber going into the Rotherhithe docks, this continued to be handled by the river port. In 1824, 2.2 million tons of merchandise entered London by coast. Of this, 8–9 per cent was coal, 14 per cent grain and 2 per cent metals. Foodstuffs, spirits and textiles accounted for less than 1 per cent.[69] Coastal cargo grew more slowly and steadily than the more volatile foreign trade, but by the later 1840s, the total tonnage of coastal vessels (including those from Ireland) entering the Port of London each year had reached 3 million, approximately a third more than in the early 1820s.[70] As Figure 4.1 shows, the number of repeat voyages made by coastal shipping meant that the tonnage of annual coastal entries continued to exceed foreign trade arrivals until 1863.

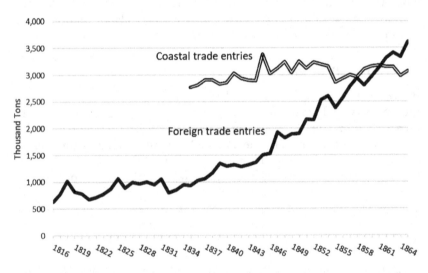

Figure 4.1 Total annual tonnage of entries into the Port of London by vessels in coastal and foreign trades, 1816–1865. (Coastal trade figures 1816–1834 unavailable.) Source: PP 1902 XLIV.1 [Cd. 1153], RC on the Port of London. Appendix, 238–42.

[68] Gordon Jackson, 'The Importance of Unimportant Ports', *International Journal of Maritime History*, 13 (2001), 1–2.
[69] Philip S. Bagwell, *The Transport Revolution from 1770* (Batsford, London, 1974), 71–2.
[70] RC Port of London (1902) Appendices, Appendix No. 6, 232–4; PP 1826 XXII.315, Account of the Number of Ships...

In the 1830s about a thousand coastal sailing vessels served London.[71] Most of these regular traders carried cargoes to and from the former Legal Quays and Sufferance Wharves. In 1842, Carpenter Smith's wharf, off Tooley Street, advertised a service to Penzance as 'the regular tin ships sail weekly'. Cotton's, another Southwark wharf, offered twenty-five destinations, including ten Irish ports.[72] But by this time, the new railways were making inroads. The South Eastern and South Western lines, terminating close to London Bridge, had already captured much of Tooley Street's south coast trade.[73] Outgoing coastal cargoes were more varied. Many of the 480 wagons and 1,700 carts reported coming into Tooley Street from the north bank via London Bridge on a single day in 1837 would have been carrying foreign cargoes imported into the docks or former Legal Quays, now destined for consumers in other parts of the country.[74]

Coastal Trades

In the late 1820s, the port handled an average of 1.9 million tons of coal every year. By the early 1840s, the figure was over 2.5 million.[75] Primarily from North East pits, it was burned in Londoners' homes for cooking and heating, with the rest used in brewing and distilling, manufacturing and, due to the growing popularity of gas lighting, also in making gas.[76] London had three gas companies in 1824, each year consuming 50,000 tons of coal. By 1851, there were fourteen, each consuming half a million.[77] Large numbers of colliers, generally measuring not more than 300 tons, came into London throughout the year.[78]

---

[71] SC Port of London, Farncomb, Q. 371.

[72] Robson's London Directory, 1842, 976–88.

[73] PP 1846 XVII.25 [719], RC Projects for Establishing Termini within Metropolis, Humphrey, Qq. 2082–3; Francis Shepherd, *London 1808–1870: The Infernal Wen* (Secker & Warburg, London, 1971), 122–157; J. R. Kellett, *The Impact of Railways on the Victorian City* (Routledge, London, 1969), 264–265; T. C. Barker and Michael Robbins, *A History of London Transport. Volume One – The Nineteenth Century* (George Allen & Unwin, London, 1975), 44–56; John Armstrong, 'Coastal Shipping and the Thames: Its Role in London's Growth and Expansion', in Roger Owen (ed.), *Shipbuilding on the Thames and Thames-Built Ships. Proceedings of a Second Symposium on Shipbuilding on the Thames, 15 February 2003* (Docklands History Group, West Wickham, 2004), 146–56.

[74] Bagwell, *Transport Revolution*, 71–2; PP 1837 XX.363, SC on the Thames Tunnel, Charlier, Q. 202.

[75] PP 1833 XXXIII.205, Quantities of Coal and Culm Imported 1826–32; PP 1846 XLIV.403, Dues for Harbour Service and Number of Tons of Coal Imported 1836–44.

[76] SC Port of London, Rowland, Q. 1908; PP 1837–38 XV.1 [475], SC Coal Trade (Port of London) Bill, Q. 3068.

[77] M. E. Falkus, 'The British Gas Industry before 1850', *Economic History Review*, 20 (1967) 494–508; Samuel Clegg, *Practical Treatise on the Manufacture and Distribution of Coal-Gas* (John Weale, London, 1853), 22.

[78] SC Coal Trade (1837-8), Appendix 6, 237.

The port had a well-established system of coal trade management. If not destined for gas works, on arrival at Gravesend a collier's papers were sent to a commission agent, 'the factor', in the City, who handled the sale to coal merchants. Between 1834 and 1845, then sporadically until the late 1850s, a coal owner combination known as 'the Vend' influenced the market by controlling the number and order of coal cargo sales. Colliers were detained downriver until their coal was sold and only then permitted by the Harbour Master to move to mooring tiers in the Lower Pool.[79] In the 1820s, there were 240 berths, but the St. Katharine's Dock and Shadwell entrance to the London Docks reduced these to 147. Even though tiers were added in the 1840s, it remained rare for there to be sufficient room. The Harbour Service red and white flag at Greenwich, signalling that tiers in the Pool of London were full, was often raised and colliers queued downriver in large numbers, in some cases for many days.[80]

Once berthed, the cargo was measured for the Corporation coal tax. It was then discharged into barges by coal heaver gangs supplied by 'coal undertakers', usually publicans, contracted by the ship's Master for transportation to coal merchant wharves. An 1841 survey found between London Bridge and Vauxhall alone twenty-six coal yards on the south bank, thirty-nine on the north.[81] A few large, well-established firms dominated the wholesale trade. Merchant and factor William Horne, whose family's involvement dated at least to the mid-eighteenth century, owned thirty-five lighters, a dozen of which would be lying off his wharf at any one time.[82] These 'first buyer' businesses sold their coal to smaller dealers, many of whom were no doubt owners of the numerous coal barges serving as floating warehouses on the river.[83]

Grain

Approximately 2 million quarters of grain arrived in the port every year between 1825 and 1840. Much of this was home-grown. Thanks to the

[79] Paul M. Sweezy, *Monopoly and Competition in the English Coal Trade* (Harvard University Press, Harvard, 1938); Raymond Smith, *Sea-Coal for London. History of the Coal Factors in the London Market* (Longmans, London, 1961).

[80] SC Coal Trade (Port of London) (1837–8), Rowlands, Qq. 3772–6; Smith, *Sea-Coal*, 207–8; Alexander Pulling, *The Laws, Customs, Usages and Regulations of the City and Port of London*, Second Edition (William Henry Bond and Wildy and Sons, London, 1854), 474–9.

[81] PP 1834 VIII.315 [559], SC Drunkeness, Moore, Q. 26, Saunders, Qq. 334, 421; SC Coal Trade (1837–8), Gouhty, Qq. 2825–39; PP 1830 VIII.1, SC State of the Coal Trade, Sanderson, 41, Apedale, 334, Griffiths, 184–7; PP 1844 XV.1, RC Metropolitan Improvement, First Report, Appendix C, 336.

[82] SC Coal Trade (1830), Horne, 85–6; SC Coal Trade (1837–8), Horne, Qq. 2855–6; Elspet Fraser-Stephen, *Two Centuries in the London Coal Trade. The Story of Charringtons* (Privately Printed, London, 1952), 34–7, 62.

[83] RC Metropolitan Improvement (1844), Appendix XVI a.

Corn Laws, there were only five years in this period when more than half came from abroad, but abolition then increased the foreign share. Local shipments of wheat and barley from Kent and Essex typically came in sixty-ton hoys, a type of sailing barge. Larger vessels carried more distant produce from Norfolk, Suffolk, Lincolnshire and Scotland. Ireland, rather than Scotland, was the major supplier of oats.[84] Overseas shipments came predominantly from Denmark, Prussia, Germany and France. British North America and the United States featured little. Much of this grain was carried by non-British shipping. Of the 1,393 vessels known to have come into London with foreign grain in 1845, 906 were foreign registered.[85]

London had a large number of granaries and warehouses for grain and flour storage, including those at the Deptford naval victualling yard.[86] In 1845, there were seventy-nine licensed for foreign grain and in some cases also flour, some also storing home-grown produce. Grain and flour for re-export had to be securely bonded, so they were still restricted to the north bank docks.[87] Many granaries were on the south bank in Southwark, Bermondsey and Rotherhithe, but by no means all. There were some in the City and a number in Wapping. These were often substantial and valuable properties. Leading grain merchant, Nathanial Palmer, claimed in 1834 that his firm's Bermondsey six-floor store, capable of holding 40,000 quarters of grain, was London's largest.[88]

Unlike coal, there were no moorings specifically reserved for grain vessels. Although certain stretches were customarily devoted to these, landing places extended over a large expanse of the river. 'The whole river, from Greenwich to Vauxhall, is one large dock for corn vessels and that corn is delivered in very large quantities over all that space', observed Corporation officer William Ruston in 1834.[89]

Most grain, sold by sample at the Corn Exchange or the Baltic Exchange if from abroad, arrived in bulk, although some from North

---

[84] PP 1834 VII.1, SC on Sale of Corn, Steed, Qq. 606, 667; PP 1843 LIII.9, Quantities of Grain ..., 71–2; Armstrong, 'Coastal Shipping', 156.

[85] Fairlie, Susan, 'British Statistics of Grain Imports from Canada and the USA, 1791– 1900', in David Alexander and Rosemary Ommer (eds.), *Volumes Not Values: Canadian Sailing Ships and World Trade* (Memorial University of Newfoundland, St. John's, 1979), 167–9; PP 1846 XLIV.591, Number of Ships Laden with Foreign Corn, 2–6.

[86] Jonathan Coad, *Support for the Fleet. Architecture and Engineering of the Royal Navy's Bases 1700–1914* (English Heritage, London, 2013), 301.

[87] PP 1845 XLVI.43, 5–7, Foreign Merchandize Permitted to be Bonded in London; PP 1840 V.475, SC on Inland Warehousing; Longlands, Qq. 2512, 2515.

[88] George Dodd, *The Food of London: A Sketch* (Longman, Brown, Green and Longmans, London, 1856), 173; David Barnett, *London, Hub of the Industrial Revolution. A Revisionary History 1775–1825* (I. B. Tauris & Co. Ltd., London, 1998), 191; SC Sale of Corn (1834), Palmer, Qq. 3000–1.

[89] SC Port of London, Appendix 1, 349; SC on the Sale of Corn (1834), Ruston, Q. 3585.

America was in barrels.[90] Kent and Essex grain, which exceptionally was in sacks, was largely exempt (allegedly as a mark of gratitude for supplying London during the Great Plague), but in all other cases, the Corporation imposed a standard metage (tax) based on quantity – the Winchester Bushel – not weight. Foreign produce paid more than home.

Traditional privileges shaped the process of grain handling. The Corporation claimed a monopoly over the porterage of all goods within its boundaries, which in the case of river-borne produce extended over the whole port. It employed those who measured the grain and collected the fees. Those who then discharged the grain for shipowners or merchants were corporation-licensed members of the Fellowship of Porters.[91] Having paid £5 to become a City Freeman plus an entrance fee, they rose through the ranks before qualifying as corn porters, the highest grade. Jobs, paid on a set scale, were allocated to gangs of porters by the Fellowship on a 'turn' system.[92] Once stored, grain was turned and screened regularly in an attempt to maintain its quality before being transferred to mills, distilleries and breweries.[93]

For centuries, grain to be ground had been barged to Thames Valley mills and the flour returned to London, again by river, for sale to bakers and households, a process that seems to have persisted well into the nineteenth century.[94] Nevertheless, although disadvantaged by lack of suitable sites for windmills, London was not without some milling capacity. Robson's 1842 Commercial Directory identifies thirty millers, most with premises on the south bank. London's first steam mill, the Albion, burned down in 1791, but by 1805, there were already six operating. Milling was a competitive business with a high attrition rate, so not all early steam mills survived.[95] However, the technology was certainly well established by the time the lease of 'a substantially brick built Steam

---

[90] Dodd, *Food of London*, 186; Graham L. Rees, *Britain's Commodity Markets* (Paul Elek Books, London, 1972), 124–9.

[91] SC Sale of Corn (1834), Fearnside, Qq. 953, 948–9. Ruston, Qq. 3503–7.

[92] Stern, *Porters*, 99–104; RC Municipal Corporations (1837), 16–17, 109–10; RC Corporation of London (1854), xxiii; Pulling, Qq. 830–839, Lawrence Qq. 7029–7064; Brown Qq. 3071, 4000.

[93] T. R. Gourvish and R. G. Wilson, *The British Brewing Industry* (Cambridge University Press, Cambridge, 1994), 79.

[94] M. Diane Freeman, 'A History of Corn Milling, c. 1750–1914, With Special Reference to South Central and South Eastern England' (Doctoral Thesis, University of Reading, 1976), 86.

[95] John Farey, *A Treatise on the Steam Engine, Historical, Practical and Descriptive*, Vol. 1 (Longman, Rees, Orme, Brown and Green, London, 1827), 443–4, 654; Richard Perren, 'Structural Change and Market Growth in the Food Industry: Flour Milling in Britain, Europe and America, 1850–1914', *Economic History Review*, New Series, 43 (1990), 422–3.

Mill', close to the London Dock, with an 'excellent four-horsepower engine, four pairs of stones for splitting beans and peas, and grinding wheat and barley', was advertised in 1831. More ambitious was the six- or seven-storied City flour mill just below Blackfriars Bridge. Built in 1852, it boasted thirty-two pairs of millstones.[96]

Foreign Trades

Beguiled by the presence of the docks and the exotic cargoes they handled, it is easy to lose sight of the continued importance of the river in London's foreign trade in the first half of the century. As already noted, in the mid-1830s, over half the shipping with overseas cargoes arriving in the port discharged here, rather than the docks. The larger vessels destined for the West India and East India systems tipped the balance of shipping tonnage towards the docks, but, at 40 per cent, the river's share of foreign trade shipping was still substantial.[97]

One reason for this was the limited impact docks had on the handling of Baltic produce. Wharves with licenses to handle foreign timber, grain and other northern European products retained these. The Rotherhithe docks had similar rights, but merchants and manufacturers were not compelled to use their facilities, and not all did so.[98] The north bank docks certainly deprived the owners of the former Legal Quays and uptown bonded warehouses of access to the port's most valuable high-duty cargoes. But the loss of sugar, wine and other businesses did not prove fatal to the prospects of the former Legal Quays, Sufferance Wharves and City warehouses. They could still handle other foreign imports and they retained the commercial advantages of waterfront premises and storage facilities close to the City of London.

In the short term, some Legal Quays came down in station. Instead of sugar and other West Indian produce, in 1820, Fresh Wharf housed cork, rags, argot, liquorice paste, lemon juice, hops and leather. Elsewhere, it was reported by a shocked customs officer, there was 'a valuable collection of pictures in the same floor with a quantity of Hams, an article liable in warm weather to breed vermin'.[99] Mundane though such produce may seem, this is a reminder that the Legal Quays and Sufferance Wharves retained the right to handle a wide

[96] *Public Ledger & Daily Advertiser*, 18 April 1831; Freeman 'Corn Milling', 40; Dodd, *Food of London*, 180–1.
[97] SC Port of London, Rowland, Q. 1826.
[98] PP 1831 XVII.459, Goods Warehoused in London, 1825–30, 461–77.
[99] TNA T92, 17, Memorial to the Commissioner of Inquiry into the Customs, 7 November 1820, 11 July 1820.

Illustration 4.3 Lighters and a sailing vessel unloading at Brewer's, Chester's and Galley Legal Quays, c. 1846. Image: Lower Thames Street. © Heritage Images/Getty Images.

range of cargoes, something still denied to London's other wharves for some years. As already noted, the Customs were impressed by the historic privileges of the Legal Quays and viewed their claims as more legitimate than those of other wharf interests.

However, it was the growth of the steam shipping trade with French channel ports, Antwerp, Rotterdam and Hamburg, and the Mediterranean that transformed Legal Quay prospects. Brewer's, Chester's and Galley Quays, owned by Joseph Barber, specialised in northern European ham, cheese and eggs. Seasonal fruit became the main business for Cox and Hammonds Quay, Fresh Wharf and the former East India Company wharf.[100] These were expanding markets. In 1839 provision merchants lobbied the Treasury to allow Sufferance Wharves to handle such imports: 'The quantity of foreign business crowded to the Legal Quays largely intermixed with Coasting Business renders it difficult for us importers of Provisions from Hambro [Hamburg], Rotterdam and c. to

---

[100] TNA T1 4133, Memorial, Quantities of Cheese, Hams, Currants, Raisins and Figs ... 23 August 1834; RC Establishing Termini within Metropolis, Tite, Q. 426.

find that accommodation, that the peculiar nature of our mode of selling (namely by shewing casks at the Bulk) requires...'[101]

Such foodstuffs were dutiable, and the Corporation charged metage, so both Customs and City officers had to be present. Handling was restricted to licensed porters, but, at least in the busy high-season fruit trade, 'unlicensed' men may also have been at work.[102]

Timber

Britain's traditional timber trade was with the Baltic, but the wartime imposition of duties of approximately 100 per cent on foreign timber by 1815 and only nominal duties on colonial produce changed this. Until timber duties began to be eased in the 1840s, in most years nationally, three-quarters of imported unsawn timber came from Canada.[103] As a west coast port, Liverpool particularly benefited, but London's proximity to northern Europe and the capital's demand for higher-quality material meant that despite duties its long-established trade with the Baltic remained important. In consequence, London imported marginally more timber from Europe than from the colonies.[104]

By the 1830s, the timber trade had the choice of the river, the basins of the Surrey or Regents Canals, or the docks. Mahogany and colonial timber were generally handled by the West India Docks and the relatively few British vessels in the Baltic trade used the Rotherhithe docks. However, large numbers of timber-carrying foreign vessels (half the total arriving in 1831) discharged in the river, even where the deals and staves were subsequently rafted to the docks. This saved the extra cost and time involved in using a dock and also economised on labour. Unlike grain, unloading could be done by the crew.[105]

July to December was the season for colonial timber entries. Vessels were then laid up until March, when they began to depart on their first return voyage of the year, which was when Baltic traders started arriving. Timber labourers, known as 'lumpers', were employed by a Master

[101] TNA T1 4133, 10 April 1839.
[102] RC Corporation of London (1854), Keeling, Qq. 1586–7, Kearns, Q. 2329; Stern, *Porters*, 258–61.
[103] J. Potter, 'The British Timber Duties, 1815–60', *Economica*, New Series, 22, (1955), 124.
[104] David M. Williams, 'Merchanting in the First Half of the Nineteenth Century: The Liverpool Timber Trade', *Business* History, 8 (1968), 104–5 [103–121]; PP 1830, XXVII.73, Timber and Wood Imported; Francis Sejersted, 'Aspects of the Norwegian Timber Trade in the 1840s and '50s', *Scandinavian Economic History Review*, 16 (1968), 139–140.
[105] PP 1835 XIX.1 [519], SC on Timber Duties, Carter, Q. 3971; SC Port of London, Gould, Qq. 2427–9.

Lumper contractor. They usually worked in gangs of four to twelve, under a foreman. Unsawn timber was dragged along the hold, using manpower and a combination of winches, tackles, chains and crowbars, then dropped gently into the river to be floated to their destination by 'rafters', who were licensed watermen. Deals (planked wood) were discharged through portholes in the vessel's stern into waiting lighters. Once ashore, deal porters, skilled men who were members of an exclusive fellowship but not licensed by the Corporation, took charge of sorting and stacking the wood.[106]

Steam Shipping

The introduction of paddle steamers into the near-European trades began modestly in 1821 with two trading to Calais, but the creation of the well-capitalised General Steam Navigation Company (GSNC) in 1824 resulted in regular steam connections with a wide range of northern European ports.[107] Already by the mid-1830s, these included Calais, Boulogne, Havre, Ostend, Antwerp, Rotterdam and Hamburg. Services were typically two to three departures a week in the summer, fewer in the winter.[108]

The joint-stock GSNC was very much a London enterprise. The founding directors had shipping experience, some already with steam, and the majority of the original 400–500 shareholders were also from the capital. By 1850, the company owned thirty-one vessels, totalling 9,676 registered tons, with operations extending over a wide sphere including river and coastal services. It dominated London's northern European steam business. In 1846, only ten of the twenty-nine British steam vessels employed in the French, Belgian and Dutch trades with London belonged to other operators.[109]

---

[106] Mayhew, Reprint, Volume 2, 271–2.

[107] Armstrong and David M. Williams, 'British Steam Navigation, 1812 to the 1850s: A Bibliographical and Historiographical Review', in John Armstrong and David M. Williams, (eds.), *The Impact of Technological Change. The Early Steamship in Britain. Research in Maritime History No. 47* (International Economic History Association, St. John's Newfoundland, 2011), 7–30.

[108] John Armstrong and David M. Williams, 'Steam Shipping and the Beginnings of Overseas Tourism: British Travel to North Western Europe, 1820–1850', *Journal of European Economic History*, XXXV (2006), 122.

[109] John Armstrong and David M. Williams, 'London's Steamships: Their Functions and Their Owners in the Mid-Nineteenth Century', *The London Journal*, 42 (2017), 11; Robert Forrester, 'The General Steam Navigation Company c.1850–1913: A Business History' (Doctoral Thesis, University of Greenwich, 2006), 32; Sarah Palmer, 'The Most Indefatigable Activity'. The General Steam Navigation Company, 1824–50', *Journal of Transport History, 3rd Series* (1982), 1–22.

Coastal steamship services developed in parallel with those to the continent. Paddle steamers owned by the London and Edinburgh Steam Packet Company, formed in 1821, provided first a weekly and, after 1826, a twice-weekly service and in 1831, the London, Leith, Edinburgh and Glasgow shipping company, which had operated a sailing packet service since 1814, introduced three more steamships on this route. Services from Kingston-upon-Hull started in 1819, from Newcastle in the 1820s and from Dublin in 1826. Weekly steam services from Aberdeen started in 1828 and those from Dundee and Perth followed. The Irish-based St George's Steam Packet Company began operating between Cork, West Country ports and London in about 1829.[110] By 1842, advertised steam services from London included three a week to Edinburgh, two to Dundee, Leith, Newcastle and Dublin and once a week to Aberdeen, Stockton-on-Tees and Cork.

Passengers and livestock, with speed and reliability at a premium, were well suited to the new technology. Cattle had long been carried by sea to London from Scotland, but the difficult voyage by sail could take a week and the animals suffered injury as well as weight loss. By 1836 some 7,000 head of cattle and 10,000 sheep each year arrived in London by steamer after a voyage that could take just two days.[111]

Some historians have been impressed by 'the rapid diffusion of steamships along the river and coasts of Britain', but even in 1850 steam shipping accounted for just 10 per cent of coastal and Irish Sea tonnage entries.[112] Several factors explain the limited impact of steam on London's coastal businesses. Fuel economy was poor, so holds filled with coal for fuel limited the space left for cargo. Capital and operating costs meant that freight rates were too high for the bulky, low-value cargoes such as coal, which characterised most of the business, where predictability was also less of an asset. In addition, at small ports on the East Coast, the volume of merchandise and the level of demand from

---

[110] Pigot's London and Provincial New Commercial Directory, 1826–7; Palmer, 'Shipping Industry', 155–79; Clive H. Lee, 'Some Aspects of the Coastal Shipping Trade: the Aberdeen Steam Navigation Company, 1835–80', *Journal of Transport History*, Second Series, 3 (1975), 94–107; R. H. Greenwood and F. J. Hawks, *The Saint George Steam Packet Company 1821–1843* (World Ship Society, Kendal, 1995).

[111] *Morning Chronicle*, 11 January 1839; Peter M. Solar, 'Shipping and Economic Development in Nineteenth Century Ireland', *Economic History Review*, New Series, 59 (2006), 725–6, 738–74; Dodd, *Food of London*, 242; Richard Perren, *The Meat Trade in Britain 1840–1914* (Routledge & Kegan Paul, London, 1978), 17–18.

[112] John Armstrong and David M. Williams (eds.), 'The Steamship as an Agent of Modernisation, 1812–1840', in *The Impact of Technological Change. The Early Steamship in Britain. Research in Maritime History, No. 47* (IMEHA, St. John's Newfoundland, 2011), 165–118; PP 1852 XLIX.25 [359], Numbers and Tonnage of Ships ... entered the Port of London from 1841–1851.

travellers were too slight to support a regular steamship service and even well-financed companies like the metropolitan-based GSNC struggled to sustain a long-term presence on certain routes.[113]

River Steam Traffic

Steam technology may have only affected a few branches of London's foreign and coastwise trade, but its impact on the port went beyond these. Activity on the river had previously been in thrall to the tides and for centuries watermen's boats had hauled sailing vessels. 'Sometimes as many as four boats with two men in each, being engaged, and thus ships of the largest class were easily moved up and down river'.[114] Now steamers could undertake this, as was soon recognised. As Harbour Master Charles Rowland explained in 1842:

Sailing vessels used to drop up on the Flood and down on the Ebb and this prac-tice was considered the Rule of the River, vessels navigated against tide did so at their own risk, but the introduction of steam vessels altered the system alto-gether, not only did the steamers themselves travel against tide but were suffi-ciently powerful to tow large vessels with them and now a great part of the home and foreign trade is carried on in vessels varying from Twenty to One Thousand Tons Burthen navigating up and down the River at all hours of the day and night against Wind and Tide.[115]

Specialist towage firms emerged in the 1820s and dedicated pad-dle tugs were probably first introduced on the Thames in 1823.[116] By the time a single steam tug was portrayed pulling the aged man-of-war *Téméraire* to a Rotherhithe breaker's yard in J. M. W. Turner's 1838 painting, such vessels were a familiar sight on the Thames. At 2,128 tons, *Téméraire* was then the most enormous ship ever to enter the Pool of London, so in reality, two were employed, as was usual in the case of larger vessels.[117] William Thackeray saw in Turner's depiction 'a little, spiteful, diabolical steamer' belching 'foul, lurid, red-hot malignant smoke' and some later commentators discerned in this extraordinary painting a prophetic insight into the outcome of a

---

[113] Palmer, 'General Steam', 9.

[114] Humpherus, *Watermen and Lightermen III*, 247.

[115] MLD, Navigation Committee Minutes, 40/PP, 1 January 1842; SC Port of London, Boy, Qq. 726–7; *London Courier and Evening Gazette*, 25 August 1835; SC Calamities by Steam Navigation, Brown, Q. 9.

[116] Advertisement Thames and Medway Steam-Towing Company; *Globe*, 18 August 1825; P. N. Thomas, *British Steam Tugs* (Waine Research, Wolverhampton, 1983), 13–14.

[117] *Times*, 13 September 1838; *Shipping and Mercantile Gazette*, 15 September 1838.

contest between sail and steam.[118] In reality the common use of steam towage to assist sailing vessels was a beneficial partnership.

The steamer portrayed by Turner was probably the twenty-five horse-power, twenty-six-ton, *Monarch*, owned by John Watkins Ltd.[119] This towage business, founded in 1833, was among the first but others soon followed. By the early 1850s, London had eight firms, together owning forty-nine tugs.[120] Many of those involved appear to have had a back-ground as watermen or lightermen, although Corporation interests were well represented in the Symington Patent Paddle Towing Company (sub-sequently the Shipowners Towing Company).[121] Using dedicated steam tugs to propel barges, later to become common, began only in 1848 when a Master Lighterman purchased a tug to use with his own craft.[122]

The Thames not only served the port, it was also a public space. For Londoners and the many visitors to the capital, it remained a major high-way. Boats and wherries piloted by watermen were the traditional means of travel, across as well as up and down the waterway.[123] Commercial steamboat operations began in 1815 with the seventy-two ton, fourteen-horsepower, *Thames* which ran to Margate. Within two years there were five serving Richmond, Margate and Gravesend. By 1835 there were at least ten companies, together operating forty vessels, engaged in services to Gravesend and beyond.[124] Most ran from City piers in the crowded Pool of London.

Initially river services were patronised by the middle and upper classes for holidays in the coastal resorts and also by those commuting daily to their London workplace. However, within just a few years, faster voy-ages, lower fares and daily excursions extended the tourist market to a less wealthy clientele.[125] Companies formed later, such as the Eagle

---

[118] Michelangelo Titmarsh [W. M. Thackeray], 'A Second Lecture on the Fine Arts', *Frasers* Magazine, 19, No. 114 (1839), 744; Martin Butlin and Evelyn Joll, *The Paintings of J.M.W. Turner*, Revised Edition Text (Yale University Press, New Haven and London, 1984), 229–31; Richard L. Stein, 'Remember the *Téméraire*: Turner's Memorial of 1839', *Representations*, 11 (1985), 186–92.

[119] Frank C. Bowen, *A Hundred Years of Towage. A History of Messrs. William Watkins Ltd., 1833–1933* (Gravesend and Dartford Reporter, Gravesend, 1933), 15–20.

[120] PP 1852–53, LXI.379 [687], Committee of the Board of Ordinance, Capabilities of the Mercantile Steam Navy for Purposes of War, 9.

[121] www.thamestugs.co.uk, accessed 5 December 2018; *Globe*, 10 March 1836.

[122] '*Times*, 27 August 1844, 3; Humpherus, *Watermen and Lightermen III*, 451.

[123] White, *London in the Nineteenth Century*, 14–15.

[124] T. C. Barker and Michael Robbins, *A History of London Transport. Volume One – The Nineteenth Century* (George Allen & Unwin Ltd., London, 1975), 40–43; Palmer, 'Shipping Industry', 142–5.

[125] John Armstrong and David M. Williams, 'The Thames and Recreation, 1815–1840', *The London Journal*, 30 (2005), 25–39; Robert Pierce Cruden, *Gravesend in the County of Kent* (William Pickering, London, 1843), 537.

Steam Packet Company, the London, Vauxhall & Westminster, the Watermans and the City, catered for shorter distance demand by offering frequent 'river-bus' services by fleets of small, purpose-built steamboats. Several of these operated mainly above London Bridge, but others provided connections within the commercial core of both City and port below London Bridge.[126]

River steamers proved immensely popular with the public, attracting those who would never have made use of uncomfortable, sometimes downright dangerous, wherries. By the late 1830s the numbers travelling on the river each year reached 2 million. 'From the peasant to the nobleman, all have availed themselves' commented one satisfied steamboat company director. They were less popular with other river users. Already in 1831 sections were 'like a crowded street' and small steamboats made congestion even worse.[127] Initially, passengers embarked and disembarked using watermen's wherries. In 1830 the first specially constructed steam wharf was opened by the St. Katharine's Dock Company and by 1839 there were six dedicated steam wharves in the Upper Pool.[128] For passengers being close to the City of London was a major consideration. In 1839 Legal Quay Fresh Wharf handled the most passengers, despite charging twice as much for landing as did St. Katharine's further downriver. The East and West India Dock Company's Brunswick Wharf at Blackwall failed to prosper until the opening of the London and Blackwall Railway in 1840 cut journey time to central London to just fifteen minutes.[129]

The Company of Watermen and Lightermen claimed that steamboat companies infringed their legal monopoly over carriage on the river. To avoid conflict, firms employed licensed watermen on their vessels, but such men were not qualified to be engineers and the 500 or so said to have obtained jobs with the steamship companies were only about a third of those who had lost employment when Thames steamers replaced wherries.[130]

---

[126] *Illustrated London News*, 'Steam Navigation of the Thames', 13 July 1844; Barker and Robbins, *London Transport*, 42–3.
[127] SC Calamities by Steam (1831), Brown, Q. 994; SC Port of London, iii.
[128] Cruden, *Gravesend*, 500.
[129] HLRO, SC on the Blackwall Railway, 1839/3, Knill, 102–3, 172; SC Port of London, Fisher, Qq. 1308, 1310; PP 1837–38 XXIII.329, Lords SC on the Carriage of Passengers for Hire upon the River, Thames, Knight, 12.
[130] SC Port of London, Hall, Q. 3; SC on the Carriage of Passengers 23, Knight, 12.

5   Port and Populace I
Maritime Industries and Communities
in the First Half of the Century

Illustration 5.1 Shipbuilding at Limehouse, 1840. Image: Limehouse. © London Metropolitan Archives (City of London). William Parrott (1813–1869).

A vessel enters the Port of London; the crew is discharged; the Man has no Location; he knows no one. Who are his Companions? To whom does he resort? There is the Public House, and there are the low Boarding Houses. He associates with the Publican, the Prostitute, and the Crimp, all of whom are interested in defrauding him of his Money, entrapping him as speedily as they can, and then getting him on board another ship.[1]

London's maritime connections extended beyond its port. Much activity in the docks and river originated in its mercantile and shipping communities, sustained by a professional cluster that included marine

---

[1] PP 1847–48 [431], House of Lords SC on the Policy and Operation of the Navigation Laws, Second Report, Hall, Q. 6933.

insurance, shipbroking, maritime law and, to a lesser extent, banking. To this list should be added the commercial intelligence provided by a specialist press. But the maritime sector, like the metropolitan economy as a whole, was not all services. There was also manufacturing. Debates on the structure of nineteenth-century metropolitan industry have focussed on the dominance or otherwise of small-scale firms, but in the case of the maritime-related industries, shipbuilding, marine engineering, sailmaking and sugar baking, large-scale wins out.[2]

The City of London, with its Baltic Exchange, coffee houses and produce markets, may have been the commercial centre, but the industrial and occupational maritime heartlands were on the north bank below the Tower of London and on the south bank towards Rotherhithe. London had many districts noted for specialities such as furniture or clock making. What distinguished the maritime districts was not a product or activity but their inhabitants' common direct or indirect dependence on sea trade for a living.

Shipowning

London was the country's busiest port and also had the country's largest registered shipping fleet. Virtually all vessels 'belonging to London' in this period were employed in the capital's trades. The small number of London steamships typically belonged to joint stock companies with many shareholders, but most sailing vessels were owned under the traditional 64th system. Shipping property was divided into sixty-four shares, with investors legally not partners but 'tenants in common', free to sell or mortgage their share as they wished. Most shareholders were Londoners, but about a fifth lived in the North East, reflecting London's coal trade connections.[3]

The majority of those investing had other occupations, but a few relied sufficiently on shipping for a livelihood to justify the description 'shipowner'. In the early nineteenth century, such specialists included Wapping firm Michael Henley & Son.[4] Originally coal merchants, they began to concentrate on shipping in the 1790s and at their wartime peak

---

[2] See M. J. Daunton, 'Industry in London: Revisions and Reflections', *The London Journal*, 21 (1996), 1–8; Paul Johnson, 'Economic Development and Industrial Dynamism in Victorian London', *The London Journal*, 21 (1996), 27–37; David Green, 'The Nineteenth-Century Metropolitan Economy: A Revisionist Interpretation', *The London Journal*, 21 (1996), 9–26.

[3] S. R. Palmer, 'Investors in London Shipping', 1820–50, *Maritime History*, 2 (1972), 46–68.

[4] Simon P. Ville, *English Shipowning in the Industrial Revolution. Michael Henley and Son, London Shipowners, 1770–1830* (Manchester University Press, London, 1987).

in 1810 owned twenty-two vessels totalling almost 6,000 tons. Coastwise coal was a core cargo for Henley vessels, but opportunities for wartime profits took them to the Baltic, the government transport service in the Mediterranean, and further afield to the West Indies, British North America and South America.[5]

Henley's business was modest in comparison with Joseph Somes. By the early 1840s, his fleet of about forty-two ships, totalling 23,100 tons, made him the country's largest private shipowner. A major government contractor, his vessels (many purchased after the breakup of the East India Company) predominantly sailed to the Far East and Australasia, but on occasion to Africa and the Americas.[6] Specialist shipowners like Henley and Somes became more common towards mid-century, but they remained a minority. The typical investor in London vessels registered their occupation as 'merchant' but mariners, shipbuilders, shipbrokers, ropemakers, mast makers, coopers and anchor smiths also feature. Such 'maritime tradesmen' often held only a small number of shares, which were frequently used to motivate and reward shipmasters, or in part-payment for shipbuilding or equipment. Wealthy men with significant shareholdings spread across a number of vessels included George Frederick Young, partner in the Limehouse shipbuilders Curling & Young, Blackwall shipbuilders Wigram and Robert Green, East India merchant and agent George Lyall, Australia trader and financier Robert Brooks and the wine and beer merchant Duncan Dunbar.[7]

Dunbar's role as a shipowner equalled his mercantile interests. When he died in 1862, he left an immense fortune of £1.5 million. By then, his fleet of seventy vessels made him, like Somes two decades earlier, reputedly the country's largest shipowner.[8] At the other end of the scale were much smaller London operators. John Long, a Woolwich coal merchant and dealer in bricks and stone, had a shipbuilding and repair business at Rotherhithe. Sole or joint owner of ten vessels in the years 1815–1828, Long shipped coals on his own account, but was prepared to carry any

---

[5] Ibid., 29, 54.

[6] ODNB, Somes, Joseph (1787–1845); PP 1844 XVII.1 [545], SC British Shipping, Somes, Qq. 251–3.

[7] See ODNB, Young, George Frederick (1791–1870), Richard Green (1803–1863), George Lyall (1779–1853); Henry Green and Robert Wigram, *Chronicles of the Blackwall Yard, Part 1* (Whitehead, Morris and Lowe, London, 1881); Frank Broeze, *Mr Brooks and the Australian Trade. Imperial Business in the Nineteenth Century* (Melbourne University Press, Melbourne, 1993).

[8] PP 1847–48 [754], Lords SC Navigation Laws, Third Report, Dunbar, Qq. 1764–71; *Inverness Chronicle*, 13 March 1862; David Dunbar-Nasmith, *Duncan Dunbar and His Ships*, www.danbyrnes.com.au/networks/periods/1800after/1800dunbar.htm, accessed 22 July 2021.

cargo anywhere in pursuit of profit. His speculations included voyages to the East Mediterranean and South America.[9]

About 10 per cent of shares belonged to those with no evident direct maritime link.[10] Asked in 1833 about investment in shipping, bill broker Samuel Gurney replied: 'There is a class of men in London who are not indisposed to pursue that line of business, and who do it as they tell me with fair advantage, but it requires a more with thorough knowledge of the business to make money out of it, coupled with a very strict economy'.[11]

Gentlemanly family connections explain some holdings, but there were those with lesser means who saw an opportunity for profit. Indeed, shipping was a business with an unusual record of upward social mobility. John Marshall, a canny ship and insurance broker, demonstrated 'how an entrepreneur could begin with one vessel and, with luck and good management, could develop a viable fleet'. Marshall owned or part-owned at least thirty vessels between 1811 and 1838.[12]

On issues of government policy, London shipowners and their counterparts in other ports worked together in the General Shipowners Society, which replaced an earlier London-based organisation in 1831. Led by free-trader Lyall and protectionist Young, both politicians and shipowners, the society promoted parliamentary investigations into the state of the industry in 1823, 1833 and 1834. Despite its public profile as a national body, support in other ports was reluctant or ephemeral. In practice, it represented a small group of larger London shipowners. Lyall, Dunbar and the Society's most enthusiastic supporter, Young, all served terms as chairman.[13]

The thirty years after 1815 were not easy for those who relied on international trade for a livelihood.[14] Like mercantile commerce more generally, growing slowly for London until the later 1840s, shipping was a risky business and depressions were sufficiently serious to merit parliamentary investigation in 1833 and 1844.[15] Even so, for those sensitive

---

[9] Sarah Palmer, 'John Long. A London Shipowner', *Mariner's Mirror*, 72 (1986), 43–61.

[10] Palmer, 'Investors', 55–9.

[11] PP 1833 VI.1 [690], SC Manufactures, Commerce and Shipping, Gurney Q. 3254.

[12] W. D. Rubinstein, *Men of Property. The Very Wealthy in Britain Since the Industrial Revolution* (Croom Helm, London, 1881), 97–8; Elizabeth Rushen, *John Marshall. Shipowner, Lloyd's Reformer and Emigration Agent* (Anchor Books, Australia, 2020), 22–34, 179–83.

[13] Sarah Palmer, *Shipping, Politics and the Repeal of the Navigation Laws* (Manchester University Press, Manchester, 1990), 30–7.

[14] Kynaston, *The City of London. Volume 1* (Pimlico, London, 1994), 36–130; David Green, *From Artisans to Paupers, Economic Change and Poverty in London, 1790–1870* (Scolar Press, Aldershot, 1995), 51.

[15] SC Manufactures; SC British Shipping (1844).

to new opportunities and with luck on their side, there was money to be made and London was the place to do it. Here were clustered the Royal Exchange, an international insurance market centred on Lloyds, the Baltic Exchange where shipping services and cargoes were traded, and coffee house commercial clubs, including the North and South American, Jerusalem, Jamaica, and Garraways. In contrast to their open eighteenth-century predecessors, these had become generally exclusive establishments, each specialising in a region or trade, whose members paid a subscription.[16] The shipping lists, foreign and national newspapers, maps and reference books provided made these establishments unparalleled sources of commercial intelligence, as well as convivial places to make deals.[17] 'Refreshment in the shape of tea and coffee, sandwiches, and wines and liquors, is often combined with business pursuits' noted Morier Evans, who also mentioned 'sandwich-bars'.[18]

Those with substantial shares in ships may have inhabited the same trading world as the merchants and brokers who also patronised the coffee houses, but their concerns were not always identical. Merchants generally favoured trade liberalisation, whereas most shipowners and shipbuilders were protectionists. Conflict with marine insurance interests over the classification of vessels, which surfaced in the 1820s, was resolved in favour of shipowners by reform of Lloyd's Register of Shipping in 1833.[19]

Something else also set shipowners apart from their City peers. Except for perhaps going to a dock to sample a cargo, a merchant might have little or no direct contact with the port that made his business possible. In contrast, a shipowner or his agent had to deal with the choice of vessel, its maintenance and repair, its equipment, its Master, its manning, its victualling, its insurance and the choice of voyage and cargo. Large shipowners were necessarily significant employers and usually had waterfront premises. Dunbar Wharf, off the tidal inlet of Limehouse Dock, still survives.[20] Successful shipowners might savour their rewards (both Somes and Dunbar had art collections), but involvement with shipping

---

[16] See Markman Ellis, *The Coffee House: A Cultural History* (Weidenfield and Nicholson, London, 2004).

[17] Hugh Barty-King, *The Baltic Exchange. The History of a Unique Market* (Hutchinson Benham, London, 1977), 62–9.

[18] David Morier Evans, *The City or The Physiology of London Business with Sketches of 'Change' and the London Coffee Houses* (Baily Brothers, London, 1845), 108–19, 122–9, 141–56.

[19] Charles Wright and C. Ernest Fayle, *A History of Lloyd's* (Macmillan, London, 1928), 328–9.

[20] Bridget Cherry, Charles O'Brien and Nicholas Pevsner, *The Buildings of England. London 5: East* (Yale University Press, New Haven, 2005), 539; *The Globe*, 5 July 1845.

demanded practical daily engagement. Somes, the son of a Master Lighterman, had a fine house in Mile End. Dunbar, like his merchant and shipowner father before him, until 1854 occupied the family house off the East India Dock Road.[21] The home of philanthropic Blackwall shipbuilder Richard Green was in the Yard and the Green family worshipped at Trinity Congregational Chapel, which they had endowed. Young, who also lived locally, was active in the community. He chaired the Stepney Board of Guardians and London Hospital Committee, as well as helping to create Victoria Park.[22]

Shipbuilding: The Yards

Building and repairing vessels was the capital's most important maritime manufacturing industry. In the early 1800s, over 3,000 men were employed in the eighteen largest shipyards, not including those in the naval dockyards.[23] There were about the same number of shipbuilding workers in 1841 and Robson's Directory lists forty-three firms.[24] For centuries, the Thames had been the country's leading merchant shipbuilding centre in terms of output, with a reputation for specialist work of the highest quality and prices to match. London shipyards served a local market. Almost half the merchant tonnage launched on the Thames over the period 1800–1812 were exceptionally large vessels built for the wealthy shipowners who provided vessels to the East India Company. Except for a few West Indiamen, the rest were under fifty tons.[25] In wartime, the yards benefited from the presence of the Admiralty. When the Royal Dockyards, including those at Deptford and Woolwich, were

[21] *Illustrated London News*, 5 July 1845; *Survey of London, XLIII*, 132–3; Dunbar-Nasmith, *Duncan Dunbar and His Ships*.

[22] ODNB, Young, Green; Tower Hamlets Local History and Archives, Records of Trinity United Reformed (formerly Congregational) Church, Poplar, http://185.121.204.36/ CalmView/Record.aspx?src=CalmView.Catalog&id=W%2FTUC, accessed 28 July 2021.

[23] PP 1813–14 VIII.1 [115], Petitions Relating to East India Built Shipping, 400.

[24] PP 1844 XXVII.1 [587], 1841 Census. Abstract of Answers and Returns. Occupation Abstract. This figure includes shipbuilders and wrights, ship carpenters, ship caulkers, ship riggers, block and mast makers in the Middlesex London maritime parishes of Bermondsey, Lambeth, Rotherhithe, Southwark, Deptford and Greenwich.

[25] Sarah Palmer, 'Shipbuilding in South-east England, 1800–1913', in Simon Ville (ed.), *Shipbuilding in the United Kingdom: A Regional Approach. Research in Maritime History. No 4*. (International Maritime Economic History Association, St. John's, Newfoundland, 1993), 57–8; PP 1812–13 VIII.59 [84], Ships Launched in River Thames for East India Company, 1770–1812; PP 1812–13 IX.451[247], Ships Launched in the Thames for the Merchant Service, 1786–1812. On the East India Company system of hiring vessels, see Anthony Webster, *The Twilight of the East India Company. The Evolution of Anglo-Asian Commerce and Politics 1790–1860* (Boydell Press, Woodbridge, 2009), 40.

unable to meet its demand for warships, the State turned to the private yards.[26] Both sectors depended upon the same skilled independent workforce of shipwrights and other highly trained men who moved between the two spheres.[27]

Most early nineteenth-century yards were in Rotherhithe or Deptford on the south bank. On the north, there was a cluster at Limehouse, shown in Illustration 5.1, the Blackwall Wigram Yard and Pitcher's at Northfleet. After Blackwall, the most productive were the two Deptford yards, Barnard's, which had four slipways (one at Rotherhithe), and Dudman's, which had five. There were seven slipways in Randall and Brent's Rotherhithe yard.[28] With the development of iron shipbuilding as a branch of engineering, from the 1830s, the industry began to extend downriver attracted by the deeper water and relatively cheap land. William Fairbairn and John Napier both established yards at Millwall on the Isle of Dogs, while the Miller & Ravenhill and Ditchburn & Mare partnerships set up at Bow Creek, the estuary of the River Lea.[29]

Leading shipyards, capable of building or repairing vessels of more than a thousand tons, were extensive enterprises. By 1842, when George Dodd described in detail the 'scene of uncommon bustling and liveliness' at Blackwall Yard, some land had been lost to the Blackwall Railway, but it still occupied a thirteen-acre site.[30] Although split when the partnership of Wigram and Green ended in 1843, nonetheless the two yards were of sufficient size to support both families' building and ship-owning interests until the 1870s.[31]

[26] Helen Doe, 'The Thames Merchant Yards in the Napoleonic Wars', in Roger Owen (ed.), *Shipbuilding and Ships on the Thames. Proceedings of a Third Symposium* (J. R. Owen, West Wickham, 2006), 10–21; Roger Knight, 'Devil Bolts and Deception? Wartime Naval Shipbuilding in Private Shipyards, 1739–1815', *Journal for Maritime Research*, 5 (2003), 34–51.

[27] Helen Doe, *Enterprising Women and Shipping in the Nineteenth Century* (Boydell Press, Woodbridge, 2009), 176–83; Chris Ellmers, 'Deptford Private Shipyards, and Their Relationship to Deptford Dockyard, 1790–1819', in *Five Hundred Years of Deptford and Woolwich Royal Dockyards, Transactions of the Naval Dockyards Society*, 11 (2018), 40–4.

[28] PP 1813–14 VIII [115], Minutes of Evidence on Petitions Relating to East India Built Shipping, Noakes, 343; Philip Banbury, *Shipbuilders of the Thames and Medway* (David & Charles, Newton Abbot, 1971), 133–5; Stuart Rankin, *Shipbuilding in Rotherhithe – The Nelson Dockyard, Rotherhithe Local History Paper 2* (Dockside Studio, London, 1996); *Shipbuilding in Rotherhithe – Greenland Dock & Barnard's Wharf, Rotherhithe Local History Paper No. 3* (Dockside Studio, London, 1999); John E. Barnard, *Building Britain's Wooden Walls. The Barnard Dynasty c.1697–1851* (Anthony Nelson, Oswestry, 1997), 63–76; Ellmers, 'Deptford Private Shipyards', 31, 39.

[29] Banbury, *Shipbuilders*, 164, 171–2, 207, 214; A. J. Arnold, *Iron Shipbuilding on the Thames 1832–1915. An Economic and Business History* (Ashgate, London, 2000), 20–34.

[30] George Dodd, *Days of the Factories or The Manufacturing Industry of Great Britain Described. Series I – London* (Charles Knight & Co., London, 1843), 459–73.

[31] *Survey of London, XLIV*, 56–74.

Most Thames shipyards were considerably smaller than Blackwall and other leading yards. Typically, they had just one or two slipways and, instead of a regular workforce of hundreds, might employ only twenty to thirty men. Even so, constructing and repairing vessels needed plenty of equipment and accommodation. An 1848 sale advertisement for medium-sized premises adjacent to the West India Dock offered: 'Two spacious dry docks for the reception of vessels of the largest class, wharf ways extensive for breaming ships' bottoms, lay-by for barges, space for building ships, mould loft, sawpits, engine-house, store-houses, joiner's shops, timber sheds, steam kiln, pitch and furnaces, landing crane, capstans, smith's shop, coal and iron yards, counting-house, lodges, landing-stairs and numerous useful appurtanences'.[32]

Even when a shipbuilding firm rented or purchased a yard with some existing facilities, the fixed capital for development needed to make a success of the business discouraged new entrants. For this reason, inheritance and family finance featured in the history of many leading yards. Shipbuilding was also an industry in which an established connection between client and builder mattered a great deal. As a London shipowner explained in 1814, since there was no way that he could check personally for shipwright deception or incompetence, he had to rely on the 'honour and integrity' of the contracting shipbuilder.[33] It was a challenging business. Winning, and then profitably fulfilling, contracts required skill, particularly when the demanding customer was the Admiralty, which imposed penalties for delay.[34] Timber and other materials had to be sourced and workmen to be recruited, managed and paid. The working capital needed was relatively modest since timber and other materials were purchased with commercial bills, shipwrights supplied their own tools and, in theory at least, customers paid in instalments as the work progressed.[35] Even so, these counted for little if workflow could not be maintained, and competition between yards for orders could be fierce.

The travails of the passage to Asia meant that the average lifespan of an Indiaman was only four years, and most ocean-going vessels were docked every time they returned to port, so outfitting, replacement, repair and maintenance were also significant sources of shipyard business. Before 1815, repair accounted for half the work in some yards, and since it was customary for vessels to be repaired where they were built, these benefited most.[36] In the depressed decades that followed, when there was less demand for new vessels and London builders also faced greater outport competition, many relied even more on repair contracts to fill their yards.[37]

The end of the East India Company's monopoly in 1813 opened Indian trade to independent shipping. This exposed London's pricey specialist shipbuilders to external competition and deprived them of their guaranteed source of custom in the East India Company ship-leasing fraternity. Freebooting sole shipowners took advantage. By the 1820s, there was an oversupply of East India shipping, resulting in lower freights and little demand for new vessels.[38] Post-war entry into the merchant fleet of prize and naval vessels depressed the shipbuilding market more generally, and, to add to the woes of leading London yards, naval contracts dried up almost entirely. Just a few, for mail packets and other small steam vessels, were awarded over the next thirty years.[39]

Almost half the nineteen leading firms that had been active in 1814 collapsed in the order crisis. Most of those who survived did so by combining wooden shipbuilding with steamship construction. In the 1820s, the new owners of Dudman's yard at Deptford, Gordon & Company, continued to build large East Indiamen but also constructed paddle steamers, including the 470-ton *Enterprize*, which made the first steam voyage to India.[40] Blackwall Yard went on to produce the distinctive Blackwall Frigates to serve the shipping interests of its owners, Money Wigram and George Green. It also constructed wooden paddle steamers for the GSNC and the Peninsular and Orient Steamship Company (P&O) among others.[41]

Iron shipbuilding on the Thames began with the launch of the first iron vessel in 1832. It was fostered by the engineering skills of firms like Maudsley, Penn and Rennie and the reputation of high-class work on the Thames.[42] By 1850, London had eight iron shipbuilding firms. All but two were owned by

---

[36] Petitions East India Built Shipping, Hughes 19–20, Dawes 363, Jordan 429; *Times* 21 September 1825.

[37] SC Shipping, Young Q. 603.

[38] Webster, *East India*, 70.

[39] Arnold, *Iron Shipbuilding*, 7.

[40] Chris Ellmers, 'Gordon & Co., Deptford – Discovering a Lost London Shipyard', in Chris Ellmers (ed.), *Proceedings of the Fifth Symposium on Shipbuilding on the Thames* (Docklands History Group, London, 2013), 43–72.

[41] Basil Lubbock, *The Blackwall Frigates* (Charles E. Lauriat, Boston, 1922), Appendix 1, 299–300; Arnold, *Iron Shipbuilding*, 171, 174; Palmer, 'The Most Indefatigable Activity', 4–6.

[42] S. Pollard, 'The Decline of Shipbuilding on the Thames', *Economic History Review*, Second Series, 3 (1950), 72.

men with an engineering background.[43] Iron hull manufacture had little in common with traditional wooden shipbuilding. Not only did metal require different techniques and skills, but the scale of operation had to be larger. With this came a greater need for substantial capital resources. Firms that ran the river's short-distance regular passenger services were major customers, altogether ordering at least forty small iron steamboats in the 1840s.[44] By then, customers of the most productive yard, Ditchburn & Mare's, at Bow Creek, Canning Town, included regional railway companies, the Post Office, P&O and the Admiralty. Status and technological leadership were responsible for sales of both wooden and iron paddle steamers to foreign clients. London's shipbuilders had broken free of home market dominance.[45]

Shipyard Workers

Constructing a wooden vessel was a complex, arduous process. It demanded, as Mayhew explained, 'not merely the customary skill and quickness of the handicraftsman, but great manual strength' as well as a degree of numeracy, literacy and draughtsmanship.[46] Shipwrights served a seven-year apprenticeship and shorter apprenticeships were also the gateway to the crafts of caulker, sawyer, block maker, joiner, or smith.[47] Access to shipbuilding was largely denied to those with no family connections. In the early 1850s, at least 70 per cent of south bank shipwrights had followed their fathers into the craft.[48]

Shipwrights had considerable control over their labour. Working in gangs of twenty to thirty men, they contracted to build the vessel for an agreed sum. In this traditional industry, all concerned knew the likely duration of the job, so the price reflected the current wage rate.[49]

[43] Arnold, *Iron Shipbuilding*, 23–34.
[44] Capabilities of the Mercantile Steam Navy for Purposes of War, 46–7, 63–5.
[45] Arnold, *Iron Shipbuilding;* Edward Sargent, 'Some Steam Warships Supplied to the Spanish Navy in the 19th Century by Thames Shipyards', in Roger Owen (ed.), *Shipbuilding on the Thames and Thames-Built Ships, Proceedings of a Second Symposium* (J. R. Owen, West Wickham, 2004), 87–104.
[46] Mayhew, *Morning Chronicle*, Reprint, Volume 5, 222.
[47] PP 1812–13 IV.941 [243], SC Petitions of Masters and Journeymen Mechanics Respecting Apprentice Laws of United Kingdom, Clark, 42, Webb, 13, Swallows, 14, Price, 18; SC Petitions East India Built Shipping, 441.
[48] Geoffrey Crossick, *An Artisan Elite in Victorian Society. Kentish London 1840–1880* (Croom Helm, London, 1978), 117.
[49] Pollard, 'Decline of Shipbuilding', 73–4; Keith McClelland and Alastair Reid, 'Wood, Iron and Steel: Technology, Labour and Trade Union Organisation in the Shipbuilding Industry, 1840–1914', in Royden Harrison and Jonathan Zeitlin (eds.), *Divisions of Labour. Skilled Workers and Technological Change in Nineteenth Century England* (Harvester Press, Brighton, 1985), 159–61; PP 1825 IV.565 [417], SC on Combination Act of 1824, Fletcher, 179, 196.

In 1800 the wage was 5s 3d, considerably more than the peace level of
3s 6d, and under wartime pressure sometimes reached seven shillings
a day. By the early 1820s it had fallen to five.[50] Such daily wages made
shipwrights and allied tradesmen among the highest-paid London artisans, but their income depended on shipyard orders and even in good
years, with work dependent on the weather, they might not be employed
for the full twelve months. Although, in shipwright John Gast's words,
'every yard is a sort of republic in itself, governed by its own rules and
its own regulations', their mutual economic concerns extended beyond
particular firms. Most subscribed to friendly societies providing sickness
and death benefits. Named after the pubs where they met, the St. Helens
served those on the south and the Hearts of Oak those on the north.[51]

In 1802, a three-month strike by shipwrights, caulkers and sawyers
successfully defeated moves by employers to reduce wages following
the brief Peace of Amiens.[52] After the war, faced with declining orders,
to cover their losses, London shipbuilders cut wages, increased hours,
replaced journeymen by apprentices and challenged shipwright autonomy in the yard.[53] When economic recovery in 1823 again filled yard
order books and created labour shortage, the shipwrights saw the chance
to reassert control. In August 1824, under the leadership of radical shipwright Gast, who had worked in Dudman's Yard for twenty-three years,
the Thames Shipwrights' Provident Union was established. Run by a
committee of yard representatives, the union rapidly gained 13,000–
14,000 members, including some in the naval dockyards. Each subscribed a penny for each day worked. The caulkers had their own union,
which operated in association with the shipwrights.[54]

What the shipwrights wanted was no reduction in the current day rate,
maintenance of apprenticeship, freedom to select gang members and
acceptance by employers of a price book drawn up by themselves. What
the shipbuilders wanted was an end to the union itself – 'the dissolution
of this unconstitutional and dangerous confederacy'.[55] In essence, the
conflict was a struggle for power in the shipyard.[56] With government

[50] John Gast, *Calumny Defeated Or A Compleat Vindication of the Conduct of the Working
Shipwrights* (John Gast, London, 1802), 5.
[51] SC Combination Act, Gast 301–2.
[52] Gast, *Calumny Defeated*; SC Combination Act, Gast, 316; Chris Ellmers, 'Industrial
Discontent in the Thames Shipyards 1795–1802' (Docklands History Group, published
online, November 2016 www.docklandshistorygroup.org.uk/Talk%20201, accessed 16
March 2021.
[53] SC Combination Act, Gast 317.
[54] Prothero, *Artisans and Politics*, 163–41.
[55] Ibid., 165; SC Combination Act, Fletcher, 189.
[56] *Hampshire Telegraph*, 15 August 1825.

support, the shipbuilders successfully lobbied for a Select Committee designed to secure restoration of the recently abolished Combination Acts. They confronted the union with new regulations which challenged established practices. In response to this provocation, with men already on strike in several yards, action now spread to others. By the end of April 1825, London's shipbuilding industry was effectively at a standstill.

To break the strikes, the employers relied on bringing in men laid off by the naval yards and from other ports. However, the Royal Dockyard shipwrights refused to black-leg, as also did those at Portsmouth, and fraternal links with outport shipwrights meant failure to recruit outsiders: 'See all the country round/All over British ground/ Unions appear', ran a verse in the Provident Society's song.[57] The strike held, and the employers' side crumbled first. After seven months of stoppage, in the heat of the moment at a shipwrights' meeting in Portsmouth in August 1825, shipbuilder Young conceded full union recognition and uniform prices in all yards.[58] A return to work followed, and the largest firm, Wigram and Green, implemented the union price book in September.[59] Employers almost immediately backtracked on the port-wide price book, putting the settlement in jeopardy.[60] With the government opening the Royal Yards to any ship needing repair, the chances of successful further strike action were much reduced and the union took the pragmatic decision to abandon this goal.[61] At Blackwall Yard, Wigram's shipwrights released the firm from the price book agreement.[62]

The shipbuilders hailed this outcome as a union defeat, but the strike action had successfully re-asserted the traditional rights of the Thames shipwrights, given notice that any threat to pay would be resisted and established the Provident Society as a presence on the Thames. Its legacy, noted by witnesses to the 1867 Royal Commission on Trade Unions, was a new day rate of six shillings, which survived until the 1850s, as well as eventual shipbuilder acceptance of the merits of the union's price book, which became the London shipyard standard.[63]

---

[57] Prothero, *Artisans and Politics*, 168; *Morning Chronicle*, 1 February 1825; *Trades Free Press*, 24 December 1826; *Public Ledger & Daily Advertiser*, 16 October 1829, 17 October 1829.

[58] *Globe*, 15 August 1825; *Hampshire Telegraph*, 15 August 1825; *Star*, 15 August 1825.

[59] *Times*, 21 September 1825.

[60] *Trades Free Newspaper*, 25 September 1825.

[61] Prothero, *Artisans and Politics*, 170.

[62] *Trades Free Press*, 23 October 1825; Prothero, *Artisans and Politics*, 170.

[63] Ibid., 305; PP 1867–68 XXXIX.375 [3980.V], RC on Trade Unions and Other Organisations, Nineth Report, Wigram, Qq. 16, 593–7, Robson, Q. 17, 614; Bayley Q. 17, 967; Green and Wigram, *Chronicles*, 58. Green and Wigram mistakenly date the strike as 1830.

The Provident Society's annual anniversary dinners, preceded by a procession through the streets 'with colours flying and to the stirring music of an excellent band', testify to the solidarity and assurance of the timber shipwrights before mid-century.[64] Iron shipbuilding had yet to undermine wooden construction, and the boilermakers, with their own union, were still just an additional trade in the shipyard workforce already divided by skill. Once the shipping and shipbuilding recession lifted in the later 1830s, order books filled and, despite a downturn in 1843, wages held up. 'The great disadvantage in London we have is the union', shipowner Joseph Somes told the 1844 Select Committee, 'the men will starve in the streets rather than work for less than 6s a day'.[65] After the 1825 strike, there were occasional disputes in individual yards but no cause for port-wide action. The union, which accumulated considerable funds, 'merged largely into a benefit society'. By 1846, it had paid out over £5,000 to support members in need.[66]

In many respects, the shipwrights epitomised the respectable London artisan. No doubt there were exceptions. In 1835, the overseer of the Poplar Poor Law, asked to identify some whose profligate spending of their good wages led them to 'throw themselves upon on the parish' when out of work, identified 'shipwrights, caulker and sawyers; shipwrights especially'. But for journalist Mayhew, struck by their intelligence, sobriety and comfortable homes with no lack of books, they represented the 'best class' of London workers.[67]

Other Maritime Industries

Shipowning and shipbuilding supported a variety of maritime services and manufacturing industries. These included firms supplying the ship's biscuits, salt beef and pork, which were the mainstay of the seaman's diet, the producers of ropes, sails and barrels and the manufacturers of navigational instruments. While generally these firms were small, exceptions included the Limehouse firm, Joseph Huddart & Co., founded by the eminent hydrographer. In 1842, this combined both rope and sail cloth manufacture on 'a very wide area of ground, and a numerous set of buildings' at Limehouse.[68]

---

[64] *Morning Advertiser*, 19 August 1846.
[65] SC Shipping, Somes, Qq. 289, 351.
[66] RC Trade Unions (1867–8), Robson, Q. 16,338; *Morning Advertiser*, 19 August 1846.
[67] PP 1834 XXVII.1–XXXIX [44], RC on the Poor Laws, Appendix A, 152; Mayhew, *Morning Chronicle*, Reprint, Volume 5, 226–7.
[68] Dodd, *Factories*, 508; David Barnett, *London, Hub of the Industrial Revolution. A Revisionary History 1775–1825* (I.B. Tauris & Co, London, 1998).

Illustration 5.2 Stepney Sugar Refinery, 1851. Image: Vincent Brooks (1814–1885), Leman Street, Stepney. © Print Collector/ Getty Images.

Processing industries, which owed their existence directly to the port, included waterfront flour milling, as we have seen, and sugar refining. In the late eighteenth century, the main cluster of 'sugar houses' were in the City, along Lower Thames Street, with a smaller group in Whitechapel. After the transfer of the sugar trade to the West India Docks, most refineries were located close to these, 'within a circle of half a mile radius immediately eastward of Aldgate'.[69] These were industrial complexes and, as George Dodd noted in 1856, 'among the largest buildings in the eastern half of the metropolis; from their numerous floors, their ranges of innumerable windows, and the nature of the processes conducted, they are in every way remarkable establishments'.[70] Illustration 5.2 shows one of at least three refineries in Leman Street, Whitechapel, in 1851.[71]

Turning raw sugar into the domed sugar loaves suitable for sale was a highly capital-intensive technical process and investment was not for the faint hearted.[72] Two-thirds of refiners, many of German extraction,

[69] Barnett, *London*, 46–7; Dodd, *Factories*, 89.
[70] Ibid., 428.
[71] Bryan Mawer, Sugar Refiners & Sugarbakers Database, www.mawer.clara.net/intro .html, accessed 1 January 2023.
[72] Dodd, *Factories*, 92–119; Charles Tomlinson (ed.), *Cyclopaedia of Useful Arts, Mechanical and Chemical, Manufactures, Mining and Engineering*, (George Virtue & Co, London and New York, 1852–54), 785–9.

appearing in insurance records for the 1820s were covered for £3,000 or more. One of these insured his steam engine, sugar house and other buildings for £9,150.[73] The national refining industry depended on the tonnage of raw sugar arriving in the Port of London. Until 1846, except for brief periods of extreme sugar shortage, foreign sugar was effectively excluded by high duties, so refineries relied entirely on imports of colonial sugar, which fell in the twenties and thirties.[74] As a result, their number declined from eighty-one in 1823 to forty-two twenty years later. Once foreign sugar had access to the British market after equalisation of duties in the 1850s, refining firms and capacity once more increased.[75]

London's Maritime Districts

Behind the Thames waterfront were London's maritime districts. They were geographically distinguished from other areas by the presence of docks and warehouses and economically as a cluster of port-related industries and occupations. Internationally, all significant seaports had such a region, but London's status as the world's largest port was reflected in its sheer scale. At the beginning of the century, the population of the principal maritime parishes of St. George-in-the-East (Wapping), Shadwell, Ratcliffe and Limehouse totalled about 46,000, or about seventy inhabitants an acre. By 1851, the figure was 103,000, or 162 an acre.[76] Running close to the river, Wapping High Street and its narrow side streets, alleys and courtyards had long been London's maritime quarter. The street clearances associated with the London Dock and St. Katharine's shifted settlement further inland. 'The docks have taken the neighbourhood', complained a public-house tenancy agent in 1830.[77] The docks penned in the High Street, increasing the attractions of the northern Ratcliffe Highway to seamen coming ashore through the dock gates.[78] The East

---

[73] Bryan Mawer, *Sugar Bakers. From Sweat to Sweetness* (Anglo-German History Society, London, 2011), 8–25; Barnett, *London*, 45–7.

[74] G. N. Johnstone, 'The Growth of the Sugar Trade and Sugar Refining', in Derek Oddy and Derek Miller (eds.), *The Making of the Modern English Diet* (Croom Helm, London, 1976), 58–64.

[75] *Morning Chronicle*, 13 July 1833; PP 1840 V.99 [601], SC Import Duties, Martineau, Qq. 891–1909; Parliamentary Debates, 55, 25 June 1840, c. 76; PP 1862 XIII.1 [390], SC Sugar Duties, Davis, Qq. 3813–16; *Pigot & Co.'s Directory 1823*; *Robson's Directory 1842*.

[76] R. Price-Williams, 'The Population of London, 1801–81', *Journal of the Royal Statistical Society*, 48 (1885), 349–432.

[77] David Hughson, *Walks Through London, Vol. I* (Sherwood & Jones, London, 1817), 18; PP 1830 X.1 [253], SC on the Sale of Beer, Bromley, 64.

[78] B. Beaven, 'From Jolly Sailor to Proletarian Jack: The Remaking of Sailortown and the Merchant Seaman in Victorian London', in Brad Beaven, Karl Bell and Robert James (eds.), *Port Towns and Urban Cultures. International Histories of the Waterfront, c.1700–2000* (Palgrave Macmillan, London, 2016), 163.

and West India Docks encouraged settlement in Poplar, but only with the opening of the London and Blackwall Railway and the growth of iron shipbuilding in the 1840s did this area begin to lose its rural character.[79]

On the marshy south bank, port-related settlement was restricted to a narrow belt of industries and housing skirting the Thames. Downriver from Tooley Street, 'the region of wharfs and granaries, of warehouses and factories, has in part given place to features of a more maritime character', wrote Charles Dodd in 1842. He remarked on the presence in Rotherhithe of sailors, 'rope-walks, anchor-smitheries, boat-builders; with outfitters, slopsellers, sea-biscuit bakers; with dealers in all the knick-knacks to which "Jack" is so much attached'. This was not, however, a prosperous area. Its docks were not large employers of labour and there was little new housing development. Moreover, as the 1844 Commission on the State of Large Towns heard, 'owing to the docks being made on the London side of the Thames, the trade was diverted, and the shopkeepers and others became distressed, and the property in the parish was greatly reduced in value'.[80] Further downriver, Deptford, with its shipyards and naval connections, was effectively an independent maritime town, although after the opening of the London and Greenwich Railway in 1836, it had significant links with the metropolis.[81]

By concentrating the handling of foreign cargoes and shipping into two dock systems, one close to the City, the other further downriver, port reform benefited the businesses of London's intervening eastern riverside parishes. Already in the early 1800s, Wapping alone had over fifty ship chandlers and, at mid-century, industries included rope-making, coopering, sail-cloth and tarpaulin manufacture, as well as shipbuilding and sugar refining.[82] Coal yards served 'manufacturing and various other establishments requiring an immense consumption of coal'.[83] Beyond the waterfront, as Thomas Beames noted in 1852, 'ship joiners – ship carpenters – mathematical instrument makers, with their signposts of gilded captains peering through telescopes, – provision

---

[79] François Bédarida, 'Urban Growth and Social Structure in Nineteenth Century Poplar', *The London Journal*, 1 (1975), 164–8.

[80] Charles Dodd in Charles Knight (ed.), *London. Volume III* (Charles Knight & Co., London, 1842), 22; PP XVII.1 1844 [572], RC into the State of Large Towns, Nottidge, Q. 2605.

[81] See Christopher Ellmers, 'Littoral, River and Sea – Exploring the Maritime History of Deptford, 1700–1850' (Doctoral Thesis, University of Portsmouth, 2020), 23–41.

[82] Derek Morris and Ken Cozens, *Wapping 1600–1800. A Social History of an Early Modern London Maritime Suburb* (East London History Society, London, 2009), 5–6, *London's Sailortown 1600–1800* (East London History Society, London, 2014), 65–71; *Robson's London Directory, 1842*.

[83] RC Improving the Metropolis, Gifford, 8.

Illustration 5.3 Henry Thomas Lambert, Wapping Sailmaker, 1858. © Museum of London.

shops – ropemakers – vendors of ship's biscuits, even ship booksellers, – iron mongers – dealers in marine stores, are strangely mixed together'.[84]

In the first half of the century, there certainly existed more social and economic diversity than might be presumed from later developments.[85] A surgeon working in the area during the 1832 cholera epidemic reported, for example, that he 'had to attend to persons of all descriptions: merchants, wharfingers, sea captains, seamen, the dock-officers, and the poor population in the neighbourhood, in lanes, courts and alley parallel to the river'.[86] Some substantial merchants, shipowners and manufacturers had both offices and homes in the maritime districts. The shipowning partnership, Camden, Calvert and King, notable for trading interests and connections stretching across the world, was based

---

[84] Thomas Beames, *The Rookeries of London: Past, Present and Prospective* (Thomas Bosworth, London, 1852), 97.
[85] Morris and Cozens, *Wapping*, 41–3.
[86] PP 1847–48 XXXII.1.57 [888.889], Metropolitan Sanitary Commission, First Report, Bowie, 1.

in Wapping, shipowner and merchant Duncan Dunbar in Shadwell and shipbuilder George Young in Limehouse. The Henley family lived on Wapping High Street, as did sailmaker Henry Thomas Lambert, whose fine 1858 portrait is reproduced above.

Even so, these were primarily poor lower-class neighbourhoods, where coal heavers were more common than coal merchants, and port labourers far more numerous than those who employed them. A statistical investigation in 1848 into a northern section of the parish of St. George-in-the-East, 'a district comprising a considerable population of the labouring classes' found that 'the number of mere labourers (in great part about the docks) exceeded those in all other trades'. Altogether about 40 per cent of men identified in this study, most with families, had maritime-related occupations, reflected in the fact that more people read *Lloyd's Gazette*, with its news of shipping arrivals, than any other paper.[87] There was a strong Irish presence here, as also elsewhere on the Thames waterfront. Bermondsey and Southwark had similar migrant colonies.[88]

There was a good reason for dock and wharf labourers to live close to where they might find work. To miss the morning call-on was to lose the chance. Those sure of employment could afford to live further away, although a journey on foot meant an early start – in darkness when it was winter. Analysis of home addresses of St. Katharine's permanent and preferable workers in 1836 reveals that about a fifth travelled two or more miles.[89] For the 1,400 or so coal heavers, it was a matter of 'belonging' to one of the eighty or so coal trade pubs between the Tower and Limehouse. Supplying gangs of men to unload colliers was in hands of publicans. Heavers were expected to drink heavily in their premises, sometimes even to pay for lodgings there, as a condition of employment. Ballast heavers similarly depended on publicans for a job.[90]

The poor residents of the waterfront attracted limited external attention until later in the century when the endemic poverty of casual labourers was central to the mythic menace of East London to Victorian civilisation. With the exception of the St. George's survey, which collected information on wages and earnings including those of some female inhabitants, criticism of their living conditions tended to focus on issues of hygiene and sanitation

---

[87] Henry Hallam, 'Report to the Council of the Statistical Society of London', *Journal of the Statistical Society of London*, 1 (1848), 193–203, 216.

[88] Lynn Hollen Lees, *Exiles of Erin. Irish Migrants in Victorian London* (Cornell University Press, New York, 1979), 56–7.

[89] MLD, SKD 1.3. Staff Records, August 1836.

[90] PP 1834 VIII.315, SC into Drunkeness [559]. Moore, Q. 26, Saunders, Qq. 334, 421; 1 SC on the Coal Trade (1837–38), Gouhty, Qq. 2825–39; Parliamentary Debates, 120, 6 April 1852, cc. 783–92; Mayhew, Morning Chronicle, Reprint, Volume 2, 232–8.

deemed relevant to epidemics.[91] It was reported to the Metropolitan Sanitary Commission of 1847 that in the riverside districts 'the crowding was excessive, the ventilation bad, the rooms, furniture, and clothes dirty'. The 1840 Select Committee on the Health of Towns heard that streets in St. George-in-the-East housing sailors and their families were lacking in sewers and 'general cleanliness of the inhabitants'.[92]

There was greater public interest in the distinctive maritime character of this part of London. 'There is fore-castle smell about the streets, a minglement of junk and rum, tar and biscuit, casks, ropes and tobacco, not unpleasant to one who is proud of the wave-washed island on which he was born' gushed a contributor to the *Illustrated London News* in 1848. Here was London's 'sailor town', a temporary home for thousands of transient seafarers. 'The stranger will find himself in a region, half land, half water, in which the population are chiefly sailors and jews, and the business all that pertains to ships and shipping', wrote the author of a London guide for visitors to the 1851 Great Exhibition, warning of 'an olio of smells more powerful than savoury'.[93] For a landsman, this part of the capital could be a disconcerting alien place that, by its challenge to social and economic norms, invited moral censure.[94] For the sailor, now free of the rigours and discipline of life at sea, Wapping and Shadwell were where he was paid attention. 'Every other shop is in some way or other devoted to *his* wants, *his* instruction, *his* recreations'.[95]

Exploiting the presence of seafarers was an industry. Those who made a living from this element of the East End's maritime economy included boarding house keepers, outfitters who supplied 'slops' (sailors' bedding and clothing), tailors, crimps who supplied men for ships, publicans, prostitutes and entertainers. The many shopkeepers ranged from 'the capitalist, whose ample window is hung round with everything to catch a sailor's eye, or sound the depths of his pocket, to the small retail tradesman whose stock in trade has exhausted his funds, and who depends almost for bread upon his daily earnings'.[96] Pubs frequented by 'sailors and girls of the town' often had a dancing room, with musicians, while

[91] Anthony S. Wohl, The Eternal Slum. *Housing and Social Policy in Victorian London* (Edward Arnold, London, 1977), 5–7.

[92] Metropolitan Sanitary Commission, First Report (1847–8), Bowie, 1; PP 1840 XI. 277 [384], SC on the Health of Towns, Moseley, Qq. 970–5.

[93] *Illustrated London News*, 29 July 1848; H. G. Clarke, *London As It Is Today, Where to Go, And What to See, During the Great Exhibition* (H. G. Clarke & Co., London, 1851), 174.

[94] Graeme J. Milne, *People, Place and Power on the Nineteenth-Century Waterfront: Sailortown*, (Palgrave Macmillan, London, 2016), 72–4.

[95] J. Saunders, in Charles Knight (ed.), *London. Volume III* (Charles Knight & Co., London, 1842), 51.

[96] Beames, *Rookeries of London*, 97.

the Prince of Denmark in Wapping offered short musical plays and ballets in its 200-seat concert hall, opened in 1839.[97] Watts Phillips, writing later in the century, commented that 'The East London Music Hall is to the Wild Tribes of Ratcliffe Highway what the Opera House is to the tamer tribes of Belgravia'.[98] Most seamen to be seen here and in the back streets of Wapping, Shadwell, Ratcliffe and Limehouse near the East India Docks were those whose voyages had ended. Men in the coastal trades or short-sea foreign trades were usually mid-voyage, so they generally remained on their ship. Like London's own local sea-going population of older married men living in Stepney and Poplar, these had no need of a place to stay on land overnight, though conditions below deck were typically primitive. With little money, they needed to be careful in how they spent time ashore. As a Welsh seaman, whose ship often waited six or seven weeks to take in return cargo for Aberystwyth, explained to Mayhew, 'It comes expensive .... there's one's bits of enjoyment on shore. I'm noways backwards in going to the play; it's a precious sight better than the public house. Indeed it does a man good ... we don't fling about money and grog ... because we haven't it to fling'.[99]

Seafarers in London with little or nothing at all to 'fling' included those from the East, principally India, known as 'lascars'. Unlike other colonial sailors, lascars were not held to be British seamen. Wartime and subsequent labour shortages permitted suspension of the Navigation Laws to allow these foreigners to serve, but they could not be used for the return voyage east. Initially, shipowners were required to repatriate them as passengers and were responsible for feeding, clothing and housing them while ashore. Then, under an act of 1823, the East India Company became solely legally responsible for the maintenance of lascars and their shipment home, even if the men had not served on its hired vessels.[100] In the 1820s, there were extensive East India Company lascar barracks in St. George-in-the-East, making a fortune for the contractor, or so it was

---

[97] Lee Jackson, *Palaces of Pleasure: From Music Halls to the Seaside to Football. How the Victorians Invented Mass Entertainment* (Yale University Press, New Haven, 2019), 49, 9; SC Drunkeness, Moore, Q. 7.

[98] Watts Phillips, *The Wild Tribes of London* (Ward and Lock, London, 1855), 23.

[99] Alston Kennerley, 'British Seamen's Missions and Sailors' Homes 1815–1970 – Voluntary Welfare Provision For Serving Seafarers' (Doctoral Thesis, Polytechnic South West, 1989), 7–8; Mayhew, *Morning Chronicle*, Reprint, Volume 4, 95–6.

[100] Shompa Lahiri, 'Contested Relations: The East India Company and Lascars in London', in H. V. Bowen, Margarette Lincoln and Nigel Rigby (eds.), *The Worlds of the East India Company* (Boydell Press, Woodbridge, 2002), 170; Conrad Dixon, 'Lascars: The Forgotten Seamen', in Rosemary Ommer and Gerald Panting (eds.), *Working Men Who Got Wet* (Memorial University, St. John's Newfoundland, 1980), 266–8.

said.[101] However, once the company lost its commercial monopoly in 1833, it became 'common practice to let the Lascars take care of themselves'. According to one account, in the early 1840s, all that was offered to these returning seamen were two sheds in the East and West India docks, 'one a long low building, with scarcely any light but from the door, and in a most wretched state, with two or three wood fires on the earth floor and a few hammocks; but chiefly, it seemed they lay on boards'.[102]

Housing was far from the only problem faced by lascars ashore. Owed wages by the *ghat serangs* who subcontracted with shipowners to recruit and employ gangs of lascars, or by the *serangs* who commanded them, under the 1823 Act, they could not receive these until discharged in India. Before then, even if paid off in London, deductions meant that they often received less than half the sum promised.[103] Furthermore, if they failed to board their vessel for the return passage, perhaps fearing a repetition of previous ill-treatment on board or being illegally put to work once out of sight of land, as deserters they would be expelled from the lascar barracks and if apprehended faced forcible deportation.

Asian seafarers survived their enforced stay in London, which could last several months, by various strategies. These included selling the East India Company clothing and bedding issued to them, stealing, and begging, which like vagrancy was a criminal offence.[104] In November 1828, six of eleven Asian seamen 'found sleeping in the open air', having failed to join their ship, were sentenced to four days in the House of Correction. However, it was not unusual for lascars who believed that they had been cheated or abused to seek redress in the Thames Police Magistrates Court or even to appeal to the Lord Mayor, occasionally with some success.[105]

In the war years, there could be as many as 1,300 lascar seamen ashore in London. Numbers fell in the depressed trade conditions of the twenties and thirties, but by the early 1850s, possibly over 3,000 arrived in Britain each year.[106] Press reports of penniless, thinly clad,

[101] *St James' Chronicle*, 30 September 1823.
[102] *Lloyd's Weekly* 11 February 1844, Letter; *The Patriot* 14 March 1842, Letter.
[103] Michael H. Fisher, 'Working Across the Seas: Indian Maritime Labourers in India, Britain, and In-Between, 1600–1800', *International Review of Social History*, 51 (2006), 21–45.
[104] Lahiri, 'Contested Relations', 171–4; Norma Myers, 'The Black Poor of London: Initiatives of Eastern Seamen in the Eighteenth and Nineteenth Centuries', in Diane Frost (ed.), *Ethnic Labour and British Imperial Trade: A History of Ethnic Seafarers in the UK* (Frank Cass, London, 1995), 7–21.
[105] Myers, 'The Black Poor', 15–19; *Public Ledger and Advertiser*, 11 November 1828, 12 November 1828, 17 November; *Times* 10 December 1841.
[106] Fisher, 'Working Across the Seas', 36.

distressed lascar seamen wandering adrift in London's streets aroused public sympathy and attracted the attention of missionary societies. 'It is for a lamentation and a reproach, that in a professedly Christian country, they are left in a state of the utmost temporal and moral destitution', wrote an evangelical clergyman in 1842.[107] However, not until 1857 did 'the utterly wretched condition of many of the Lascar seamen, and others from kindred climes – friendless, homeless and destitute' result in the opening of the Strangers Home for Asiatics, Africans and South Sea Islanders on the West India Dock Road.[108] Not everyone saw such strangers as pitiable. According to a magistrate in 1817, the population of Shadwell consisted of 'foreign sailors, Lascars, Chinese, Greeks and other filthy dirty people', and racist attitudes to lascars as workers were commonplace in shipping circles.[109]

Boarding house keepers, many of whom were crimps, had little interest in lascars or those who stayed on their ships berthed in the London and St. Katharine's docks. In contrast, mariners discharged from East India ships were a valuable commodity. During their time in port, 'turned out from their ships' under the East and West India dock regulations, such seamen needed board and lodging, safe storage for their chest of personal possessions and hammock and new clothing. These necessities offered an unscrupulous operator the lucrative chance to take almost total control of a seaman's life ashore. Homeless and probably penniless when they came ashore, but due in a few days to be in possession of a substantial lump sum in wages owed, a seaman depended on credit to tide him over. Crimps and their associates were happy to oblige. Nor did his value end once, with their aid, his new-found wealth had evaporated. When the man signed up for his outward voyage, he received an advance for normally two months' wages in the form of a 'note', cashable once the ship sailed, paid for sea-going clothing and settlement of outstanding debts. Discounting the advance note was yet another opportunity for crimps, outfitters and their associates to benefit.[110]

The seafarer's circumstances made him an easy target. After long and hard months at sea, these typically young unmarried men were looking to have a good time in pubs, dance halls and other sources of entertainment, and

[107] Joseph Salter, *The Asiatic in England. Sketches of Sixteen Years' Work Among* Orientals (Seeley, Jackson and Halliday, London, 1873), 3.
[108] Ibid., 38–40, 66–71; *Times*, 2 June 1856.
[109] PP 1817 VII.1 [233], SC State of the Police of the Metropolis, Röhde, 51; Rozina Visram, *Asians in Britain. 400 Years of History* (Pluto Press, London, 2002), 30–2.
[110] Milne, *People, Place and Power*; Conrad Dixon, 'The Rise and Fall of the Crimp, 1840–1914', in Stephen Fisher (ed.), *British Shipping and Seamen, 1630–1960. Exeter Papers in Economic History* (University of Exeter, Exeter, 1984), 49–67.

in the company of women. Apart from the Green's home on the East India
Dock Road established in 1841 for employees, the only non-commercial
accommodation on offer was the Sailor's Home, opened as a charitable
venture six years' earlier in Well Street near the London Dock.[111] Neither
home was free for occupants or particularly inexpensive (board and lodging at Green's cost twelve shillings a week, at Well Street fourteen shillings), but the facilities were good. The Well Street Sailors' Home also ran
a Savings Bank and acted as a manning agency.[112] In 1842, this had 242
'berths', but an average daily occupancy of 126 that year suggests that it
was not always as popular as its promoters wished. Even so, almost 5,000
men stayed there for short or long periods in 1848, a boom year for trade.[113]

For those who fell on hard times, there was the Destitute Sailors'
Asylum, close to the Sailors' Home and under the same management
from the later 1830s. 'We find that sailors have a great hesitation in
going even there', reported the asylum's secretary in 1844, regarding
being forced to use what was known as 'the straw yard' as the ultimate
sign of degradation. 'I should be very badly off before I went there – very
hard up indeed', a seaman 'of very sedate appearance' told Mayhew.[114]
Other than this, the main practical charitable venture directed at seamen was the floating Seamen's Hospital off Greenwich, first in the hulk
of the *Grampus* and after 1831 in that of the *Dreadnought*.[115] However,
once recovered but still unfit to work and with no money, the discharged
former patient might find himself in the asylum, or eking out a living as
an illegal vagrant on the streets.

Common lodging houses – 'hotels for the poor' – were a familiar feature in nineteenth-century London, but providing temporary housing
for seamen was a specialist business.[116] Standards varied. According to
Mayhew, the 'best class' of private boarding houses for seamen offered a

[111] Roald Kverndal, *Seamen's Missions. Their Origin and Early Growth. A Contribution to the History of the Church Maritime* (William Carey Library, Pasadena, California, 1986), 330–40.
[112] Kennerley, 'Seamen's Missions', 77–82; PP 1844 VIII.279 [431], SC on Merchant Seamen's Fund, Pierce, Qq. 1057–1064; Mayhew, *Morning Chronicle*, Reprint, Volume 4, 106–113, 117–20.
[113] *Morning Advertiser*, 20 May 1842; Mayhew, *Morning Chronicle*, Reprint, Volume 4, 110.
[114] SC Merchant Seamen's Fund (1844), Pierce, Q. 1100; Mayhew, *Morning Chronicle*, Reprint Volume 4, 112–13.
[115] Gordon C. Cook, *Disease in the Merchant Navy. A History of the Seamen's Hospital Society* (Radcliffe Publishing, Abingdon, 2007) 129–164; Mayhew, Morning Chronicle, *Morning Chronicle*, Reprint, Volume 4, 179–82.
[116] Tom Cook, 'Accommodating the Outcast: Common Lodging Houses and the Limits of Urban Governance in Victorian and Edwardian London', *Urban History*, 35 (2008), 414–36.

homely environment, typically decorated with shells and 'sea curiosities'. They charged much the same for bed and board as the more institutional Well Street Sailor's Home. 'We consult the men's tastes more than they can do at places carried on strictly by rule', one boarding house master told him. At the other end of the scale were 'low' boarding houses, some associated with brothels, offering more basic accommodation and run by crimps or their allies.[117] It is impossible to know how many seamen's boarding houses there were, but securing customers was certainly competitive. Boarding house masters took advantage of the time that vessels had to spend at Gravesend 'reporting entry' by touting for business aboard. Seamen also encountered crimps at the dock gates, or on the quayside, and porters who undertook to carry the seamen's heavy belongings ashore were often in their pay. Outfitters and tailors connected with the Sailors' Home also employed runners to direct seamen there.[118]

Outside observers found much in sailor town to shock them. Drunkenness and prostitution were by no means unique to its streets. But when associated with parading throngs of seamen enjoying the rewards of their labour, the effect was 'to challenge respectable visions of urban space on many levels', as sailortown historian Graeme J. Milne has pointed out.[119] By allegedly encouraging profligate spending, unruly behaviour, drinking and immorality, crimps and other 'land sharks', were held responsible for the area's moral degradation. For a witness to the 1834 Select Committee on Drunkeness [sic], dancing rooms 'full of sailors and girls of the town', were 'disgraceful places', and according to sensationalist Watts Phillips, Ratcliffe Highway at night was 'the headquarters of unbridled vice and drunken violence – of all that is dirty, disorderly and debased'.[120]

Not everyone went so far, but the perception that seamen were particularly in need of protection from crimps influenced charitable interventions by seamen's missions, the founding of the London Sailor's Home and Green's and, later in the century, State intervention. There was little recognition that those said to prey on seafarers were empowered by the shipping industry's payment practices, which entangled their workers in a web of debt. Or indeed that the men themselves might be resigned to a system they were powerless to challenge, as well as resistant to well-meaning attempts to deprive them of whatever freedom and fun they had when ashore.

[117] Mayhew, *Morning Chronicle*, Reprint Volume 4, 113–6, 154–6.
[118] Ibid., Mayhew, 121–4, 156–8.
[119] Milne, *People, Place*, 63–4.
[120] Phillips, *Wild Tribes*, 19.

Part II

The Steam Era

6   Emporium of the World
Docks, Shipping and Cargoes

Figure 6.1 Annual entrances and clearances of vessels with cargo in foreign and colonial trades in all United Kingdom ports and the Port of London, 1853–1910. Sources: Annual Statements of Trade and Navigation 1853–1872; Annual Statements of Shipping and Navigation 1873–1910; David J. Starkey (ed.), *Shipping Movements in the Ports of the United Kingdom, 1871–1913. A Statistical Profile* (University of Exeter Press, Exeter, 1999).

> There is no doubt that the bulk of the imports entering the Port are consumed or used by the vast population immediately surrounding it, and that the growth of the trade of the Port in recent years is chiefly due to the increase in the numbers and wealth of the inhabitants of London and its environs.[1]

The total tonnage of shipping the Port of London handled continued to increase over the second half of the nineteenth century. By 1900 entrances in the foreign and colonial trades were five times the level in 1850. However, as a southern port it did not benefit from northern

[1] PP 1902 XLIII.1 [Cd 1151], RC on the Port of London, Report, 21.

147

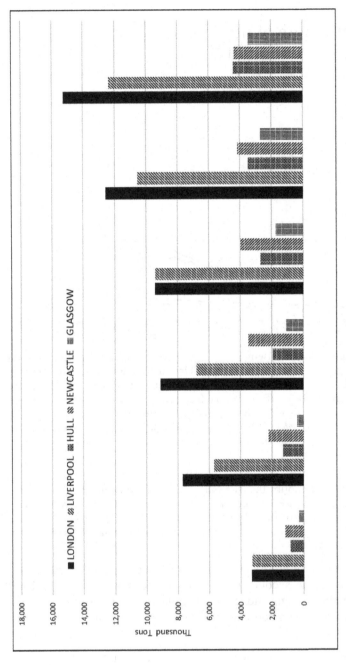

Figure 6.2 Total annual entrances and clearances of vessels with cargo in foreign and colonial trades at leading ports, 1850–1900. Sources: PP. 1851 LII.213 [656], Return of Number of Vessels Inwards and Outwards at Twelve Principal Ports of the United Kingdom, 1816–50; Annual Statements of Trade and Navigation 1860–1870; David J. Starkey (ed.), *Shipping Movements in the Ports of the United Kingdom, 1871–1913. A Statistical Profile* (University of Exeter Press, Exeter, 1999).

industrial expansion and, as Ranald C. Michie has pointed out, 'the trend in bulky was definitely away from London' so its national share fell.[2] Thanks to a lead in export business, at mid-century Liverpool was close to overtaking London, but its tonnage growth subsequently faltered in some years, so the capital remained the country's premier general cargo port, albeit not by a great margin (see Figures 6.1 and 6.2).[3] With limited direct competition between the two leading ports and a growing metropolitan market for port services, relative port-city status mattered little to dock companies and wharfingers, still less to the port workforce. Nevertheless, London's co-existence with another great port, similarly global in its connections and shaped by the same economic forces, yet free of its organisational complexity, encouraged unfavourable comparison that influenced Londoners' attitudes to the port in their midst.

Protectionist trade policy shaped the reformed Port of London in its first half century, but steam technology was prime mover in the second. In 1850 London had a steam fleet of over 300 vessels. As already noted, for thirty years or so, paddle steamers had been at work in its coasting, Irish Sea and short-sea continental trades and every year transported thousands of passengers up and down the Thames. However, as Alfred Holt later commented, these were the only routes where 'the old mode of conveyance for cargo by sailing vessel [was] seriously invaded by the new'. Both the ocean-going P&O and the Royal Mail Steam Packet Company, for reasons of prestige, registered their subsidised mail contract oceanic fleets in London, but these ran from Southampton rather than the capital.[4] Not least because of the development of iron shipbuilding on the Thames, historians Armstrong and Williams are not wrong to claim that 'in the new technology of the steamship, London was by far the most dominant port in the UK'.[5] But this is faint praise. In 1850, steam shipping accounted for just 8 per cent of all vessels arriving in London, 14 per cent of total shipping tonnage.[6] Steamers had certainly had a significant effect on some river-based trades, but apart from construction of specialised wharves, they made little physical impact on the port, which had been able to accommodate the new type of vessel without difficulty.

---

[2] Ranald C. Michie, *The City of London. Continuity and Change, 1850–1990* (Macmillan, London, 1992), 34.
[3] Francis E. Hyde, *Liverpool and the Mersey. An Economic History of a Port 1700–1970* (David & Charles, Newton Abbot, 1971), 96–7.
[4] Alfred Holt, 'Review of the Progress of Steam Shipping During the Last Quarter of a Century', *Minutes of the Proceedings of the Institution of Civil Engineers*, 51 (1878), 2–11.
[5] John Armstrong and David M. Williams, 'London's Steamships: Their Functions and Their Owners in the Mid-Nineteenth Century', *The London Journal*, 42 (2017), 238–256.
[6] RC Port of London, Appendix, 244–5.

The technical problems of the early steamers, which until the second half of the nineteenth century restricted them to certain routes and types of traffic, are well documented. To maintain immersion of the paddles, vessels had to be 'long, lean and narrow', but the paddles added width. This, together with the space needed for fuel, affected cargo capacity and hence commercial viability. Improved marine engines reduced coal consumption to a degree, but this remained a fundamental defect. Vibrations caused by engine, crankshaft and paddles also proved a problem for wooden hulls. After much experimentation, in the 1840s, such shortcomings began to be tackled. By 1851, forty-seven of the eighty-nine British steamers regularly running to and from London in foreign trades had iron hulls, and half of these were also screw propelled.[7] Progressive, if piecemeal, improvements in engine efficiency in the 1850s were followed by the development of the compound engine in the 1860s. Steam shipping now became profitable not only for liner business but also for many European bulk cargoes, including those from the Mediterranean. Even so, it was not until 1872 that the tonnage of foreign and colonial steamship entries into London overtook that for sailing vessels.[8]

Sailing ship design also benefited from a switch to iron hulls and was far from moribund in the most distant trades.[9] Coal consumption was the major impediment to adoption of steam on oceanic passages, but this halved by the 1870s, leading to lower freight rates. Combined with the opening of the Suez Canal in 1869, such fuel economy also reshaped London's long-standing connections with the Far East. Further refinements of the compound engine in the eighties and nineties, together with steel hulls and refrigerated capacity, largely completed the oceanic

[7] Ibid., 448.
[8] 'Capabilities of the Mercantile Steam Navy' (1852), 4; P. L. Simmonds, 'On the Rise and Progress of Steam Navigation in the Port of London', *Journal of the Royal Society for the Encouragement of Arts, Manufactures and Commerce*, 8 (1860), 153–170; Charles Capper, *The Port and Trade of London. Historical, Statistical, Local and General* (Smith, Elder & Co., London, 1862), 167; Basil Greenhill, 'Steam Before the Screw', in Robert Gardiner (ed.), *The Advent of Steam. The Merchant Steamship before 1900* (Conway Maritime Press, London, 1993), 11–23; Armstrong and Williams, 'London's Steamships', 238–56.
[9] Gerald S. Graham, 'The Ascendancy of the Sailing Ship, 1855–1885', *Economic History Review*, 9 (1956), 134–46; Charles K. Harley, 'The Shift from Sailing Ships to Steamships, 1850–1890's Study in Technological Change and its Diffusion', in D. N., McCloskey (ed.), *Essays on a Mature Economy: Britain after 1840* (Methuen, London, 1971); David M. Williams and John Armstrong. 'An Appraisal of the Progress of the Steamship in the Nineteenth Century', in Gelina Harlaftis, Stig Tenold and Jesús M. Valdaliso (eds.), *The World's Key Industry. History and Economics of International Shipping* (Palgrave Macmillan, Basingstoke, 2012), 43–63.

transition. By 1900, three-quarters of foreign and colonial trade vessels (90 per cent of tonnage) arriving in London were steam-powered. With iron hulls and steam came progressive increases in vessel size. The average size of all foreign-trading vessels (steam and sail) entering London in 1885 was 651 tons, roughly double that in 1865. By the end of the century, it reached 850 tons.[10]

The first commercial victory for screw steamers was in London's coal trade. *John Bowes*, the earliest commercial iron screw collier built, arrived in the Poplar Dock with 540 tons of coal in August 1852. This was a sufficiently notable event to attract the attention of the *Illustrated London News*.[11] Once water ballasting proved feasible, investment in steam colliers proceeded apace. By 1865, more coal arrived in screw colliers than by sail. Ten years later, they dominated the trade, and the river clogged with sail colliers became a past problem.[12] High productivity, as well as new steamer types like the 'flat iron', introduced in 1878 by the London Gas Company to take coal upstream under London's bridges, meant that coastal shipping successfully competed with rail and by the 1890s handled most of the coal trade to London.[13] Heavy demand from large liners coaled in docks or in the river at Gravesend meant that average collier size nearly doubled between 1870 and 1890.[14]

Express screw steamers made rapid inroads into the coastal liner business and the sea-borne cattle trade proved resilient in competition with railways.[15] Although rail had the greater share of the Scottish trade south

---

[10] RC Port of London, Appendix, 448, 235–7.

[11] *Illustrated London News*, 28 August 1852; C. M. Palmer, 'On the Construction of Iron Ships', *Report of the Twenty-Third Meeting of the British Association for the Advancement of Science* (John Murray, London, 1864), 696–701; Robin Craig, *The Ship. Steam Tramps and Cargo Liners 1850–1950* (HMSO, London, 1980), 6–13.

[12] PP 1860 XIII.1 [530], SC on Merchant Shipping, xiv; Robin Craig, *The Ship. Steam Tramps and Cargo Liners 1850–1950* (HMSO, London, 1980), 6–1366; R. Morton, 'The System of Coaling at the Works of the Late London Gaslight Company, Nine Elms', *Proceedings of the Institution of Civil Engineers*, 78 (1884), 357–60; D. Ridley Chesterton and R. S. Fenton, *Gas and Electricity Colliers* (World Ship Society, Kendal, 1984), 6, 40.

[13] John Armstrong, 'Late Nineteenth-Century Freight Rates Revisited: Some from the British Coastal Coal Trade', *International Journal of Maritime History*, 5 (1994) 68–9; 'Climax and Climacteric: The British Coastal Trade, 1870–1930', in David J. Starkey and Alan G. Jamieson (eds.), *Exploiting the Sea. Aspects of Britain's Maritime Economy Since 1870* (University of Exeter Press, Exeter, 1998), 37.

[14] MLD, EWID TIL14, J. R. Scott's Evidence to the SC on Private Bills, East and West India Docks Extension Bill, 1 March 1882.

[15] Nick Robins, *Coastal Passenger Steamers of the British Isles* (Seaforth Publishing, Barnsley, 2011), 36–8.

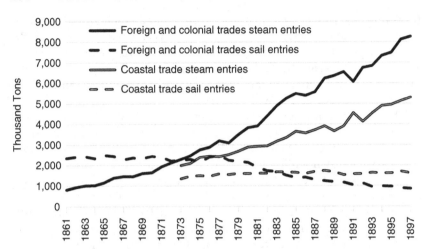

Figure 6.3 Port of London tonnage of annual entrances by sail and steam vessels (cargo and in ballast) in foreign and colonial trades, 1860–1897 and in coastal trades 1873–1897 (figures unavailable for earlier years). Source: PP. XLIV.1 [Cd. 1153], 1902 RC on the Port of London, Appendices, 244–7.

by 1870, in the 1890s, Aberdeen Steam Navigation Company steamers still ran to London three days a week in summer and twice-weekly in winter.[16] Low fares and luxurious accommodation ensured that East Coast express passenger steamers remained competitive with railways, profitably running to London wharves until the First World War.[17] Despite the impact of steam shipping on London's coal, livestock, and passenger trades, small sailing vessels continued for many years to serve more distant parts, in particular the West Country. Approximately a fifth of vessels in the coasting trade that arrived in the Port of London in 1895 were sailing ships, although they accounted for just 5 per cent of total tonnage[18] (see Figure 6.3).

---

[16] G. Channon, 'Pooling Agreements Between the Railway Companies Involved in Anglo-Scottish Traffic, 1851–1869' (Doctoral Thesis, University of London, 1975), 386; PP 1894 LXIX.267 [293 C.7511] Departmental Committee on Transit by Water and the Embarkation and Landing of Animals Carried Coastwise, Beattie, Qq. 5566–72.

[17] Robins, *Coastal Passenger Steamers*, 36–62; A. M. Northway, 'The Tyne Steam Shipping Co: A Late Nineteenth-Century Shipping Line', *Maritime History* 2 (1972), 74.

[18] *Post Office London Directory 1895*, 2753–6; PP 1896 LXXXIII.529 [C. 8089], *Annual Statement of the Navigation and Shipping of the UK for* 1895, Tables 26–7, 160–63.

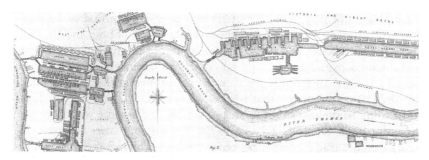

Map 6.1 London's Lower Docks, 1885. Image: Leveson Francis Vernon-Harcourt, *Harbours and Docks. Their Physical Features, History, Construction Equipment and Maintenance II* (Clarendon Press, Oxford, 1885), Plate X.

New Docks

In the first half century there were dock construction phases in the 1800s and 1820s. The transition to steam shipping led to several more. Some were associated with entirely new joint stock companies, others with dock and improvement projects by established companies. Replacement of sailing vessels by steamers and the increase in average vessel size that came with this placed additional demands on existing facilities. London, with its combination of waterfront wharves and docks, responded with relative ease, not least because it took several decades for the shipping industry to complete the transition. Sea-going steamers continued to make their way upriver, as they had done since the 1820s. The attractions of the central London wharves, with their proximity to the produce market, endured. Even at the end of the century, steamers, varying from 600 to 1,000 net tons, bringing fresh and dried fruit to London discharged at the former Legal Quays.[19] The upper docks, although built for another age, also proved capable of handling small steam vessels, particularly after the London Dock Company's Shadwell entrance opened in 1852, and the East and West India Dock systems could accommodate the largest steam vessels arriving in London, at least until the 1880s.

The mid-century Port of London was not in crisis. There was certainly no urgent immediate need for additional commercial docks, as the early port historian Joseph Broodbank seems to imply.[20] However,

---

[19] PP 1884–85, VIII.47, SC on Corporation of London – Bridge Bill, Tatham, Qq. 5662–6, Carew Hunt, Qq. 9941–4, Appendix 1, 631; RC Port of London, Minutes, Isaacs, Q. 9475.
[20] Broodbank, *Port of London, Volume I*, 193; John Marriott, 'West Ham: London's Industrial Centre and Gateway to the World' I: Industrialisation, 1840–1910', *The London Journal*, 13 (1987), 121–142.

increasing trade in the 1850s created opportunities for property developers, which was the original context for construction of both the Victoria and Millwall docks. The decade also saw the London Dock Company add a new basin and entrance to its system and significant reconstruction work by the Commercial Dock Company, but neither these companies, nor the railway company that built the Poplar Dock, were particularly responding to the transition to steam, which, at this time was more the exception than the rule. By the 1870s the situation was different. In many oceanic trades, steam propulsion was becoming the norm. The existing dock companies now sought to gain an advantage by investing in new and improved facilities, with the Albert extension to the Victoria Dock and distant Tilbury docks the most substantial results.

Poplar

Given the entrepreneurial drive and willingness to accept financial risk that characterised railway promotion, it is unsurprising that railway interests seized the initiative. When the North West Railway Company's Poplar Dock opened in 1851 (soon to welcome the first screw collier as we have seen), it was the first significant extension to London's dock system since 1828. A dock within a dock, created from a timber pond, its seven and a half acre site was leased from the East and West India Dock Company for £1,200 a year and dock dues. It cost £36,886 to construct.[21] Used by the North London, Great Eastern and the Great Western railway companies, in the mid-1870s it was extended to serve barges. Poplar became London's prime railway freight terminal, handling seaborne and inland coal, bulk cargoes like grain and timber and general merchandise. Its systems were technologically advanced: hydraulic cranes transferred coal from colliers to railway wagons (the first-time mechanised cranes were used systematically in the port), and shutes fed inland coal from wagons into barges.[22]

Victoria

The Victoria Dock was built next. Unlike the earlier north bank commercial docks, its creation owed nothing to mercantile or shipping

---

[21] RC Port of London, Minutes, Baggallay, Qq. 941, 946, Dunn Q. 1366; Shaw, Q. 11788: RC Port of London, Appendix, 832.

[22] *Survey of London*, 43, 336–41. W. Armstrong, 'The History of the Modern Development of Water Pressure Machinery' and 'Discussion Proceedings of the Institution of Civil Engineers', 50 (1877), 64–88; Tim Smith, 'Hydraulic Power in the Port of London', *Industrial Archaeology Review*, 14 (1991), 64–88.

interests but everything to an appreciation of the profits to be made from London's expanding commerce. Its promoters were contractors and civil engineers, Sir Morton Peto MP, Edward Ladd Betts, Thomas Brassey and George Bidder, whose many interests included the Eastern Counties Railway, which terminated at Stratford. Bidder had developed property and railways in West Ham, and his chosen site for the 100-acre dock was Plaistow marshes.[23] The group had no interest in becoming dock managers and in 1852, they approached the St. Katharine's Dock Company with an amalgamation proposal. Although tempted by the chance to handle larger vessels, its directors were unconvinced of the Victoria's commercial viability. They turned down the offer, consigning their company to a war of attrition with the Victoria Dock Company, which lasted until the property was sold to the newly amalgamated London St. Katharine's Dock Company in 1864.[24]

Thwarted by failure with St. Katharine's and with parliamentary authorisation to double the original capital to £800,000, the associates pushed on independently. Under a novel financial arrangement with the newly formed Victoria Dock Company, they contracted to undertake construction in return for a twenty-one-year lease of the dock, with an annual payment of 5 per cent 'rent' to the company. This meant a guaranteed dividend and a first claim on any profits, without any of the public scrutiny associated with a joint stock enterprise. Unsurprisingly, the shareholders were content, and at least one of those present at an Extraordinary Meeting in October 1852 was pleased that there was no prospect of amalgamation with St. Katharine's Dock Company, which 'really did appear to him as if a young, handsome girl of eighteen was going to marry an old gentleman of seventy'.[25]

The water-logged uninhabited site, which 'contained nothing but fat oxen, and a few manufactories, too disagreeable even for London' was cheap and easy to excavate.[26]

---

[23] *Illustrated London News*, 9 September 1854; W. R. Powell (ed.), *A History of the County of Essex: Volume VI* (Oxford University Press, Oxford, 1973), 47–9; J. Abernethy et al., 'Discussion. Description of the Entrance, Entrance Lock, and Jetty Walls of the Victoria (London) Dock', *Minutes of the Proceedings of the Institution of Civil Engineers*, 18 (1859), 477–89; Marriott, 'West Ham', 129–130.

[24] MLD, LDC 191, Special Committee Minutes, 17 September 1852, 14 October 1852, 21 October 1852. (These SKDC minutes are catalogued as LDC records.); MLD, SKD 247, 26 October 1852.

[25] *London Daily News*, 30 October 1852; *The Economist*, 25 November 1854.

[26] PP 1861 IX.1, Select Committee on Poor Relief (England), First Report, Cane, Q. 13436.

Under the direction of Bidder, with Peto, Betts and Brassey as labour contractors, construction began in 1854, and the almost mile-long dock officially opened for business on 26 November 1855.[27] The new dock, which had two stations for workers, was well out of London, but with good communications; the Great Northern connected it with the Midlands and the Eastern Counties Railway with the City.[28] In contrast, neither the London Dock nor St. Katharine's had railway connections. The East and West India Dock Company got its first in 1840, when the London and Blackwall Railway, initially rope-hauled and powered by stationary steam engines, connected the Brunswick Wharf with the City. A series of extensions eventually (in 1865) joined the East and West India docks to the Great Eastern Railway's services to the North of England.[29]

J. C. Scott, the Joint Docks Committee chairman at the end of the century, disparaged the Victoria Dock as 'much more of a pond than a dock', but its first facilities included hydraulic cranes and projecting jetties, which enabled cargoes unloaded one side to be transferred into barges opposite. With free trade, there was no need for high walls or expensive secure premises. There were initially four warehouses and wine and spirit vaults on site, but to provide storage in the City, the promoters acquired warehouses near Fenchurch Station and on the river.[30] As usual the final costs exceeded the original estimates, but the million pounds spent on the Victoria Dock compared favourably with the substantial initial investment that had been required for the earlier docks.[31] At seventy-four acres, it was the largest dock to be built in the Port of London and remained so until Tilbury opened in 1886.

The Victoria Dock was a major industrial incursion into West Ham.[32] It was sometime before many other new enterprises were established, but it quickly attracted large numbers of labourers who became 'Londoners beyond the Borders'.[33] Already by 1861, there were about 9,000 residents.[34] Appalling living conditions in Canning Town and Hallsville

[27] *Illustrated London News*, 16 February 1856.

[28] Dave Marden, *London's Dock Railways, Part 2, The Royal Docks, North Woolwich and Silvertown* (Kestrel Railway Books, Southampton, 2013), 2.

[29] Marden, *London's Dock Railways, Part 1*, 1–3; John Christopher, *The London & Blackwall Railway. Docklands' First Railway* (Amberley Publishing, Stroud, 2013), 21–48.

[30] RC Port of London, Minutes, Scott, Q. 5584; Broodbank, *Port of London, Volume I*; *Illustrated London News*, 16 February 1856; Vernon-Harcourt, *Harbours and Docks*, 497–8.

[31] PP 1857, Session 2, XIX.505 [19], Reports of Board of Trade on Private Bills for Harbours, Docks and Navigations; Capper, *Port and Trade*, 160.

[32] Powell, *County of Essex VI*, 43–50.

[33] Marriott, 'West Ham', 130.

[34] Jim Clifford, *West Ham and the River Lea. A Social and Environmental History of London's Industrialized Marshland, 1839–1914* (UBC Press, British Columbia, Canada, 2017), 60.

(associated with C. J. Mare's shipyard) built by unscrupulous developers mirrored the worst London slums.[35] Coal merchant William Cory's installation of hydraulic cranes in the Victoria Dock reduced coal prices, encouraging further industrial development. As a result, West Ham grew rapidly after 1870, with the later Albert Dock adding to its maritime profile. By 1900, it had become 'a great seaport and manufacturing town'.[36]

Millwall

By the late 1850s the Isle of Dogs shoreline was dominated by shipbuilding and manufacturing activity yet, apart from the West India Dock area, much of the interior remained marshy pasture.[37] Oil merchant and Millwall wharf owner, Nathanial John Fenner, with civil engineer, Robert Fairlie, devised a scheme to develop dry docks and wharfage frontage along a canal across the island, with a branch extending north. In 1864 the Millwall Canal, Wharfs and Graving Docks Bill gained parliamentary approval. By then the proposal had become a contractor speculation. Public works specialists, John Aird & Son and John Kelk, builder of a new dock for the Commercial Company, had elbowed out the original promoters. Their aim was to induce the East and West India Dock Company to take over all or part of the scheme, for which they were the designated builders, but the offer was rejected. Faced with finding an alternative, the company joined others promoted by the Credit Foncier and Mobilier, one of a number of 'rip-off finance houses' operating in the City of London in the 1860s.[38] Four Credit Foncier nominees became directors, and the company name was changed to the Millwall Land and Dock Company. With the canal ruled out on cost grounds, the new name made marketing sense. 'As a land company, the present undertaking has enormous advantages', claimed the company prospectus, which unpropitiously appeared in *The Times* on 1 April 1865, citing: 'The great demand for wharves, sites for manufactories, shipbuilding yards, and graving docks within the Port of London, which the natural increase of trade, combined with the removal of existing water frontage by the formation of the Thames Embankment and other metropolitan improvements, has created'.[39]

---

[35] 'Londoners Over the Border', *Household Words*, 390, 12 September 1857.
[36] John Marriott, *Beyond the Tower. A History of East London* (Yale, New Haven & London, 2011), 249.; Powell, *County of Essex VI*, 47; Clifford, *West Ham*, 25–6.
[37] For a detailed account of the origin and construction of the Millwall Docks, see *Survey of London*, *43*, 345–56 and Peter Guillery, 'Building the Millwall Docks', *Construction History*, 6 (1990), 3–21.
[38] David Kynaston, *The City of London. Volume 1. A World of Its Own 1815–1890* (Pimlico, London, 1994), 223.
[39] *Times*, Advertisement, 1 April 1865.

Shares were taken up and excavations, employing about a 1,000 men, began in July 1865.[40] However, all was not well on the financial front. Shareholders became suspicious once it became known in August 1865 that to support the launch Aird and Kelk had agreed to pay a considerable fee of £100,000 to the Credit Foncier financier Albert Grant. Also undisclosed was an agreement that the payment of interest on shares during construction would last only two years. The £600,000 contract with Kelk and Aird covered Grant's fee, miscellaneous expenses, shareholder interest payments and engineering and structural costs. With land costs, the total reached £700,000, more than the borrowing permitted under its act.

With legal proceedings threatened on grounds of a fraudulent prospectus, many subscribers failed to respond to the second share call and 'the company began to fray at the edges', as the *Survey of London* puts it.[41] The Millwall Land and Dock Company now relied on bank loans and debenture shares to meet commitments. Shareholder prospects looked dire, but the company was saved by the intervention of Acton Smee Ayrton, who became its champion and chairman. Ayrton, the radical Liberal MP for Tower Hamlets, was an industrious metropolitan politician.[42] Under Ayrton's leadership, finances were shakily reconstructed, and work continued. In the wake of the 1866 financial crisis and its effect on the Isle of Dogs industries, the market for wharfage premises or graving services collapsed.

The East and West India Dock Company continued to spurn approaches, so the only remaining option was to change direction and run Millwall as a commercial trade dock. Former Victoria Dock superintendent George Birt and his colleague Frederic Eliot Duckham were recruited as General Manager and Clerk of Works. The dock began operating in March 1868 'as a makeshift establishment where only essential work had been completed', but financial complications remained.[43] There followed lawsuits, with some shareholders pressing for liquidation. Eventually, in December 1868, a compromise agreement was reached. Having steered the enterprise through this challenging period, Ayrton bowed out. He was replaced by Charles Henry Parkes, parliamentary agent and subsequently Chairman of the Great Eastern Railway Company. In 1870, the company's name changed to the Millwall Dock Company.

---

[40] *Times*, 20 November 1865.
[41] *Survey of London*, 43, 349.
[42] ODNB, Acton Smee Ayrton (1816–1886).
[43] *Survey of London*, 43, 350.

Despite its chequered financial history and truncated final 'L' shape, the thirty-six-acre Millwall dock was an impressive addition to London's dock estate. It was as deep as the Victoria Dock, and its 80-foot wide, 450-foot-long entrance lock could potentially handle the largest vessels then afloat, with the exception of the *Great Eastern*. Apart from hydraulic cranes, at first Millwall had limited mechanical apparatus and storage facilities. Within a few years, however, grain handling and other equipment introduced by its talented chief engineer Duckham established Millwall as the most technically advanced of London's docks. By 1887 warehousing capacity, originally just 17,000 tons, had expanded to 135,000.[44]

Dock Improvements

Although reported that the Victoria Dock proposal 'had put the older establishments upon a defensive movement', it did not need the threat of competition to persuade the London Dock Company that its facilities needed updating.[45] A few years earlier, the company had built a huge five-story warehouse specifically to house tea, but as the Directors told shareholders in October 1852, the forty-five-foot Shadwell entrance, opened twenty years before, was now 'not large enough for the China and Far Eastern business' since 'the increase in the size and tonnage of vessels within the last few years had been considerable'.[46] There were also the large sailing vessels of the wool trade to consider. Work began in 1854, and the new Shadwell Basin, designed by J. M. Rendel and constructed by Cubitts, opened four years later. Costing almost a million pounds, this was an ambitious project. The basin was both bigger and deeper than its predecessor, but the two sixty-foot entrance locks were twenty-foot narrower than those at the Victoria Dock.[47] On the Surrey bank, similar considerations encouraged the Commercial Dock Company to purchase the East Country Dock, which gave them a second entrance to the Thames. As its directors told proprietors, 'the present docks were constructed when ships averaged about 300 tons, but now they required a depth of water for the entrance of ships of 1,500 tons'.[48]

---

[44] Edward Sargent, 'Frederic Eliot Duckham, M.I.C.E., and the Millwall Docks (1868–1909)', *Transactions of the Newcomen Society*, 60 (1988), 49–71; *Survey of London, 43*, 351.

[45] *John Bull*, 30 October 1852.

[46] MLD, LDC141, 28 February 1832; LDC145, 12 October 1852; *Times*, 5 January 1853; *Illustrated London News*, 27 September 1855.

[47] *Public Ledger*, 18 October 1858.

[48] *Globe*, 21 December 1850.

One reason why the East and West India Dock Company resisted offers to buy the Millwall Dock was that it was already involved in a major development of its own. The London Dock Shadwell improvements had been directed at large sailing vessels, but by the mid-1860s the shift from sail to steam was well underway and both docks were at a disadvantage competing for steamers with the Victoria Dock. In 1866, the East and West India directors approved a scheme, devised by company officers and worked up by civil engineer Sir John Hawkshaw, to turn the former City Canal and adjacent timber pond into a third dock. Work began in October 1866 but was delayed by flooding of the excavation and then the collapse of dock walls due to water pressure, both caused by the neighbouring Millwall Dock.[49] The twenty-seven-acre dock at South Dock eventually opened in March 1870. Including warehouses, sheds, bridges and railways, the cost was about £750,000.[50]

The width of the eastern lock of the East and West India's South Dock was fifty feet less than the Victoria dock lock and in length it was 150 feet shorter than that at Millwall. Noting that vessel length was increasing, some experts correctly predicted that it would soon prove too small. The company took more account of the increase in breadth and draught of vessels when making improvements to the East India Dock. When opened in 1806, the forty-seven-foot entrance lock, designed for East India shipping, was the widest in the Port of London. Such dimensions now severely limited its use, so a new sixty-five-foot entrance further downriver was added in 1879. In order to fit into the site, this lock was only a 100 feet long, effectively half the length of the older narrow East India Dock locks, so it entirely failed to resolve the problem of size.[51]

The Victoria Dock's Albert Extension

The original Victoria Company plan had been for two docks, and enough land had been purchased. Nine years after acquiring the Victoria Dock, the amalgamated London St. Katharine's Dock Company completed the project. Designed by engineer Sir Alexander Rendel and constructed by the Millwall builders, the Royal Albert Dock was opened with great ceremony by Queen Victoria's third son, the Duke of Connaught, in June 1880, an indication of the project's public status.[52] Linked

[49] *Survey of London, 43*, 277–80.
[50] Broodbank, *Port of London, 1*, 216–7; Vernon-Harcourt, 167–77.
[51] Vernon-Harcourt, *Harbours and Docks*, 495.
[52] RC Port of London, Minutes, Baggallay, Q. 818; *East London Observer*, 2 August 1879; *Illustrated London News*, 26 June 1880, 3 July 1880; Greeves, *London Docks*, 13.

with the Victoria by a short canal, and costing £2.3 million, the eighty-four-acre Albert Dock and basin was unlike London's previous docks. Long and narrow, without jetties and with quays served by travelling hydraulic cranes and electric lighting, it was designed specifically for the latest generation of steamers. Even so, the entrance lock turned out to be 'inadequate for the growing traffic of ships and barges and did not give sufficient depth of water for the increasing draught of ships'. In 1886, a deeper second entrance had to be added.[53]

Along the Albert Dock northern boundary was the company's own railway with stations, for transporting 'artisans, mechanics and daily labourers', connected with the Great Eastern Railway's northern branch. It also served the steamer terminal and hotel at Gallions Reach. The Great Eastern took over the service in 1896, but although it no longer owned the locomotives, the stations, signal boxes and crossing continued to be manned by dock company employees.[54]

Tilbury Dock

The Albert Dock was eight miles from the historic heart of the Port of London in the City, but the next new dock extended activity well beyond the capital. Opened by the East and West India Dock Company in 1886, the Tilbury Dock in Essex was twenty-seven miles away. Little over ten years in operation, the company's South Dock could not cope with steamers over 500 feet long. Threatened with competition from the Royal Albert and an independent proposal for a dock at Dagenham, the East and West India Dock Company saw salvation in deeper water down-river.[55] Apart from its fort, Tilbury itself was largely uninhabited marsh-land and the 450-acre site, purchased before the project was announced, was cheap. Nevertheless, there existed a station. Since 1854, passengers had been able to alight from the Gravesend ferry onto a pontoon in the river and up a ramp to join the London, Tilbury and Southend Railway for the journey to London. Its London connections to national trunk lines made it an essential element of the project.[56]

Excavation began in July 1882, but the site proved geologically challenging for the original contractors and progress was slow. Lucas and

---

[53] Vernon-Harcourt, *Harbours and Docks*, 497–9; B. H. Martindale, 'Demolition of the North-East Wall of the Gallions Basin, Royal Albert Docks, on the 23rd April, 1886', *Proceedings of the Institution of Civil Engineers*, 86 (1886), 329.

[54] Marden, *London's Dock Railways Part 2*, 87–8.

[55] *Times*, 1 October 1881.

[56] Peter Kay, *The London, Tilbury & Southend Railway*, Vol. 1 (Peter Kay, Teignmouth, 1996).

Aird, who had worked on the Millwall and Albert Docks, replaced them in October 1884 and finished the work. Designed in-house by the company's engineer, in scale and layout, Tilbury differed from other dock systems. Entry was through a seventeen-and-a-half-acre tidal basin, open to the river, with projecting timber jetties on both sides to allow passengers to disembark before the steamer moved to its berth. There was also a coaling jetty and two large graving docks. Eighty-foot-wide locks, with a combined length of 946 feet, led to a fifty-two-acre main dock divided into three branches with berths, each with access to the London, Tilbury and Southend Railway. Besides electric lighting, facilities included the most up-to-date hydraulic and other machinery. Sheds were provided for berths, but there were no warehouses. A Whitechapel depot, with display facilities, was available as temporary storage for goods passing through London. As well as the magnificent Tilbury Hotel at the entrance to the dock basin overlooking the Thames, the dock premises contained houses of varying sizes for company officers and 'workmen's dwellings' to house 500 families. However, it was anticipated that most labourers would come by rail from London.[57]

Total investment of almost £11 million by London's dock companies, new and old, made the Port of London physically fit for the steam shipping era. That this was only £1.3 million more than had been spent by the older enterprises earlier in the century was largely due to geographical good fortune – the availability of suitable sites. In the case of the established companies, sufficient capital was ensured. The solidity suggested by historic status, and generally stable – in the case of the East and West India Dock Company high – dividends reassured ordinary stockholders, the 'Proprietors' and those holding preference shares or debentures, both paying a fixed rate of return. Open to public scrutiny as joint-stock enterprises, published half-year reports contained current information on shipping tonnage handled, quantities of goods warehoused, costs and revenue. But, as we shall see, their short-term focus obscured underlying problems, not publicly exposed until the later 1880s.

Wharves

Investment in the later nineteenth-century Port of London was not limited to docks. New or updated riverside warehouses and industrial premises,

---

[57] J. F. Scott, 'The Construction and Equipment of the Tilbury Docks', *Proceedings of the Institution of Civil Engineers*, 120 (1896), 276–88; *Southend Standard and Essex Weekly Advertiser*, 18 March 1886, 22 April 1886.

Illustration 6.1 Hay's Wharf, 1857. Image: Alderman Humphery's Dock and Hay's Wharf, 1857. © Heritage Images/Getty Images.

as also the embanking of the Thames and the construction of Tower Bridge, altered conditions in the river port. In contrast to the scruffy, increasingly defunct, north bank coal wharves, at mid-century, many of the thriving Southwark foreign and coasting trade wharves had fine extensive modern warehouses, with impressive river frontages. A major 1856–8 reconstruction by Cubitt of Hay's, Humphery's and Cotton's included a long and narrow dock, the only privately owned commercial one in the port, to take barges and sailing vessels (Illustration 6.1). The famous Tooley Street Fire of June 1861, the capital's worst since the Fire of London, destroyed much of this work, but rebuilding was completed within a few years.

A stream of successful new applications for landing and storage privileges in the early 1860s were followed by wharf and warehousing improvements that continued, on and off, for the rest of the century.[58] As business grew, the wharfingers developed their premises to meet the increased demand of trade. 'The natural law of supply and demand has had full play', the chairman of the Wharfingers', Warehousekeepers' and Granarykeepers' Association told the 1902 Royal Commission on the Port of London. By then, most had hydraulic or steam power, gas or electricity, and a few boasted all four. Altogether over a million pounds was invested by seventy-seven waterfront firms (about three-quarters of the total number) in the 1890s.[59]

Proximity to the City was important to these wharves since their value as property diminished with the distance from London Bridge. But there were also several sites developed further downriver to handle foreign live-stock. In the early 1850s, the proprietors of the British and Foreign Steam Wharf (at the entrance to the St. Katharine's Dock) adapted this for cattle by adding a jetty and slaughterhouses.[60] The GSNC leased two adjoin-ing wharves at Poplar from the East and West India Dock Company for its livestock business. The unfortunate animals were driven from these through the streets to Islington.[61]

Odam's wharf near Victoria Dock, with a railway connection to Islington, was opened for landing and slaughter of foreign cattle in 1866.[62] Government intervention to curb the spread of livestock disease then closed the upper livestock wharves and animals arriving at Poplar completed their journey by rail. Much further downriver, the Thames Haven Dock Company, a group of livestock dealers and shipowners, began landing animals from the conti-nent.[63] Facilities in 1866 included piers, cattle pens, cranes and sheds and after 1889 enlarged wharf frontage suited for larger ships.[64]

The Corporation of London, owners of the Metropolitan Cattle Market where foreign and domestic cattle mixed, came under pressure from the Privy Council in 1860 to provide a separate foreign market. It eventually

---

[58] Chris Ellmers and Alex Werner, *London's Lost Riverscape. A Photographic Panorama* (Viking, London, 1988), 57, 100–2; Aytoun Ellis, *Three Hundred Years on London River. The Hays Wharf Story 1651–1951* (Bodley Head, London, 1952), 63–9; Customs Third Report, 1859, 10–11; Eighth, 1864, 27–8, Ninth, 1865, 31–2, Tenth, 1866; SC Tower Bridge Bill, Hunt, Qq. 9929–31.

[59] RC Port of London, Appendix, 1–3, 208–14; Minutes, Smith, Q. 2466.

[60] PP 1867–8, XII.1, SC on the Metropolitan Cattle Market Bill, First Report, Engledew, Qq. 8272–90.

[61] *Survey of London*, 44, 618–20; Forrester, 'General Steam', 71.

[62] SC Metropolitan Cattle Market, Robinson, Qq. 1683–4; Odam, Qq. 1856–8; Edward G. Howarth and Mona Wilson, *West Ham. A Study in Social and Industrial Problems* (J. M. Dent and Company, London, 1907), 141.

[63] Kay, *Thames Haven Railway*, 19–23.

[64] PP 1870 LXI.1 [61], Committee on the Transit of Animals by Sea, Irwin, Qq. 4–5, 21–3; B. E. Cracknell, 'The Petroleum Industry of the Lower Thames and Medway', *Geography*, 37 (1952), 80; Kay, *Thames Haven Railway*, 27–33.

opted for the nearby former naval dockyard at Deptford, although 'very inconveniently situated for its present purpose at an out-of-the-way spot on the wrong side of the river', purchasing this from its private owner.[65] The Deptford Foreign Cattle Market, where all imported cattle arriving in London had by law to be slaughtered, opened in 1871.[66] Deptford wharf itself could not cope with the largest American livestock carriers once these started arriving in the Port of London, so animals waiting in ocean-going steamers in the docks, off Gravesend or Thames Haven, were transhipped there in small Corporation steamers.[67] With the continental livestock business in terminal decline due to government regulation and American competition, Odam's switched to guano and in the 1880s, the GSNC abandoned the trade.[68] Thames Haven's ability to berth transatlantic vessels enabled it to survive until 1896, when an official decision that sheep as well as cattle had to be slaughtered on landing ended its involvement.[69]

Petroleum was another cargo progressively excluded from the metropolis. In the 1860s, barrels were often stored at wharves alongside other types of produce, but it soon became clear from fires on petrol-carrying vessels in the Thames that this was an extremely hazardous substance. Under the 1871 Petroleum Act, the Thames Conservancy introduced by-laws restricting such vessels to the river below Thames Haven, where the petrol could be transferred in the stream to covered barges, itself a dangerous process. In 1880, the enterprising 'Petroleum Storage Company' founded the Lower Thames petroleum industry by providing tanks for bulk storage here on a former cattle trade site.[70]

Foreign and Colonial Trades

1895 is the first year for which it is possible to compare the value and volume of London's imports.[71] In terms of declared value, in the lead

---

[65] *Morning Post*, 8 November 1870; Charles Dickens, *Dicken's Dictionary of the Thames from its Source to the Nore. An Unconventional Handbook* (Macmillan & Co., London, 1885), 70.
[66] RC Amalgamation of City and County of London; PP 1902, XV.33 [Cd. 4661], Departmental Committee on Combinations in the Meat Trade, Appendix VII, 308.
[67] RC Amalgamation, Appendix III, 83; RC Port of London, Minutes, Williams, Q. 2170.
[68] Forrester, 'General Steam', 137; Report of Veterinary Department, 68–9; RC Port of London, Minutes, Cattarn, Q. 3399.
[69] Kay, *Thames Haven Railway*, 28.
[70] SC Fire Protection, Miles Qq. 4067–8; Cracknell, 'Petroleum Industry', 80–1.
[71] Statistical analysis of London's trade is constrained by the content of the *Annual Statements of Trade and Navigation* and subsequent *Annual Statements of Trade*. These

were wool, worth £20 million, followed by grain, provisions and tea, each at 10 million. Together these accounted for 66 per cent of the value of the capital's imports. In contrast, in terms of quantities handled, sugar imports of 10 million cwts placed these second to grain with 28 million cwts, followed by wool with 5 million. Since cargo handling charges were based on size and weight, which also determined labour requirements, it was the volume of produce handled, not their market value, which mattered to London's port business.

Table 6.1 shows the quantity of London's leading imports at ten-year intervals 1865–1905, with their percentage share of the UK total. Decennial statistics are necessarily a snapshot, and fluctuations in domestic and overseas trading conditions mean that not too much emphasis should be placed on the results for individual years, but trends are evident.

Until 1895 imports of provisions, timber, tea, sugar and wool increased, in most cases modestly. Grain imports trebled impressively, coffee rose then declined, as did livestock, but overall they reflect a port settled in its trading relationships, but not gaining an increased share of national trade.

Most of London's trade continued to be with northern Europe, which accounted for 52 per cent of shipping arriving in 1861 and 44 per cent by the end of the century.[72] Good rail connections with the coast and new terminals at Charing Cross and Victoria meant that London's continental passenger trade declined.[73] However, traditional provision trade with a variety of near European destinations, including Antwerp and Hamburg, was more than sufficient in 1870 to support twenty GSNC regular sailings, some for cargo-only services were reduced in the depression decades that followed, but London's regular steamer connections

included shipping movements on a port-by-port basis since the late eighteenth century, but until 1857, there was no comparable treatment of port cargo trade. From then on, detailed tables itemise the type and quantity of imported produce, exported and re-exported at major ports. These make it possible to track changes in the quantity of particular goods arriving over time (excluding illegal trade), but not the *total* volume of a port's trade. The variety of units of measurement ('lbs' of tea, but 'loads' of wood and 'great hundreds' of eggs, for example) rule this out. Declared trade values, which replaced 'official values' in 1854, are an inadequate substitute but can indicate trends. However, total port import values were not published until 1872, and disaggregation by type of produce only from 1895. See also B. R. Mitchell, *British Historical Statistics* (Cambridge University Press, Cambridge, 1988), 442–447; David J. Starkey (ed.), *Shipping Movements in the Ports of the United Kingdom. A Statistical Profile* (University of Exeter Press, Exeter, 1999), xi–xxxi.
[72] PP 1861 LX.1 [2984], Annual Statement of Trade and Navigation 1860, 426; Starkey (ed.), *Shipping Movements*, 22.
[73] Customs Reports, 1860–1875.

Table 6.1 *Quantities of London leading imports and their United Kingdom percentage share, 1860–1905*

LONDON IMPORTS (Thousands)	1860	1865	1870	1875	1880	1885	1890	1895	1900	1905
Coffee (Cwts)	649	1,159	824	1,433	1,357	842	802	737	531	721
% Share UK	88	94	98	90	88	81	93	95	72	78
Grain (Cwts)	4,403	10,128	17,781	18,779	30,230	24,028	33,804	28,791	39,358	30,976
% Share UK	26	28	25	25	24	27	23	29	31	27
Provisions* (Cwts)	1,047	997	927	1,240	6,177	2,226	5,683	4,823	7,378	7,708
% Share UK	46	31	27	18	49	18	35	25	29	29
Sugar (Cwts)	4,846	4,542	4,094	6,588	7,906	9,756	9,449	10,024	11,065	9,238
% Share UK	55	41	32	34	39	39	37	32	36	31
Tea (Cwts)	747	1,045	1,255	1,758	1,846	1,892	1,991	2,266	2,654	2,698
% Share UK	94	97	100	100	100	100	100	100	99	98
Wool (Cwts)	994	1,323	1,893	2,538	3,212	3,661	4,526	5,541	3,689	3,897
% Share UK	75	70	80	78	78	80	79	78	1	67
Livestock (Number)	338	658	476	835	802	674	332	515	330	212
% Share UK	85	58	57	69	62	63	33	35	38	28
Timber (Loads)	651	1,023	847	1,176	1,483	1,445	5,034	1,500	2,116	1,695
% Share UK	23	27	21	23	28	23	70	20	21	19
Spirits, Wine (Gals)	16,104	17,220	17,139	21,062	16,973	15,270	17,753	16,291	15,364	10,968
UK% Share	71	71	52	61	62	62	62	63	56	57

* Cheese, butter, fresh and preserved meats and lard.
Sources: PP, Annual Statements of Trade and Navigation, 1861–1876; Annual Statements of Trade, 1881–1906.

with Europe remained an important element of port business well into the next century.[74] The GSNC benefited considerably from buoyant European livestock imports, investing in three large iron paddle steamers in the early 1860s to cater specifically for these.[75] Continental outbreaks of cattle plague periodically led to import restrictions, but the business continued to grow. In 1876 it reached the high point of 941,412 animals landed. Thanks to further outbreaks of disease on the continent, the cross-channel trade dwindled to almost nothing in 1893 and failed to recover.[76]

Within a few years of introduction, screw steamers had a presence in London's European bulk trades. By 1865, they dominated the Mediterranean fruit business as well as carriage of cotton from Egypt. In 1868 the Customs reported that 'sailing vessels of the smaller class, particularly those used to bring grain, no longer arrive in the Port of London, one steam vessel carrying as large a cargo as several used to do'. However, on the more distant Black Sea and Eastern Mediterranean routes, sail remained competitive with steam for longer, so London continued to receive European grain by both steam and sail into the late 1870s.[77] Sail also proved tenacious in the northern European timber trade, where British shipowners were a minority, and steam only began to overtake sailing vessel tonnage in the mid-1880s.[78]

Oceanic Trades

Since the seventeenth century, almost all imported tea came via London and its trading community and warehousing facilities ensured that this continued. Throughout the nineteenth century, benefiting from the increase in tea drinking, the Port of London still handled virtually all tea imported into the UK, whether for home consumption, re-export or transhipment. No other port offered similar facilities for the inspection

---

[74] Forrester, 'General Steam Navigation Company', 113–4.
[75] Ibid., 70.
[76] PP 1877 XXVII.515 [C. 1727], Report of the Veterinary Department of the Privy Council for 1877; PP 1894 XXVII.5 [C. 7258], Board of Agriculture, Annual Report of the Veterinary Department for 1893, Tables XVIII-XIX; Perren, *Meat Trade*, 172–3.
[77] PP 1867–68 XXII.591 [4046], Customs Twelfth Report, 1868, 45; Max E. Fletcher, 'The Suez Canal and World Shipping, 1869–1914', *Journal of Economic History*, 18 (1958), 557. Gelina Harlaftis, *A History of Greek-Owned Shipping. The Making of an International Tramp Fleet, 1830 to the Present Day* (Routledge, London, 1996), 119–20; Stephanos Xenos, *Depredations; or Overend, Gurney and Co, and the Greek and Oriental Steam Navigation Company* (Stephanos Xenos, London, 1869), 20.
[78] RC Port of London, Appendix, 200.

and quality testing needed.[79] For a long time, tea came exclusively from China, but from 1854 on, Indian and then Ceylon tea gradually gained market share, superseding Chinese by the 1890s.[80] Sugar was a different story. London had no monopoly in its import, storage or refining, so it faced competition from other British ports. In 1860 importation was almost all raw cane sugar, including foreign produce, but by the end of the century, this had been largely replaced by continental beet sugar, refined and unrefined. The change hit London's long-established sugar baking industry hard, as well as dock company business, in particular that of the East and West India Dock Company.[81] European beet sugar imports remained important for London, by 1900, over twice the level in 1870, but the sugar trade no longer had the prominence it had enjoyed earlier in the century.[82]

Opening of the Suez Canal in 1869 extended the triumph of steam over sail to European connections with Asia. By eliminating the need to circumnavigate Africa, the canal shortened voyage distance and time, so reshaping shipping trades. The new route, with good access to coal stations for refuelling, was particularly well suited to the independent power of steamers. Within a decade, most high-value cargoes reaching London from the East Indies came by steamer, as so did tea from China.[83] Until freight rates started to fall in the 1880s, the canal had less impact on the transportation of lower-value bulk cargoes from Asia, the Pacific and elsewhere. Large, iron-hulled, modern sailing vessels used the well-established, low-cost Cape route to carry other bulk cargoes, such as rice, to London.[84]

[79] RC Port of London, Appendix, 282, 803; PP 1902 XLIII [Cd 1151], RC Port of London, Minutes, McEwan, Q. 866; R. C. Michie, 'The International Trade in Food and the City of London Since 1850', *Journal of European Economic History*, 25 (1996), 380.

[80] PP 1898 LXXXV.1 [C8706], Customs Tariffs of United Kingdom, 204; PP 1900 LXXIX.425 [351], Statements of Imports of Tea and Coffee into Principal Countries of Europe and United States, Table X, 9; P. Mathias, 'The British Tea Trade in the Nineteenth Century', in Derek Oddy and Derek Miller (eds.), *The Making of the Modern English Diet* (Croom Helm, London, 1976), 92–4.

[81] John M. Hutcheson, *Notes on the Sugar Industry of the United Kingdom* (James M'Kelvie, Greenock, 1901), 115–6,120; Philippe Chalmain, *The Making of a Sugar Giant: Tate and Lyle, 1859–1989*, Translated by Eric Long-Michalke (Routledge, London, 1990), 27–9.

[82] Annual Statements Trade, PP 1871 C. 437, 106; PP 1901 LXXVI Cd. 549, Annual Statement of Trade, 664; PP 1884 LXXIV.371 [325], Report to Board of Trade, Progress of the Sugar Trade.

[83] D. A. Farnie, *East & West of Suez. The Suez Canal in History, 1854–1956* (Oxford University Press, Oxford, 1969), 157–212; Max E. Fletcher, 'The Suez Canal and World Shipping, 1869–1914', *Journal of Economic History*, 18 (1958), 561; J. Forbes Munro, *Maritime Enterprise and Empire. Sir William Mackinnon and his Business Network, 1823–1893* (Boydell Press, Woodbridge, 2003), 121–53.

[84] Graham, 'Ascendancy of the Sailing Ship', 84–5; R. V. Jackson, 'The Decline of the Wool Clippers', *The Great Circle*, 2 (1980) 88–9, 96–7.

Illustration 6.2 The London Dock Company new wool warehouse, 1850.
© *Illustrated London News*/Mary Evans.

In the 1870s the speed and reliability of steamships opened up transatlantic trades. Liverpool became the major receiver of foreign cattle as well as chilled and frozen meat.[85] However, London also gained transatlantic business. In the early twentieth century, on average, 236,000 animals from the United States and Canada were landed in the Port of London each year, but this was a quarter of European livestock imports in the 1880s.[86] The port's provision trades had long included bacon, ham and relatively small quantities of fresh meat from the Continent, but nothing matched the scale of the novel oceanic trade in chilled and frozen carcases. Unlike the trade in live animals, where the key had been steamer efficiency, technologically its development depended on advances in shipboard refrigeration and frozen storage capacity on land.[87] The

[85] Perren, *Meat Trade*, 114, 157–165; C. Knick Harley, 'Steers Afloat: The North Atlantic Meat Trade, Liner Predominance, and Freight Rates, 1870–1913', *Journal of Economic History*, 68 (2008), 1034.
[86] PP 1906 XXIII.37 [Cd.2893], Board of Agriculture and Fisheries. Annual Report of Proceedings Under the Diseases of Animals Act, Table VIII, 75.
[87] Derek J. Oddy, 'The Growth of Britain's Refrigerated Meat Trade, 1880–1939', *Mariner's Mirror*, 93 (2007), 269–72 [269–80].

trade to London began with United States beef in 1879, followed by Australasian mutton and lamb two years later. From a modest start with 856,000 cwts in 1882, when the London St. Katharine's Dock Company opened the first cold store in the capital, the quantity of non-European meat arriving in the Port of London reached almost 3.5 million cwts by the end of the century.[88] Improvements in steamer efficiency also stimulated the transatlantic grain market. In 1870 most wheat imported was Russian. Ten years on, two-thirds came from the United States.[89] Liverpool became the leading wheat port, but European grain remained an important London cargo.[90]

Until the 1830s, London's raw wool imports, primarily from Germany or Spain and meagre compared to domestic supply, were relatively unimportant. After this, Australian wool progressively displaced these in Britain's voracious mills. The quite dramatic rise in this new colonial trade had a considerable impact on port facilities (Illustration 6.2.). Dedicated warehouses were opened by leading wool merchants, the London Dock Company and, less successfully, the Millwall Dock Company in 1870.[91] By 1870, London, the nexus of the wool trade, was importing 3 million cwts, two-thirds from Australia.[92] Sailing clippers continued to dominate wool shipment from Australia in the 1870s, but their resilience in competition with steam should not be exaggerated. From the mid-1880s to the mid-1890s, steamers carried about half of wool exports to Europe. Thereafter the switch from sail to steam gathered pace, along with increasing steamer size, which disadvantaged London's upper docks. By 1900 the steam transition in London's wool trade was complete.[93]

Another London bulk trade still dominated by sail in the 1870s was guano. Cargoes of the fertiliser began arriving from islands off Peru, and briefly Africa, in the 1840s, at first finding a ready market among

[88] James Troubridge Crittell and Joseph Raymond, *A History of the Frozen Meat Trade*, (Constable & Co., London, 1912); Rebecca J. H. Woods, 'Breed, Culture and Economy: The New Zealand Frozen Meat Trade, 1880–1914', *Agricultural History Review*, 60 (2012), 288–308.

[89] PP 1882 XIV.1, 45,493, [C.3309-1 C3309.II], RC Depressed Condition of Agricultural Interest. Final Report, Harris, Q. 66, 318; PP 1887 LXXV.299, Number of Quarters of Wheat and Flour Imported into the United Kingdom, 1866–86.

[90] Francis Hyde, *Liverpool and the Mersey. An Economic History of a Port 1700–1970* (David & Charles, Newton Abbot, 1971), 98–9; Rodman W. Paul, 'The Wheat Trade Between California and the United Kingdom', *Mississippi Valley Historical Review*, 45 (1958), 405–6.

[91] Alan Barnard, *The Australian Wool Market 1840–1900* (Melbourne University Press, Melbourne, 1958), 20–26, 85–87, 132–4, Table VI, 218; Rees, *Commodity Markets*, 320–30.

[92] 1871 Trade and Navigation; PP 1901 LXXVI Cd. 549, 664, Annual Statement of Trade 1899.

[93] Jackson, 'Wool Clippers', 87–98; RC Port of London Minutes, Daniels, Qq. 8915–20, Blackburn Q. 8884.

Britain's farmers.[94] In the face of growing price and product competition from manufactured fertilisers, imports peaked in the late 1850s but remained substantial for some years after.[95] Sailing vessels were ideally suited to guano, found in remote places, away from sources of coal and, in most cases, habitation. Free at source, although extracted at great human and ecological cost, the cargo could be loaded straight into the hold. Guano carriers could be large for sailing ships. Those dispatched in 1860 by Anthony Gibbs and Co., which held the Peruvian government monopoly, averaged 863 registered tons.[96]

Petroleum, which first arrived in London in any quantity in 1857, was also carried in barrels on sailing vessels.[97] This was an unfamiliar cargo, a witness to the 1862 Select Committee on Fires in the Metropolis described it as 'earth oil', but it soon found a market in the buoyant domestic oil lamp industry.[98] Cheap, smelly and extremely dangerous to use, it fuelled 'the poor man's light', as also his stove.[99] Nationally, petroleum imports grew from 791,000 gallons that year to approaching 6 million by 1870, and over 100 million in the 1890s. By then, purpose-built steam tankers carrying petroleum in bulk were superseding sailing vessels and barrels.[100]

Not all goods arriving in the Port of London were destined for the home market. Having earned the dock companies and other owners of bonded warehouses income from rent and services, some were re-exported. The time lag between import and re-export means that there is no direct relationship between the two for any particular year, but comparisons over time suggest an overall reduction in the re-export of coffee, sugar, tea and wool from 10 per cent of these imports in the 1860s and 1870s to 5 per cent at the end of the century.[101] That said, London's exceptional ability 'to assemble sufficiently large cargoes of miscellaneous goods for shipment to specific destinations' remained a strength.[102]

[94] Robin Craig, 'The African Guano Trade', *Mariner's Mirror*, 50 (1964), 25–55; W. M. Matthew, 'Peru and the British Guano Market, 1840–1870', *Economic History Review*, 23 (1970), 112–28.
[95] Ibid., Matthew, 118, 124.
[96] RC Unseaworthy Ships. Preliminary Report, Appendix X, 472–3.
[97] PP 1896 XII.1 [331], SC on Petroleum, Appendix 29, 739.
[98] PP 1862 IX.1 [222], SC on Fires in the Metropolis, Drummond, Q. 1754.
[99] PP 1867, XI.1, 319 [471, 471.I], SC on Fire Protection, Miles, Qq. 4083–4090; PP 1894 XIV.503 [244], SC on Petroleum, Majendie, Q. 118; PP 1897 XIII.109 [309], SC on Petroleum, Norman, Q. 249.
[100] SC on Petroleum (1897), Bowring, QQ. 4017, 4095; SC on Petroleum (1896), Appendix 29, 739; Robin Craig. *The Ship. Steam Tramps and Cargo Liners* (HMSO, London, 1980), 19–22.
[101] Calculated from Annual Statements of Trade and Navigation, 1865, 1875; Annual Statements of Trade, 1885, 1895, 1905.
[102] Richie, *City of London*, 34–5.

Re-export was not the same as transhipment, although these can be confused. Overseas transit cargoes, never landed, were not recorded as imports. Improvements in international transportation and communications, with direct trade between producers and consumers, progressively undermined London's role as intermediary, turning northern continental ports into rivals. The range of produce transferred through London narrowed. At the end of the century, London's main transhipment cargoes, at most half the quantity of re-exports, were tea, wine and spirits. There was no systemic decline in tea, but transhipments of wine and spirits fell from 3 million gallons in the 1870s to 1 million in the 1890s.[103]

By 1900, the Port of London was no longer the global hub to the extent it had been earlier in the century. The 1902 Royal Commission on the Port of London concluded that this was an inevitable result of the direct shipment of foodstuffs, so generally beyond London's control. Even so, progressive reduction in re-exports had consequences for dock company warehouse facilities.[104]

The Steam Port

In the new age of distant oceanic services, no other national or foreign centre could yet match London's world-wide commercial networks or immense local market, so its deeper docks attracted major steamer lines. In the early 1870s, the port gained both Glasgow's Glen Line and P&O and foreign steamship lines: Austrian Lloyd, Messageries Maritimes, the Russian Steamship Company and the German Steamship Line. Companies operating from London by 1882 included the Castle Line, which ran to South Africa, the Ducal (Eastern Shipping) Line to India, the National and the Atlantic to the United States. A few years later, steam connections with New Zealand were established by the New Zealand and the Shaw, Savill and Albion lines.[105]

The remarkable expansion of world trade as new routes and sources of supply opened in the later nineteenth century strengthened the City of London's role as an international financial and commercial hub. Subsidised mail-carrying steamers considerably improved international postal services. Shipping intelligence published in *Lloyd's List* remained important, but by the 1870s, shipowners and managing agents in London also had access to a world-wide information network, 'an immense girdle

---

[103] RC Port of London, Appendix, 279–86.
[104] RC Port of London, Report, 23; Michie, 'International Trade', 379–80.
[105] RC Port of London, Minutes. Sutherland, Q. 1936; Farnie, *East and West of Suez*, 155; *Post Office London Directory for 1882*, 2422–24.

of telegraph wires radiating from London'.[106] Up-to-date information on prices and markets enabled imports to be tailored more accurately to demand. By the 1870s, arrivals of tea cargoes in the Port of London extended over six months, instead of the frantic few weeks usual in the days of sail.[107]

The capital had owed its creation to trade and shipping, but by the close of the century, the relationship had largely been reversed. The port now owed its existence to the metropolis that housed it. The enormous increase in Greater London's population, from 2.6 million in 1851 to 6.5 million in 1901, guaranteed import growth.[108] As Douglas Owen, author of several contemporary port studies, told the 1902 Royal Commission on the Port of London, 'London's local consumption trade is secured to her, and probably this is the bulk of the trade of the port'.[109]

With the construction of new docks further downriver, but London's commercial heart still the City, London progressively became 'a barge port' where many cargoes were landed in its huge downriver docks and transferred to wharves upriver in lighters.[110] Steam tramps and sailing vessels continued to bring timber and grain cargoes into the Surrey Commercial and the river, but by 1900 liners dominated most activity. In dock company boardrooms, directors wrestled with acute problems of rising costs, wharf competition and falling profits. Dealing with liner shipping was a more predictable, straightforward, business than handling sailing vessels. Liners needed specialised berths, so owners rented quayside and shed space on an annual basis. However, high capital and running costs made owners or managers determined to work their vessels hard, placing greater demands on dock companies, wharfingers and others dealing with shipping and cargoes. 'The large increase of steamers trading to London and the constant pressure by shipowners urgently demanding that not a moment's delay should take place in the discharge

[106] John Tully, 'A Victorian Ecological Disaster: Imperialism, the Telegraph, and Gutta-Percha', *Journal of World History*, 20 (2009), 563, 559–79; Yrjö Kaukiainen, 'Shrinking the World: Improvements in the Speed of Information Transmission, c. 1820–1870', in Lars U. Scholl and Merja-Liisa Hinkkanen (eds.), *Sail and Steam. Selected Maritime Writings* of Yrjö Kaukiainen (IMHA, St. John's Newfoundland, 2004), 231–60; Byron Lew and Bruce Cater, 'The Telegraph, Co-ordination of Tramp Shipping and Growth in World Trade, 1870–1910', *European Review of Economic History*, 10 (2006), 147–73.
[107] *The Economist*, 14 March 1874, 8 and 9 March 1879.
[108] Ball and Sunderland, *Economic History of London*, 42.
[109] RC Port of London, Minutes, Owen, Q. 5157.
[110] Robin Craig, *British Tramp Shipping, 1750–1914* (IMHA, St. John's Newfoundland, 2003), 15–39; Gordon H. Boyce, *Information, Mediation and Institutional Development. The Rise of Large-Scale Enterprise in British Shipping, 1870–1919* (Manchester University Press, Manchester, 1995), 19–20, 29–41.

of their vessel tax to the utmost the energies of the whole department', complained the Customs Commissioners in 1863.[111]

City mercantile interests and connections had been at the heart of dock business originally and remained so at mid-century. But as steam shipping took hold, such connections between dock companies and their customers, some based in other ports or overseas, became rare. Dock company fortunes depended less on choices made by merchants or their agents, more on the decision of a liner company to adopt one of their berths, and dependence on a few major clients left them open to commercial blackmail. In such dealings, the dock companies often found themselves at a disadvantage, not least because they were faced with some formidable shipping magnates, including Sir Thomas Sutherland of P&O, Sir Donald Currie of the Castle Line and Sir Alfred Jones of Elder Dempster & Co.[112]

Port and Capital

As we have seen, in the 1830s government interest in the management of the river was a response to port user concern. Discussion about the state of the London Thames next moved beyond the port issues of access and water depth to public concerns about 'a river front that was clearly unworthy of the growing magnificence of London'.[113] It was not only 'the offensive mud-banks and mean and unsightly buildings which disfigured the shores of the river' but more pressingly the polluted sewage-ridden Thames water associated with 'The Great Stink' of 1858.[114] Bazalgette's 1856 scheme for a sewer running under a north bank embankment, with more embankments further upriver and on the south bank, offered both a practical and aesthetic solution. The creation of the Metropolitan Board of Works, parliamentary support, effective financing and engineering expertise provided the means.[115]

---

[111] PP 1863 XXVI.109 [3157], Customs Seventh Report, 1863, 27.

[112] P. N. Davies, *Sir Alfred Jones, Shipping Entrepreneur Par Excellence* (Europa, London, 1978); ODNB, Sir Thomas Sutherland (1834–1922); Andrew Porter, *Victorian Shipping Business and Imperial Policy* (Boydell, Woodbridge, 1986).

[113] David Owen, *The Government of Victorian London 1855–1899. The Metropolitan Board of Works, the Vestries and the City Corporation* (Belknap Press, Cambridge, MA, 1982), 74; Stuart Oliver, 'The Thames Embankment and the Disciplining of Nature in Modernity', *The Geographical Journal*, 166 (2000), 227–238.

[114] Percy J. Edwards, *History of London Street Improvements* (London County Council, London, 1898), 125.

[115] Edward Bazalgette, 'The Victoria, Albert and Chelsea Embankments of the River Thames', *Proceedings of the Institution of Civil Engineers*, 10 (1878), 1–26; Owen, *Government Victorian London*, 74–101; Dale H. Porter, *The Thames Embankment. Environment, Technology and Society in Victorian London* (University of Akron Press, Akron Ohio, 1998); Stuart Oliver, 'Thames Embankment', 227–38.

Illustration 6.3 Photograph of the Pool of London and Tower Bridge, 1901. © Mary Evans Picture Library.

The Victoria Embankment, opened in 1870, ran between Westminster and Blackfriars. It dislodged a number of wharves and waterfront businesses, including the Temple coal yards, but passenger steamer companies got new piers and floating platforms, and others were able to relocate elsewhere on the river. Even so, the plans were vigorously opposed, costing the Board of Works almost £300,000 to settle forty-four compensation claims.[116]

London's three new solid granite-faced embankments have been characterised as emblematic of modernity; a re-engineering of the river that displaced unsightly, traditional 'natural' uses like wharves. They have also been seen as a victory for land 'in the capital's centuries-long struggle between land and water'.[117] Even so, the denial of commercial access to parts of the London shoreline barely infringed the established hold of port trading interests. The docks at Poplar and Limehouse

[116] Porter, *Thames Embankment*, 160–64; Owen, *Government Victorian London*, 83.

[117] Oliver, 'Thames Embankment', 236; Vanessa Taylor, 'Water and Its Meanings in London, 1800–1914', in Bill Luckin and Peter Thorsheim (eds.), *A Mighty Capital Under Threat. The Environmental History of London 1800–2000* (University of Pittsburgh Press, Pittsburg, 2020), 162.

now handled much metropolitan coal distribution, so the upriver coal wharves were already becoming less important. In the judgement of the Thames Embankment Commissioners, 'public convenience no longer necessitates the continuance of either of the coal or any other trade in this immediate locality'. The Commissioners viewed lower wharves differently, ruling out any interference on grounds of their commercial importance.[118] For this reason, they rejected a Metropolitan Board of Works proposal for a southern embankment extending below London Bridge, which would have affected the river port's most valuable property, including the Tooley Street wharves. As the Embankment commissioners observed, this 'would involve a vast expenditure of money, and cause a great disturbance of the trade and commerce of that part of the metropolis'.[119] It is not necessary to invoke the family and business connections between Commission chairman William Cubitt and Alderman Humphery, proprietor of Hay's Wharf, to explain an undoubtedly sensible decision, even though it left a flooding issue unresolved.[120]

Proposals in the 1870s for a new crossing downstream from London Bridge were potentially a greater threat to port interests than embankment. The congested London Bridge remained the lowest road link between the two banks of the Thames. Brunel's foot tunnel between Wapping and Rotherhithe had become a railway tunnel and the 1871 'Tower Subway', used by a million foot passengers a year, including port workers, was only seven feet in diameter and effectively just a pipe.[121] 'That the 890,000 inhabitants on the sixteen square miles to the north-east could only communicate with the 655,000 on the southeast, by going Westward to London Bridge, has struck me as something completely ludicrous' observed one of a growing number of those convinced that this situation should not be allowed to continue.[122] There was less agreement on what the solution should be, who should be responsible and how it should be financed.[123]

---

[118] PP 1861 XXXI.267 [2872], RC Embanking the River Thames, 2.

[119] PP 1862 XXVIII.61 [3043], Thames Embankment Commission (Surrey Side), Snooke, Q. 181.

[120] Porter, *Thames Embankment*, 162.

[121] Ben Weinreb, et al., 'The Thames Tunnel', in *The London Encyclopaedia*, 3rd ed. (Macmillan, London, 2008), 913, 912; John Wolfe Barry, *The Tower Bridge. A Lecture* (Noot, Son and Carpenter, London, 1894).

[122] W. Hora, *Bridge or Tunnel for Improved Communication Across the River Thames Below London Bridge* (London, 1884), Bristol Selected Pamphlets, University of Bristol Library, www.jstor.org/stable/60241338, accessed 22 October 2018; PP 1884, XIV.1 [255], SC Metropolitan Board of Works (Thames Crossings) Bill, iv.

[123] Peter Matthews, *London's Bridges* (Shire Publications, Botley, 2008), 165–173; J. E. Tuitt, *The Tower Bridge, Its History and Construction from the Date of the Earliest Project to the Present Time* ('The Engineer', London, 1894), 32–51.

Two Board of Works schemes having failed to gain government support, the Corporation proposed a low-level 'bascule' bridge, running close to the Tower of London across the river to the end of Tooley Street. This would open to allow shipping to pass through. Although outside City limits, the new bridge would be financed from its Bridge House Estates.[124] This, like other proposals, faced opposition from river users. It was claimed that the bridge would drive the provision and fruit trade in ocean-going steamers away from the Upper Pool wharves to the docks or other ports, that the narrow passage between the bridge piers would be a danger to barge and steamer traffic, and that the bridge would have to remain open for three hours to allow for the tides.

Aware of the self-interested nature of their claims, at a time of well-known hardship suffered by port workers, some wharfingers emphasised their role as employers of day labourers, and by extension the impact any decline in wharf business would have on these men. The workers themselves were not united. A petition 'with numerous signatures' claimed that the bridge would deprive many thousands of a livelihood and 'destroy the navigation of the river which has made London the greatest commercial city of the world'. But another argued that it would be a boon to the working classes and the Secretary of the Labour Protection League union told Members of Parliament that the bridge would give them 'great facilities to get to their work'.[125]

With the interests of many thousands of Londoners weighed against those of the river port, there was little doubt that the Corporation project could go ahead. Wharfingers achieved a right to limited compensation if it could be shown that the bridge caused danger or damage to vessels using their facilities and shipowners gained the services of a Corporation steam tug to help navigate through, but this was probably the best they could hope for. Compensation for loss of business awarded to 171 watermen totalled £5,480 and the Thames Subway owners received £11,500.[126] Tower Bridge was opened by the Prince of Wales with great pageantry in June 1894, having taken eight years to build.[127]

The bridge's opponents had overstated its impact on shipping. In the expectation that the bascules would have to be raised for at least two hours a day, Barry's design included a high-level pedestrian walkway.

[124] John Wolfe Barry, *The Tower Bridge. A Lecture* (Noot, Son and Carpenter, London, 1894), 15.

[125] SC Tower Bridge Bill, Chairman's comments, 461–2, Hunt, Q. 9952; Moore, Q. 7821; Keen, Q. 3521, Beard, Qq. 482–484; Humphrey Qq. 9036–7; Furber, Q. 5638.

[126] *Times*, 15 January 1897; PP 1906 XLI. 1 [Cd. 2752], RC London Traffic, Appendix 43, 496; *Times*, 9 January 1896.

[127] *Times*, 7 August 1885,

As it turned out, the average delay to bridge traffic was just six minutes. Since it was quicker and easier to wait for the bridge to re-open than take the lift or stairs, the walkway was seldom used. It closed in 1906.[128] When the Embankment was being planned twenty years earlier, doing no damage to the commerce of the river had been an important consideration. By the 1880s, London itself had moved on, and much port activity had moved out. Wharves were doing well as accessories to the lower dock system. As Illustration 6.3 suggests, barges, not ocean-going ships, had become the upper river port's main users.

[128] Matthews, *London's Bridges*, 169; J. Wolfe Barry, 'Discussion on the Tower Bridge', *Minutes of the Institution of Civil Engineers*, 127 (1897), 63–4; *Times*, 1 May 1906.

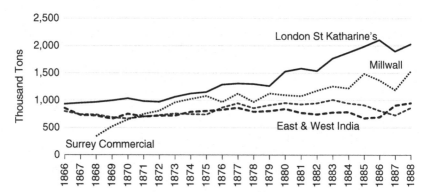

Figure 7.1 Total registered tonnage of vessels with cargo annually entering the Port of London company docks, 1865–1888. Source: PP 1902 XLIV.1 [Cd.1153], RC on the Port of London. Appendix, 42–3, 79, 198.

> Without labour, useless would be our employers' warehouses; useless would be their ships, wharfs or docks; useless their machinery for working the goods intrusted to their charge, unless directed and controlled by manual labour.[1]

In the 1850s the north bank companies faced two main problems: wharf competition and the failure of earnings to keep pace with an increase in the shipping and cargoes handled. Adding to these challenges from the 1860s was accommodating steam shipping by investment in facilities, including new docks, and in the 1880s a resurgence of fierce rivalry between themselves. Their common response to diminishing profitability was a refashioning of original employment systems to the detriment of the lives and livelihoods of a resistant workforce.

[1] The Waterside Labourers' Statement, *Times*, 28 July 1853.

Dock Companies 1850–1865

The companies continued to compete, but earlier agreements on charges had eliminated cut-throat contests. Now their mutual concern was to counter 'the formidable rivalry and competition which has sprung up, mainly only from recent relaxations of privileges in favour of the Wharves'. Having found that a moderate reduction in charges had little impact on the lightering away of goods to their waterfront competitors, in May 1854 all landing and storage rates were cut by a substantial 15 per cent, an indication of the extent to which the wharves were undermining dock business. Faced with aggressive competition from the Victoria Dock, in 1859 the panicking established companies reduced rates even more.[2]

In a bolder concerted move, they introduced similar private bills authorising them to charge on lighters and barges for entering their docks, to which 'The Merchants, Traders, Wharfingers, Warehouse-Keepers, Lightermen and Granarymen of London and the Metropolitan Districts', as well as the Corporation, a waterfront property owner, responded aggressively.[3] Asserting that 'the Thames, an imperial river, is the property of the nation' their campaign contrasted the 'large establishments, vast capital, business on a gigantic scale' of the dock companies with the much smaller, although in several cases certainly wealthy, wharf owners. For the *Economist* and *Times*, the bills were evidence of greed.

Private bills were usually considered in committee, but arguments that this was a matter of public interest ensured that in 1855, the East and West India Dock Company's bill came before the whole House of Commons. Only its chairman and the St. Katharine's Dock Company director W. S. Lindsay spoke in favour. Despite meetings with the President of the Board of Trade, the dock companies signally failed to convince the government, which opposed the bill. It was denied a Second Reading, and the other companies withdrew.[4] Coming in the wake of the recent Customs trouble, this was further humiliation. The Free Water Clause did not cease to rankle over the following decades and there was a weaker attempt at removal when the London Dock Company and

---

[2] Anon, *The London Dock Companies: An Inquiry into Their Present Position and Future Prospects, with Suggestions for Improvement of Revenue and Dividends* (Richardson & Co., London, 1861), 21–2, 25; MLD SKD 009, 18 October 1859.

[3] MLD EWID 012, 6 January 1854, SKD 008, 14 March 1854; *Economist*, 2 December 1854, 20 January 1855; Humpherus, *Watermen and Lightermen, IV, 1850–1883*, 45; *Economist*, 2 December 1854, 3 February 1855, 17 February 1855, 20 January 1855; *Times*, 19 February 1855.

[4] Humpherus, *Watermen and Lightermen, IV*, 46; Parliamentary Debates, 3rd Series, 136, 19 February 1855, cc. 1505-1511.

St. Katharine's Dock Company amalgamated in 1864, but not until 1900 did they again risk bringing a similar bill before Parliament.[5]

Competition was not the only problem. From the 1850s, the proportion of wage costs to earnings was higher than in the 1840s, averaging about 1 per cent more for the St. Katharine's Dock Company and 3 per cent for the other companies.[6] St. Katharine's identified its cramped site and 'incessant restowing' as factors, but all docks were affected by the labour-intensive process of clearing cargoes from more congested quays. One solution was the replacement of manually operated cranes and capstans by hydraulic power to speed things up.[7] William Armstrong's 1846 patented crane rapidly gained acceptance. By 1853 hydraulic cranes had been installed at the Regents Canal Basin, at railway depots, in the London Dock Company's new wool warehouse and in other major ports. By 1858 all north bank docks, including Victoria, had this technology.[8]

A competitive metropolitan labour market ruled out wage cuts in the early 1850s. A strike in 1853 of dock and warehouse labourers for higher wages was evidence of labour militancy. It forced the London Dock Company into substantial concessions, including enlarging its permanent labour force, which meant greater labour costs. St. Katharine's initially focussed on pensioning off salaried officers 'who through age and infirmity are unable to render efficient service', lowering pay levels for new appointments, and monitoring officer performance. In the 1860s companies broke with their historic adherence to day-pay. Except for particularly fine articles such as silk and feather or delicate operations with drugs or oils, piecework replaced timework as the norm in warehouses.[9]

Despite the continued growth of the port's trade and their investment in improved facilities in the 1850s, the finances of the St. Katharine's Dock Company and London Dock Company failed to improve. Inflated by the Shadwell development, the London's interest payments bore

---

[5] PP 1864 LIV.1 [19], Reports on Railway and Canal Bills, and Bills Relating to Harbours, Docks and Tidal Waters, 127–8, 167–8; *London Evening Standard*, 10 August 1864; Parliamentary Debates, 4th Series, 83, 15 May 1900, cc. 160–308.

[6] MLD SKD 125, 21 June 1852, EWID 011, 22 July 1853, EWID 012, 12 May 1854, 147, 28 June 1860, LDC 102, EWID 019, 28 June 1870.

[7] Sir William Armstrong, 'The History of the Modern Development of Water Pressure Machinery', *Proceedings of the Institution of Civil Engineers*, 15 (1877), 64–88; Tim Smith, 'Hydraulic Power in the Port of London', *Industrial Archaeology Review*, 14 (1991), 64–88; MLD SKD 125, 21 June 1852.

[8] MLD EWID 011, 18 March 1853, EWID 012, 1 January 1854, 12 May 1854, SKD 008, 7 July 1853, SKD 009, 13 July 1858; Smith, 'Hydraulic Power', 65.

[9] MLD, LDC193, 4 October 1853, SKD 125, 21 June 1852, EWID 012, 12 May 1854, EWID 019, 28 June 1870.

heavily on annual earnings and drained reserves. Dividend on ordinary shares, which had been 5 per cent for fourteen years, was cut to 4.5 per cent in 1858 and by 1861 was 2.5 per cent. St. Katharine's dividends fell to 3 per cent in 1862, but drawing on still substantial accumulated balances enabled the East and West India Dock Company to maintain 6 per cent.[10]

By 1860 the Victoria Dock was well established. It handled more shipping tonnage than either London or the St. Katharine's and, thanks to the London and Blackwall Railway link to its warehouses in the City, also competed for the storage of wine and spirits. When the Crown disposed of its warehouse monopoly in 1857, the Victoria captured tobacco storage and it also seized the contract with the guano monopolist William Gibbs from the East and West India Dock Company.[11] These successes owed much to ruthless rate-cutting strategy, but downriver location and facilities proved particularly attractive to the coal trade. By the early 1860s, a third of the seaborne coal arriving in the port was discharged in the Victoria Dock.[12]

In May 1859, the Victoria Dock Company again offered sale or amalgamation to the St. Katharine's Dock Company. In theory, opportunists Peto, Betts and Brassey were in a strong position, but they were probably operating at a loss and other speculations had landed Peto in serious financial trouble.[13] Dubious about outstanding commitments to the Victoria's investors, the St. Katharine's initially rejected this overture. However, the London Dock Company shareholders were publicly restive about its performance and the wisdom of continuing to compete with the St. Katharine's Dock for a similar range of cargoes. In a complex settlement, the two companies united on equal terms and purchased the Victoria Dock Company.[14] The amalgamated London St. Katharine's created a more powerful rival to the East and West India but did nothing to tackle the on-going problem of wharf competition.

Amalgamation and speculation were also featured across the river. The 1850s were boom years for the timber trade, and the Commercial

---

[10] Anon, *London Dock Companies*, 5–14; MLD, LDC 150, General Meeting Minute Book, SKD 125; Palmer, 'Port Economics', 33–4; RC Port of London, Appendix, 424.

[11] Anon, *London Dock Companies*, 24; PP 1857–58 XXV.389 [2357], Second Report Customs, 12–13; PP 1859 Session 2, XIV.67 [2540], Third Report Customs, 10, 13–14.

[12] PP 1863 XII.1 [454], SC on Conservancy River Thames, Cory, Qq. 4709, 4783–6.

[13] MLD, SKD 009, 31 May 1859; Adrian Vaughan, *Samuel Morton Peto. A Victorian Entrepreneur* (Ian Allan Publishing, Hersham, Surrey, 2009), 164–76.

[14] *Times*, 24 October 1859; Anon, *London Dock Companies*, 62; 18 & 19 Vict. c. cxxxiv; PP 1854–55 L. 423, Reports of Board of Trade on Private Bills for Harbours, Docks, and Navigations, 15.

company's dominance of the Baltic and North American business was such that the East and West India followed its lead on charges. Once its enlarged East Country Dock opened in 1855, the Commercial Dock Company could handle the largest timber-laden vessels.[15] For years, the neighbouring Grand Surrey Canal system failed to make profits and posed little threat. But in the mid-1850s, under more enterprising management and with Bidder the Victoria Dock promoter as a consulting engineer, it rebranded itself as the 'Grand Surrey Docks and Canal Company', ensured that its act permitted amalgamation with the Commercial Dock Company, and financed a new deep-water dock, basin and lock. Better facilities attracted business, enabling it to pay 6 per cent dividends by 1860.[16] But its directors were not diverted from their prime speculative objective and negotiations with the Commercial Dock Company began.[17]

It has been suggested that competition for timber business marked by 'a ruinous period of rate cutting competition' was responsible for this decision. In fact, far from 'beggaring themselves', both companies were now equally profitable, but there were obvious advantages from combining interests. For the Commercial Dock Company, it solved the problem of inadequate facilities to cope with growing activity, while the other achieved the desired amalgamation on favourable terms.[18] In January 1865, the Surrey Commercial Dock Company, with equal representation for both former companies, met for the first time and the following year the two systems were physically connected. Amalgamation cemented the Commercial's success. In the decades that followed, the Surrey Commercial Dock Company paid 6 per cent dividends and was not afflicted by the competition problems encountered by other dock companies. The East and West India concentrated on 'exotic' hardwoods while with other types of timber the two companies routinely operated rate agreements.[19]

[15] MLD EWID 010, 4 April 1851, EWID 012, 27 January 1854, 10 February 1854, EWID 013, 25 July 1856.

[16] Griffin, *Surrey Commercial Docks*, 9, 16; *Sussex Advertiser*, 28 November 1854, 'Grand Surrey Canal'; 18 & 19 Vict. c. cxxxiv; L.423 [118], Reports Private Bills (1854–55), 15.

[17] *Sussex Advertiser*, 28 November 185; 18 & 19 Vict. c. cxxxiv; PP 1854–55 L.423 [118], Reports Private Bills (1854–55), 15; *London Daily News*, 18 April 1862; CDC 571, 27 May 1859; Griffin, *Surrey Commercial Docks*, 19–20.

[18] Rankin, *Surrey Commercial* Docks, 13; *Evening Standard*, 29 July 1863; *London Daily News*, 1 August 1863.

[19] Griffin, *Surrey Commercial Docks*; 20; MLD, R. B. Oram, *An Outline History of the Surrey Commercial Docks*, Unpublished Typescript, 1970, 20; RC Port of London, Minutes, Malcolm, Q. 1803.

Dock Companies 1865–1900

With Millwall, the Port of London had four dock companies. The East and West India continued to be based on the Isle of Dogs and Blackwall, but the London St. Katharine's responsibilities included both two old docks in central London and modern deep docks much further east. On the opposite bank was the enlarged Rotherhithe system. The London St. Katharine's led in shipping tonnage, but specialist niches gave the Surrey Commercial and Millwall docks a significant share of Port of London business (Figure 7.1).

Opened in 1868, Millwall Dock quickly gained a foothold. It never seriously challenged the Commercial's timber dominance but led in the transhipment and storage of grain, accounting for a third of the port's grain imports in 1900.[20] Thanks to bold investment in advanced grain handling equipment and its internal railway system, it was exceptionally efficient. In 1884, five new warehouses and a purpose-built nine-story granary doubled storage capacity.[21] How far such innovation was translated into profits is uncertain. The company appeared to be doing reasonably in the mid-1880s, paying 4.5 per cent dividends. However, the discovery in 1898 that to maintain share price its able secretary Birt had for years fraudulently overstated earnings casts doubt on its financial success.[22] As the port's only major dock enterprise since St. Katharine's opened in 1828, it was less constrained by past practices than its predecessors, although it necessarily colluded with these on charges. From the beginning, it relied on sub-contracting most labour and from 1884 permitted shipowners to arrange their own cargo discharge.[23]

Integrating the Victoria, London and St. Katharine's companies proved challenging. It took until 1869 to establish a new administrative structure, with a single superintendent responsible for all three docks, under the General Manager.[24] With mutual competition eliminated, it increased charges and joined the West and East India and waterfront businesses in further rises following the 1872 dock strike.[25] Ten years on, warehousing charges were reduced under a traditional working agreement.[26] 'Something like a Trades Union existed between them',

---

[20] MLD, MDC 552, 10 August 1883.
[21] Sargeant, 'Duckham', 49–71.
[22] Broodbank, *Port of London I*, 226.
[23] MLD, MDC 554, 15 August 1854; PP 1888 XXI.1 [448], Lords SC on Sweating System, Second Report, Birt Q. 14, 235–43.
[24] MLD, LSKD 194, 11 May 1866; LSKD 638, 27 July 1869.
[25] *Economist*, 18 February 1865.
[26] *Lloyd's List*, 18 July 1872; MLD EWID 021, 12 July 1872, 24 June 1873, LSKD 638, 25 July 1872, EWID 025, 5 June 1877, EWID 026, 5 March 1878; *Times*, 30 January 1878, 25 February 1884.

the Select Committee on Tonnage observed in 1881.[27] In another concerted move, in 1883 the north bank companies matched wharfingers' loyalty discounts, uniting their shipowner customers in outrage by increasing previously notional unloading charges to compensate for the loss of income.[28]

The London St. Katharine's pulled well ahead of the East and West India Dock Company (Figure 7.1). In 1882, its docks handled almost three times the tonnage of foreign and colonial shipping compared to its rival.[29] The company served at least a dozen ocean lines, including Anchor, National, British India, Orient, Messageries Maritimes and P&O, whereas the East and West India had only the Castle and Glen lines.[30] Despite muted competition and growing tonnage of shipping arrivals, earnings failed to keep pace. Average income per thousand registered tons arriving fell from £902 in the 1870s to £619 in the years 1880–1888, largely due to reduced warehousing income.[31] Demand for swift turnround by steamship lines increased the hours worked, so labour costs rose. Figure 7.2, covering the period 1865–1888, shows dividend levels, annual earnings and operating costs, together with the total paid out in ordinary share dividends, interest on loans, preference shares and up to £3 million of debenture stock. Such commitments left little room for reserves.

From the 1860s, the East and West India was in far greater financial difficulty than its rival, but subventions from large historic reserves obscured this. Its new South Dock and improved East India Dock proved no match for the London St. Katharine's West Ham system, so the tonnage of shipping handled barely responded. As overside delivery to wharves increased and more sugar went to downriver refineries, warehousing income declined. Even before the impact of the 1872 wage settlement, despite attempts to improve productivity, outlay on wages and salaries had risen steadily from 33 per cent of earnings in the mid-1850s to 41 per cent in 1868.[32] The outcome of all this is revealed in Figure 7.3, which shows East and West India Dock Company's annual earnings net of costs, debenture interest, preference

---

[27] PP 1881 XLIX.1.43 [C.3074], Royal Commission on Tonnage, Report, xxxiv.
[28] MLD, LSKD 638, 30 January 1883, 31 July 1883; *Times*, 14 February 1883, Letters, 15 February 1883, 2 March 1883.
[29] RC Port of London, Appendices, 42–3.
[30] *Times*, 24 September 1881, Letter Robert Capper; MLD, EWID TIL3, 28 January 1882; Post Office London Directory, 1882; MLD, EWID 104, 18 January 1887.
[31] MLD, LSKD 638.
[32] MLD, EWID 019, 6 June 1869, 29 June 1869, 28 June 1870; *Morning Post*, 15 January 1870; *Standard*, 14 January 1871; Palmer, 'Port Economics', 60.

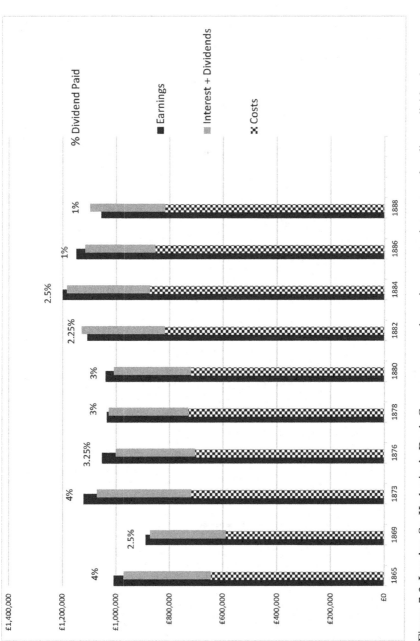

Figure 7.2 London St. Katharine's Dock Company, annual earnings, costs, interest and ordinary dividend payments, 1865–1888. Sources: MLD, LSKD 638; PP 1902 XLIV.1 [Cd.1153], RC on the Port of London. Appendix, 28.

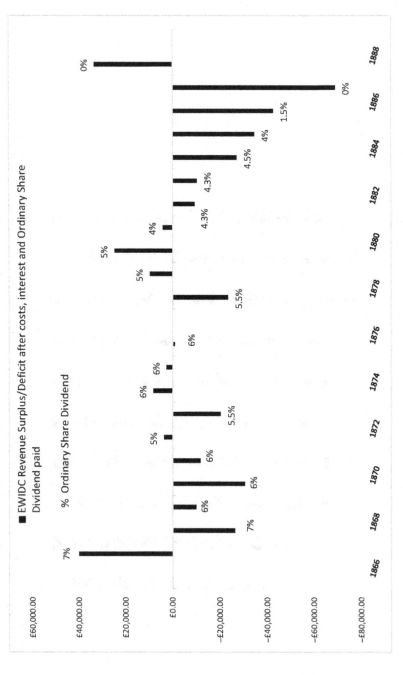

Figure 7.3 East and West India Dock Company. Annual Revenue Surplus/Deficit 1866–1888. Source: PP 1902 XLIV.1 [Cd.1153], RC on the Port of London. Appendix, 29.

share interest and the ordinary share dividend. Only by drawing on previous balances was the company able to afford the dividends shown. Directors were large shareholders, so as long as funds were available, it is unsurprising that these payments remained as high as they did.

Amalgamations led to large boards: thirty-nine members for the East and West India and forty-four for the London St. Katharine's. As in the past, these men were appointed for their trade connections; links with the City's mercantile and financial establishment remained strong. When the London Chamber of Commerce was formed in 1881, almost the whole London St. Katharine's Dock Company board was elected to its Council.[33]

Achieving overall oversight of these extensive enterprises was more challenging than at mid-century. Most directors lacked expertise in port operations, so strategic decisions relied strongly on the quality of senior officer advice. This was a point made forcibly by Broodbank in relation to the East and West India, his employer for much of his career. He blamed 'timid policy' between 1840 and 1870 on Secretary George Collin, who lacked relevant practical management experience. Broodbank's scathing conclusion was that it became 'effete in its policy and slack in its administration'.[34] In contrast, Broodbank admired Collin's successor, Colonel John Lowther du Plat Taylor, who joined from the General Post Office.[35] He considered Plat Taylor to be an outstanding manager and moderniser, while conceding lack of judgement with the Tilbury scheme. However, both an unsuccessful wool warehouse venture and his handling of dock labour issues suggest that Tilbury was not the man's only flaw.[36] The London St. Katharine's secretary after 1873 was another military man, Colonel Ben Hay Martindale. A Royal Engineer, Martindale had served as commissioner of railways and public works in New South Wales and at the War Office. George Birt, Chairman and manager of Millwall, also had a military background but had previously held a similar position at the Victoria Dock.[37]

The East and West India refused an 1873 amalgamation offer from its rival but by 1880, the Albert Dock, as well as the threat of a new

---

[33] *The Engineer*, 23 September 1881; Steven Reginal Burdett Smith, 'British Nationalism, Imperialism and the City of London 1880–1900' (Unpublished Doctoral Thesis, Queen Mary University of London, 1987), 37.

[34] Broodbank, *Port of London I*, 215.

[35] *Times*, 8 March 1904.

[36] Broodbank, *Port of London I*, 214–8; *Standard*, 9 January 1874; *Dickens's Dictionary*, 111; MLD, EWID 499, 13 January 1879, EWID 026, 12 March 1878, 25 June 1878, 28 January 1879, 11 February 1879.

[37] *Australian Dictionary of Biography, Volume 5*, Ben Hay Martindale (1824–1804); SC Sweating System, Second Report, Birt, Qq. 14, 230–3.

dock at Dagenham, were serious concerns.[38] As company engineer Augustus Manning pointed out to directors in 1881, their docks could not accommodate the largest steamers and lacked railway links to main lines, as well as dry docks, coaling space and facilities for grain and cattle traded. His solution was 'an earning machine of great value' in the form of a deep-water dock at Tilbury, mainly designed by himself. Manning's scheme assumed that shipping lines and their customers would be attracted by a dock so far from London and, despite the absence of detail on commercial prospects, the directors agreed. As major shareholders, they may have been influenced by Manning's observation that, in the event of amalgamation, a new dock 'of great earning capacity' would enable the company 'to dictate their terms, instead of being treated as a retrogressive undertaking, and having their stock forced down to the same level as their opponents'.[39]

Four years later, Tilbury was open, existing agreements were terminated and the foreshadowed contest for shipping lines was underway.[40] When the London St. Katharine's retaliated by lowering rates, this forced the East and West India to lower charges in all its docks. Most shipowners had little enthusiasm for Tilbury. When the bill was before the Select Committee, the East and West India's parliamentary agent was only able to persuade existing customer Castle's Donald Curry to speak in favour, others invited were 'out of town'. Those few steamship companies that transferred steamships exacted considerable concessions on charges and premises.[41] Some river port interests were actively hostile. Grain importers Ralli Brothers barred discharge at Tilbury in their Bill of Lading and a boycott by the Millers Association was only averted by generous reductions. Lighterage firms either demanded high rates or refused the work. The twenty-mile trip, one had told the Select Committee, 'would be like taking the Port of London down to the ship instead of bringing the ship up to London'.[42]

The East and West India financed Tilbury by property and stock sales, debentures, mortgages and borrowing, facilitated by its banker chairman Harry Hankey Dupree. But construction costs rocketed to almost three

---

[38] *Times*, 1 December 1873, 3 December 1873, 1 July 1881; *The Engineer*, 23 September 1881.

[39] MLD, EWID TIL 6, 15 September 1881, 1 October 1881, 18 October 1881, 24 February 1881.

[40] *Times*, 28 January 1887.

[41] MLD, EWID 514, 10 December 1886, 21 December 1886, EWID 032, 30 November 1886, 14 December 1886; *Times*, 16 April 1888.

[42] MLD, EWID 514, 28 September 1886, EWID, TIL 3, 14 October 1881, TIL 14, Minutes SC on Private Bills, Edmunds; Broodbank, *Port of London I*, 241.

times the original estimate, and the company became embroiled in a costly legal dispute with contractors.[43] Twelve months from its opening, Tilbury was almost empty, handling fewer than 200 vessels. Earnings tumbled to £33,000, not sufficient to cover working expenses, let alone interest payments, which led to further borrowing. Failing to meet some mortgage repayments, the East and West India Dock Company declared itself bankrupt in March 1888.[44]

Insider Broodbank blamed Dobree's 'fatal financial policy' for the catastrophe. For other observers, it was the inevitable result of excessive dock company competition. Certainly, the Tilbury venture was influenced by long-standing rivalry, but until then collusion had more often typified the relationship. Although Hay's Wharf proprietor Humphery later claimed that 'the competition of the wharfingers took a very small part in dock company troubles, disingenuously adding that 'the wharves were established many years before the docks', the impact of wharf competition on dock income cannot be dismissed.[45] Neither can be the financial challenge of adaptation to steam shipping by investing in new facilities. Tilbury brought matters to a head for both companies, but their problems were evident decades earlier.

The London St. Katharine's retaliatory rate cuts meant that its finances were not in good shape either. Faced with a dividend of just 1 per cent and deteriorating stock values, shareholder criticism mounted and pressure for amalgamation extended to East and West India proprietors. Discussions began in May 1887 but, since the East and West India was unwilling to suspend rate competition and London St. Katharine's at first refused to open its accounts to a competitor, little progress was made. Meanwhile, the East and West India finances were daily more dire, so frustrated East and West India Dock Company shareholders appointed their own four-man committee to assist directors in pursuing amalgamation. With relations between the two companies publicly acrimonious and agreement a distant prospect, a joint working arrangement became the only option. A month after East and West India Dock Company's collapse, separate shareholder meetings simultaneously endorsed this way forward. In January 1889, after almost a century of rivalry, the two undertakings started to be 'worked as one', under a London and India Joint Docks Committee.[46]

---

[43] Ibid., 239–40; MLD, EWID 104, 20 January 1886, 18 January 1887.
[44] RC Port of London, Appendices, 29, 43; Broodbank, *Port of London I*, 241–2.
[45] Broodbank, *Port of London I*, 218; RC Port of London, Minutes, Humphrey Q. 2897.
[46] *Globe*, 31 January 1888, *Times*, 18 April 1888.

Dock and River Labour 1850–1900

The north bank dock workforce division into permanent salaried and waged staff and those casually employed continued. By the late 1880s, the number of permanent employees in both systems was almost double that at mid-century. There were over 3,000 permanent positions at the London St. Katharine's upper docks alone and the smaller East and West India's establishment numbered 2,000. Even so, compared with the total casual dock workforce of as many as 18,000 men at the busiest times, appointed labourers were still a minority.[47]

With a regular weekly income of 20 to 30 shillings a week, annual paid leave, pension entitlement, recognised status and sufficient income to afford housing far from their workplace, such men 'lived a life remote from that of the dock casual'.[48] Even so, for a regular labourer, usually assured of work if available, a permanent post had its drawbacks. 'It is difficult to make clear to men of this class in life the advantage of a permanent situation with its prospects of promotion, clothing etc.', observed the East and West India Secretary in 1873.[49] Set against such 'advantage' was the compulsion to work a continuous six-day week and the loss of personal freedom to choose where this was. Permanent labourers in the East and West India had annual contracts, but the penalty for leaving without notice was three-month imprisonment; a consideration said to have caused the suicide of a permanent labourer during the 1889 dock strike.[50]

Within the casual workforce, the old categories persisted. The 'preferables', known in the East and West India Docks as 'Royals', were guaranteed hiring when there was work available. Preferables were part of the regular dock workforce, as so too were those extra labourers who were frequently employed. Expertise differentiated such men from their fellows. Although the leanly managed Millwall and the Surrey Commercial had few permanents or designated preference workers, most of the work in these docks was undertaken by regulars. Grain and timber demanded particular strength and proficiency, so handling was highly specialised. Whether

---

[47] LSE, Beatrice Webb, *Diary*, Typewritten Transcript, Vol. 10, 23 March 1887, 109, https://digital.library.lse.ac.uk/collections/webb; SC Sweating System. Second Report, Appendix B, 545–6, Plat Taylor, Q. 13,973, Martindale, Q. 17,055; PP 1893–94, XXXIII.681 [C. 6894-VIII], RC on Labour, Vol. III, Booth, Q. 24,735.

[48] Charles Booth, *Life and Labour of the People in London, First Series: Poverty* (Macmillan, London, 1902), 22, 24, *Second Series: Industry* (Macmillan, London, 1903), 396.

[49] Pattison, 'Nineteenth-Century Dock Labour', 273.

[50] PP 1892 XXXV.1 [C. 6708–V], RC on Labour. Vol. I, Brien, Q.11; *Times*, 28 August 1889.

employed by large contractors at Millwall, or by sub-contracted master labourers at the Surrey Commercial Docks, corn and timber porters maintained strong and exclusive occupational groupings.[51] Stevedores, loading ships in the docks or river for shipowners, also had enduring skill-based identities and at the other end of the status scale, so too did coal porters and ballast heavers. Recruitment at the 100 or so principal wharves, which by the end of the century employed about a third of port workers, tended to be more regular than on the docks, but at busy times the workforce could double. With some significant exceptions, wharves were relatively small-scale businesses, directly employing about a hundred casual labourers and most operating a preference system.[52]

Unlike permanents, such casually employed regular 'professional' dock or wharf labourers could not count on employment. This still depended on the ebb and flow of trade, as also weather. Rain might interfere to an extent, but, as Charles Booth noted, 'there is no cure for fog; when it is dense work must stop at the docks'.[53] Informal attachment counted for little when business was slack or the day was too murky. Employers recognised no obligation to those they laid off. As a charity worker reported in 1886:

I know a man well who is now out of work, and who had for many years been continuously employed. He had been employed at the [Commercial] docks on a superior class of work. Together with a mate he was discharged in January, the men being told that their services would not be wanted until July. Immediately afterwards the employer subscribed fifty guineas to the fund for the unemployed.[54]

But even for the less skilled, there was still an advantage in being known, so port labourers rarely looked for a job elsewhere. There was nothing to stop them from doing so, but failure to be available risked being struck off the list.[55] As in the past, foremen recruited men at the daily call-on, as shown in Illustration 7.1.

[51] SC Sweating System. Second Report, Birt, Qq. 14,303, 14,253, Martindale, Qq. 16,966–7, Plat Taylor, Qq. 13,977–8; John Lovell, *Stevedores and Dockers. A Study of Trade Unionism in the Port of London, 1870–1914* (Macmillan, London, 1969), 130; Geoffrey Crossick, *An Artisan Elite in Victorian Society. Kentish London 1840–1880* (Croom Helm, London, 1978), 64–5.
[52] PP 1896, C. 8230, Board of Trade, Third Annual Report, Abstract of Labour Statistics, 74–5; SC Sweating System, Second Report, Tillet, Qq. 13,355, 13,458, McCarthy, Qq. 15,345–47, Brand, Q. 13,875; PP 1892 C. 6795-VIII, RC on Labour, Answers to Schedule of Questions (Group B), 82.
[53] Charles Booth, 'Inaugural Address', *Journal of the Royal Statistical* Society, LV (1892), 546.
[54] Charity Organisation Society, *On the Best Means of Dealing with Exceptional Distress. The Report of a Special Committee, November 1886* (Cassell, London, 1886), 55.
[55] Gareth Stedman Jones, *Outcast London. A Study in the Relationship Between Classes in Victorian* Society (Penguin Reprint, London, 1984), 81–2.

Illustration 7.1 'Call On' at the West India Dock, 1886. © *Illustrated London News* Ltd/Mary Evans.

The north bank dock companies originally set great store on directly recruiting, controlling and securing the loyalty of all employees, including extra labourers. A new generation of directors in the 1850s, bent on reducing labour expenditure, found this policy costly and impractical. Faced in 1872 with a port-wide increase in hourly wages following strikes, the London St. Katharine's introduced sub-contracting, with 'sets' headed by former preference workers. In 1888, there were 257 such sub-contractors in the London Dock alone. The East and West India experimented with using external subcontractors in its warehouses but returned to direct employment in 1872. Thereafter it combined piecework incentive with hourly pay. A foreman acted as a contractor by selecting labourers for a particular task, paying them an hourly rate, based on how long the job should take. If the work was completed faster than expected, the labourers received a share of the cost-saving, known as 'The Plus', which the men treated as regular remuneration.[56]

---

[56] SC Sweating System, Second Report, Martindale, Qq. 16,884–5, 16931, Plat Taylor, 13.894, 13951, Tod, Qq. 15084–15091; MLD, EWID 019, 28 June 1870; PP 1890, XVII.257 [169], Lords SC on the Sweating System, Fifth Report, Lxxiv, 80–81, 98.

At Millwall, contractors (thirty in 1888) were entirely responsible for cargo handling, tallying and clerical services at their warehouses and quays, employing gangs of labourers who divided payment between themselves.[57] On the south bank, the Surrey Commercial awarded annual timber contracts for dock 'districts' to leading deal porters working on an equal footing with a group of mates, who in turn employed casual labourers as needed. When discharging grain, it employed seven-man corn porter gangs on piece-work rates but used permanent workers supplemented by day-pay casual labourers in the granaries.[58]

Sub-contracting dock employment had wider consequences. In the competition to recruit extra labourers, it was in the interest of contractors or foremen to maintain a pool of potential recruits by distributing the chance of work among as wide a group, then taking on the fewest possible and driving them hard. Losing the chance of future jobs deterred men from complaining and the system encouraged bribery and treating. The opportunity for corruption and injustice that went with sub-contracting led to resentment and demoralised the labourers.[59]

The maximum working in the docks in the early 1890s had not much increased since mid-century. Contemporaries identified several reasons for this: reduction in long-term warehousing due to the impact of the telegraph and the steamship on commercial practices, replacement of imports of cane sugar by beet sugar which went straight from dock to refinery, more transhipment of goods immediately on arrival and greater use of labour-saving machinery. Trade unions blamed also 'feverish working' when discharging steamers and the 'sweating' of workers.[60]

Yet the number of those seeking port employment was far greater than earlier in the century. Social investigator Charles Booth estimated that on average as many as 22,000 men competed for work every day in 1891–1892, whereas in theory the demand could be met by 16,000 working on a more permanent regular basis, supplemented by outsiders at the busiest times. Stedman Jones has suggested an association between the number of competing wharf employers and port labour oversupply, but since wharf sector expansion began decades earlier, this is unpersuasive. Instead, it is more significant that an enduring surplus of underemployed

---

[57] SC Sweating System, Second Report, Birt Qq. 1423, 1452–53; SC Sweating System, Fifth Report, Lxxvii, 95.
[58] Mayhew, *Morning Chronicle*, Reprint, Volume 5, 55–61; RC on Labour, Vol. I, Griffin, Q. 6708, 6080–6082.
[59] SC Sweating System, Fifth Report, lxxv.
[60] SC Sweating System, Second Report, Birt, Q. 14,340, Tillett, Qq. 12,624–35, 13,605, Steward Q. 13, 215; Stedman Jones, *Outcast London*, 118–24.

extra labourers coincided with the adoption of sub-contracting in the two largest dock systems.[61]

In 1888, trade unionist Ben Tillett contrasted those men for whom dock work was a trade, a profession, with 'outsiders' recruited from London's abundant supply of other casual labourers.[62] The port's need for labour remained irregular and sometimes pressing. Indeed, as the steamship and rapid turnround penetrated ever more trades, the difference between busy and slow times grew more extreme. A minority of outsiders were 'loafers' or vagrants who otherwise subsisted on charity or the earnings of others. More commonly, they were seasonal workers or had been ousted from employment elsewhere. Fruit and vegetable costermongers, for example, often worked at the London Dock when the winter wool sales were on. A greater number were forced into casual port work by factors such as cyclical depression in building, decline in the demand for some types of skilled work such as sugar baking and shipbuilding, bankruptcy or death of an employer, termination of army service or personal problems like alcoholism or ill-health. Mayhew's observation at mid-century that 'we find every kind of man' at work in the docks still held true forty years later.[63]

Unlike regular port labourers, completely casual workers potentially had the advantage of mobility, but this was constrained both by their own economic and physical limitations, as well as the extended geography of the Port of London.[64] Lighter labour was most on offer at the London and St. Katharine's docks, where outsiders congregated. Only when opportunities had been exhausted would they travel downriver. The complacent author of *Three Years of a Wanderer's Life*, a fit middle-class young man who worked for a few days in the London Dock, found wheeling a hand truck for eight or nine hours a day 'little more than healthy exercise'. For hungry impoverished labourers, restricted by lack of muscle to where they could get truck work, even this was hard toil.[65]

Much cargo handling had always been tough, dangerous work, but possibly became even more so as mechanisation increased. Hobsbawm's statement that 'in the late 1880s there was, with the exception of quays,

---

[61] RC on Labour, Vol. III, Booth, 24, 940–3. (Booth's figures excluded stevedores, lightermen and coal porters as well as 'outsiders'.); Stedman Jones, *Outcast London*, 64.

[62] SC Sweating System. Second Report, Tillett, Qq. 12,651–2.

[63] Stedman Jones, *Outcast London*, 73–90, 121–2; Mayhew, *Morning Chronicle*, Reprint, Volume 1, 66; Lovell, *Stevedores and Dockers*, 31–2.

[64] Phillips and Whiteside, *Casual Labour*, 34–6.

[65] John F. Keane, *Three Years of a Wanderer's Life, Vol. I* (Ward and Downey, London, 1887), 232; SC Sweating System, Second Report, Birt, Q. 14,444; Howarth and Wilson, *West Ham*, 53–5, 399–400.

cranes, winches and dockside railways, virtually no mechanical equipment at all' is misleading.[66] Certainly much labour involved basic equipment like hooks, trucks and trolleys; as late as the 1880s, the fruit trade relied on men carrying boxes on their backs. But there was a world of difference between the hand or steam-powered fixed cranes of the past and the movable hydraulic cranes and steam hoists of the steamer port.[67] Working with or alongside machinery only added to the risks. Sub-contracting enabled employers to evade responsibility for conditions, so with pressure to labour faster and nonstop, poor maintenance, a lack of training and, in the words of an 1889 *Lancet* report, 'sheer weakness in men irregularly occupied, underpaid and therefore underfed', accidents were inevitable.[68] It concluded that trade union claims that over five years at least half of all dockers would have a serious accident were no exaggeration.[69]

Industrial Conflict in the Fifties and Seventies

In August 1853 London experienced a wave of strikes in response to rising prices, which affected the port as well as other metropolitan industries. Well-supported action by about 2,000 south bank wharf labourers, mostly regular workers not easily replaced, succeeded in raising their hourly wage from three pence an hour, the rate for fifty years, to four pence. In the London Dock, a strike for higher pay by quayside extra labourers spread to men working on the Australian and East India ships and to the tea warehouses. Some permanent and preferable labourers joined in and within a few days, only the wine vaults were still at work. Labourers at St. Katharine's and the East and West India docks also struck, 8,000 processing along the East India Dock Road 'with banners, flags, bands of music and large placards' to a meeting in Victoria Park with workers from other docks.

---

[66] Eric Hobsbawm, *Labouring Men. Studies in the History of Labour* (Weidenfeld & Nicolson, London, 1964), 207.

[67] PP 1894 xxx.9 [C.7421], RC Labour, Fifth and Final Report, 183; SC Sweating System. Second Report, Tillett, Qq. 12,631, 13,341–2, McCarthy, Q. 1411; PP 1892 XXXV.1 [C. 6708-V], RC Labour, Minutes (Group B), Vol. I, Cridge Q. 4085, Griffin, Q. 6,105; PP 1900 XI.249 [Cd. 223], Inspector of Factories and Workshops Report 1899, 75–6. 9.

[68] P. J. Rawlings, '"Without Feeling and Without Remorse"? Making Sense of Employers' Liability and Insurance in the Nineteenth Century', *British Insurance Law Association Journal*, 126 (2013), 1–16; PP 1886 VIII.1 [192] SC on Employers' Liability Act, Ruegg, Qq. 444, 540–2; SC Sweating System, Fifth Report, lxxv.

[69] Michael Quinlan, 'Precarious Employment, Ill Health and Lessons from History: The Case of Casual (Temporary) Dockworkers 1880–1945', *International Journal of Health Services*, 43 (2013), 724–9.; *The Lancet*, 'Accidents Among Dock Labourers', 13 April 1889, 756; *The Lancet*, 'The Dock Strike', 31 August 1889, 444; SC Sweating, Fifth Report, lxxvii, lxxx; RC Labour, Fifth and Final Report, 163–5.

Slow progression of the strike from dock to dock gave time for companies to counterattack and 'the rural districts around London were energetically beaten up for recruits'. By the time the Poplar labourers came out, 500 police at the London and St. Katharine' gates allowed in new and returning hands and work restarted. The East and West India Dock Company could not afford grain discharge to be delayed, so these workers gained extra per ton, but otherwise held out. Two weeks later, with many destitute through lack of work, London's first port-wide strike of dock labourers came to an end.[70] Other workers did better. Action by south bank coal heavers resulted in victory, though not those on the north, and a nine-day strike in September by journeyman lightermen achieved double pay for Sundays and a substantial rise for nightwork.[71]

Had the striking extra labourers in the three docks acted in concert from the beginning, they might have shocked more employers into concessions. The strikers did not lack organisation. Press reports refer to the use of committee rooms and in preparation for the East and West India strike, the leaders set up 'large tables with memorials on them for higher wages being exhibited for the signatures of the labourers'. But they needed central leadership, and their bargaining position was weakened by their opponents' ability to bring in replacement workers with police support. The companies blacklisted the most active strikers and twenty-five London Dock Company permanent labourers involved were sacked. However, at this busy time of the year, it was not in the employer's interest to be more punitive. The St. Katharine's Dock Company re-employed strikers known to be efficient workers and the London increased the number and pay of permanent workers from 16s 6d to 18 shillings a week, with long-term consequences for labour costs.[72]

The next wave of port-wide strikes came not until the early 1870s, when activity was on the rise after years of depression. In July 1871, the East and West India Dock Company's Plat Taylor, newly recruited from the General Post Office bringing with him 'a Post-Office economy and a Post-Office broom', replaced sub-contracted piecework in up-town warehouses by fixed hourly pay.[73] With reduced hours and less call for overtime in the winter months, the East and West India's

---

[70] *Shipping and Mercantile Gazette*, 3 August 1853; *Morning Post*, 6 August 1853; *Morning Advertiser*, 9 August 1853; *Reynolds News*, 14 August 1853; *Lloyd's Weekly*, 7 August 1853; *Times*, 9 August 1853; *Morning Post*, 10 August 1853.

[71] *Morning Post*, 24 August 1853; *London Daily News*, 1 September 1863, 9 September 1853; *London Evening Standard*, 10 September 1853.

[72] *Reynolds Newspaper*, 7 August 1853; SKD008, 16 August 1853; LDC193, 4 October 1853.

[73] *Times*, 8 March 1904.

warehouse workforce of 300–400 men faced a cut in earnings. A brief November strike by tea labourers for a return to the old system or higher wages failed to shift Plat Taylor who threatened strikers with blacklisting. The men capitulated, but a meeting in December established the 'Labour Protection League', with wider ambitions for port labour than redressing the grievances of East and West India Dock Company's warehouse workers.[74]

In its first six months alone, membership of the Labour Protection League expanded to take in other occupational groups, some already unionised, looking for improvements in wages and conditions. These included stevedores, dock and waterfront labourers, corn porters and employees of the short-sea shipping companies, predominantly the GSNC. In June, agitation on the south bank achieved an increase in the hourly rate from four pence to five pence and 5,000 or 6,000 East and West India extra labourers struck for sixpence, as did also those at London St. Katharine's and Millwall. These two companies quickly settled, but the East and West India Dock Company held out for longer. Having failed to recruit replacement labour, it conceded the advance and reinstated piecework.[75] Both dock companies then increased their permanent workforce. In the case of the London St. Katharine's Dock Company, this almost doubled to 625 men, approximately an eighth of labourers. However, both companies discovered that secure employment offered little protection against calls from even permanent workers for higher pay, which they were sometimes forced to concede. Until a downturn in the later 1870s, docks and wharves were generally busy, and workers were able to take advantage.[76]

Industrial Conflict in the Eighties

Unionisation in the Port of London continued to advance, with some successes, but not as a mass movement. After the achievements of the early 1870s, support for the Labour Protection League waned everywhere except among stevedores and south bank corn porters. Significantly, Millwall corn porters, stevedores and labourers who struck in May 1876 against the employment 'of men from the country' to work by the week

---

[74] Lovell, *Stevedores and Dockers*, 61–2; *Hackney and Kingsland Gazette*, 22 November 1871; *Shipping and Mercantile Gazette*, 22 November 1871; *Standard*, 25 November 1871; *Times*, 25 November 1871.

[75] Lovell, *Stevedores and Dockers*, 66; *Shipping and Mercantile Gazette*, 2 July 1872; *Times*, 5 July 1872.

[76] MLD, LDC 167, 22 August 1873; EWID 021, 10 September 1872, 12 November 1872, 10 December 1872; EWID 023, 3 November 1874.

rather than the job failed to secure backing from workers elsewhere.[77] In April 1880, a strike for sixpence an hour by West India Dock labourers collapsed, but they gained a guaranteed day's work, and a thirty instead of twenty minutes mealtime midday break. London St. Katharine's labourers refused to join the West India action but independently struck for sixpence with success.[78]

Progress was most marked in skilled occupations. The Amalgamated Society of Watermen and Lightermen was founded after successful strikes by lightermen in 1871 and 1872. Members had little in common with other London port workers. Besides pay rises, journeymen lightermen, a 'society within a society', were bent on equal representation with Master Lightermen on the court of the Watermen's and Lightermen's Company and the preservation and enforcement of restrictions on entry to the trade. In contrast to the dying occupation of waterman, lightering was expanding and men who had not served an apprenticeship, so ineligible for a Company license, were entering the trade with licenses issued by the Thames Conservancy.[79] The stevedores, whose work could take them anywhere on the waterfront, had Labour Protection League branches in Poplar, Stepney, Millwall and Canning Town. An 1872 strike achieved much improved wages, union recognition, acceptance of their rule book and, most important, the right of their members to preference over non-members in hiring. In 1881 some stevedores formed the separate Stevedores Union, others stayed with the Labour Protection League.[80]

In 1887, resistance to a wage reduction in the London St. Katharine's Cutler Street warehouse resulted in the formation of a Tea Operatives' and General Labourers' Association and the company backed off. Led by the talented and pugnacious Ben Tillet, the association's objective, reforming 'the present system of contract and sub-contract upon a basis conducive to greater regularity of employment', went beyond immediate wage concerns to the institutional origins of the daily struggle for existence.[81] Tilbury preference workers received the East and West India Dock Company hourly rate of five pence, but ordinary casual labourers,

[77] *Lloyd's Weekly Newspaper*, 28 May 1876; Lovell, *Stevedores and Dockers*, 74–5.
[78] *East London Observer*, 17 April *1880*; *Times*, 23 April 1880; SC Sweating System. Second Report, Martindale, Q. 16,885; H. Llewellyn Smith and Vaughan Nash, *The Story of the Dockers' Strike Told by Two East Londoners* (T. Fisher Unwin, London, 1889), 38.
[79] J. Thomson and Adolph Smith, *Street Life in London* (Sampson Low, Marston, Searle & Rivington, London, 1977), 64–6; Cecil Llewellyn Wheble, 'The London Lighterage Trade; its History, Organisation and Economics' (Unpublished M.Sc. Thesis, London School Economics and Political Science, 1939), 152–7.
[80] Lovell, *Stevedores and Dockers*, 77–88.
[81] Jonathan Schneer, *Ben Tillett: Portrait of a Labour Leader* (Croom Helm, London, 1982).

most of whom travelled from London and had to meet the cost of fare and lodgings, were paid the local labour rate of just four pence. At the new union's instigation, 500 Tilbury dock labourers struck for higher pay in October 1888. The company directors rejected their appeal, citing the pending company amalgamation. Men brought from the company's other docks were persuaded to turn back, but the union could not prevent recruitment of agricultural labourers from the surrounding area, so after a month without pay, the desperate Tilbury men gave in.[82]

This resounding defeat was a personal disappointment to Tillett. In despairing evidence to the Lords Select Committee on Sweated Industries (1888–90), he contrasted sectional success with the experience of organising the mass of casual labourers. The poverty and the uncertainty of employment that ruled out regular union subscriptions, the lack of solidarity engendered by the divisive contract system, the problem of excluding outsiders, employer blacklisting of activists and absence of support from skilled workers were among the factors that Tillett considered made their unionisation 'impossible'.[83] Yet about ten months later, those same dock and wharf labourers, together with stevedores, lightermen, carmen, sailors, firemen and others, were involved in what became the port-wide 1889 Great Dock Strike, famous for its place in the unskilled 'new-unionism' phase of British labour history.

The wider metropolitan setting of the strike was a summer of unusually full employment and the remarkable success of the gas workers union in achieving an eight-hour day. Workers in the two dock systems, now with the same Joint Committee employer desperate to cut costs, faced deterioration in wages and conditions. Its chairman Charles Norwood was an unsympathetic figure, with public notoriety as the shipowner who had unsuccessfully sued the popular safety-at-sea campaigner, Samuel Plimsoll, for defamation.[84] The context included greater public awareness of port working conditions resulting from Charles Booth's investigations and the on-going public exposure of the dock labour system by parliamentary investigation of sweated labour. The Select Committee, in response to an excoriating Board of Trade report on conditions in East End trades, at first focussed on workshop and home-work industries, conventionally identified as 'sweating' labour, and refused to include

---

[82] Ibid., 33–6; *East London Observer*, 22 October 1888; *Times*, 1 November 1881.

[83] SC Sweating, Second Report, Tillett, Qq. 1348, 12,837–9, 1284, Driscoll Qq. 13,774–5, Todd, 15070; Schneer, *Tillett*, 33–5.

[84] Henry Pelling, *A History of British Trade Unionism*, Fourth Edition (Penguin Books, London, 1987), 83–93; *East London Observer*, 22 October 1888; ODNB, Charles Morgan Norwood (1825–1891).

dock and wharf labour. A protest meeting at Mile End in August 1888 changed their mind.[85] Committee chairman Lord Dunraven's draft report, rejected by the rest of the committee, made it clear that he was more convinced by the testimony of the labour representatives than what East and West India's Plat Taylor, London St. Katharine's Martindale and Millwall's Birt had to say: 'The opinion of the authorities at the docks generally is that there is a good deal of professional agitation at work, exciting discontent among the labourers, and although it is entirely possible that such influences are not entirely absent, yet this explanation will by no means account for the complaints which the labourers make...'

The final report, agreed under a new chairman, was anodyne: 'the state of the casual dock labourer was very miserable, the work uncertain, the wages low'. But the evidence on the system of employment, reported in considerable detail by *The Times*, spoke for itself.[86]

The 1889 Great Dock Strike

The 1889 strike originated in Tillett's Tea Operatives' Association response to an attempt by a new rival union to organise labourers at the East and West India's South Dock, where labourers threatened to stop work over the 'plus' allowed for discharging a vessel, a not unusual occurrence. Tillett took charge, persuaded the men to return to work and set out their demands, with a twenty-four-hour ultimatum, to the Joint Committee: 'No man to be taken on for less than four hours at a stretch, contract and piecework to be abolished, and wages to be raised to sixpence an hour with eight pence overtime'.[87] The Joint Committee refused and on 14 August 1889, the strike went ahead. With a foothold in the West India docks, Tillett now looked to the London St. Katharine's Victoria and Albert workers. Despite the fact that their employment in the most prosperous of London's docks made them relatively well-paid and with 'no definite grievances, except a general objection to contract work', they were persuaded to join the action.[88] The same company's workers at London and St. Katharine's, where the contract system was deeply engrained, were more reluctant to become involved and, with the memory of the earlier unsuccessful strike still fresh, so too were Tilbury workers. But by Monday, 19 August, all Joint Committee docks and Millwall were affected.

---

[85] PP 1887 LXXXIX.253 [331], Report to Board of Trade on Sweating System at East End of London; *Times*, 29 February 1888; *Times*, 20 September 1888, 31 August 1888, 29 August 1889.

[86] SC Sweating System, Fifth Report, xxii, lxxviii.

[87] Smith and Nash, *Dockers' Strike*, 33; Schneer, *Tillett*, 39–46.

[88] Smith and Nash, *Dockers' Strike*, 38.

What turned the dock labourers' action into the 'Great Dock Strike', with a port-wide dimension, was the stevedore decision to come out in support. Working every day up- and down the river in docks and wharves, and opposed to black-leg labour, stevedores were necessarily affected. Their support encouraged groups (some like the stevedores recognised as skilled workers) with particular demands of their own to stop work. These included lightermen, coal heavers, steamship workers, wharf and warehouse labourers, and the southside corn porters. By Thursday, 22 August, the port was effectively at a standstill and remained so until victory for the strikers on Saturday, 14 September.

The dramatic involvement of large numbers of less-skilled casual labourers, as also the Dock, Wharf, Riverside and General Labourers' Union of Great Britain and Ireland that resulted, positioned the strike within the so-called 'New Unionism' of the late nineteenth century, although this contemporary label has long been contested by historians of labour.[89] However, as already shown, the port was no stranger to organised labour before this and, despite the risks, even casual labourers had sometimes been prepared to strike and in a number of cases, this had proved an effective weapon against employers. This is not to deny the difficulties identified by Tillett earlier, or that the same sectional interests that fostered occupational unions militated against the development of more broadly-based associations.

The action was prompted by a minor issue, but its spread across the port is explained by long-standing grievances. 'For many years discontent has been sullenly smouldering among the dockers. Employment has been shrinking, and what has remained has become more uncertain and irregular'.[90] The considerable administrative talents several of the leaders brought to the strike, a flair for publicity, use of political allies and ability to maintain support were key factors in its ultimate success. Without these, it would almost certainly have failed. But although socialist ideas certainly influenced its leaders, opponents who blamed the dispute on political agitators were wide of the mark. Even before the events of 1889, London's port workers were further along the path of joint action than might be assumed.

There was never a golden age for dock labourers, but the contract system and the use of the 'plus' were deeply unpopular. In a combative 1991

---

[89] See A. E. P. Duffy, 'New Unionism in Britain, 1889–1890', *Economic History Review*, New Series, 14 (1961), 306–19; E. H. Hunt, *British Labour History 1815–1914* (Weidenfeld & Nicolson, London, 1981), 295–310; Wolfgang J. Mommsen and Hans Gerhard Husung, *The Development of Trade Unionism in Great Britain and Germany, 1880–1914* (Routledge, London, 1985).

[90] Smith and Nash, *Dockers' Strike*, 29.

article, Derek Matthews argues that, despite claims to the contrary by historians Hobsbawm, Lovell and Schneer (as well as Tillett himself) that dock work had intensified, there is no 'quantitative evidence that dockers worked harder in 1889 than they had ten or twenty years before'.[91] The 'quantitative' here is a telling reservation, but the crux of the 1889 strikers' case was not that they were having to work harder, but that the payment system was unjust and should be replaced by non-contracted piecework, at the rate of sixpence an hour. This 'docker's tanner', caught the public imagination, but, as the first historians of the dock strike, Smith and Nash, pointed out, the dispute was not about this. Sixpence an hour was already guaranteed for many and it was 'the amount of possible earnings per week that really matters to the labourer, and the question of wages is thus intimately bound up with that of irregularity of work'.[92]

Examining East End political culture in this period, Marc Brodie notes prevalent complaints about contractors. He argues that by employing, 'even within an apparent socialist framework', traditional radical concepts of Old Corruption, leading trade unionists referenced long-standing resentments. Brodie also suggests that working-class anger was individualised and 'directed at a corrupt foreman rather than the employer's system of wages'.[93] This may have been true for other East End workers but did not apply to most striking dock labourers in 1889. They accepted the trade union argument that the system itself was rotten; the dock companies rather than their middlemen, in some cases workers like themselves, were the target. Moreover, since some could recall a time before the widespread use of contractors, it did not seem far-fetched or impractical to envisage its replacement by a different scheme.

The Course of the Strike

Strategy and finances were handled by a United Strike Council, which met daily at stevedore headquarters Wades Arms, Poplar, with a committee at Sayes Court Deptford representing the south side. Eight district centres distributed food tickets. Daily meetings at Tower Hill and processions into central London gained public attention. Decorated floats and bands added a festive, theatrical air, while the range of occupations

---

[91] Derek Matthews, '1889 and All That. New Views on the New Unionism', *International Review of Social History*, 36 (1991), 42.
[92] Smith and Nash, 54.
[93] Marc Brodie, *The Politics of Poverty. The East End of London 1885–1914* (Oxford University Press, Oxford, 2004), 139–42, 202.

Illustration 7.2 The Dock Labourers Great Strike in London, 1889.
© *Illustrated London News* Ltd./Mary Evans.

represented reminded watchers of the port-wide nature of the strike.[94]
Better-off Londoners' fears that these large gatherings would threaten
their comfortable, propertied lives were confounded. The respectability, moderation and stress on orderliness of the strike leaders reinforced
Liberal views of trade unionism as a force for good.[95] The generally
restrained conduct of the strikers should not be attributed solely to their
leadership. Those who daily laboured in the docks or on the waterfront
were well-accustomed to disciplined behaviour.

With the press generally sympathetic to the strikers, the dock companies' Joint Committee had 'to contend throughout against a hostile

[94] Smith and Nash, 131; Lovell, *Stevedores and Dockers*, 109; Janice Norwood, 'The
Performance of Protest: the 1889 Dock Strike On and Off the Stage', in Peter Yeandle,
Katherine Newey and Jeffrey Richards (eds.), *Politics, Performance and Popular Culture.
Theatre and Society* (Manchester University Press, Manchester, 2016), 250–4.

[95] Pitts Theology Library, Henry Edward Manning, MSS 002, 'Paper on the London
Strike and Political Economy' (Undated); United States, Reports from the Consuls,
No. 109, October 1889, 24 August 1889, 296; Henry Hyde Champion, *The Great Dock
Strike: In London, August* 1889 (Swan Sonnenschein, London, 1890), 6; Stedman Jones,
Outcast London, 15–7.

public opinion'.[96] Donations flowed in, most from within London. Street collections alone raised a thousand pounds, an East End benefit concert at the New Palace of Varieties produced thirty-one, the metropolitan *Pall Mall Gazette* and *London Evening News*, as well as the left-wing nationals *Star* and *Reynold News*, channelled contributions. Local organisations set up relief committees and organised collections. Middle or upper-class donors (including Catherine Gladstone, the statesman's wife) attracted attention, but much of the £13,430 raised came from working people. With £4,473 from trade unions and societies and over £30,000 from Australia in the last weeks of the strike, the eventual total reached over £18,000.[97]

Picket lines, set at every dock and on boats in the river, succeeded in turning back men brought in by the Joint Committee from Liverpool and Southampton, as well as American sailors from the cattle ships.[98] There was little to fear from 'amateurs, clerks from the City' whose attempts at discharging vessels, *The Times* reported, 'were slow, and barren of results'.[99] A greater risk was the recruitment of 'outsiders', attracted by 20 shillings a week and a permanent post offered by the Joint Committee.[100] Strike notices warning blacklegs of serious consequences, and the threatening presence of pickets, were intended to deter them and may well have done so. 'That a certain amount of violence *was* used, I am prepared to admit', wrote the socialist Henry Champion.[101]

Joint Committee claims that picketing was intimidation, and therefore illegal, were rejected by the Metropolitan Chief Police Commissioner and the Home Secretary. Only a few cases of open assault by pickets reached the courts. The relatively low-paid police constables may have sympathised with the strikers, but they had good reason not to stir up additional trouble by excessive intervention or seeming to side with the employers. Norwood badgered the Commissioner 'by letter, by telegram and by word of mouth, but all in vain'; his messages were dismissed by officers as 'over-excited'; and maintaining order on dock premises was deemed the responsibility of the dock police, not the metropolitan force.[102]

---

[96] Smith and Nash, 97; *Times*, 4 October 1889.
[97] Champion, *Great Dock Strike*, 7; *Lloyd's Weekly*, 8 September 1889; Ann Stafford, *A Match to Fire the Thames* (Hodder and Stoughton, London, 1961), Appendix.
[98] *Times*, 23 August 1889. 24 August 1889, 30 August 1889; Reports from the Consuls, 11 September 1889, 314; Lovell, *Stevedores and Dockers*, 107.
[99] Times, 30 August 1889.
[100] *Times*, 23 August 1889, 24 August 1889, 30 August 1889; Reports from the Consuls, 11 September 1889, 314; Lovell, *Stevedores and Dockers*, 107.
[101] Champion, *Great Dock Strike*, 25.
[102] Joan Ballhatchet, 'The Police and the London Dock Strike', *History Workshop*, 32 (1991), 54–68.

The Joint Committee did not cope well. Some directors and senior officers were on holiday when the strike started, so over a week elapsed before their robust rejection of the strikers' demands appeared. A meeting with union leaders on 22 August achieved nothing. In a revealing misjudgement of the issues, they offered to replace the 'plus' at the East and West India Docks by the contract system operating at the London and St. Katharine's docks. This was rejected, and the stoppage continued.[103]

With more than 300 vessels waiting to load or unload, the Joint Committee was also in dispute with dock customers. At an acrimonious meeting with seventy shipowners led by P&O's Thomas Sutherland, they heard that the labourers' demands were justified and should be met. A later deputation, headed by the less combative Sir Donald Currie, who had several large ships stranded in the East India Dock, proposed settling the strike by allowing shipowners to discharge their own vessels. This too was refused.[104] But if the Joint Committee was obdurate, the equally affected wharfingers and granary owners were not. The manager of the large Butlers Wharf agreed to sixpence an hour, followed by other wharfingers and some private warehouses. However, so long as the lightermen stayed on strike, only vessels berthed alongside could resume work.[105]

By September the outlook for the strikers looked bleak. After almost four weeks of stoppage, union funds were depleted and food tickets unaffordable, so charities were feeding possibly 50,000 people each day. Pickets, some paid, were not always assiduous and the job was hard. Strike Committee inspectors found that, 'in the chilly hours before dawn', those on guard sometimes 'strayed to warmer quarters'. Despite reports of price rises due to meat and vegetable shortages, factories suffering from a lack of coal and the City's tea and spice traders doing little business, there was evidence of increasing activity in the warehouses and on the river. Keeping men on strike proved particularly difficult at the London and St. Katharine's docks, where there was less commitment to the cause. Lovell's conclusion that 'the picket lines held, but only just' seems correct, and unsurprisingly the struggle to keep the upper hand took its toll on the men's morale.[106]

---

[103] *Times*, 23 August 1889, 67; *London Daily News*, 23 August 1889.

[104] *Morning Post*, 24 August 1889; Joan Ballhatchet, 'The Police and the London Dock Strike', *History Workshop*, 32 (1991), 54–68, 24 August 1889; Reports from the Consuls, 24 August 1889, 309–10; *Lloyd's Weekly*, 8 September 1889.

[105] Smith and Nash, *Dockers' Strike*, 127–8; *Lloyd's Weekly*, 8 September 1889; Lovell, *Stevedores and Dockers*, 111.

[106] Smith and Nash, *Dockers' Strike*, 103; *Times*, 7 September 1889; Reports from the Consuls, 31 August 1889, 311; Lovell, *Stevedores and Dockers*, 107–8.

Illustration 7.3 1889 Great Dock Strike commemoration poster.
© Mary Evans Picture Library.

With no end in sight, militants on the Strike Committee led by Tom
Mann independently published the 'No-Work Manifesto' calling for all
London workers to stop work. A rash and risky move, there was little evidence of a potential positive response and moderates objected
that the threat of a general strike would alienate the wider public. The
'No-Work Manifesto' was not put to the test. When news of a substantial donation from Australian waterfront unions arrived, it was with-
drawn. As a commemorative poster with the banner headline 'The New
World Unites With The Old World to Help Dock Labourers' acknowl-
edged, the gift saved the strike (Illustration 7.3). Relief committees were
now able to meet the demand for food tickets, and, with daily processions no longer vital for fundraising, the campaign focussed on meetings
and picketing efforts.[107]

---

[107] Smith and Nash, *Dockers' Strike*, 75–6, 119–252; *Lloyd's Weekly Newspaper*, 1 September
1889; *Times*, 28 August 1889; Schneer, *Tillett*, 43; P. F. Donovan, 'Australia and the
Great London Dock Strike 1889', *Labour History* 23 (1972), 17–26.

The strike was reinvigorated, but the Joint Committee refused to negotiate and showed no sign of surrender.[108] Up to this point the Lord Mayor had rejected calls from the Chamber of Commerce to intervene, but despite the Joint Committee's insistence that the dispute was a private matter, its impact on London made it incontrovertibly a London matter. On 30 August the deputy Lord Mayor and Cardinal Edward Manning, many of whose Irish parishioners were port labourers and was himself the son and brother of former dock company chairmen, met the Joint Committee. It was not a successful encounter. The directors did not take kindly to being treated as 'a merciless, money-grubbing set of men'. On his part the Cardinal observed that 'I never in my life preached to so impenitent a congregation'.[109]

The initiative then passed to a six-member Mansion House Committee of Conciliation. Lord Mayor Sir James Whitehead was a self-made man, with a successful commercial past and radical views, his deputy Sir Andrew Lusk was a shipowner and Liberal banker Sir John Lubbock MP chaired the London Chamber of Commerce.[110] Manning and Sidney Buxton MP had links with the Strike Committee, and the Bishop of London had heard evidence of dock worker poverty when serving with Manning on the 1885 Royal Commission on the Housing of the Working Classes. Apart from the Anglican bishop, who told a fellow cleric that 'my heart is with the dockers, my head is with the directors', the weight of opinion in this metropolitan group was that the strikers deserved a settlement.[111] In fact, Tillett subsequently characterised the role of the committee, or possibly just Cardinal Manning, as acting on behalf of the men.[112] London MPs backing the dockers were not all Liberals. Frederick Wootton Isaacson, the Conservative MP for Stepney, was a supporter, but the Conservative member for Limehouse, London St. Katharine's Dock Company director Edward Norris, vigorously promoted the dock company case in the press.[113]

[108] *Lloyd's Weekly*, 8 September 1889.
[109] *Times*, 28 August 1889, 31 August 1889; Sidney Holland Viscount Knutsford, *In Black and White* (Edward Arnold & Co., London, 1928), 110; Edmund Sheridan Purcell, *Life of Cardinal Manning, Vol. II* (Macmillan, London, 1896), 662.
[110] Andrew Connell, '"I feel I am placed at a very great disadvantage". Sir James Whitehead: the Parliamentary Travails of a Liberal Meritocrat', *Journal of Liberal History*, Vol. 92 (2016), 25–33; J. Ewing Ritchie, *Famous City Men* (Tinsley Brothers, London, 1884), 78; ODNB Sir Andrew Lusk, (1810–1909), John Lubbock, (1834–1913), Frederick Temple, Frederick (1821–1902); H. L. Malchow, *Gentlemen Capitalists: The Social and Political World of the Victorian Businessman* (Stanford University Press, Stanford, 1992), 351.
[111] Ann Stafford, *A Match to Fire the Thames* (Hodder & Stoughton, London, 1961), 21.
[112] RC Labour, Minutes (Group B) Vol. 1, Tillett, Qq. 3379–81; RC Labour Fifth and Final Report, 185.
[113] Alex Christian Windscheffel, 'Villa Toryism? The Making of London Conservatism, 1868–1896' (Unpublished PHD thesis, Royal Holloway, University of London, 2000), 131–5.

The Joint Committee felt obliged to engage with the conciliators but resented their intervention. Chairman Norwood subsequently complained that 'the most effective aid and encouragement given to the strikers, next to the inaction of the government and the police authorities, was the constant and ill-timed interference of outside and irresponsible persons'.[114] The ensuing negotiations were fraught and came close to breaking down, but eventually the Joint Committee grudgingly conceded the sixpence an hour, to start in January 1890. This was initially accepted by the delighted strike leaders, even though it meant that the strikers would have to wait for their reward effectively until April, since little dock work was available in the slack winter months. On mature reflection, faced with explaining this decision to their associates, they withdrew their agreement and the chance of victory receded.

Skilful intervention by Cardinal Manning averted disaster. At a long meeting on their home ground in the East End, he persuaded the Strike Committee to agree to an immediate return, with a compromise of 4 November as a date for the new hourly and overtime rates and the replacement of the contract system. Agreement was reached on Saturday, 14 September, and work resumed on Monday. Even so, the lightermen's dispute with the Masters was not finally resolved in the men's favour until the end of November.[115] However, enforcement of the Mansion House agreement in respect of meal-time pay proved particularly problematic on the wharves, leading to several local strikes over the following months.[116]

Aftermath

Unable to lower charges to cover the increase in wages, some wharves permanently lost business to rail and competing continental ports may have made some long-term transhipment gains from the strike, but overall London's trade recovered quickly.[117] Support for the stevedore and lightermen unions strengthened and in mid-September 1889, Tillett's Tea Operatives' Association, now with 18,000 members, became the Dock, Wharf, Riverside and General Labourers' Union of Great Britain and Ireland, a title reflecting aspirations more than reality.

[114] *Times*, 4 October 1889.

[115] John Temple, *History of the Origin and Progress of the Company of Watermen and Lightermen of the River Thames*, Vol. 5, 1883–1920 (Lavenham Press, London, 2008), 57–60, 62; ODNB Thomas Brassey (1836–1918).

[116] Smith and Nash, *Dockers' Strike*, 136–153; PP 1893–4 C. 6894-VIII, RC on Labour Volume III, Frey, Q. 16,746; PP 1892 C. 6795.VII, RC on Labour, Answers to Schedules of Questions, 51, 160.

[117] RC Port of London, Minutes, Gomme, Qq. 7836–7; *Times*, 31 July 1890.

In the port as a whole, far from reducing occupational sectionalism, the strike enhanced it. A separate South Side Labour Protection League was established and steamship workers, tugboat men and those working with port machinery were inspired to set up their own associations. Refusing to join the Docker's Union, foremen and permanent workers created their own. As Lovell argues, trade unionism in the London's port after 1889 was 'a house divided'.[118] It was also a house built on the favourable economic conditions of 1889–90. Over the following decade, faced by depressed trade and an aggressive fightback by anti-union employers, membership fell and still shallow-rooted mass unionism withered.

Some 1889 achievements survived beyond the end of the century, including the new pay rates and minimum four hours' work, but others proved short-lived.[119] The Joint Committee replaced piecework by hourly pay, cutting three pence off a day's pay by excluding the lunchtime half-hour. Union representatives, under the Mansion House agreement allowed to monitor piecework sub-contracting and to control hiring, were ousted.[120] Other developments also weakened union influence. In September 1890, shipowners nationally banded together in the Shipping Federation, 'a fighting machine to counter the strike weapon' by supplying 'free-labour'. As a result, strikes by stevedores and dockers in the autumn of 1890 in support of seafarers and a dockers strike in June 1900 collapsed.[121]

Faced with the free-labour threat and withdrawal of recognitions by some employers, even the powerful stevedores were forced to concede the rule-book amendment. Within a few years, control over recruitment was threatened by the movement of the port downstream, which created practical difficulties in keeping out non-unionists. It was also jeopardised by the increasingly dominant large shipping lines, which preferred to employ their own stevedores and were hostile to trade unions.[122]

The Joint Committee reorganised dock labour along lines advocated by Booth. The number of permanent workers increased, and casual labourers

---

[118] Lovell, *Stevedores and Dockers*, 112–121, 130; RC on Labour, Answers to Schedule of Questions, 9; Schneer, *Tillett*, 50–1.

[119] RC Port of London, Appendices, 20th Day No. 10, 814–5.

[120] LSKD 638, 31 July 1890; RC Labour, Fifth and Final Report, 145–6; RC Labour, Minutes (Group B) Vol. 1, Hubbard, Q.4778; Lovell, *Stevedores and Dockers*, 134–5.

[121] L. H. Powell, *The Shipping Federation. A History of the First Sixty Years 1890–1950* (Shipping Federation, London, 1950), 5; Alessandro Saluppo, 'Strikebreaking and Anti-Unionism on the Waterfront: The Shipping Federation, 1890–1914', *European History Quarterly*, 49 (2019) 573–80; Jonathan Schneer, *London 1900. The Imperial Metropolis* (Yale, New Haven & London, 1999), 51–61; Lovell, *Stevedores and Dockers*, 138–40, 145–8.

[122] Ibid., 77–88.

were divided into three registered categories. The 'A' list labourers were those regularly employed and paid weekly, but not entitled to sick pay and pensions; hourly paid 'B' men had a preferential right to work next, followed by those on the 'C' list. These were the 'ticket' men. If any vacancies were left, they went to what an observer of the call-on at the London Dock in 1902 described as 'strangers of no status at all' – the casuals.[123] By 1900, almost two-thirds of the dock labourers in the north bank docks were permanent. The system, Beveridge explained, 'put a premium upon regular attendance for work and good behaviour, since men were to be moved up and down the list according to their merits'.[124] There were echoes here of arrangements earlier in the century designed to cement a dependent, controlling association between workers and employer.[125] Stedman Jones points out that middle-class observers saw such decasualisation as a major achievement because in their eyes it distinguished between the respectable working class and the residual fringe of loafers and idlers.[126] However, there were other port employers and the Joint Committee docks employed only a fifth of Port of London labourers.[127] Extending full-time employment in the docks left fewer vacancies for those on the 'B' and 'C' lists, who then had to compete for work on wharves and elsewhere. The benefits of decasualisation for some meant increased underemployment and depressed earnings for the rest.[128]

The Joint Committee now allowed steamship lines to unload their own vessels, and most chose to do so.[129] Dispensing with this loss-making survival of a time when landing and storage were linked made economic sense. But there was an additional reason. As P&O's Sutherland explained: '... the great dock strike in 1889 and the subsequently disturbed state of labour in the East End of London showed that if the dock company continued to discharge all the ships, as up to that time they had done, the risk of labour agitation against the company would be very great'.[130]

Transferring loading and discharge to shipowners or their contractors worsened call-on conditions. As a 1907 report on West Ham noted,

[123] George R. Sims, *Living London. Its Work and Its Play, Its Humour and Its Pathos. Its Sights and Scenes. Vol. I.* (Cassel and Co., London, 1902), 170.
[124] Booth, *Life and Labour of the People of London. Second Series: Industry, Volume 3* (Macmillan, London, 1903), 413–5; W. H. Beveridge, *Unemployment. A Problem of Industry* (Longmans, Green and Co., London, 1909), 88.
[125] Beveridge, *Unemployment*, 89; Lovell, *Stevedores and Dockers*, 137.
[126] Stedman Jones, *Outcast London*, 319–20; Phillips and Whiteside, *Casual Labour*, 51–3.
[127] RC Port of London, Minutes, Sutherland, Q. 1951; RC on Labour, Vol. I, Birt Qq. 6980–2.
[128] Beveridge, *Unemployment*, 92.
[129] RC Port of London, Scott, Q. 6516.
[130] Ibid., Sutherland, Q. 1951.

these had no concern for continuity of employment and 'any attempt at organisation would be looked on with disfavour with foremen, who like to have a wide margin of choice'.[131]

Despite all this, 'the struggle of 1889 was a real landmark', as Mann wrote later.[132] A longer historical perspective reminds us that the strike transformed the character of labour relations in the Port of London. However emasculated and unsuccessful London's new port unions turned out to be in the short term, there was no going back to when permanent unions were the exception rather than the rule, less-skilled workers lacked representation and most dock companies and wharfingers only occasionally had reason to fear worker militancy. Whether they resisted or accepted trade unions, port employers now had to take account of their existence.

The strike revealed a side of the East London and its inhabitants obscured by images of hopeless degeneracy and fecklessness, proving in Buxton's words, 'that the average docker was himself by no means the "failure", the ne'er-do-well, the hopeless wreck of humanity, of popular fancy'.[133] Distinguishing between a mass of 'respectable' casual labourers and a smaller 'residuum' comforted those who feared the influence of socialism on their fellow Londoners. 'They might have made a revolution; instead of which they acted as constitutional Socialists', observed the socialist Henry Champion. Indeed, Stedman Jones argues that the strike ended fears of revolution: 'the casual residuum was no longer a political threat – only a social problem'.[134]

Before the publicity generated by the strike, there was limited public knowledge of the parlous financial situation of London's major dock companies. Even Manning was surprised to learn that they were not the prosperous businesses he had assumed when first involved. With their directors' high-handed behaviour during the dispute encouraging greater scrutiny, the issue of their privileged status as private enterprises – long the target of critics – became the subject of wider discussion.[135] This was part of the context that made the reform of the Port of London a pressing issue, not only just for port users and trade unions but also the Corporation and newly created London County Council.

---

[131] Howarth and Wilson, *West Ham, 200,* 215.

[132] Tom Mann, *Tom Mann's Memoirs. With a Preface by Ken Coates* (MacGibbon & Kee, London, 1923, 1967 Edition), 65.

[133] Sidney Buxton, Introduction, Smith and Nash, *Dockers' Strike,* 17; Stedman Jones, *Outcast London,* 283–91.

[134] Schneer, *Tillett,* 43; Stedman Jones, *Outcast London,* 321.

[135] Purcell, *Manning,* 658; *Lloyd's Weekly,* 1 September 1889; Broodbank, *Port of London II,* 277; RC Labour, Fifth and Final Report, 348–9.

8   Port and Populace II
Maritime Industries and Communities in the Second Half of the Century

Illustration 8.1 View across Bow Creek, Blackwall, to Mare's Shipyard, 1854. © *Illustrated London News* Ltd./Mary Evans.

> Let it be well noted that the inhabitants of Wapping Island are perhaps exceptionally well off for labouring people. They are nearly all workers on the river … men whose toil is about the hardest, but whose pay is also about the best, of London labourers. It is precarious, and as it comes it goes; but there is more room for providence in Wapping Island than in most of our courts and alleys.[1]

In 1850, the East India Docks still remained the port's outer limit and there was just a fringe of industry along the Isle of Dogs waterfront. The opening of the Victoria Dock in 1858 stretched London's dock system

---

[1] *East London Observer*, 14 January 1871.

214

downriver to West Ham, bringing industrialisation and urbanisation with it. Along with these developments came major changes in the lives and livelihoods, not only of those who handled cargoes but also those employed in London's maritime industries. The iron shipbuilding industry boomed then declined, beet sugar refining replaced sugar baking and steam-powered milling transformed grain handling.

Shipbuilding

At mid-century, London was both the producer of high-quality timber sailing vessels and the national leader in iron shipbuilding and marine engineering. Over the next decade, the iron side expanded mightily, trouncing sail. In 1866, the leading yards launched twenty-five iron steamships and just seven sailing ships, two with iron hulls.[2] London's shipbuilding capital became the Isle of Dogs – transformed from a pastoral backwater to a place of noise and furnaces.

There was no comparable large-scale development on the more constricted south bank, but its well-known engineering firms prospered.[3] New players came into London shipbuilding, most with an engineering rather than commercial background. The seven major firms operating in the period 1854–59 were huge ventures. Thames Ironworks and Millwall took advantage of the 1856 introduction of limited liability and incorporation to extend their resources.[4] Incorporated or not, virtually all newcomers operated as personal fiefdoms, but only Joseph Samuda, Member of Parliament, and member of the Board of Works, achieved comparable metropolitan prominence to that of the Wigram family in an earlier age.[5] The 1850s were generally good years for London shipbuilding and marine engineering, despite a post-Crimean War slump and a sharp fall in orders in 1859. As in the past, the industry benefited from lucrative government contracts, and there were still sufficient shipowners, at home and abroad, prepared to pay elevated London yard prices. Technologically these were far from backward, but they did not lack equally capable rivals elsewhere, especially on the Clyde.[6] Financing and managing a large order book proved a problem for some, including John

---

[2] PP 1867 LXXX.127 [417], Trade and Navigation Accounts. Return of Vessels above Fifty Tons built at each port of the United Kingdom.

[3] Barry, P., *Dockyard Economy and Naval Power* (Sampson, Low, Son and Co., London, 1863), 22, 294–7; Crossick, *Artisan Elite*, 49–50.

[4] Arnold, *Iron Shipbuilding*, 7, 54–64.

[5] S. ODNB, Joseph D'Aguilar (1813–1885).

[6] Butt, John, 'The Industries of Glasgow', in W. Hamish Fraser and Irene Maver (eds.), *Glasgow. Vol. II: 1830–1912* (Manchester University Press, Manchester, 1996), 117.

Scott Russell, builder of the *Great Eastern*, whose yard folded. However, shipyards were valuable physical assets and typically re-emerged under new owners.

London did well from a feverish nationwide explosion in ship-building orders between 1860 and 1865, benefiting particularly from mail contract steamer contracts. The collapse of the Overend Gurney Bank, a direct and indirect investor in shipping, brought the boom to a sudden halt in 1866. Although Scottish and other northern centres recovered fairly quickly, there was no such respite for London's yards, which closed for lack of orders.[7] Contemporary commentators blamed speculative ventures, high wages and union resistance to reductions. But these were hardly new. Ultimately, more significant was London's distance from supplies of coal and iron.[8] Faith in London builders had also been damaged before the Overend Gurney crisis. After the bankruptcy of Mare's yard in 1855, the GSNC, a formerly loyal customer, only once ever used a Thames yard again. P&O also had a bad experience. After its reputation was damaged by the disastrous performance of nine vessels built by London yards, it returned to Clyde builders.[9]

London shipbuilding was decimated, but not annihilated. Output, almost 10 per cent of national tonnage before the crisis, averaged only 3 per cent annually over the next two decades.[10] The mid-1870s were slightly better years, but a severe cyclical downturn in 1878 was followed by severe depression in 1885 and 1886. A naval shipbuilding boom brought recovery in the 1890s.[11] The historic Blackwall firms, by now builders in both wood and iron, proved tenacious. Wigram's disposed of the yard in 1877 to concentrate on shipowning, but Green's prospered by expanding the repair side of its business. Samuda's well-equipped

[7] RC on Trade Unions (1867–68), Ninth Report, Dudgeon Qq. 16878–9; Arnold, *Iron Shipbuilding*, 61–98, 86–8; *Survey of London XLIV*, 672–675; *Times*, 28 November 1866; RC Trade Unions (1967–68), Ninth Report, Samuda, Q. 16746.
[8] Sidney Pollard, 'The Decline of Shipbuilding on the Thames', *Economic History Review, Second Series*, 3 (1950), 79–85.
[9] Robert Edward Forrester, 'The General Steam Navigation Company c.1850–1913: A Business History', Doctoral Thesis, University of Greenwich, 2006; Crosbie Smith, *Coal, Steam and Ships, Engineering, Enterprise and Empire on the Nineteenth-Century Seas* (Cambridge University Press, Cambridge, 2018), 330, 333–38, 355.
[10] Sarah Palmer. 'Ship-building in South-east England, 1800–1913' in Simon Ville, *Shipbuilding in the United Kingdom: A Regional Approach. Research in Maritime History, No.4* (IMEHA, St. John's, Newfoundland, 1992), 60; Sidney Pollard and Paul Robertson, *The British Shipbuilding Industry 1870–1914* (Harvard University Press, Cambridge, 1979), 26.
[11] Pollard and Robertson, *Shipbuilding Industry*, 26–30; *London Evening Standard*, 13 February 1886; Arnold, *Iron Shipbuilding*, 12, 104–5, 125–7.

yard did well with naval orders, yachts and small commercial vessels, but after his death went into voluntary liquidation in 1892.[12] On the south bank, firms focussed successfully on merchant shipping and repairs, essential in a busy port, proved a lifeline for many yards.[13] By the end of the century, Thames shipbuilding was a combination of 'highly sophisticated naval ships and often very basic commercial and private boats', tied to the fortunes of two companies. Thames Ironworks, a successful survivor of the 1866 crisis, focussed on Admiralty work. Yarrows, founded in 1865, was a major international supplier of torpedo boats. The departure of Yarrows from the Thames in 1904 and the collapse of Thames Ironworks in 1912 dealt the final blow to London shipbuilding on any scale.[14]

The Shipbuilding Workforce

In the boom year 1865, Thames shipbuilding and marine engineering firms altogether employed about 27,000 men.[15] Most were skilled, but there were also large numbers of labourers. The transition to iron shipbuilding fundamentally changed the organisation of shipyard work.[16] Now traditional workers, including shipwrights, caulkers, riggers and sailmakers, all unionised, found themselves working alongside men with expertise as ironworkers, boilermakers and engineers. Some hailed from Scotland or northern England, bringing their own customs and practices to the Thames waterfront.[17] Timber work was still essential. In 1867, despite high shipbuilding unemployment, London shipwrights demonstrated their industrial muscle when they refused to accept a cut from seven shillings a day, which established this as the standard for the rest of the century, although piecework was the norm

---

[12] *Survey of London*, 44, 535–6, 569–74.
[13] Crossick, *Kentish London*, 49–50; Graham G. Jones, 'Victorian Suburban Society, A Study of Deptford and Lewisham' (Doctoral Thesis, Birkbeck College, University of London, 1980), 487.
[14] *Times*, 27 March 1886. Pollard, 'Decline of Shipbuilding', 79–88; Banbury, *Shipbuilders*, 181–6, 289–91, 253–7; Arnold, *Iron Shipbuilding*, 89, 106–22, 128, 134–49.
[15] Pollard, 'Decline of Shipbuilding', 79–84, 88; RC Trade Unions (1867–68), Ninth Report, Samuda, Q. 16079, Divers, Q. 16,998, 17,166–9, Wigram, Q. 1658; RC Labour, Answers, 226; Pollard, 'Decline of Shipbuilding', 88.
[16] Keith McClelland and Alastair Reid, 'Wood, Iron and Steel: Technology, Labour and Trade Union Organisation in the Shipbuilding Industry', in Royden Harrison and Jonathan Zeitlin (eds.), *Divisions of Labour. Skilled Workers and Technological Change in Nineteenth Century England* (Harvester Press, Brighton, 1985), 151–184.
[17] Thomas Wright, *Some Habits and Customs of the Working Classes by A Journeyman Engineer* (Tinsley Brothers, London, 1867), 252–3; RC Trade Unions, Ninth Report, Divers, Q. 17,009, Samuda, Q. 16711.

for repairs.[18] However, as with other former sail trades, demand for their traditional skills fell away with the progress of steam shipping. 'Not much is heard by the outside world of their misfortunes: they are proud men and have a history', observed Booth in 1903.[19]

Like wooden shipbuilding, iron construction involved a number of different unionised trades, including boiler-making, engineering, plating, riveting, turning and pattern making.[20] The most prominent unions, both established in the early 1850s but with many antecedents, were the United Society of Boilermakers and Iron Shipbuilders and the Amalgamated Society of Engineers, which spanned a range of industries.[21] All ironwork unions controlled entry through apprenticeships and provided friendly society benefits, including out-of-work pay. A tight labour market in these skilled trades meant that shipyard wages invariably rose at busy times, so unions focussed not on raising wages but on resisting reductions in the downturn. A bitter five-month engineers strike in the 1879 trade depression, a response to a concerted attack on wages by leading employers, ended in failure. But within two years, economic recovery ensured a rise to previous levels.[22]

Not all disputes were about wages. Demarcation and controlling entry were issues. When Wigram's recruited boilermakers to train its shipwrights in iron work in the early 1850s, the trainers were blacklisted in other yards. Employment of non-union men led to an unsuccessful six-month strike in 1890.[23] Shipbuilding unions opposed overtime. They regulated working hours and break times, but outside the normal

---

[18] Pollard and Robertson, *Shipbuilding Industry*, 153; *Times*, 4 February 1867; RC Trade Unions, Ninth Report (1867–68), Robson, Qq. 17,675–9; PP 1896 XCIII.277 [C. 8232], Statistical Tables, Trade Unions Eighth Report, 39; PP 1906 CXII.1 [55], Reports of Friendly Societies, 589; W. C. Steadman, 'Shipbuilding', in Frank W. Galton (ed.), *Workers On Their Industries* (Swan Sonnenschein & Co., London, 1896), 64–5.

[19] Statistical Tables, Trade Unions Eighth Report, 39; Friendly Societies, 589; Steadman, 'Shipbuilding', 64–5; Charles Booth, *Life and Labour of the People in London. Second Series: Industry I* (Macmillan, London, 1903), 275–81; Hersh, Mark 'Sailmakers: The Maintenance of the Craft Traditions in the Age of Steam' in Royden Harrison and Jonathan Zeitlin (eds.), *Divisions of Labour. Skilled Workers and Technological Change in Nineteenth Century England* (Harvester Press, Brighton, 1985), 87–113.

[20] John Glover, 'On the Decline of Shipbuilding on the Thames', *Journal of the Statistical Society*, 32 (1869), 292.

[21] J. E. Mortimer, *History of the Boilermakers' Society. Volume 1 1832–1906* (George Allen & Unwin, London, 1973), 17–56; James B. Jefferys, *The Story of the Engineers 1800–1945* (EP Publishing, London, 1945), 27–3; Pollard and Robertson, *British Shipbuilding*, 156–63.

[22] RC Trade Unions (1867–68), Ninth Report, Allen, Qq. 17,543–8, Robson, Q. 17658; RC Labour, Minutes, Group A, Hills, Qq. 24,896–900; RC Labour, Answers, 314; Jefferys, *Engineers*, 63, 98–9; Pollard and Robertson, *Shipbuilding*, 164–5; *London Evening Standard*, 10 February 1879, 12 February 1879.

[23] RC Trade Unions (1867–68), Ninth Report, Allen, Qq. 17,543–8, Robson, Q. 17,658; RC Labour Group A, Hills, Qq. 24,896–24,900; RC Labour, Answers, 314.

working day, hours were unrestricted and breaks were not guaranteed.[24] A projected union ban on overtime was the London focus of a famous three-month lockout by engineering employers in 1852. In Lancashire, at issue was also the introduction of piecework and non-union labour, but London's gang labour tradition of indirect employment made these less significant here. This dispute ended in short-term union defeat, but even at the end of the century, most London shipyard unions retained considerable autonomy in the labour process.[25]

In 1851 the Engineers had explained that working long hours through overtime 'deprives them of rational enjoyment, prevents them from using opportunities for culture, and weakens their physical powers ... there is no necessity for it, because hundreds are begging to be allowed to take their share of the work'.[26] But opposition was not a question of welfare and fairness. Members' unemployment affected union finances. Most shipbuilding unions paid out-of-work benefits, and even the shipwrights, who did not, tried to discourage the practice by not paying allowances for accidents that happened after normal hours.[27] Nevertheless, despite employer claims to the contrary, it was accepted that overtime was sometimes unavoidable. Union leaders also recognised that earning extra income was tempting. For these reasons, while systematic overtime remained 'a standing grievance', by the 1890s, their rules generally specified a limited number of overtime hours.[28]

The context for opposition to overtime and wage cuts was insecurity of employment. Although relatively well-paid, the work was intermittent, and the launch of a new vessel meant unemployment for its makers. Even in good times, a man's income could vary and as a former engineer wrote, shipyard workers were used to weathering the shipbuilding cycle, 'in one way and another they contrive to exist till the turn of trade comes'.[29] But the impact of the 1866 shipbuilding crisis was greater than anything London's shipbuilders and their families had ever experienced.[30] Not only were the Poplar yards affected, but there was similar hardship across the river at Deptford and Greenwich, where

---

[24] RC Trade Unions, Ninth Report, Robson, Qq. 17,622–624, 17,633.
[25] Hunt, *Labour History*, 251–2; Jefferys, *Engineers*, 38–42. Thomas Hughes, 'Account of the Lock-Out of Engineers 1851–52', *Trades Societies and Strikes. Report of the Committee on Trades Societies, National Association for the Promotion of Social Science* (John. W. Parker and Son, London, 1860).
[26] Hughes, 'Lock-Out', 188.
[27] RC Trade Unions (1867–68), Ninth Report, Robson, Q. 18,025.
[28] Hughes 'Lock-Out', 252; Sidney Webb and Harold Cox, *The Eight Hours Day* (Walter Scott, London, 1891), 154–5; RC Labour Fifth and Final Report, 105.
[29] Wright, *Habits and Customs*, 253–4, 257–60.
[30] *Times*, 7 February 1867, 19 March 1867.

bread riots broke out in February 1867.[31] Some builders left London for opportunities in northern England or Scotland, where they originated. Others took advantage of passage money and clothing offered by emigration societies to go to Canada and Australia.[32] Unskilled yard labourers had no such options. Depressed dock and wharf employment, as well as freezing weather, meant alternative job opportunities were few, leaving them reliant on the Poor Law or charity to survive.[33] To stave off this fate, shipwrights, iron workers and engineers, 'the more provident class' as a Poor Law Inspector described them, at first relied on savings or union benefits, then on selling off possessions until forced to seek help.

Poor Law funds were overwhelmed and charitable efforts were impeded by opposition from the leading shipbuilding employers, who considered that 'the distress was not so great as it was represented to be'.[34] Eventually, London merchants persuaded the Lord Mayor to establish a Mansion House relief committee to solicit donations and allocate funds to local charities. Much of the £16,244 raised came from the City, and it did not pass unnoticed that, apart from Robert Wigram and Henry Green, employers were not among the donors.[35] The plight of London's shipbuilders, 'respectable' skilled artisans, gained sympathy, 'but notably less than the parallel crisis on the docks and wharves'.[36] Referring to union resistance to wage cuts, a magistrate observed that 'the shipwrights have brought this dreadful state of things in a great measure on themselves'.[37] The relief committee was wound up after a month, but there was little revival along the river.[38] Shipyard employment fell to 9,000 in 1871 and whole streets were emptied as former occupants moved away.[39] Privation continued for those who remained but in time they too faced becoming paupers.[40] One of six famished families living

---

[31] *Kentish Chronicle*, 2 February 1867; *Kentish Independent*, 17 August 1867.

[32] *Times*, 5 August 1867, 8 January 1868.

[33] *London City Press*, 9 February 1867.

[34] David R. Green, *Pauper Capital, London and the Poor Law, 1790–1870* (Routledge, London, 2010), 209; *Morning Advertiser*, 21 January 1867.

[35] *London City Press*, 26 January 1867, 30 March 1867.

[36] Baldwin Leighton, *Letters and Other Writings of the Late Edward Denison* (Richard Bentley and Son, London, 1875), 153–5, 241–2.

[37] *Clerkenwell News*, 20 August 1870, 27 August 1870, 12 September 1870, 31 December 1870; *Times*, 30 December 1870.

[38] Twentieth Annual Report of the Poor Law Board, 122; *London City Press*, 30 March 1867, 6 April 1867.

[39] Pollard, 'Shipbuilding', 84, 88; Cole, 'Isle of Dogs', 96–7.

[40] PP 1867–68 XXXIII.1 [4039], Twentieth Annual Report of the Poor Law Board, 122–3; *London City Press*, 30 March 1867; Thomas J. Cole, 'Life and Labor in the Isle of Dogs: The Origins and Evolution of an East London Working-Class Community, 1800–1980' (Doctoral Thesis, University of Oklahoma, 1984), 95; *Times*, 7 February 1867; *Kentish Chronicle*, 2 February 1867, *Kentish Independent*, 17 August 1867.

together, 'all connected with the iron shipbuilding', Catherine Spence and her baby boy starved to death in January 1869.[41]

Sugar Baking and Flour Milling

London's two major processing industries changed considerably in the later nineteenth century. Soft sugar replaced loaf and the new factory industry was dominated by large manufacturers. Flour milling similarly became more concentrated. However, whereas London's sugar industry was almost entirely focussed downriver by the 1880s, there continued to be large mills along the London waterfront supplemented by three huge West Ham mills. In 1864, twenty East London sugar baking firms produced almost 120,000 tons of hard sugar a year and ten soft sugar refineries produced 52,000.[42] Twenty years on, baking was in terminal decline. Only one older firm, Martineau's, survived, having moved early to processing beet sugar, cheaper than cane.[43] Changing consumer tastes and the growth of the jam and confectionary industry increased national demand for soft sugar, but London lost business to lower-cost northern centres and competed with subsidised refined foreign sugar in export markets.[44]

In 1881–5 London imported 350 tons of raw sugar annually, less than 200,000 by the late 1890s. By then, the raw material was continental beet sugar, not cane sugar, which mattered to the London's older dock companies. Imported in bags not casks, this change seriously affected demand for coopers.[45] Only larger, more technologically advanced enterprises were equipped to meet such challenges, with the result that there remained in London only two refining firms of any scale.[46] Both were led by men new to the capital, but with funds and experience. In 1878, Liverpool grocer and refiner, Henry Tate and Sons, opened a factory on

---

[41] *Times*, 29 January 1869, 30 December 1870.
[42] PP 1881 LXXXIII.681 [317], Memorandum Respecting Production of Refined Sugar, 10, 14.
[43] PP 1888 XCIII [353], Return on Production of, and Trade in Sugar, 26–7; Philippe Chalmin, *The Making of a Sugar Giant. Tate and Lyle 1859*–1989. Translated by Eric Long-Michalke (Routledge, London, 1990), 55, 65; PP 1878–79 XIII.1 [321], SC Sugar Industries, Martineau, Qq. 10, 20–130; Howarth and Wilson, *West Ham*, 166; *The Globe*, 9 May 1879.
[44] PP 1867 XXXVIII Pt I.1,579 127, Pt II.1 [3844-I 3844-II], RC on Railways, Appendices, 250–257; John M. Hutcheson, *Notes on the Sugar Industry of the United Kingdom* (James M'Kelvie, Greenock, 1901), 121.
[45] Hutcheson, *Sugar*, 115–6, 120; Charles Booth, 'The Inhabitants of Tower Hamlets (School Board Division), Their Condition and Occupations', *Journal Royal Statistical Society*, 50 (1887), 342.
[46] Chalmin, *Tate and Lyle*, 65.

a waterfront site in Silvertown, close to the Victoria Dock. A short distance away, the Lyle refinery, owned by Greenock shipowner and refiner Abram Lyle, began operating in 1883.[47] A 'London beyond the borders' location for these new refineries made sense. Instead of the overcrowded East End, this region offered 'cheaper ground, a riverside position, and room for everything likely to help economical working'.[48]

In 1900, London sugar refining was barely recognisable as the same industry that had had such a presence earlier in the century. Extremely concentrated in terms of ownership and located far from its traditional centre, it was relatively smaller. Financially, both firms struggled initially, but in due course, each prospered by finding a market niche, though competition was intense.[49] For the Tate family, exploiting a patent for a new type of hard sugar, 'the sugar lump', designed for the domestic market, proved highly profitable, while the combination of golden syrup (then a luxury consumer product) and competitively priced soft sugar had a similar positive impact on the fortunes of its neighbour.[50]

An estimated 1,200 sugar bakers had lost their jobs before the 1880s, as well as other trades indirectly involved. As temporary migrants, many German sugar-bakers returned home, but more settled men, particularly those with families, diversified into other German-dominated trades such as baking, found work in the Silvertown refineries or joined London's pool of casual labourers.[51] Both sugar companies brought managers and skilled men with them to London from Liverpool and Scotland, respectively, but they also employed daily casual labourers when needed. The relatively small workforce included women packers and can fillers.[52] The skilled job of sugar boiler went only to those who had served a three-year apprenticeship, but between 1895 and 1912, Lyle's basic hourly wage

---

[47] *The Grocer*, 5 May 1883. Reprinted in Oliver Lyle, *The Plaistow Story* (Tate & Lyle, London, 1960), 252–4.

[48] Hutcheson, *Sugar*, 22.

[49] Lyle, *Plaistow*, 40.

[50] ODNB, Sir Henry Tate (1819–1899), Abram Lyle (1820–1891); *Illustrated London News*, 25 June 1910; Chalmin, *Tate and Lyle*, 75–105; Antony Hugill, *Sugar and All That … A History of Tate & Lyle* (Gentry Books, London, 1978), 60–73.

[51] Memorandum Refined Sugar, 1864 and 1881, 14–15; *Shipping and Mercantile Gazette*, 11 September 1880; Horst Rössler, 'Germans from Hanover in the British Sugar Industry', in Stefan Manz, et al. (eds.), *Migration and Transfer from Germany to Britain 1660–1914* (K. G. Saur, Munchen, 2007), 55, 58–9; Jerome Farrell, 'The German Community in 19th Century East London', *East London Record*, 13, (1990).

[52] *Essex Herald*, 17 April 1874; Booth, *Life and Labour: Industry, Vol 3*, 98–101; PP 1913 LXXIX.1 [Cd. 7019], Census of England and Wales 1911, Table 13; *Illustrated London News*, 25 June 1910.

for unskilled adult workers was 24 shillings.[53] Both firms were to some extent unionised, but by different unions: Tate's by the Workers Union, Lyle's by the less militant Gas Workers and General Labourers. Charles Lyle was among the local manufacturers, including Arnold Hill of Thames Ironworks, politically active in the 'Municipal Alliance', formed in 1899 in opposition to socialist West Ham council.[54] Even so, Lyle's 1960 house history describes a good union relationship in the 1900s, but not at Tate's Thames Refinery. Although Henry Tate was notably philanthropic, it was possibly significant for workforce relations that the Lyle family was more directly engaged in daily operations.[55]

Until mid-century, London's waterfront flour mills mainly processed domestic grain from Kent and eastern England. Increasing grain imports following the abolition of the Corn Laws and a subsequent influx of American wheat, together with the introduction of roller milling, transformed London's handling of grain.[56] The Millwall Docks benefited particularly from American grain imports and along the waterfront, enterprising stone millers upscaled their works. Most of the new steam-powered stone mills were on the south bank but in the 1870s, the City of London Flour Mill at Blackfriars was the largest, with thirty-two pairs of stones.[57] Transition to roller milling, mechanically more efficient and better suited to hard North American grain, followed. By 1890, there were several roller mills on the south bank, one in East London on the River Lea, as well as McDougall's at Millwall Dock, the first dockside mill in London. Often architecturally as well as technologically ambitious, these substantial buildings were impressive additions to the metropolitan riverscape.[58] The fixed capital requirements of roller milling

---

[53] Frank Lewis, *Essex and Sugar* (Phillimore, London, 1976), 92–3; Booth, *Life and Labour Industry. Vol. 3*, 98–101.

[54] John Wesley Marriott, 'London Over the Border: A Study of West Ham During Rapid Growth, 1840–1910' (Doctoral Thesis, University of Cambridge, 1984), 177–8.

[55] Lyle, *Plaistow*, 43–4,183.

[56] Martin and Sue Watts, *From Quern to Computer: The History of Flour Milling*, https://new .millsarchive.org/2016/09/06/from-quern-to-computer-the-history-of-flour-milling/, accessed 23 July 2022; Richard Perren, 'Structural Change and Market Growth in the Food Industry: Flour Milling in Britain, Europe and America, 1850–1914', *Economic History Review, Second Series*, XLIII (1990), 425.

[57] Mildred Cookson, 'City of London Flour Mills, a Millstone Mill', *Milling and Grain*, August 2018, 14–15; 'The Sun Flour Mills Bromley by Bow', *Milling and Grain*, June 2018, 12–15; Peter Sinclair, *The Brown Family. Ten Flour Mills in a Hundred Years* (The Mills Archive, Reading, 2017), 26; Jennifer Tann and R. Glyn Jones, 'Technology and Transformation: The Diffusion of the Roller Mill in the British Flour Milling Industry, 1870–1907', *Technology and Culture*, 7 (1996), 39.

[58] Martin and Sue Watts, *Quern to Computer*; Perren, 'Flour Milling', 429; Mildred Cookson, *Roller Mills of London*, https://catalogue.millsarchive.org/roller-flour-mills-of-london, accessed 4 August 2022.

resulted in greater industrial concentration. Some of the older generation of London millers had strong City connections, but leadership passed to outsiders who took advantage of London's lower docks and their transport connections.[59] In 1901, the Co-operative Wholesale Society mill opened in Silvertown. Close to the Victoria Dock, backing on to the Great Eastern Railway, this had extensive river frontage for barges.[60] There followed Joseph Rank's Premier Mill and, within the Victoria Dock itself, the Millennium Mill, owned by Birkenhead's William Vernon and Sons.[61]

Stone milling did not need large numbers of workers, and roller mills were no different. Apart from engineering, much of the work was unskilled handling, warehousing and packing, but it was fairly regular. Weekly pay for such labourers was 16 shillings a week, but 'the roller men' tending the machines could make twice that. The National Millers Union, founded in 1889, and open to both skilled and unskilled, had only four small branches in London, but the industry's concentration proved a strength when negotiating with London's master millers.[62]

South Bank Maritime Communities

In the 1890s, Charles Booth considered the south shore, apart from Deptford, as 'not exactly London, but still to be described in terms of London' and disappointingly lacking 'an independent life'.[63] This was wide of the mark.[64] The region was certainly bound up with the rest of the metropolis, but it did not lack identity and retained a distinctive maritime character for longer in the century than the waterfront parishes on the opposite bank. Indeed, Booth himself commented that 'London south of the Thames strikes the observer as a compound of tanyard, factory and warehouse', but was thrilled to discover that 'in Rotherhithe we have a seaport'.[65]

---

[59] Mildred Cookson, *Roller Mills of London*, https://catalogue.millsarchive.org/roller-flour-mills-of-london, accessed 4 August 2022; PP 1905 XXXIX.217 [Cd. 2644], RC Supply of Food and Raw Material in Time of War, Taylor, Q. 3694.

[60] Percy Redfern, *The Story of the C.W.S: The Jubilee History of the Co-operative Wholesale Society Ltd 1863–1913* (Co-operative Wholesale Society, Manchester, 1913), 231–2.

[61] ODNB, Joseph Rank (1854–1943); Mildred Cookson, 'The Mills of the Co-operative Wholesale Society', *Milling and Grain*, March 2018, 12–15.

[62] Booth, *Life and Labour, Industry, Volume 3*, 101–8.

[63] Booth, *Life and Labour, First Series Volume 1*, 275.

[64] E. J. Hobsbawn, (ed.), 'The Nineteenth-Century London Labour Market', in *Worlds of Labour. Further Studies in the History of Labour* (Weidenfeld and Nicolson, London, 1984), 139.

[65] Charles Booth, *Life and Labour of the People of London. Third Series: Religious Influences, Volume 4* (Macmillan, London, 1902), 140.

Despite redevelopment, it maintained established industrial patterns. The wharfingers and warehouse owners of Southwark and Bermondsey generally prospered, as did Rotherhithe's docks. Organisationally, the Surrey Commercial differed little from earlier in the century. Timber and grain remained the specialism, and sub-contracting persisted. Unlike the north bank dock companies, its managers did not see a need to experiment with new employment systems. Not having been compelled by steam shipping to expand downriver, it still occupied a single site.

Deptford's heavy industries, still relatively new in the 1850s, proved resilient in the face of the 1866 crisis and shipbuilders continued to be significant local employers, as did the GSNC repair works. Many skilled workers lost jobs following naval dockyard closure in 1869, but this proved a temporary blow to the area. In 1871, the population was a fifth of that ten years earlier, but numbers recovered with the opening of the new Foreign Cattle Market that year. A settlement of cattlemen, slaughterers, butchers and 'gut-girls' who cleaned out the carcasses, developed around the market.[66] The navy's Royal Victoria victualling yard, the largest in the country and both a manufacturing and storage facility, employed 400–500 men in the 1870s and 1880s.[67] Occupational divisions were notably strong, with the workforce consisting of skilled men employed in factories, shipyards, large and small engineering works or on the river as lightermen or stevedores. Less skilled labourers worked in docks, mills, granaries, warehouses and on wharves. There were limited employment opportunities for women. A small middle class meant fewer jobs in domestic service and distance from the centre of the clothing industry reduced chances of outwork. In 1861, 15 per cent of women over the age of twenty were employed as servants or making clothes. Forty years on, they also worked in jam manufacturing, sack making and 'fur-pulling' rabbit skins.[68]

A sense of common cause and different interests for north bank workers were reflected in the 1872 Southside Labour Protection League and separate organisations in the 1889 General Strike. Even so, despite the presence of the most modern types of industry, the traditional culture of exclusivity and disdain for the unskilled survived

---

[66] Crossick, *Kentish London*, 49–50; Jones, 'Victorian Suburban Society', 59–60, 235, 283.
[67] PP 1870, XLVI.797 [56], Arrangements on HM Victualling Yards, 5; Nathan Dews, *The History of Deptford in the Counties of Kent and Surrey*, Second Edition (Simpkin, Marshall and Co., London, 1884), 278; Jonathan Coad, *Support for the Fleet. Architecture and Engineering of the Royal Navy's Bases 1700–1914* (English Heritage, Swindon, 2013), 312–314.
[68] PP 1863, Cd 3221, Census of England and Wales 1861, 30–34; Booth, *Life and Labour: Religious Influences, Volume 4*, 164; Margaret Elise Harkness, *Toilers in London or Inquiries Concerning Female Labour in the Metropolis* (Hodder and Stoughton, London, 1859), 68–70.

among the region's accomplished unionised employees.[69] Moreover, south bank casual labourers and their families were certainly at least as desperately poor as those in the East End waterfront parishes. In 1861 Hollingshed considered their 'dirty, neglected and degrading' living conditions to be even worse and Booth's investigators reached much the same conclusion in the late 1890s. Although Deptford had more skilled workers than some other districts, it too had streets marked by severe deprivation.[70]

Rotherhithe was familiar to Irish migrants before the famine years. During the peak July to January months, these came from Ireland to work handling imported timber.[71] At mid-century, there were therefore already enclaves of Irish people settled close to the waterfront wharves. With 18 per cent of Irish-born people in 1861, Southwark's St. Olave parish was London's most Irish district.[72] Settlement was encouraged by familial and religious links. In 1860, there was one Catholic Church in Southwark, by the 1900s, there were three. However, the importance of religious affiliation should not be overstated. Deptford had possibly 6,000 Irish residents in 1900, but only 1,400 attended mass regularly.[73]

Local conditions encouraged putting down roots. Until Tower Bridge opened, cross-Thames transport links were limited. Although areas close to London Bridge lost housing to railways and warehousing, there was nothing comparable to dock expansion and slum clearance on the north side to disrupt neighbourhoods.[74] For more skilled workers, such as shipbuilders and engineers, work relationships created communal attachments. Even though Deptford shipwrights could afford the rents of newly developed artisan properties, in the 1870s many still continued to live in their traditional neighbourhood closer to the river.[75]

---

[69] H. E. Malden (ed.), *A History of the County of Surrey, Volume 4* (London, 1912), 17–24; Crossick, *Artisan Elite*, 60–1.

[70] John Hollingshed, *Ragged London in 1861* (First printed 1861. Reprint. Read Books Ltd., London, 2013), 132; Booth, *Life and Labour, Religious Influences, Volume 4* (Macmillan, London, 1902), 163–4.

[71] Mayhew, *Morning Chronicle*. Reprint, Volume 4, 272.

[72] Lees, *Irish Migrants*, 55–88; PP 1863, Cd. 3221, Census of England and Wales 1861, 30–4.

[73] Jones, 'Victorian Suburban Society', 175; Hugh McLeod, *Class and Religion in the Late Victorian City* (Croom Helm, London, 1974), 34–5, 77; Richard Mudie-Smith (ed.), *The Religious Life of London* (Hodder and Stoughton, London, 1904), 59, 263; Booth, *Life and Labour, Religious Influences, Volume 4*, 17, 127.

[74] Booth, *Life and Labour, Religious Influences, Volume 4*, 123.

[75] Jones, 'Victorian Suburban Society', 493.

North Bank Maritime Communities

At mid-century, London's main maritime districts were still around the London and St. Katharine's docks and along the Wapping and Shadwell waterfront in Stepney, with outposts at Limehouse and Blackwall.[76] Encouraged by industrial development and the Victoria Dock, settlement then spread to the Isle of Dogs and the rest of Poplar, as well as downriver to West and East Ham. The presence of other trades and occupations in these newer areas of settlement made them less distinctly maritime in character. Clearance for the Shadwell Basin, new roads and railways increased residential overcrowding. So too did housing improvement schemes. In 1875, the demolition of over 200 dilapidated properties close to the London Dock displaced over 2,000 dock or waterfront labourers and their families, mainly Irish. Needing to remain close to the source of work, those forced out crammed into already packed nearby streets and courtyards.[77] Mayhew and many others documented the dismal, overcrowded slums inhabited by London's casual poor. Dilapidated tenements, high rents and irregular earnings consigned numbers of men, women and their families to lives of extraordinary bleakness. In this environment, the street became a significant social space, particularly for women, as did the public house for men. Increasingly out of place in a world of shipping companies and the international telegraph, remaining merchants and shipowners retreated to their country estates. Apart from clergy and mission workers, by the 1870s residentially the district had become almost entirely working class.

In the traditional maritime district, sugar baking and shipbuilding declined and much marine manufacturing followed the new docks downriver. Some seaborne coal, increasingly brought in by steam collier or lighter, was still landed at Wapping. More went directly to gas works, to Poplar Dock, the Regent's Canal Limehouse Basin or to coal derricks with hydraulic cranes in the Thames. There was now less call for traditional coal handling methods, so heavers, together with their

---

[76] Percy J. Edwards, *History of London Street Improvements 1855–1897* (London County Council, London, 1898); T. F. T. Baker (ed.), *A History of the County of Middlesex, Volume 11, Stepney, Bethnal Green*, ed. (London, 1998), *British History Online*, www .british-history.ac.uk/vch/middx/vol11/pp7-13, accessed 3 September 2022, 7–13; Bridget Cherry et al., *The Buildings of England. London 5: East* (Yale University Press, New Haven and London, 2005), 39.

[77] PP 1882 VII.395, SC Artizans' and Labourers' Dwellings Improvement, Liddle Qq. 281–286; William Denton, *Observations on the Displacement of the Poor By Metropolitan Railways and By Other Public Improvements* (Bell and Daldy, London, 1861), 5–11; D. L. Munby, *Industry and Planning in Stepney* (Oxford University Press, London, 1951), 24–5; PP 1884–5 XXX.1 [C. 4402], RC Housing of the Working Classes, First Report, 18.

Illustration 8.2 Derricks discharging coal on the river, 1896. Image: William Wylie (1851–1931) 'The coal traffic on the Thames: William Cory and Son's coal derricks at work'. © *Illustrated London News* Ltd/ Mary Evans.

employment system, departed the waterfront.[78] As a result, the London St. Katharine's docks became the most important source of casual maritime employment in the East End.[79] Their labourers, faced with increasing competition for a day's work, lived alongside other inhabitants serving the ready-made clothing industry.[80]

Many dock labourers had Irish origins, although contemporaries possibly overstated their dominance.[81] Not all were casual labourers. In the

[78] PP 1893–94 XXXIV.1 [C.6894-IX], RC Labour, Group C, Volume III, Gardner, Q. 27598; Booth, *Life and Labour. Industry, Volume 3*, 433–440; LSE Booth Archive, BOOTH/B/144, 87; Alan H. Faulkner, 'The Regent's Canal Dock, Part 1', *Journal of the Railway & Canal Historical Society*, 2 (2002), 77–80.

[79] Booth, *Life and Labour First Series. Poverty*, 18–19.

[80] Munby, *Stepney*, 51–63; J. E. Martin, *Greater London. An Industrial Geography* (G. Bell and Sons, London, 1966), 2–4; Peter H. Hall, *The Industries of London Since 1861* (Hutchinson, London, 1962), 53–55; Stedman Jones, *Outcast London*, 22, Appendix 2, Table 6, 366–7.

[81] Charles Booth (ed.), *Life and Labour of the People of London. Volume III, Blocks of Buildings, Schools and Immigration* (Macmillan & Co., London, 1892), 87–91.

early 1860s, Irish politician William Urquhart-Pollard reported that some had been promoted to permanent posts, 'without any regard of country or creed'. This is unsurprising. The companies had little choice except to recruit foremen and sub-contractors from the ranks of regular casual labourers, whatever their background. Irishmen had, as Llewellyn-Smith expressed it, 'a grip on waterside work'. At the end of the century, a quarter of London's skilled stevedores had been born in Ireland and a high proportion of the rest had similar origins.[82] Such Irish London citizens were blamed for slums. 'Rookeries are bad, but what are they to Irish rookeries?', wrote one commentator in 1851.[83] Twenty years on, *The Builder* described appalling living conditions in 'Wapping Island', between the two London Dock entrances to the river.[84] For the artisan editor of the *London Observer* (quoted at the start of this chapter), such people were feckless, so beyond help, but as Urquart-Pollard pointed out in 1862, a shortage of decent lodgings gave his fellow countrymen little choice except to live where they did.[85]

Occupationally, Poplar was more mixed than Stepney. Settlement gathered pace when shipbuilding and other industries took hold on the Isle of Dogs and Limehouse in the forties and fifties.[86] After the 1866 crisis, a mixture of large-scale factories, including the Thames Ironworks, and small workshops predominated. Investment in steam shipping facilities ensured that the West and East India docks remained important. In 1851, about a tenth of male Poplar residents were port workers and this proportion remained constant into the twentieth century.[87] In 1861, over half the women in St. George's parish, Stepney, undertook paid work, many no doubt wives of dock workers, with ready-made clothing manufacture the most common. In contrast, a third of women living in Poplar were not employed. This may have been due to distance from the centre of the outwork clothing industry, higher household income due to skilled male workers or under-reporting for fear of prejudicing charitable or Poor Law assistance. By 1900 the development of the local food and chemical industries gave Poplar women more chances of finding work locally.[88]

---

[82] Booth, *Life and Labour, Blocks of Buildings*, 92.

[83] Montague Gore, *On the Dwellings of the Poor*, 3rd ed. (James Ridgeway, London, 1851), xx.

[84] *The Builder*, 7 January 1871. *East London Observer*, 14 January 1871.

[85] Urquhart-Pollard, 'Irish Labourers' 745–6.

[86] Wright, *Habits and Customs*, 253–4, 257–60; 1861 Census for England and Wales, Table 11; Cole, 'Isle of Dogs', 45–7.

[87] François Bédarida, 'Urban Growth and Social Structure in Nineteenth-Century Poplar', *The London Journal*, 1 (1975), 168–71.

[88] 1861 Census for England and Wales; Edward Higgs and Amanda Wilkinson, 'Women, Occupations and Work in the Victorian Censuses Revisited', *History Workshop Journal*, 81 (2016), 17–38; Bédarida, 'Urban Growth', 170; Cole, 'Isle of Dogs', 108–9.

The 'Myth' of Outcast London

At mid-century, Mayhew provided a nuanced London 'panorama of poverty' and Booth's influential forensic investigations of the London poor, published between 1887 and 1903, did much to dispel ill-informed generalisation. But over the intervening decades, a sensationalist slum journalism genre identified East London as populated by a largely undifferentiated mass of poverty-stricken, criminally inclined slum dwellers.[89] Others followed suit. For Matthew Arnold in 1868, its inhabitants were 'vast, miserable, unmanageable, masses of sunken people'.[90] 'Outcast London', allegedly populated by a 'residuum' left behind as the rest of Victorian London advanced, became not only a subject for middle class curiosity or regret, but also a source of anxiety. Fears of urban physical and moral degeneration and a sense of looming political threat increasingly influenced attitudes.[91] In 1889, George R. Sims, after 'a journey into this dark continent that is within easy walking distance of the General Post Office', warned that 'this mighty mob of famished, diseased, and filthy helots is getting dangerous, physically, morally, politically'.[92]

Although far from uncontested by reformers and local interests, such stigmatising mythical portrayals took firm hold among the wider public.[93] By lumping together occupationally and culturally diverse inhabitants, not only individual identity was denied but also that of the groups to which they belonged. Long-standing prejudices against the Irish, heightened by simian caricatures, found a ready outlet here.[94] Their presence in the maritime districts loomed large in this imagined East London, much more so than reputedly respectable Scottish shipbuilders and German sugar bakers.

Sensationalist descriptions gave little hint of the East End's commercial and manufacturing activity, still less of the contribution its maritime sector made to London's trade and prosperity. The 'respectable artisan', beloved of middle-class commentators, was seemingly absent.

---

[89] H. J. Dyos, 'The Slums of Victorian London', *Victorian Studies*, II (1967), 12–20; Marriott, *Beyond the Tower*, 158–68.
[90] Matthew Arnold, *Culture and Anarchy* (1869), Dover Wilson (ed.) (Cambridge University Press, Cambridge, 1932), 193.
[91] Stedman Jones, *Outcast London*, 281–296.
[92] George R. Sims, *How the Poor Live and Horrible London* (Chatto & Windus, London, 1889), 1.
[93] Marriott, *Beyond the Tower*, 150–173; William J. Fishman, *East End 1888. A Year in a London Borough Among The Labouring Poor* (Gerald Duckworth & Co., 1988, Reprinted Five Leaves Publications, Nottingham, 2009), 9; Geoff Ginn, 'Answering the "Bitter Cry": Urban Description and Social Reform in the Late-Victorian East End', *The London Journal* 31 (2006), 179–200.
[94] Steven Fielding, *Class and Ethnicity. Irish Catholics in England, 1880–1939* (Open University Press, Buckingham, 1993), 5–13.

Yet skilled male workers are estimated to have been 40 per cent of East End inhabitants in 1861 and 31 per cent in 1891.[95] Whether or not those in the maritime industries both lived and worked locally, and many certainly did, their organisations had a presence. Union officers used local public houses or school rooms to conduct business, as did friendly societies. The stevedores operated their 'turn' system from the Wade's Arms.[96] Union benefit distribution, annual dinners and celebratory processions reflected and encouraged social connections between members.[97] In common with other parts of London, there were also artisanal working-men's clubs. In the 1880s, the Tower Hamlets United Radical Club had 800 members.[98]

As we have seen, skill provided no immunity from hardship. Severe downturns, as in the 1860s and 1880s, caused privation, but short-term unemployment could be weathered. It was different for the unskilled genuinely casual labourer. Booth concluded that over 11 per cent of East End men and women were 'very poor', living in chronic want.[99] Shocking though this revelation was, and indeed still is, it has distorted perceptions of the district. Booth's focus on the near-destitute overstated the prevalence of casual employment, and by extension the magnitude of East London poverty more generally.[100] As he himself commented, 'the numbers [of casual workers] are not very large, considering the great public concern which has been aroused on this subject', pointing out that only dock work was significantly casualised.[101] Even so, in Stepney's St. George-in-the-East parish, closest to the upper docks, only just under 10 per cent of heads of households were casual labourers.[102] Unlike some other contemporary commentators, Booth did not confuse those 'loafers' and vagrants who appeared sometimes at the dock gates, with the 'very poor' who were there regularly but only got a few days' work. He observed

[95] Stedman-Jones, *Outcast London*, 350–57, 388–9.
[96] PP 1896 XCIII.277 [C.8232], Statistical Tables, Trade Unions Eighth Report, 1894–95; PP 1889 113, Reports of Chief Registrar of Friendly Societies, 1887, II A; Brian Harrison, 'Pubs', in H. J. Dyos and Michael Wolff (eds.), *The Victorian City: Images and Realities Volume 1* (Routledge and Kegan Paul, London and Boston, 1973), 175–6.
[97] Wright, *Habits and Customs*, 83.
[98] Laurence Marlow, 'The Working Men's Club Movement 1862–1912: A Study of the Evolution of a Working Class Institution' (Doctoral Thesis, University of Warwick, 1980), 283; John Davis, 'Radical Clubs and London Politics 1870–1900', in David Feldman and Gareth Stedman Jones (eds.), *Metropolis – London. Histories and Representations since 1800* (Routledge, London, 1989), 103–28.
[99] Charles Booth, 'Condition and Occupations of the People of East London and Hackney, 1887', *Journal of the Royal Statistical Society* 51 (1888), 278.
[100] Brodie, *Politics of the Poor*, 1–7.
[101] Booth, 'The Inhabitants of Tower Hamlets', 336.
[102] Booth, 'Conditions and Occupations' (1888), 360.

that 'to the rich the very poor are a sentimental interest: to the poor they are a crushing load. The poverty of the poor is mainly the result of the competition of the very poor'.[103]

Whatever the truth or otherwise of this judgement, regular port labourers appear not to have recognised such a division. 'Outsiders' waiting at the dock gate with little or no experience of the work were resented, but not as much as foremen or gang leaders perceived as corrupt or unfair. As Booth conceded, the line between casual and irregular employment was 'most difficult to draw'.[104] The formality of dock company workforce structures could deceive. As we have shown, daily employment of casual men was not a totally random process. Moreover, while there was a considerable difference in pay and skill status between a stevedore paid a daily wage of eight pence an hour in the 1890s and a dock extra labourer receiving sixpence, both were casually employed.[105] This should not be interpreted as an absence of poverty among the slightly better off and their families. Those who managed to get work only a day or two a week were indeed as desperate as Booth reported.

The Sailor Economy

A maritime connection that sensationalist writers did not ignore was the presence of seafarers. London's sailortown boomed in the 1850s and 1860s, expanding eastward into Limehouse, to the dismay of the Rector, who noted more 'low lodging houses and a corresponding increase in immorality' and exodus of 'more respectable families'[106]. On average an estimated 283 seamen arrived daily in London from overseas in 1850. By 1870, the number was 385.[107] On Census night, April 1861, not a particularly busy month for the port, 5,439 seamen were recorded as present in St. George-in-the-East and Poplar. Although some must have been local residents, this is a substantial number.[108]

---

[103] Ibid., 299.
[104] Ibid., 284.
[105] Booth, *Life and Labour, Industry*, Vol. 3, 406, 428–9; PP 1887 LXXI.303 [C.5258], Condition of the Working Classes, iv–vi, 108–9.
[106] Quoted in J. G. Birch, *Limehouse Through Five Centuries* (The Sheldon Press, London, 1930), 123–4.
[107] Alston Kennerley, 'British Seamen's Missions and Sailors' Homes 1815–1970, Voluntary Welfare Provision for Serving Seafarers' (Doctoral Thesis, Polytechnic South West, 1989), Appendix 1e.
[108] 1861 Census for England and Wales; Richard Rowe, *Jack Afloat and Ashore* (Smith, Elder & Co., London, 1875), 102.

Illustration 8.3 The Strangers' Home for Asiatics, Africans and South Sea Islanders, c. 1857. Image: Strangers' Home, Stepney. © London Metropolitan Archives (City of London).

Most seafarers lodged in private boarding houses, not Well Street Sailors' Home, but in 1857 another charity opened the Strangers Home for Asiatics, Africans and South Sea Islanders. This was on the West India Dock Road, close to the docks serving trades to the Far East.[109] The home also housed the Board of Trade's Lascars' Shipping Office, a recruiting and repatriation centre. Following repeal of the Navigation Laws, colonial Asian seamen were redefined as British, so they could legally man outbound vessels. Starting with P&O, liner companies increasingly employed these low-wage crews and preferred to keep men working on board when in dock.[110] As foreigners, Chinese sailors tended to stay with their compatriots when ashore. Despite sensationalist accounts of Limehouse opium dens and trade union hostility, the number serving in British vessels was insignificant.

---

[109] Joseph Salter, *The Asiatic in England. Sketches of Sixteen Years' Work Among Orientals* (Seeley, Jackson and Halliday, London, 1873), 38–40, 66–71; *Times*, 2 June 1856.
[110] *London Evening Standard*, 29 May 1872; Visram, *Asians in Britain*, 54–61; Raminder K. Saini, '"England Failed to do Her Duty Towards Them": The India Office and Pauper Indians in the Metropole, 1857–1914', *Journal of Imperial and Commonwealth History* 46 (2018), 235.

In 1895, 12,492 lascars shipped from the Victoria Docks, but just 412 were Chinese.[111]

Public appetite for revelatory accounts of lower-class existence, stimulated by Mayhew's *Chronicles*, encouraged other travellers to London's 'unknown' regions. In 1852, Stepney's St. George-in-the-East was included in Thomas Beames, *The Rookeries of London* as among districts 'which bear away the palm of vice, misery, and filth'. Graphically describing the worst sailors' lodgings and public houses, he also wrote sympathetically, even romantically, about daytime Ratcliffe Highway, '… every fourth man you meet is a sailor; you will hear German, Spanish and even modern Greek, spoken by those whose dress at once connects them with our mercantile marine'.[112] However, for Watts Phillips and others, the Highway was 'the headquarters of unbridled vice and drunken violence, 'all that is dirty, disorderly, and debased'.[113] Such images proved enduring. Popular author Richard Rowe conceded in 1875 that Ratcliffe Highway 'had improved, to a certain extent', but melodramatically described serious brawls where 'knives flash in the gaslight and inflict deadly stabs in the dark'.[114]

As well as the traditional stereotype of seamen ashore as boisterous, drunken and irresponsible, a common theme running through many sailortown descriptions was alleged unworldliness, gullibility and inexperience which made them easy victims. In the words of one concerned MP, 'although the sailor was gallant and enduring at sea, he was soft and yielding on land'.[115] However, there was a parallel, somewhat inconsistent, narrative also in circulation, where foreign seamen were knife-carrying villains who menaced Englishmen. A spike in knife assaults on Radcliffe Highway and in Liverpool in 1864 prompted calls to ban sailors from carrying sheath or dagger knives.[116] Public opinion was selective in its condemnation of knife attacks. When 'a poor Irish lad in the hands of an East End Jew' was sentenced to death for his murder by stabbing, the resulting outcry led to the lesser penalty of transportation for life.[117]

[111] PP 1903 LXII.15, Committee on Certain Questions Affecting our Mercantile Marine III, Appendices G. 1, G. 2.

[112] Thomas Beames, *The Rookeries of London: Past, Present and Prospective* (Thomas Bosworth, London, 1852), 19, 96–105, 185–90.

[113] Watts Phillips, *The Wild Tribes of London* (Ward and Lock, London, 1855), 19; Ewing Ritchie, *The Night Side of London* (William Tweedie, London, 1858), 83–4.

[114] Rowe, *Jack Afloat and Ashore*, 72, 76.

[115] Robert Lee, 'The Seafarers' Urban World: A Critical Review', *International Journal of Maritime History*, 25 (2013), 23–64; Parliamentary Debates, 3rd Series 162, cc. 324–51.

[116] Parliamentary Debates, 3rd Series 173, 1364–1451.

[117] *Old Bailey Proceedings Online*, www.oldbaileyonline,org, accessed 13 May 2022, March 1862 trial of Patrick Devereux; *Morning Chronicle*, 7 March 1862; *Cork Examiner*, 29 July 1862.

There is no evidence that knife crime was a significant problem in St. George's-in-the-East.[118] Serious protests in 1859 and 1860 by a largely working-class local 'mob' opposed to High Church ritualism were stronger evidence of local lawlessness than the actions of a few sailors.[119] However, moral panics and truth are not usually close relations, so an effect of the knife issue was to reinforce Ratcliffe Highway's reputation as dangerous and unruly. Highlighting the presence of foreigners, as well as routine emphasis in sensationalist depictions on the role of Jews as publicans, outfitters and boarding house keepers, further contributed to an imagined status as an alien place.

It was a far from poor district for some who made their living out of seamen's temporary wealth, including shopkeepers with windows 'hung round with everything to catch a sailor's eye, or sound the depths of his pocket'.[120] It also meant big business for Benjamin Jones, who owned fifty brothels in St. George-in-the-East and Whitechapel, as well as for John Harris, a leading outfitter, public house owner, money lender and shipping agent. In the 1870s, he was also a Poor Law Guardian and vestry member.[121]

As public attention to conditions in East London grew, so too did concern for the souls of the inhabitants. For some in the Anglican Church and other denominations, they became subjects of a religious crusade.[122] Conversion and charity featured but so did concern about poor housing.[123] High churchman Charles Lowder, a prominent 'slum priest' who

[118] Brad Beaven, '"One of the Toughest Streets in the World": Exploring Male Violence, Class and Ethnicity in London's Sailortown, c. 1850–1880', *Social History*, 46 (2021), 6–13.

[119] Owen Chadwick, *The Victorian City. Part One 1820–1859* (SCM Press, London, 1970), 497–501; David Kent, 'High Church Rituals and Rituals of Protest; the 'Riots' at St. George-in-the-East, 1859–1860', *The London Journal*, 32 (2007), 145–66.

[120] Beames, *Rookeries*, 97.

[121] *East London Observer*, 15 May 1909, *Morning Advertiser*, 11 August, 25 August 1860; *Reynolds News*, 26 August 1860; PP 1878 XVI.77 [205], SC on Merchant Seamen Bill, Harris, Qq. 5264–5456.

[122] *London Evening Standard*, 18 August 1862; Arthur Miall, *Religion in London. Statistics of Church and Chapel Accommodation in 1865. An article reprinted from the 'British Quarterly Review', No. 85. With an appendix of tables* (Jackson Walford and Hodder, London, 1866), Appendices XXI–XXV, 14–16; David McIllhiney, *A Gentleman in Every Slum. Church of England Missions in East London 1837–1914* (Pickwick Publications, Eugene, Oregon, 1988), 16–17.

[123] Wohl, *Eternal Slum*, 50–53. Harry Jones, *East and West London, Being Notes of Common Life and Pastoral Life in St. James' Westminster and Saint George's-In-The-East* (Smith, Elder, & Co., London, 1875), 9, 168, 217–8; C. F. Lowder, *Ten Years in S. George's Mission Being an Account of its Origin, Progress and Works of Mercy*, (C. J. Palmer, London, 1867), 3; C. F. Lowder, *Twenty-One Years in S. George's Mission. An Account of Its Origin, Progress and Works of Charity* (Rivingtons, London, 1877); R. H. Hadden, *An East End Chronicle: St. George's-In-The-East Parish and Parish Church* (Hatchards, London, 1880), 32–5, 110–14.

ran a creche for the infants of absent sailors' wives so that they could find work other than prostitution, remained appalled by much he encountered. In contrast, Rector Harry Jones celebrated port and maritime connections. 'Our contact with distant places is fresh, our people are related to sailors', he wrote in 1875.[124] Seafarers themselves remained the concern of specialist missions, by now generally mature enterprises. Most restricted activity to distributing religious tracts, but a few combined spiritual care with direct practical responses to the perils of life ashore.[125] The British and Foreign Sailors Society opened effectively a club in Shadwell in 1856. Facilities included religious services, a reading room, a coffee room, classrooms, a savings bank and washing facilities.[126] These were 'free to all seafaring people', but in 1871, the Norwegian Crown Prince launched a church and mission for Scandinavian seamen close to the Commercial Dock. However, the Catholic Seaman's Club catered for all religions and nationalities.[127] Despite evangelical origins, the Wells Street Sailors' Home did not force religious instruction on boarders. It remained the only institution that sought to improve the lives of seamen ashore by directly countering the power of the crimp and his associates.[128]

For different reasons, the government was similarly concerned about the corrupting influence of 'land sharks'. An 1836 Select Committee, consular reports and debates about the Navigation Laws raised concerns about the behaviour of British merchant seamen, the source of naval manpower in wartime, particularly their drunkenness,.[129] When Labouchere, President of the Board of Trade, embarked in the early 1850s on merchant service reforms, these included interventionist measures to curb the power of crimps.[130] Board of Trade shipping offices

---

[124] Jones, *East and West London*, 168.

[125] Sampson Low, *The Charities of London in 1861* (Sampson Low, London, 1862), 279–80; Thomas C. Garland, *Leaves from My Log of Twenty-Five Years of Christian Work Among Sailors and Others in the Port of London* (T. Woolmer, London, 1882), 3; Sarah Palmer, 'Seamen Ashore in Late Nineteenth Century London: Protection from the Crimps', in Paul Adam (ed.), *Seamen in Society* (International Commission for Maritime History, 1980), 60.

[126] Roald Kverndal, *Seamen's Missions. Their Origin and Early Growth* (William Carey Library, Pasadena California, 1986), 369–72; Kennerley, 'Seamen's Missions', Appendix 8a.

[127] David Redvalksen, 'The Two Kingdoms: The Norwegian Seamen's Church in London 1865–1905', *Journal of Religious History*, 42 (2018), 6–22; Daniel Renshaw, *Socialism and the Diasporic 'Other'* (Liverpool University Press, Liverpool, 2018), 207.

[128] Palmer, 'Seamen Ashore', 58–9.

[129] PP 1876 LXVI.333 [C. 1398], Report on Recent Legislation Concerning Merchant Ships and Seaman; Palmer, *Repeal of the Navigation Laws*, 171.

[130] Roger Prouty, *The Transformation of the Board of Trade 1830–1855; a Study of Administrative Reorganisation in the Heyday of Laissez Faire* (William Heinmann Ltd., London, 1957), 87–98.

were established in London and other major ports. Here, crews had to be paid off and signed on. Subsequent legislation added saving banks, where seamen could deposit and withdraw wages, and a money order system to transfer money to dependents.[131]

London's offices were established in Green's Sailors' Home, East India Dock Road, Poplar and Well Street Sailors' Home. In 1874 Green's Home closed and the Board of Trade took over the entire Poplar building.[132] Two years earlier it had left Well Street for new premises at Tower Hill. Concerted attempts to discredit the home by lodging housekeepers and outfitters may have influenced the move, but efficiency was the prime motive.[133] Facilities included 'a capacious waiting room … a more orderly and rapid system of engagement and discharge, and greater facilities for investing in the Seamen's Money Orders before they quit the discharge rooms and fall under the influence of crimps and low characters'.[134]

These measures had little immediate impact. Delay between a sailor's discharge and payment of wages continued and relatively few seamen took advantage of savings banks or money orders. Indeed, encouraging seamen to gather outside shipping offices actually made it easier for crimps to operate.[135] Supplying men to ships, uncommon in London because of the large number of seamen available, needed a licence, but the entrenched advance note credit system was said to create 'a free-masonry between the crimp and the sailors, and they do not break faith with the crimp, who encourages their getting into debt'.[136]

It was illegal to go on a vessel before its arrival in port without permission from the Master. However, given the profit to be made out of a sailor, due perhaps to receive £40 or £50 in wages, the derisory £5 penalty was no deterrent.[137] The Thames Police, a Metropolitan

---

[131] 13 & 14 Vict. c. 93; 17 & 18 Vict. c. 93; SC on Merchant Shipping (1860), Farrer, Q. 5676; 1896 XLI.113,137 [C. 8167 C8168], Departmental Committee on the Mercantile Marine Fund, Swain, Qq. 8932–38.

[132] PP 1852 XLIX.283 [308], Amount of Income and Expenditure under the Mercantile Marine Act, 1850–51.

[133] Palmer, 'Seamen Ashore', 58–9; Kennerley, 'Seamen's Missions', 122.

[134] PP 1875 LXVIII.319 [132], Memorandum on Improvements Effected by the Board of Trade.

[135] Henry Toynbee, 'On Mercantile Marine Legislation As Affecting The Number And Efficiency Of British Seamen', *Journal of the Society of Arts*, 15 (1867), 125–7; Kennerley, 'Seamen's Missions', Appendices 3a, 11a.

[136] 1859 Session 1, VI.1 [2469], RC Manning of the Navy, Elliot, Q. 841.

[137] Merchant Shipping Act 1854, 17 & 18 Vict., cap. 104, s. 237, s. 238; Conrad Dixon, 'Seamen and the Law: An Examination of the Impact of Legislation on the British Merchant Seaman's Lot, 1588–1918' (Doctoral Thesis, University College London, 1981), 116; PP 1893–94 LXXX.397 [C. 7179], Transmission of Seamen's Wages, Pitman, Q. 3.

Police division, policed the river and in 1867 began boarding ships below Gravesend, ejecting 'improper persons' and occasionally charging them.[138] The Board of Trade then took over, appointing a naval officer, Captain Robert Pitman, to 'suppress crimping on the river', with sufficient staff to run the more ambitious Midge System, named after the Board's patrol steamer.[139]

Under Pitman's 1896 Transmission of Wages Scheme, an inbound sailor could be signed off in the dock or on board instead of the Shipping Office. He could then be taken to the railway station and, with the aid of a rail ticket and a loan of some cash, immediately travel to the Marine Office in his home port. Here he could collect the wages due to him. Back in London, the Shipping Office in due course collected the sailor's wages from his employer.[140] Transmission of wages, making the sailor 'valueless to the crimp', was a striking extension of State involvement in the maritime sector. There were some legal challenges by crimps, but the courts ruled in favour of the Shipping Office.[141] Advance notes were abolished in 1880 but legalised nine years later. Some sailors still needed funds to equip themselves for a voyage, so shipowners had simply turned to other types of promissory notes. Even so, outward-bound crimping became rare in London, in part because more British vessels discharged their cargoes and crews in continental ports before returning to London.[142]

Despite its claims to the contrary, Board of Trade intervention was not solely responsible for the almost total eradication of London crimping.[143] Stopping crimps boarding vessels must have had an impact but did not stop touting at dock gates or outside shipping offices. The transmission system was only relevant to British seamen with homes in places with a shipping office, and the sums handled were small compared with the total paid out by shipping offices every day.[144] In fact, as Milne notes,

---

[138] PP 1872 XXX.261 [C. 652], Report Commissioner of Metropolitan Police, 1871; Dixon, 'Seamen and the Law', 185; Memorandum on Improvements.

[139] SC Merchant Seamen Bill, Pitman, Qq. 4436–9, 4444.

[140] Transmission of Seamen's Wages, Pitman, Q. 3, 42.

[141] PP 1903 LXII.15 [Cd. 1608], Committee on Certain Questions Affecting Our Mercantile Marine II, Pitman, Q. 63; Dixon, 220–221, 246–7.

[142] David M. Williams, '"Advance Notes" and the Recruitment of Maritime Labour in Britain in the Nineteenth Century', in Lars U. Scholl (ed.), *Merchants and Mariners: Selected Maritime Writings of David M. Williams* (International Maritime Economic History Association, St. John's Newfoundland, 2000), 253–72; PP 1886 LIX.197 [C. 4709], Report on Supply of British Seamen, Appendix H; Dixon, 'Seamen and the Law', 187–8, 190–1, 219; Transmission of Seamen's Wages, Pitman, Q. 111.

[143] Transmission of Seamen's Wages, Pitman, Qq. 7–8, 57–60.

[144] Kennerley, 'Seamen's Missions', 113–4.

'sailortown rose and fell with the age of sail'.[145] With liner steam shipping came predictable voyages and regular wages with no need for an
advance. There was now a greater chance of a settled homelife and a
more domesticated lifestyle. In 1887, there were 2,298 seamen with families living in East London, over half in Poplar.[146] Others settled closer
to the Victoria and Albert Docks, the centre of London's liner trades.
The 1891 West Ham Census records 2,203 males and seven females as
employed in the merchant navy.[147]

Thanks to the 1889 Great Dock Strike, the publication of Booth's
surveys and the efforts of those dissenting from the darkest conventional
portrayals, by the end of the century, outsider views of East London had
altered. The problem of underemployment, most acute in port work, was
no less than it had been, but the revelation that a respectable working
class existed within the East End changed perspectives. Notwithstanding
fears of conflict between the local population and foreign seamen
expressed to the 1903 Royal Commission on Alien Immigration, most
contemporaries had little doubt that London's sailor town district had
altered for the better. 'The low public houses and other dens which
abound in the neighbourhood of the docks ... have greatly decreased,
probably half of them are closed altogether, and the character of some
localities has undergone a complete change', Captain Pitman already
reported in 1886 and in 1898, a Booth investigator found 'fewer sailors,
one cause of less vice'. Even so, prostitution remained common, as were
public houses. But the Highway was different in atmosphere from how it
had been in the past. Author Besant found it 'a lively, cheerful street ...
growing in respectability'.[148]

---

[145] Graeme J. Milne, *People, Place and Power on the Nineteenth-Century Waterfront* (Palgrave
Macmillan, London, 2016), 213.

[146] Stan Hugill, *Sailortown* (Routledge & Kegan Paul, London, 1967), 126; Kennerley,
'Seamen's Missions', 117; Williams, 'Advance Notes', 272; Booth, 'Condition and
Occupations' (1888), 316–7, 322–3, 326–7; Milne, *People, Place and Power*, 143.

[147] PP 1893–94 CV.1 [C.7058], Census of England and Wales 1891, III, Table 7; V.
C. Burton, 'A Floating Population: Vessel Enumeration Returns in Censuses, 1851–
1821', *Local Population Studies*, 38 (1987), 36–43.

[148] Walter Besant, *East London* (The Century Co, New York, 1901), 73.

Illustration 9.1 'The Busy Port of London A Probable State Property'. *Illustrated London News*, 4 April 1908. © *Illustrated London News* Ltd./Mary Evans.

To inquire into the present administration of the Port of London and the water approaches thereto; the adequacy of the accommodation provided for vessels and the loading and unloading thereof; the system of charge for such accommodation and the arrangements for warehousing dutiable goods; and to report whether any change or improvement ... is necessary for the promotion of the port and the public interest.[1]

Over the course of the later nineteenth century, the state of London's port again became a question for national government, eventually leading to the creation of the Port of London Authority (PLA) in 1909. Amalgamation of the leading players was a practical commercial solution to the financial crisis faced by the dock companies in the late 1880s, requiring no external intervention. However, the attempt which followed by the united London and India Dock Company to establish jurisdiction over their water space by abolishing the Free Water Clause challenged the compromise between dock and river port interests that had underpinned the 1799 settlement fashioned by government. This reminder that its port's business was never only a matter for London resulted in the appointment of the Royal Commission on the Port of London, which provided the basis for eventual reform in 1908.

The reforms of 1799 and 1908 were not the only attempts by government to intervene in the management of the capital's port. In 1857, it created the Thames Conservancy Board with responsibility for river management. The Corporation had been a government collaborator in the reform of London's port, but by mid-century, it was no longer obvious that its Navigation Committee should continue with this role. The problem of 'shoals and banks', identified by the 1836 Select Committee, featured again in evidence to the 1840 Select Committee on the Thames Embankment, as well as the Royal Commission on Tidal Harbours.[2] Its 1845 report commented that 'the Thames ... the high road of the commerce of this great empire, for want of systematic conservancy and efficient dredging, has shoals with only eleven feet depth over them'. The 1854 commission that investigated the Corporation, having concluded that 'regulation of the Port of London requires an access to more extensive interests and a greater command of technical knowledge', recommended that another authority should take over. As a result, also in settlement of the seemingly interminable conflict with the Crown over

---

[1] RC Port of London, Report, 3.
[2] SC Thames Embankment; PP 1845 XVI.269, RC Tidal Waters, First Report; PP 1846, 692, RC Tidal Harbours, Second Report, xxvi.

ownership of the riverbed, in 1857 the Thames Conservancy Board was established.[3]

The Thames Conservancy

'The City of London was at length and finally expelled from the ancient office it had enjoyed and exercised during the large part of seven hundred years', wrote conservancy historian Fred S. Thacker in 1914.[4] It was not quite the dramatic severance he suggested. There were seven Corporation nominees and the only external members represented Trinity House, the Admiralty and the Board of Trade. This excited 'considerable remonstrance and opposition' on the grounds, as the Board of Trade suggested, that 'the Corporation of London will continue to possess the real power, whilst they will be no more competent, and even less responsible for its exercise, than they are at present'.[5] Six years on, the Select Committee on Thames Navigation endorsed representation of the two governmental 'Imperial interests', plus Trinity House as pilotage authority, but recommended adding six representatives of 'local interests' and reduction of Corporation representation to three. Predictable Corporation opposition ensured that it retained its seven members when an enlarged Thames Conservancy Board was established in 1864. Membership now also included two elected representatives of shipowners, one elected by passenger steamboat companies, two elected by lighterage and steam tug owners and one by dock companies and wharfingers.

In 1866 the Thames Conservancy also gained responsibility for the non-tidal river above Staines. A second representative of the Board of Trade and four elected representatives of the Upper Thames were then added. Membership remained at twenty-three until 1894, when representation of riparian county councils and water interests increased it to thirty-eight. Direct charges on shipping, in the form of tonnage dues and tolls, were the Conservancy's primary source of income: 38 per cent of total revenue in 1876 and half by the 1890s.[6]

---

[3] PP 1854 XXVI.1 [1772], RC State of the Corporation of the City of London, xxvi; Taylor, 'Water and Its Meanings in London, 1800–1914', 62.

[4] Thacker, *Thames Highway*, 235.

[5] Bill Luckin, *Pollution and Control. A Social History of the Thames in the Nineteenth* Century (Adam Hilger, Bristol, 1986), 144–5; Parliamentary Debates, 3rd Series 146, cc. 1118–1151; PP 1857 Session 2, XIX.515 [2], Report upon Private Bills for Harbours, Docks, Navigations & c. 585.

[6] PP 1863 XII.1 [454], SC Conservancy of River Thames, iv; RC Port of London, Minutes, Phillipson, Q. 2; RC Port of London, Report, 33–7; Luckin, *Pollution*, 147–9; PP 1877 XVII.1 [367], SC Thames Floods Prevention, 218–21.

Illustration 9.2 The *Princess Alice* disaster, 1878. Image: Port of London. © London Metropolitan Archives (City of London).

Conservancy representation was narrowly focussed on trade and transport. It took slight account of the wider interests of the London community the river served. The infrastructural responsibilities of the Metropolitan Board of Works (established in 1855) included sewage outflows into the Thames, but despite several attempts, the Board failed to secure a seat on the Conservancy.[7] According to the Conservancy vice chairman in 1863, it had 'nothing whatsoever to do with the river ... except bringing sewage into the river at Barking'. Conservators treated the Metropolitan Board of Works as a polluting enemy, poisoning the water and impeding navigation by creating mudbanks. In turn, the Board saw the Conservancy as fatally compromised by its connections with wharfingers and steamboat companies, 'the very parties who ought to be put under control instead of being made the controlling parties'.[8] Festering acrimony between the two organisations publicly surfaced in the late 1870s with a renewed Conservancy claim that lower river outfalls were seriously affecting water quality, seemingly supported by

[7] David Owen, *The Government of Victorian London 1855–1899. The Metropolitan Board of Works, the Vestries and the City Corporation* (Belknap Press, Cambridge, MA, 1982) 31–46; Luckin, *Pollution*, 145–7.
[8] PP 1866 XII.491 [871], SC Thames Navigation Bill, Thwaites, Qq. 3798, 3842.

reports that passengers thrown into the river by the sinking of steamboat *Princess Alice* choked on untreated sewage (Illustration 9.2).

The disaster, caused by a collision with a collier, prompted a Board of Trade investigation into the regulation of traffic on the river from which the Conservancy did not itself emerge entirely unscathed. The final report conceded that its 'maintenance and improvement of the physical condition of the river has been efficiently performed', but other than commenting that 'rules which are not habitually enforced are apt to be habitually neglected', it did not challenge complaints by some witnesses of inattention to other responsibilities.[9] Meanwhile, the Conservancy was becoming increasingly successful in directing public attention to the sewage pollution issue. Unlike the Metropolitan Board of Works, it could draw on its members' connections. In 1882, a General Committee of merchants, owners of ships, barges and steamboats, along with dock company and wharf interests, petitioned the government for a Royal Commission. Signatories included the Medical Officer of the Port of London, employed by the Corporation, which had become the sanitary authority for the Port of London. By demanding that the Metropolitan Board of Works improve treatment at the outfalls, the 1884 Royal Commission on Metropolitan Sewage implicitly endorsed the Conservancy's criticisms, but by then its own performance was under attack.[10]

In February 1887 *The Times* published a forthright letter from leading London liner companies, shipping agents and marine insurers. Addressed to the Conservancy, its authors complained of failure to deal with shallows in the river entry to the Victoria and Albert Docks and also at Gravesend, which threatened any vessel above eighteen-foot draft with grounding. They stressed the poor value received from the tonnage dues paid by shipping. Published when the rivalry of the two dock companies was at its height, with the London St. Katharine's Dock Company potentially threatened by its rival's Tilbury dock, the letter's motivation was suspect.[11] Even so, it drew unwelcome public attention to the Conservancy, which, while acknowledging the depth problem, seemingly did little in response.

In 1893 the new London County Council (LCC), keen to bring the Port of London into its sphere of influence, succeeded in gaining three representatives on the Conservancy. When the bill amending its

[9] PP 1878–79 [c. 2338], Thames Traffic Committee, Reports, xxxiii, xlix.
[10] PP 1884 LXII.443 [323], Thames (pollution), Correspondence, 38–44; RC Port of London, Minutes, Collinson, Q. 3647; Luckin, *Pollution*, 147–8.
[11] *Times*, 1 February 1887, 189–90.

constitution was before Parliament the following year, P&O chairman Sir Thomas Sutherland MP went on the offensive. In an echo of complaints earlier in the century, he alleged that by failure to dredged sufficiently, 'the Thames Conservancy been improperly obtaining money for the improvement of the Port of London, while they had failed to expend it on the improvement of the port'. Sutherland's motion having been carried, despite Thames Conservancy opposition, a three-man Lower Thames Navigation Commission, appointed by the Board of Trade, concluded that the Conservancy should dredge a low water channel from the estuary and, if necessary, obtain parliamentary powers to take steps to do so.[12] However, with no indication of how the work would be financed and dubious that the government would support granting additional financial powers, the Conservators decided to take no action, but to continue with a more modest programme. 'We were quite prepared to lower the river if we had the funds', their chairman told the Royal Commission on the Port of London in 1900, a 'do-nothing' strategy which was unlikely to convince critics.[13]

Other River Authorities

Establishing the Thames Conservancy in 1857 did nothing to reduce the historic mix of authorities with responsibilities for river management. Indeed, the 1872 Public Health Act added one more by making the Corporation Sanitary Authority, a choice presumably dictated by its wealth as well as past health responsibilities. The Sanitary Authority's considerable responsibilities for a district covering ninety-one miles of river and a strip of land on each bank included control of infectious disease and inspection of cargoes for health hazards. Its operations sometimes led to conflict with the Customs and local authorities but were not generally a cause of complaint.[14] In contrast, resistance from river users to the Waterman's Company licensing of river craft and labour and Trinity House's pilotage regulations resulted in parliamentary investigations.

The 1854 Royal Commission on the Corporation of London had recommended abolition of the Company of Watermen and Lightermen. An 1859 Act, still in force in 1900, removed its general monopoly but

---

[12] RC Port of London, Report, Appendix A, 126–30; Broodbank, *Port of London Volume 1*; Rodwell Jones, *Geography of London River*, 121–3.
[13] RC Port of London, Minutes, Hartland, Qq. 1432–5, 1606–7, 1676.
[14] 'The Public Health Act, 1872', *British and Foreign Medico-Chirurgical Review* (1873), 1–5 [1–28]; 'The Port of London Sanitary Committee', *British Medical Journal*, 2 (1876), 536; RC Port of London, Minutes, Collingridge, Qq. 3647–54; Report, 59–60.

Illustration 9.3 Workers on the 'Silent Highway', 1877. Image: J. Thomson and Adolph Smith, Street Life in London (Sampson Low, Marston, Searle & Rivington, London, 1877). © London School of Economics Digital Library.

still limited navigation to licensed freemen or their apprentices. The Company's contention that the unique difficulty of Thames navigation required exceptionally experienced men had proved stronger than the barge owners' counterargument that it was not in their interest to employ incompetent bargemen. Over the next forty years, it successfully repelled attempts by both the Thames Conservancy and barge firms to end this restriction.

Compulsory Thames pilotage and the role of Trinity House Corporation, which had jurisdiction as London's lighthouse and licensing authority, were other grievances. Under the 1854 Merchant Shipping Act, the obligation to have a pilot on board was continued where it already existed. Though with little practical justification, coasters, vessels without passengers in northern European trades and those in ballast were therefore exempt. A campaign by the Shipowners' Society to end all obligatory pilotage, as well as gain representation on Trinity House similar to that it enjoyed on the Thames Conservancy, made no progress and an 1870 bill failed to gain parliamentary supporters. In 1879 the Select Committee on Thames Traffic recommended that manning of both passenger steamers and barges should 'be thrown open entirely'.[15] The 1888 Select Committee on Pilotage, mainly dealing with national grievances, concluded that compulsion should be a local matter, which in the case of London left the decision to Trinity House.[16] Like the barge owners, opponents of compulsory pilotage had found themselves up against the Port of London's still powerful entrenched traditional interests.

A Port and Harbour Authority for London

If London needed a comprehensive harbour authority similar to other ports, the focus on sectional grievances and the failings of existing institutions, which, no less than in earlier decades, marked the 1870s and 1880s, was not going to achieve this. But three developments in the late 1880s – the financial crisis in the largest dock companies, the Great Dock Strike and the ambitions of the LCC – drew public attention both to the Port of London's problems and possible solutions.

In the early 1880s, *The Times* published several letters from a single correspondent advocating a public trust similar to that in Bombay and in 1889, it carried an editorial headlined 'The Coming Dock Trust', which referred to supporters in the City, among them the GSNC Chairman.[17] The previous year's legislation establishing the London St. Katharine's and East and West India joint working union had been opposed by shipowners on the grounds that this 'would substitute a monopoly with all its attendant evils for the competition which now exists between the two great dock-owning companies'. Totally dependent on the largest docks, major customers P&O, British India and British India Associates particularly feared cancellation of agreements that guaranteed them the same charges as paid by their competitors.[18] Given the severity of the

---

[15] PP 1859 Session 1 XIII.41 [13], Reports of Board of Trade on Private Bills, 98–9; RC Port of London 1902 Report, 57; Jon Temple (ed.), *History of the Watermen's Company* (Watermen's Company, London, 2008), 73–7.

[16] PP 1870 IX.1 [343], SC on the Pilotage Bill; PP 1871 LXI.495 [263], Memorial ... Change in Constitution of the Trinity House; SC Thames Traffic (1878–9); PP 1888 XIV.85 [324], SC Pilotage.

[17] *Times*, Letters 6 October, 22 October 1881, 24 January 1882, Editorial 25 September 1889; *Pall Mall Gazette*, 28 August 1889.

[18] TNA, MT10 513 H4032, H3824, H3852; *Shipping Gazette and Lloyd's List*, 11 May 1888.

dock company crisis and the practical nature of the proposal, self-serving arguments by wealthy businesses carried little weight and the bill passed. 'The shipowners have failed again', a Board of Trade official noted.[19]

For the Progressive Group of Liberal and Labour men on the LCC, gaining representation on the Thames Conservancy was only an interim victory.[20] Commitment to port municipalisation, made topical by the 1889 strike, was added to their programme in 1891. As Fabian socialist LCC member Sidney Webb wrote:

The substitution for the Conservancy Board of either a committee of the County Council or a 'representative Dock and River Trust' with power to take over property of the four great companies ... appears to be the best practicable means of organising the demoralised dock labourers, and so healing the spreading social ulcer of the East End.[21]

In 1891 *The Times* continued its campaign by publishing two long articles on 'The Problem of the Ports'. These were highly critical of the Progressives municipalisation policy but admiring of the Mersey Docks and Harbour Board and the Clyde Ports Trust. Such public bodies were nationally very much on the political agenda, with their introduction under discussion elsewhere.[22] With the financial future of London's dock companies still uncertain, in 1896 rumours circulating about the formation of a large dock trust were said to account for a rise in dock company stocks. Mindful of possible compensation, the dock companies were not averse to their eventual replacement by a trust or even the LCC, but the rumours were probably just that.[23]

The Travails of the Joint Committee

With competition eliminated, agreements with wharfinger interests in place and an increase of 25 per cent in charges on goods and shipping, more than compensating for the rise in wages achieved by the Great Dock Strike, the Docks Joint Committee companies expected a turnround in

[19] TNA, MT10 513, H4736.
[20] John Davis, 'The Progressive Council, 1889–1907', in Andrew Saint (ed.), *Politics and the People of London. The London County Council 1889–1965* (Hambledon Press, London, 1989), 27–36.
[21] Sidney Webb, 'The Municipalisation of the London Docks', *Fabian Tract No. 35* (London, 1891); *Reynolds News*, 6 December 1891; Charles Harrison, 'The River Thames. Its Port and Conservancy', London Reform Union Pamphlet (1895); Paul Thompson, *Socialists, Liberals and Labour. The Struggle for London 1885–1914* (Routledge & Kegan Paul, London, 1967), 106.
[22] *Times*, 3, 13, 21 August 1892.
[23] *Liverpool Shipping Telegraph*, 30 June 1896; *Shipping Gazette & Lloyd's List*, 30 June 1895.

fortunes. Instead, warehousing business continued to drain away to the river wharves. The weaker of the two companies, the East and West India, lacked capital for necessary improvements. Failing to persuade the Admiralty to purchase Tilbury, it was compelled to borrow from its Joint Committee partner. Between 1890 and 1898, the East and West India paid no dividend on ordinary shares. London St. Katharine's managed 2.5 per cent in most years, but its proprietors were restive for better dividends.[24]

The Joint Committee decided to generate more income by exploiting their monopoly power. Discharging vessels was no longer a major source of earnings since most shipping lines undertook this themselves, so in 1897 the dock companies announced they would forgo fixed rent on liner berths and instead charge shipping companies for unloading produce. Recognising the potential impact of the change on their costs, the shipowners aired their opposition in the press. The Joint Committee retreated, but the public furore was an unhelpful reminder of the role of unaccountable private companies in the country's premier port.[25]

In 1900, two Joint Committee private bills, one uncontroversial, the other much less so, went before Parliament. After eleven years of working in tandem, earlier mutual distrust was largely eliminated, but duplication of operations was inefficient and legal separation created problems in raising capital. The proposal to join the two companies came from the East and West India, which was facing an organised shareholder revolt. Despite the title, the Amalgamation bill effectively authorised its sale to the London St. Katharine's, as was reflected in the new name: the London and India Docks Company. It was an ignominious end to an enterprise that, not entirely unfairly, had for decades considered its management and connections superior to that of its slightly more junior rival. The bill received the Royal Assent at the end of July 1900. After the final meeting of the East and West India Dock Company on 29 January 1901, someone wrote 'Goodbye' at the end of the minutes.[26]

The Joint Committee's other bill, which authorised companies to charge on craft using its docks, was a direct challenge to the Free Water Clause.[27] The Watermen and Lightermen's Company, wharfingers and shipowners, as well as the London Chamber of Commerce, the Corporation of London and the LCC were united in their opposition.

---

[24] MLD, EWID 037, 31 July 1894; RC Port of London, Appendices, Second Day, No. 6.
[25] MLD, EWID 037, 23 February 1897; Broodbank, *Port of London 1*, 265–7; *St James Gazette*, 2 March 1896.
[26] MLD, EWID 038, 19 July 1898, 15 November 1898, 2 October 1900; *Times*, 12 April 1900.
[27] *Shipping Gazette & Lloyd's List*, Editorial, 25 November 1899.

Urged by all the 'great representative bodies' to set up an inquiry, the President of the Board of Trade, Charles Ritchie, on the grounds that the future of the Port of London was 'not only a local but a national question', appointed a Royal Commission. Seemingly certain of vindication, the Joint Committee dropped its private bill.[28]

The Royal Commission on the Port of London

Dock company opponents had often called for simply a 'dock trust', but Ritchie envisaged an investigation that would also cover the entire port and its final terms of reference were certainly broad. A technocratic businessman, former Conservative member for Tower Hamlets and the minister responsible for the act that created the LCC, Ritchie was well-versed in the troubles of the Port of London.[29] His tenure at the Board of Trade was short, but no other ministry including the Customs had so much history, sometimes difficult, of direct engagement with London's maritime sector.

The Commission, Ritchie explained to the Commons, would not be 'partial or partisan', or represent particular interests. At least formally, those appointed reflected this. The original chairman having resigned on grounds of ill health, his replacement was merchant banker, Lord Revelstoke. The other members were former Board of Trade statistician Sir Robert Giffen, Quaker coal owner John Ellis MP, Rear Admiral Sir John Hext, lawyer Alfred Lyttleton MP, LCC member William Peel MP and civil engineer Sir John Wolfe-Barry.[30] While unconnected with the port, when it came to arriving at recommendations, some commissioners may not have been entirely without prejudice. Wolf-Barry, the architect of Tower Bridge, was a member of the 1896 committee that supported shipowners against the Conservancy by recommending dredging a thirty-foot channel.[31] Peel was a member of the LCC's Conservative-associated Mutual Reform Party opposed to municipalisation. Hext had served for fifteen years on the Bombay Port Trust, established in 1873. His inclusion suggests that the Board of Trade saw the Bombay Trust as a potential imperial model for London, as much as the home example of the Mersey Docks and Harbour Board. The government of the Port of

---

[28] *Lloyd's List*, 15 March 1900; Parliamentary Debates 4th Series 83, 15 May 1900, cc. 160–86.

[29] ODNB, Charles Thomson Ritchie, first Baron Ritchie of Dundee (1838–1906).

[30] *Lloyd's List*, 27 June 1900; ODNB John Baring, second Baron Revelstoke (1863–1926), Sir Robert Giffen (1837–1910); Alfred Lyttelton (1857–1913), William Robert Wellesley Peel (1867–1937) and Sir John Wolfe Wolfe-Barry (1836–1918).

[31] RC Port of London Report, Appendix A, 126–30.

Bombay included not only municipal representatives but also nine government nominees, including its chairman.[32]

The Royal Commission began work in June 1900. As well as receiving written submissions and visiting some British and north European ports, members examined more than a hundred witnesses between November and the following July. The LCC's clerk, Lawrence Gomme, was among the best prepared. In 1895, its Rivers Committee had asked him to gather material on all aspects of the port's operations. Gomme, an extraordinarily industrious man, had gone about this task with a will. As a result, the reports and tables he had originally provided for his employers served as the factual underpinning of the Commission's final report.[33] Far less well prepared and seemingly unaware of the threat to its survival was the Thames Conservancy chairman. Commissioners were unimpressed that he had to be pressed to submit a proposal to raise revenue but rigidly defended its commitment to limited dredging. However, no one could accuse the London and India Dock Company chairman Charles Cater Scott, who endured five successive days of questioning, of being uninformative, or indeed lacking stamina.[34]

The Commission's report was published in July 1902. This steered a judicious course. While accepting the argument of shipowners and merchants that the Port of London was unable to meet the needs of modern commerce, it contended that the dock companies deserved sympathy as 'the victims of a change in circumstances which has dispossessed them gradually of the advantages that they once enjoyed'. At the same time, it considered that to attempt to resolve their financial difficulties by eliminating the Free Water Clause would be unjust to the wharfingers, on whom much of the trade of the modern port depended. Although evident, the Commission's disapproval of the Conservancy's performance was muted. Indeed, its most direct criticism was reserved for the only port workers mentioned, the licensed lightermen: 'river traffic was too much under the control of a limited class of men'.[35]

Except for submissions by the London and India, Millwall and Commercial Dock companies, the Commission found 'a powerful consensus of opinion in favour of the consolidation of powers at present divided, and the creation of a single public Authority for the control of

---

[32] W. R. S. Sharpe, *The Port of Bombay* (Bombay Port Trust, Bombay, 1900), 21; Adrian Jarvis, *Liverpool Central Docks, 1799–1905. An Illustrated History* (Alan Sutton, Stroud, 1991), 15.

[33] London County Council, *Royal Commission on the Port of London, 1900, Statement of Evidence by Clerk of the London County Council*, 3 December 1900.

[34] RC Port of London, Report, 9, 42.

[35] Ibid., 82, 37.

the Port'.[36] That this was the core recommendation is therefore unsurprising. More astonishing was the range of responsibilities it envisaged for London's new port government. As the *Shipping Gazette* commented, these did not show 'a too tender consideration for vested interests'.[37] Besides acquiring the dock companies, including the still profitable Surrey Commercial, the port authority would replace the Conservancy on the Lower Thames and possibly take over Thames pilotage and buoying rights from Trinity House. The Company of Watermen and Lightermen would be abolished, except as a charity. Other than passenger vessels, the licensing of craft and those who navigated them would cease. To avoid unfair competition between the warehouses formerly owned by the dock companies and those in private hands, the new authority would be required to sell or lease those that were not closely connected with dock operations.[38]

The Commission recommended the creation of interest-bearing port stock, which dock company investors would receive in return for their shares. Noting that both the Corporation and the LCC had shown an 'earnest and public spirited' desire for port improvement, either or both the Corporation and the LCC should grant a £2.5 million capital sum needed for river improvement. They would also guarantee interest on a further £4.5 million needed for dock improvement, which would be raised through the issue of port stock. The port authority's revenue would come from tonnage dues on shipping entering the port and using the docks, a new charge on goods landed anywhere in the port and an annual license fee for river craft.

Although commenting vaguely that there were signs that the Port of London might be losing out in competition with other British and foreign ports, the Commission's primary interest in these was whether any might serve as a model for London's port authority. In the light of London's 'enormous population and the magnitude of the interests affected', it rejected a predominantly elected body in favour of a majority of nominated members. 'In Liverpool a distinguished merchant or shipowner is known throughout the whole community. In London such a man is often neither a member of the London County Council, nor of the City Corporation, and, in the vast aggregate of individuals gathered there, his capacity is known only among a section'.[39]

---

[36] Ibid., 112.
[37] *Shipping Gazette*, 19 June 1902.
[38] RC Port of London, Report, 112–4.
[39] Ibid., 121.

About forty members were suggested, fourteen elected by port interests and twenty-six nominated. Eleven might represent the LCC, three
the Corporation. The Admiralty, Board of Trade, Trinity House, Kent
and Essex County Councils would also nominate. Two would be from
the London Chamber of Commerce and five would be nominated by
the Governors of the Bank of England, a final five might come from 'the
mercantile community of London'. Closer in structure to Bombay than
Liverpool, though much larger than both those authorities, the proposed
size and membership seemingly reflected the mercantile City interests of
the Commission's chairman more than a need for an effective governing
body for the Port of London.[40]

Political Challenges to Port Reform

The Board of Trade responded swiftly to the 1902 Royal Commission
report. By the following April its Port of London Bill was before
Parliament. In the intervening months it became clear that opposition
to some Commission recommendations was not limited to those most
directly affected. Involving the Corporation and LCC in port reform
touched on wider issues of metropolitan government and politics. In the
autumn of 1902, a committee, convened by the Lord Mayor and representing the Corporation, LCC, port, shipping, mercantile and banking
interests, tried to arrive at a common position to put to Gerald Balfour,
the President of the Board of Trade. Most were in favour of a port authority. Predictably the dock companies, Trinity House and the Conservancy
were against it. There was general agreement that mercantile interests
on the authority should be elected, not nominated. However, apart from
the LCC itself, many opposed local government involvement as port
stock guarantor, arguing that this would throw port development on the
rates. It was argued that the reformed port's progress would be sufficient
security.

Gerald Balfour's Port of London bill was opposed at second reading only by the discredited Conservancy chairman and the Surrey
Commercial Dock Company, for whom compulsory purchase of all
London's docks was 'socialistic, communistic legislation'.[41] The bill
took some account of objections to Royal Commission recommendations. Trinity House, a practical but elite establishment body with political friends, would retain its Thames role and the new authority would
have forty members, but more than half would be elected. However,

[40] Ibid., 115–122.
[41] *Times*, 14 May 1903.

there was still much to enrage critics. The government did not accept arguments that the new authority would be able to finance port development investment on its own account and, since the Corporation had declined to be a guarantor of port stock, this would fall to the LCC alone. It also decided that to compel the new port authority to sell off wharf and warehouse facilities would impede its progress, so private wharfingers and warehouse operators faced its competition. There was also the issue of port authority membership. As many as twenty-seven councils and organisations, including the LCC and Corporation, petitioned either to be granted representation or for this to be increased. The Commons and Lords Joint Committee on the Port of London Bill also had to consider arguments against other aspects of the bill presented by their Counsel or agents. With some justification, critics of the proceedings contended that its fourteen sittings, seemingly rushed to enable the bill to become law in that parliamentary session, were insufficient for such an important and controversial measure.[42] But it was the Joint Committee's decision that the LCC should have nine members and the Corporation just one that sealed the bill's fate.[43]

For London's shipping companies and traders, establishing the port authority was far more urgent and important than its membership or financial settlement. But for the dock companies, the Corporation's supporters and Conservative opponents of the LCC these were priorities. 'It may also answer certain partisan views to keep the influence of the County Council as much as possible', commented the P&O's Sutherland. Balfour faced down a Lord Mayor's deputation, which demanded he withdraw his bill, but fearing defeat in the Commons, orchestrated by City members, announced that it would be carried over to the following year.[44]

The weakened Conservative and Unionist government did not reintroduce its bill. A somewhat similar LCC bill for a forty-member authority, giving it twenty-four representatives and reducing port and trade interests to twelve, was rejected by the Commons in 1905. Since the LCC bill was supported by the Liberal opposition, as well as some municipalist conservatives, the margin of defeat was not large. For the first time port reform had become a party issue. Three years were to pass before Parliament, under a different government, returned once more to the question.[45]

[42] *Times*, 22 August 1903.
[43] PP 1903 VIII.1 [288], Joint SC report, xi.
[44] *Times*, 16 July, 1, 11, 22 August 1903; *Eastern Post*, 22 August 1903.
[45] Broodbank, *Port of London II*, 331–2; *Times*, 14 April 1905.

In the meantime, those interests most threatened by a port authority sought to consolidate their position. In 1904, the London India attempted to ensure its survival by a bill that, besides turning the Conservancy into a port authority by strengthening its powers, would have enabled it to raise the capital to enlarge the Royal Albert Dock. In the absence of government support, it was unable to proceed. Increased charges had improved revenue sufficiently to permit modest dividends, but improvements were stymied by a lack of capital. Under a new chairman, the Conservancy did somewhat better, by gaining parliamentary authority in 1905 to double tonnage tolls and borrow £3 million for investment in dredging equipment, quays and jetties.[46]

The 1902 Royal Commission had asserted that London's problems were 'not due to any physical circumstances, but to causes which may easily be removed by a better organisation of administrative and financial powers', hence the need for a port authority. Not all subsequent commentators were convinced that all the port's problems were organisational. The Conservancy Act's reference to quays and jetties, and a similar mention in the LCC's bill, reflected increasing public discussion of major waterfront improvements as the answer to the Port of London's need for ever deeper berths. This arose out of sometimes flimsy adverse comparisons with London's transit-trade foreign competitors, Antwerp, Rotterdam and Hamburg, all of which were ocean trade river ports. Suggested projects for London deep water included piers, a basin above Tilbury and a barrage at Gravesend to create 'a freshwater lake'.[47]

Lloyd George's Port of London Bill

With Liberal electoral victory in 1906 came expectations of fresh legislation to establish a port authority. No longer blocked by a Conservative government, the LCC Progressives had hopes of early success. However, unlike the new President of the Board of Trade, David Lloyd George, the Cabinet was in no hurry to deal with such a notably complex and contentious issue, so the government undertook to introduce legislation in the 1908 session. The Liberal government was not ignorant of the Port of London's problems. Postmaster-General Sidney Buxton, the popular member for Poplar and supporter of the 1889 Dock Strike,

[46] Broodbank, Ibid.; Parliamentary Debates, 4th Series, 146, 12 July 1905, 459–604; PP 1906 XCVIII.723 [130], Thames Conservancy General Report, 1905.
[47] T. W. Barber (ed.), *The Port of London and the Thames Barrage* (Swan Sonneschein, London, 1907), 6–11; *Times*, 12 November 1907.

had introduced the LCC's Port of London bill and Chancellor of the Exchequer Herbert Asquith, soon to succeed Campbell Bannerman as Prime Minister, was a legal expert on port matters and an Elder Brother of Trinity House. The LCC Progressives might have expected to influence the forthcoming Port of London legislation. However, electoral defeat by the Conservative's Moderate Party in March 1907 put an end to their ambitions for a municipalised port, helping Lloyd George to arrive at a settlement acceptable to his parliamentary opponents.[48] When he introduced his bill, it had Conservative support.

Lloyd George's Port of London bill reflected many months of careful preparation. He had seen for himself the much-vaunted port facilities of London's continental rivals, visiting in turn Antwerp, Hamburg and Rotterdam over the 1907 Whitsun break. With him were senior Port of Trade officials, the Progressive leader and coal merchant Sir Edwin Cornwall MP, and his Parliamentary Secretary, the grocery magnate Hudson Kearley, who as Lord Devonport was to become the first chairman of the PLA. The group concluded that re-engineering the Thames waterfront was not the answer to London's need for deep draught facilities. 'The docks are necessary'.[49]

Pressure from port users and other bodies had led the previous legislative attempts to founder once before Parliament. To avoid a repeat, Lloyd George, according to a gas company chairman, 'showed a very reasonable spirit in his efforts to draft the Bill, and talked the matter over in a friendly way with representatives of the various interests'.[50] His biographer, Bentley B. Gilbert, suggests that Lloyd George was not much involved in negotiations with the dock companies. Given the financial expertise required in this case, and urgent other issues demanding his attention, this may well be correct. However, he was certainly not disengaged. There are several reports of meetings with port interests.[51]

Ongoing discussions confirmed widespread support for a powerful port authority and the proposal for a reasonable charge on goods in return for a better Port of London was generally acceptable. The shipowner lobby,

[48] Clifton, Gloria 'Members and Officers of the LCC, 1889–1965' in Andrew Saint (ed.), *Politics and the People of London. The London County Council 1889–1965* (Hambledon Press, London, 1989), 1–26; *Times*, 20 November 1907.
[49] TNA, CAB 37/85 1906; ODNB, Sidney Charles Buxton, Earl Buxton (1853–1934); Ian Ivatt, 'Lloyd George's Presidency of the Board of Trade', *Journal of Liberal History*, 103 (2019), 27–9 [23–9]; ODNB, Hudson Ewbanke Kearley, first Viscount Devonport (1856–1934); PP 1908 XCIII.931 [109], Port of London Bill Memorandum.
[50] *Times*, 29 May 1908; Port of London Bill Memorandum.
[51] Bentley Brinkerhoff Gilbert, *David Lloyd George: A Political Life. The Architect of Change 1863–1912* (B. T. Batsford Ltd., London, 1987), 327.

long vocal in its support for reform, took no persuading. The powerful wharf interests, with their City supporters, were a different matter. There was never any possibility that the private wharves might be purchased. Practical and political considerations ruled this out. But the waterfront wharf interests would not benefit directly from the charges to be imposed on their traffic. Instead, they faced PLA competition. Board of Trade negotiations with wharfingers were therefore particularly challenging.[52]

Examination of the London India books by a government-appointed accountant confirmed that current revenue could not both finance new projects and reward shareholders out of current revenue but would be sufficient to pay interest on port stock. The new LCC administration ruled out any guarantees, in any case now judged unnecessary. Most important, terms were agreed to buy the property of the London India, Millwall and (with greater difficulty) the Surrey Commercial companies, avoiding compulsory purchase, arbitration and any involvement by an infant PLA.[53] The front page of the *Illustrated London News* (Illustration 9.1) was not entirely wide of the mark.[54]

By the time the Port of London bill came before Parliament in April 1908, those issues with the greatest potential to derail its progress had been eliminated. Only a delay beyond 31 December 1908, when the dock company agreements expired, could do this. The Lloyd George bill owed little to its Conservative predecessor, much to his fresh approach and outstanding negotiating skills. As expected, as well as the docks, the Authority would take over the Lower Thames responsibilities of the Thames Conservancy and those of the Company of Watermen and Lightermen. But it would not have forty members. 'It is better to have a small body to transact business than to discuss' Lloyd George told the Commons, so there would be just twenty-five.[55] To discourage sectionalism, he proposed that the majority would be elected by a general constituency of fifteen port users, wharfingers and owners of river craft, the payers of port and dock charges. The remaining appointed members would represent the Admiralty, Board of Trade, LCC, Corporation and Trinity House. Except for the chairman and vice chairman, members would be unpaid.[56]

---

[52] Lincoln Gordon, 'The Port of London Authority', in William A. Robson (ed.), *Public Enterprise. Developments in Social Ownership and Control in Great Britain* (George Allen & Unwin, London, 1937), 24.
[53] Port of London Bill Memorandum, *Times*, 29 May 1908.
[54] *Illustrated London News*, 4 April 1908.
[55] Parliamentary Debates, 4th Series 187, 2 April 1908, c. 712.
[56] Port of London Bill Memorandum.

Lloyd George became Chancellor within days of the bill's first reading, so the next stages of the Port of London bill were handled by his successor, Winston Churchill. The government, committed to a small membership, stood firm at the committee stage in the face of most demands for representation, many from riparian county councils and boroughs. It did, however, introduce or accept some other changes in membership. Wharf interests were placated by being awarded a special representative elected only by themselves, as well as being included in the broader electorate of port users.[57] The number of appointed members remained ten, but the Corporation gained an extra representative at the expense of the LCC. The final composition of the authority was eighteen elected and ten appointed by the Board of Trade. Two would be its own nominations and the Admiralty and Trinity House were allotted one each. The LCC was allowed four representatives, the Corporation two. In both these cases, half those nominated could not be drawn from their members. Thanks to the efforts of members with labour connections, most representing East London constituencies, one each of those nominated by the Board of Trade and by the LCC were to be 'representative of labour'. The PLA's Chairman and Vice Chairman, who did not have to be board members, would also be government appointees.[58]

The State's role in the authority went beyond such appointments. The Board of Trade 'is to be found in thirty-four of the sixty-three sections of the Act', ruefully noted Broodbank. In William Robson's 1937 edited collection, *Public Enterprise*, the first chapter deals with the PLA. However, as far as day-to-day business was concerned, it was to operate independently and political influence over its policy was in practice constrained. On the grounds that it was an independent body, in July 1912, the Common's Speaker rejected a motion that dealt with port traffic congestion and decasualisation. By then, the Liberal government that fathered the PLA had already discovered that it could not control its infant.[59]

The Port of London Authority

Lloyd George's bill was not without opponents, among them some recalcitrant Thames Conservancy figures, but they were a minority. With

---

[57] PP 1908 X.1 [288], Joint SC Port of London Bill, ix, Fitzgerald, 19.

[58] George J. D. Tull, *The Port of London Authority 1909–1959* (Unpublished), 10. In the ownership of the author, this detailed summary of the Board minutes was issued only to Board Members and Officers of the Port of London, 'with the object of assisting them in their functions and duties'; Parliamentary Debates, 4th Fourth Series 193, 23 July 1908, cc. 294–496.

[59] Broodbank, *Port of London II*, 345; Robson, *Public Enterprise*, 29–33.

cross-party support and the deadline for purchase agreements due to expire, on 21 December, it received the Royal Assent.[60] Thereafter, things moved swiftly. On 16 March 1909 the PLA held its inaugural meeting. Lord Devonport was chairman, Vice-Chair was Owen Crosby Phillips, managing director of the Royal Mail Steampacket Company. With time too short for elections, the Board of Trade had appointed the representatives of port users, wharfingers and owners of river craft. Effectively these were their nominees. There was no contested election in 1913 and in some years thereafter. The Board of Trade representatives were Broodbank, the former secretary of the East and West India Dock Company and Harry Gosling, the well-known champion of river workers. Stevedore James Anderson was LCC's labour representative. Including a temporary member permitted 'as a person of experience in dock management', the authority had thirty members, seven of whom had served on the Thames Conservancy.[61]

Most of the Act establishing the PLA 'for the purpose of administering, preserving and improving the Port of London' dealt with its rights, powers, finances and membership. It was generally unspecific on how it should improve the port – with one exception. Under Section 8(1), it should 'take such steps as they should think best calculated to diminish the evils of casual employment and to promote the more convenient and regular engagement of such workmen or any class thereof'.[62] Dealing with casual employment was high on the Liberal agenda. The Royal Commission on the Poor Laws (1905–1909), a Local Government Board inquiry (1908) and an investigation by the Charity Organisation Society (1908) had all heard evidence of a connection between port labour and pauperism.[63]

Of course, there was nothing at all new about endemic underemployment in the port industry. What was novel was the political will to intervene. Under Churchill's 1909 Labour Exchange Act, it was possible for the Board of Trade, already with this role in relation to seamen, to set up its own employment offices to serve the docks and wharves. Any programme for decasualisation depended on the co-operation of employers, including shipowners and wharfingers. These proved resistant, so

[60] 8 Edw. VII, Ch. 68.
[61] Tull, *Port of London*, 10–13; Broodbank, *Port of London II*, 346–7.
[62] Tull, Ibid., 105.
[63] PP 1909 XXXVI1.1 [Cd. 4499], RC Poor Laws and the Relief of Distress, 1145–53; PP 1908 XCII.483 [Cd. 4391], Dock Labour in Relation to Poor Law Relief; Charity Organisation Society, *Special Committee on Unskilled Labour. Report and Minutes of Evidence, June 1908* (COS, London, 1908), 25–36, 114–63.

the Board of Trade trusted that the PLA would take the lead. But any possibility of progress was undermined by extremely hostile industrial relations between 1911 and 1913, to the extent that the PLA became 'a truculent adversary' of decasualisation.[64]

Port Labour and the Port of London Authority

The creation of the PLA resolved some but not all of the Port of London's problems. Although still constrained by financial considerations, it was able to embark on a major programme of investment, with dredging a deep channel and modernisation of the lower dock systems the priorities. Both were delayed by war, but the George V dock, parallel to the Albert Dock, opened in 1921.[65] The failure of the 1908 Port of London Act to have any effect on the port's casual labour system is unsurprising. The dock workforce was consolidated, but there remained many employers, including the anti-union liner companies, which hired their own dockers and stevedores. Even if the PLA had been more accommodating and others less determined to retain their freedom, further obstacles to decasualisation included doubt or antipathy in the workforce. However, trade union leaders had no rooted objection, provided they could influence recruitment. Hoping for substantial labour representation and greater cooperation, they had campaigned for a port authority for London.[66]

Neither turned out to be the case. Labour representation on the PLA was both niggardly and indirect, and the PLA's Lord Devonport revealed himself to be at least as fierce an opponent as Norwood had been in 1889. In September 1911, London's transport unions came together in the National Transport Workers Federation. Although the initiative was Tillett's, the Dockers Union was moribund, so the Federation was dominated by the more successful skilled worker unions. Its President and General Secretary, Gosling and Anderson, were PLA members. Their unions had adapted to the challenge of competition from outsiders by greater willingness to enrol them as members, so had more in common with the general Dockers Union than in the past.[67] As Gosling later recalled:

---

[64] Gordon Phillips and Noel Whiteside, *Casual Labour. The Unemployment Question in the Port Transport Industry 1880–1970* (Clarendon Press, Oxford, 1985), 84–5; Tull, *Port of London Authority*. 105, 111.
[65] Greeves, *London Docks*, 19–25.
[66] Phillips and Whiteside, *Casual Labour*, 55–67; Tull, *Port of London Authority*, 111.
[67] Lovell, *Stevedores and Dockers*, 150–4; Schneer, *Ben Tillett*, 150–2.

It had been twenty-two years since any real improvement had been made in the conditions of the dockers and other transport workers. The hours of work were atrocious ... while the wages of the men, the majority of whom where casually employed, were wretchedly low. These same twenty-two years had, on the other hand, brought a steady advance in prosperity to the employers connected with riverside work.[68]

With the London economy booming and unemployment low, unions saw an opportunity. On 29 June, with strikes by sailors affecting other British ports and sympathetic action likely to break out in London, the dockers demanded that the PLA, wharfingers, shipowners and granary keepers increase wages to eight pence an hour for regular work and a shilling for overtime by 3 July. The Lightermen made a similar claim, but the Stevedores already received this, so were not involved. Threatened with a general stoppage, the employers agreed to negotiate, and the deadline passed.

Three conferences between these and the National Federation followed. This was the first time in the port's history that they had ever met face-to-face, seemingly as equals, across a table. The trade union side had in its sights recognition by all port employers and the same hourly pay rate across the entire Port of London. It achieved neither and the final provisional agreement, which did not apply to all types of port work and in some cases involved arbitration, was for seven and nine pence an hour. When Gosling and Tillett put the settlement to a mass meeting in Mile End, it was thrown out. 'There was a bold new spirit in them, and they found it hard to realise we had done the best we could', later observed Gosling.[69]

The National Federation misjudged the men, just as they had misjudged the PLA. Devonport had taken the lead in rejecting the full pay claim and refused to shift. Spontaneous walkouts by coal porters and dockers followed, and, accepting the inevitable, the transport workers declared an official strike on 3 August, which the stevedores joined five days later. With stoppages spreading and food cargoes rotting in the port, the Board of Trade intervened. Thanks in large part to the Board's expert conciliator, George Askwith, the last of the strikes ended by 23 August with agreements, which in most cases favoured the men, who got their eight pence and shilling. It was a remarkable victory.[70]

---

[68] Gosling, 148.

[69] Lovell, *Stevedores and Dockers*, 157–163; Gosling, Ibid., 150; Schneer, *Ben Tillett*, 153–4.

[70] George Ranken Askwith, *Industrial Problems and Disputes* (John Murray, London, 1920), 156–7; Lovell, Ibid., 167–97; Gosling, Ibid., 156; Schneer, Ibid., 156.

However, for the employers, the outcome of the 1911 conflict was a temporary truce, not a peace. In May 1912 the lightermen struck in response to a refusal by some barge owners to pay the new wage rate and a refusal by the lighterage employers to adhere to the traditional closed shop. Stevedores, already in dispute with shipowners over the recruitment monopoly issue, along with dockers and carmen, came out in support. Buoyed by the previous year's triumph, on 23 May, the National Federation called a port-wide strike, and more men joined the action. With the Port of London at a standstill, again the government intervened, appointing a public inquiry into the strike and attempting conciliation.[71]

This time the employers refused to be involved. Led by Devonport, they were determined to defeat the unions once and for all. To force matters to a head, the Federation then called a national strike. It was a disastrous move. Despite its name, the National Federation had little support outside the metropolis, where the struggle continued. Funds for strike pay began to run out, and, beaten by starvation, support slowly dwindled. On 27 June, the strike was called off, though some men stayed out longer. Thirteen thousand black legs had been recruited by the employers, and conflict with some caused serious riots in August. The aftermath of this exceptionally bitter dispute predictably followed the historic pattern: those who had held permanent posts lost their jobs and not all strikers were reinstated.[72] Far from the 1908 Port of London Act leading to improvements in labour relations, it accomplished the opposite. The PLA was a much more formidable union opponent than its dock company predecessors had ever been. In due course, the demands of the wartime economy reduced casualism, or made the system work more efficiently, and seemingly achieved a better understanding between port employers and unions. But such gains proved temporary and wholesale decasualisation remained elusive for many years to come.[73]

In a neat symmetry, this book began and ended with major port reform. Indeed, the involvement of government was a recurrent theme. In the intervening years the port, like the rest of London, had undergone considerable change. Docks had once been seen as the height of modernity, their directors as symbols of enterprise and progress. A century later, docks were bywords for poor management and outdated

[71] Lovell, Ibid., 194–99; Gosling, Ibid., 159–60.
[72] *London Evening Standard*, 11 June 1912; Askwith, *Industrial Problems*, 222–5; Gosling, 163; Lovell, Ibid., 201–2.
[73] Phillips and Whiteside, *Casual Labour*, 113–45.

facilities. In a curious reversal, waterfront wharves, once the poor relation, had become essential elements in port operations. Most obvious
was the transformation in shipping. London had become a downriver
steam port. What changed the least was port work. Whether permanent or casual, whether in old or newer workplaces, the basic job of
cargo handling altered little. As in the past, industrial relations were
fragile, the hold of unions tenuous, and a culture of sectional interest
persistent.

Bibliography

Archives

The National Archives
BT 36, MAF 41, MT6, T10, RAIL 1066, T1 4133, T10, T76, T108.

British Library
Chatham Papers

Merseyside Maritime Museum
Mersey Docks and Harbour Board

Museum of London Docklands
Corporation of London Navigation Committee Minutes
Minutes and other records of:
  Commercial Dock Company
  Docks Joint Committee
  East and West India Dock Company
  East India Dock Company
  Grand Surrey Dock and Canal Company
  London & St Katherine's Dock Company
  London Dock Company
  St. Katharine's Dock Company
  Society of West India Merchants
  West India Dock Company
Vaughan Papers

London Metropolitan Archives
Society of Merchants Trading to the Continent

264

London School of Economics and Political Science

Digital Library Collections:
  Beatrice Webb's Diaries
  Charles Booth Archive

Parliamentary Archives

Lloyd George Papers

Tower Hamlets Local History and Archives

Records of Trinity United Reformed (formerly Congregational) Church, Poplar

Internet

Old Bailey Proceedings Online
Emory University, USA, Pitts Digital Collections, Manning Papers
Bryan Mawer, Sugar Refiners Database www.mawer.clara.net/intro.html

Parliamentary Papers

1795–1796, 102, Committee Appointed to Enquire into the Best Mode of Providing Sufficient Accommodation for the Increased Trade and Shipping of the Port of London.
1796–1797, 12, SC on Finance, Fourth Report.
1798–1799, 124, SC Improvement of the Port of London, Second Report.
1799–1800 CXXXII, 260, SC Improvement of the Port of London, Third Report.
1808, 337, Account of Quantities of Articles Imported and Exported for England, 1790–92 and 1799–1802.
1812 VI.117 [151,182] SC Affairs of the East India Company, Fourth Report.
1812–13 IV.941 [243], SC on Petitions of Masters and Journeymen Mechanics Respecting Apprentice Laws of United Kingdom.
1812–13 VIII.59 [84], Return of Ships Launched in River Thames for East India Company, 1770–1812.
1812–13 IX.451 [247], Return of Ships Launched in the Thames for the Merchant Service, 1786–1812.
1813–14 VIII [115], Minutes of Evidence on Petitions Relating to East India Built Shipping.
1814–15 V.1491 [472], SC Gauging in the Port of London.
1817 VII.1 [233], SC State of the Police of the Metropolis.
1820 VI.559 [46], Commission of Inquiry into the Customs and Excise, First, Second, Third, Fourth, Fifth and Sixth Reports.
1821 VI.1 [186], SC Foreign Trade (Timber Trade).
1821 V.281 [609], SC Present State of London Bridge.

1821 X.283, Commissioners of the Customs, Ninth Report (Port of Liverpool).

1823 IV.265 [452], SC on Law Relating to Merchants, Agents and Factors.

1823 IV.489 [411], SC on Improving and Maintaining Foreign Trade (West India Docks).

1824 VI.1 [416], SC Foreign Trade (Pilotage), First Report.

1824 VI.287. [431], SC Foreign Trade (London Port Duty), Third Report.

1825 IV.565 [417], SC on Combination Act of 1824.

1825 XX.207 [119], Account of the Progress of the Works of the London Dock Company.

1826 XXII.315, Account of the Number of Ships...

1828, XIX.583, Return of Ports to which Privilege of Warehousing has been Extended.

1830 VIII.1 [663], SC State of the Coal Trade.

1830 X.1 [253], SC on the Sale of Beer.

1830 XXVII.73, Account of the Timber and Wood Imported.

1831 V.225 [320A], SC on the Affairs of the East India Company.

1831 VIII.1. [335], SC on Calamities by Steam Navigation.

1831 XVII.459, Account of Goods Warehoused in London, 1825–30.

1831–32 VIII.1–XIV.1 [734–735], SC on the Affairs of the East India Company.

1833 VI.1 [690], SC on Manufactures, Commerce and Shipping.

1833 XXXIII.205, Quantities of Coal and Culm Imported 1826–32.

1833 XXXIII.117, Account of Payments out of the Consolidated Fund.

1834 VII.1 [517], SC on Sale of Corn.

1834 VIII.315 [559], SC into Drunkeness [sic].

1834 XVI.1 [600], SC on Metropolis Sewers.

1834 XXVII–XXXI.1 [44], RC on the Poor Laws.

1834 XLIX.705, Return of Warehouses of Special Security in Port of London.

1835 XIX.1 [519], SC Timber Duties.

PP 1835 XLIX.1 [52], Tables of Revenue, Population and Commerce of the United Kingdom and Dependencies.

1836 XIV.1 [557], SC on the State of the Port of London.

1836/2. Vol. 15. HLRO, SC on the Blackwall Railway Bill.

1837 XX.363 [499], SC on the Thames Tunnel.

1837 XXV.1 [239], RC Municipal Corporations, Second Report (London and Southwark; London Companies).

1837 XXXI.127,321 [546-I 545-II], Third Annual Report of the Poor Law Commissioners.

1837–38 XV.1 [475], SC on the Coal Trade (Port of London) Bill.

1837–38 XXIII.329, SC of the House of Lords on the Carriage of Passengers for Hire on the River Thames.

1837–38, XLV. 317 [88], Return of Vessels with Cargoes from Foreign Ports.

1840 V.99 [601], SC on Import Duties.

1840 V.475 [464], SC on Inland Warehousing.

1840 XI.277 [384], SC on the Health of Towns.

1840 XII.271 [554], SC Thames Embankment.

1842 XXVI.275 [73], Return related to Friendly Societies.

1843 LIII.9, Statement of the Quantities of Grain of Each Kind ... Imported into the Port of London.

1843 XXIX.77 [480], Report of the Commissioners of Revenue Inquiry into Customs Frauds.

1843 XXIX.133 [481], Report of the Commissioners of Customs to the Lords of the Treasury on the Customs Frauds.

1843 XXIX.157 [502], Commissioners of Customs, General Report on Commissioners of Revenue Inquiry.

1844 XV.1 [15], RC Means of Improving Metropolis, First Report.

1844 XVII.1 [572], RC for Inquiring into the State of Large Towns, First Report.

1844 IX.93 [531], SC on Medical Relief to Sick Poor under the Poor Law Act.

1844 VIII.1 [545], SC on British Shipping.

1844 VIII.279 [431], SC on Merchant Seamen's Fund.

1844 XXVII.1 [587] 1841 Census of England and Wales.

1845 XVI.269 [665], RC on Tidal Waters, First Report.

1845 XLVI.483 [214], Return of Articles of Foreign Merchandize Permitted to be Bonded in London.

1846 692, RC Tidal Harbours, Second Report.

1846 XVII.25 [719], RC to Investigate Projects for Establishing Termini within Metropolis.

1846 XLIV.403, Return of Amount of Dues for Harbour Service and Number of Tons of Coals Imported, 1836–44.

1846 XLIV.403, Return of the Number of Merchant Ships....

1846 XLIV.591, Return of the Number of Ships Laden with Foreign Corn Entered Inwards.

1847 VIII.273 [640], SC on Smithfield Market.

1847 XII.151 [504], SC on Thames Conservancy (Recommitted) Bill.

1847–48 [340], House of Lords SC on the Policy and Operation of the Navigation Laws, First Report.

1847–48 [431], House of Lords SC on the Policy and Operation of the Navigation Laws, Second Report.

1847–48 [754], House of Lords SC on the Navigation Laws, Third Report.

1847–48 LVIII.527 [400], Account of Sugars Imported into United Kingdom, 1793–1847.

1847–48 XXXII.1.57 [888, 895], Metropolitan Sanitary Commission, First Report.

1849 XIV.1 [458], SC Friendly Societies Bill.

1849 XIX.243 [420], SC Smithfield Market.

1851 [209], SC on the Customs, First Report.

1851 [604], SC on the Customs, Second Report.

1852 [498], SC on the Customs.

1852 XLIX.25 [359], Numbers and Tonnage of Ships ... entered the Port of London 1841–1851.

1852 XLIX.283 [308], Income and Expenditure under the Mercantile Marine Act, 1850–51.

1852–53 LXI.379 [687], Committee of Board of Ordinance on Capabilities of the Mercantile Steam Navy for Purposes of War, Report.

1852–53 1691–1, 1851 Census of England and Wales.

1854 XXVI.1 [1772], RC State of the Corporation of the City of London, Report.

1854–55 L.423 [118], Reports of Board of Trade on Private bills for Harbours, Docks, and Navigations.

1857 Session 1 III [2186], Commissioners of the Customs, First Report.

1857 Session 2, XIX.505 [19], Reports of Board of Trade on Private Bills for Harbours, Docks and Navigations.

1857 Session 2, XIX.515 [2], Report upon Private Bills for Harbours, Docks, Navigations &c.

1857–58 XXV.389 [2357], Commissioners of Customs, Second Report.

1859 Session 1, VI.1 [2469], RC Manning of the Navy

1859 Session 1 XIII.41 [13], Reports of Board of Trade on Private Bills for Habours, Docks, Navigations &c.

1859 Session 2. XIV.67 [2540], Commissioners of Customs, Third Report.

1860 XIII.1 [530], SC on Merchant Shipping.

1861 IX.1, [180], Select Committee on Poor Relief (England), First Report.

1861 XXXI.267 [2872], RC to Inquire into Plans for Embanking the River Thames.

1862 XIII.1 [390], SC on Sugar Duties.

1862 IX.1 [222], SC on Fires in the Metropolis.

1862 XXVIII.61 [3043], Thames Embankment Commission (Surrey Side).

1862 XXX.495, Return of Sums Advanced and Repaid for Rebuilding London Bridge.

1863 VI.303 [424], SC on Inland Revenue and Customs Establishments.

1863 XII.1 [454], SC Conservancy of River Thames.

1863 3221, Census of England and Wales 1861.

1864 LIV.1 [19], Reports of Board of Trade on Railway and Canal Bills, and Bills Relating to Harbours, Docks and Tidal Waters.

1866 XII.491 [871], SC Thames Navigation Bill.

1867 XII.431 [135], Commission to Inquire into Local Government and Taxation of Metropolis.

1867 LXXX.127 [417], Trade and Navigation Accounts. Return of Vessels above Fifty Tons built at each port of United Kingdom.

1867 XXXVIII Pt I.1, 579 127, Pt II.1 [3844-I 3844-II] RC on Railways, Appendices.

1867 XXXII.1 [3873], RC on Trade Unions, First Report.

1867 XXXII.289 [3952], RC on Trade Unions, Fourth Report.

1867, XI.1, 319 [471, 471.I], SC on Fire Protection.

1867–68 XII.1 [227], SC Metropolitan Cattle Market Bill, Report.

1867–68 XII.479,599 [599], SC on the Metropolitan Cattle Market, Third Report.

1867–68 XXII.591 [4046], Commissioners of the Customs, Twelfth Report.

1867–68 XXXIII.1 [4039], Twentieth Annual Report of the Poor Law Board.

1867–68 XXXIX.375 [3980.V], RC on Trade Unions, Ninth Report.

1870 IX.1 [343], SC on Pilotage Bill.

1870, XLVI.1 [56], Arrangements on HM Victualling Yards.

1870 LXI.1 [61], Report of the Committee on the Transit of Animals.

1870 LXI.329, Return of Articles subject to Import Duties 1840–69.
1871 C.437, Annual Statement of Trade and Navigation.
1871 LXI.495 [263], Memorial … Change in Constitution of the Trinity House.
1872 XXX.261 [C.652], Report by Commissioner of Metropolitan Police, 1871.
1873 XXXVI.315,335 [C.853 C.853-1], RC on Unseaworthy Ships, Preliminary Report.
1875 LXVIII.319 [132], Memorandum on Improvements Effected by the Board of Trade.
1876 LXVI.333 [C.1398], Report on Recent Legislation Concerning Merchant Ships and Seamen.
1877 XVII.1 [367], SC Thames Floods Prevention.
1877 XXVII.515 [C.1727], Report of the Veterinary Department of the Privy Council.
1878 XVI.77 [205], SC on Merchant Seamen Bill.
1878–79 XIII.1 [321], SC. on Sugar Industries.
1878–79 XLI.245 [C.2328], SC Thames Traffic.
1881 XLIX.1.43 [C.3074.1], RC on Tonnage.
1881 LXXXIII.681 [317], Memorandum Respecting Production of Refined Sugar, 1864 and 1881.
1882 VII.395 [358], SC on Artizans' and Labourers' Dwellings Improvement.
1882 XIV.1, 45, 493 [C.3309 C.3309-1 C.3309 II], RC on Depressed Condition of Agricultural Interests, Report.
1884 LXII.443 [323], Thames (Pollution), Correspondence.
1884 LXXIV.371 [325], Report to Board of Trade, Progress of the Sugar Trade.
1884, XIV.1 [255], SC on Metropolitan Board of Works (Thames Crossings) Bill.
1884–85, VIII.47 [228], SC on the Corporation of London Tower Bridge Bill.
1884–85 XXX.1 [C.4402], RC on the Housing of the Working Classes, First Report.
1886 LIX.197 [C.4709], Board of Trade Report on Supply of British Seamen.
1886 VIII, [192], SC on Employers' Liability Act.
1887 LXXI.303 [C.5258], Condition of the Working Classes, Tabulation.
1887 LXXV.299, Number of Quarters of Wheat and Flour Imported into the United Kingdom, 1866–86.
1887 LXXXIX.253 [331], Report to Board of Trade on Sweating System at East End of London.
1888 XIV.85 [324], SC Pilotage.
1888 XXI.1 [448], SC of the House of Lords on the Sweating System, Second Report.
1888 XCIII [353], Return on Production of, and Trade in Sugar.
1889 C.113, Reports of Chief Registrar of Friendly Societies, 1887 Volume II.
1889 LXXXIV.147 [C.5808], Statistical Tables and Report on Trade Unions, Third Report.
1890 XVII.257 [169], SC of the House of Lords on the Sweating System, Fifth Report.
1890 LXVIII. 591 [375], Return of Average Number of Hours Worked Per Week.
1890–91 XCII.73 [C.6475], Statistical Tables and Report on Trade Unions, Fourth Report.

1892 XXXV.1 [C.6708-V], RC on Labour, Minutes of Evidence (Group B) Volume I.

1892 C.6795.VII, RC on Labour, Answers to Schedules of Questions.

1892 C.6795-XII, RC on Labour, Rules of Association of Employers and of Employed.

1893–4 C.6894 VIII, RC on Labour, Minutes of Evidence, Appendices (Group B) Volume III.

1893–94 XXXII.5 [C.6894-VII], RC on Labour (Group A) Volume III, Minutes.

1893–94 XXXIV.1 [C.6894-IX], RC on Labour (Group C) Volume III, Minutes.

1893–94 CV.1 [C.7058], 1891 Census of England and Wales.

1893–94 LXXX.387 [C.7179], Transmission of Seamen's Wages.

1894 XXXV.9 [C.7421], RC on Labour, Fifth and Final Report.

1894 LXIX.267, 93 [C.7511], Departmental Committee on Transit by Water and the Embarkation and Landing of Animals Carried Coastwise.

1894 XIV.503 [244], SC on Petroleum.

1894 XXVII.5 [C.7298], Board of Agriculture, Annual Report of the Veterinary Department, 1893.

1894, XVII.1, XVIII.1 [C.7493, C.7493-1, C.7493-II], RC to Consider Amalgamation of City and County of London.

1896 XLI.113,137 [C.8167, C8168] Departmental Committee on the Mercantile Marine Fund.

1896 C.8230, Board of Trade, Third Annual Report, Abstract of Labour Statistics.

1896 LXXXIII.529 [C.8089], Annual Statement of the Navigation and Shipping of the UK for 1895.

1896 XCIII.277 [C8232], Statistical Tables, Trade Unions, Eighth Report.

1896 XII.1 [331], SC on Petroleum.

1897 XIII.109 [309], SC on Petroleum.

1898 CIIi.127 [C.9013], Statistical Tables and Report on Trade Unions, Tenth Report.

1898 LXXXVIII.1 [C.8975], Report on Changes in Rates of Wages and Hours of Labour.

1898 LXXXV.1 [C.8706], Customs Tariffs of United Kingdom.

1900 LXXIX.425 [351], Statements of Imports of Tea and Coffee into Principal Countries of Europe and United States.

1900 Cd.166, Agricultural Returns for Great Britain.

1900 XI.249 [Cd.223], Inspector of Factories and Workshops Report, 1899.

1901 LXXVI [Cd.549,664], Annual Statement of Trade.

1902, XV.33 [Cd.4661], Report of the Departmental Committee on Combinations in the Meat Trade.

1902 XLIII.1 [Cd. 1151], RC on the Port of London, Report.

1902 XLIII.201 [Cd. 1152], RC on the Port of London, Minutes.

1902 XLIV.1 [Cd.1153], RC on the Port of London, Appendices.

1903 LXII.15 [Cd.1608], Committee on Certain Questions Affecting our Mercantile Marine, Volume II.

1903 LXII.737 [Cd.1609], Committee to Inquire into Certain Questions Affecting the Mercantile Marine, Volume III.

1903 VIII.1 [288], Joint SC Port of London Bill.
1905 XXXIX.217 [Cd.2644], RC on Supply of Food and Raw Material in Time of War.
1906 XXIII.37 [Cd.2893], Board of Agriculture and Fisheries. Annual Report of Proceedings Under the Diseases of Animals Act.
1906 XLI.1 [Cd.2752], RC on London Traffic, Volume III, Report.
1906 CXII.1 [55], Reports of Friendly Societies.
1908 X.1 [288], Joint SC Port of London Bill.
1908 XCII.483 [Cd. 4391], Report Dock Labour in Relation to Poor Relief.
1908 XCIII.931 [109], Port of London Bill, Memorandum.
1909 XXXV11.1 [Cd. 4499], RC Poor Laws and the Relief of Distress, Report.
1913 LXXIX.1 [Cd.7019], Census of England and Wales 1911.
Annual Statement of Trade and Navigation 1854–1875.
Annual Statement of Navigation and Shipping 1876–1913.

Serials and Reference Works

Acts of Parliament
Australian Dictionary of Biography
Bibliography of Printed Works on London History to 1939
Oxford Dictionary of National Biography
Parliamentary Debates
The History of Parliament
The London Encyclopaedia

Printed Primary Sources

'Accidents Among Dock Labourers', *The Lancet*, 13 April 1889.
A Digest of Proceedings and Reports of the Committee of London Merchants for Reform of the Board of Customs (Effingham Wilson, London, 1853).
East and West India Docks, Regulations and Rates on Shipping (Charles Skipper and East, London, 1839).
Facts Plainly Stated: In Answer to a Pamphlet Entitled 'Plain Statement of Facts Connected with the Proposed St. Katharine's Dock' By a London-Dock proprietor (J. M. Richardson, London, 1824).
Information Useful to Owners, Masters, Pilots, Or Persons in Charge of Vessels About to Enter, Whilst Lying In. Or Departing from The St Katharine Docks (London, 1837).
Report of the Trial of an Indictment Prosecuted at the Instance of the West India Dock Company Versus John Smith, Walter Foreman, Samuel Hucks and Daniel Hall, for an Alleged Conspiracy (C. Teulan, London, 1821).
Table of the Rates and Charges of the London Dock Company (J. Metcalfe, London, 1832).
The British Metropolis in 1851 (Arthur Hall, Virtue & Co., London, 1851).
The London Dock Companies: An Inquiry into Their Present Position and Future Prospects, with Suggestions for Improvement of Revenue and Dividends (Richardson & Co., London, 1861).

'The Port of London Sanitary Committee', *British Medical Journal*, 2 (1876), 536.

'The Public Health Act, 1872', *British and Foreign Medico-Chirurgical Review* (1873), 1–28.

'The Dock Strike', 31 August 1889, *The Lancet*.

Abernethy, J. Murray, et al., 'Discussion: Description of the Entrance, Entrance Lock, and Jetty Walls of the Victoria (London) Docks', *Minutes of the Proceedings of the Institution of Civil Engineers*, 18 (1859), 477–89.

Armstrong, William, 'Discussion: The History of the Modern Development of Water-Pressure Machinery', *Minutes of the Proceedings of the Institution of Civil Engineers*', 50 (1877), 64–102.

Arnold, Matthew, *Culture and Anarchy (1869)*, in Dover Wilson (ed.) (Cambridge University Press, Cambridge, 1932).

Askwith, George Ranken, *Industrial Problems and Disputes* (John Murray, London, 1920).

Barber, T. W., (ed.), *The Port of London and the Thames Barrage* (Swan Sonnenschein, London, 1907).

Barry, John Wolfe, *The Tower Bridge; A Lecture* (Boot, Son and Carpenter, London, 1894).

Barry, John Wolfe, 'Discussion on the Tower Bridge', *Minutes of the Institution of Civil Engineers*, 127 (1897), 63–4.

Barry, Patrick, *Dockyard Economy and Naval Power* (Sampson, Low, Son and Co., London, 1863).

Bazalgette, Edward, 'The Victoria, Albert and Chelsea Embankments of the River Thames', *Proceedings of the Institution of Civil Engineers*, 10 (1878), 1–26.

Beames, Thomas, *The Rookeries of London: Past, Present and Prospective* (Thomas Bosworth, London, 1852).

Beesley, Edward S., 'The Amalgamated Society of Carpenters', *Fortnightly Review*, 7 (1867), 319–34.

Besant, Walter, *East London* (The Century Co., New York, 1901).

Beveridge, William H., *Unemployment: A Problem of Industry* (Longmans, Green and Co., London, 1909).

Booth, Charles, 'The Inhabitants of Tower Hamlets (School Board Division), Their Condition and Occupations', *Journal of the Royal Statistical Society*, 50 (1887), 326–401.

Booth, Charles, 'Condition and Occupations of the People of East London and Hackney, 1887', *Journal of the Royal Statistical Society*, 51 (1888), 276–331.

Booth, Charles, 'Inaugural Address', *Journal of the Royal Statistical Society*, LV (1892), 521–57.

Booth, Charles, *Life and Labour of the People in London. Volume III, Blocks of Buildings, Schools and Immigration* (Macmillan & Co., London, 1892).

Booth, Charles, *Life and Labour of the People in London. First Series: Poverty* (Macmillan & Co., London, 1902).

Booth, Charles, *Life and Labour of the People in London. Third Series: Religious Influences*, Vol. 4 (Macmillan, London, 1902).

Booth, Charles, *Life and Labour of the People in London. Second Series: Industry* Vol I (Macmillan, London, 1903).

Booth, Charles, *Life and Labour of the People in London. Second Series: Industry.* Vol. 3 (Macmillan, London, 1903).

Booth, Charles, *Life and Labour of the People in London. First Series.* Vol. I (Macmillan, London, 1904).

Capper, Charles, *The Port and Trade of London: Historical, Statistical, Local and General* (Smith, Elder & Co., London, 1862).

Champion, Henry Hyde, *The Great Dock Strike: In London, August 1889* (Swan Sonnenschein, London, 1890).

Charity Organisation Society, *On the Best Means of Dealing with Exceptional Distress: The Report of a Special Committee, November 1886* (Cassell, London, 1886).

Charity Organisation Society, *Special Committee on Unskilled Labour: Report and Minutes of Evidence, June 1908* (COS, London, 1908).

Clarke, H. G., *London as It Is To-day: Where to Go, And What to See, During the Great Exhibition* (H. G. Clarke & Co., London, 1851).

Clegg, Samuel, *Practical Treatise on the Manufacture and Distribution of Coal-Gas* (John Weale, London, 1853).

Clifford, Frederick, *A History of Private Bill Legislation*, Vol. II (Butterworths, London, 1887).

Cock, S., *The Case of the London Dock Company* (M. Richardson, London, 1824).

Colquhoun, Patrick, *A Treatise on the Commerce and Police of the River Thames* (J. Mawman, London, 1800).

Cormack and Semple, 'The Hospitals of London No. 5', *London Journal of Medicine*, 3 (1851), 480–83.

Cruden, Robert Peirce, *Gravesend in the County of Kent* (William Pickering, London, 1843).

Cummings, D. C., *A Historical Survey of the Boiler Markers' and Iron and Steel Ship Builder' Society* (R. Robinson & Co., Newcastle-on-Tyne, 1905).

Denton, William, *Observations on the Displacement of the Poor, by Metropolitan Railways and by Other Public Improvements* (Bell and Daldy, London, 1861).

Dews, Nathan, *The History of Deptford in the Counties of Kent and Surrey*, 2nd ed. (Simpkin, Marshall and Co., London, 1884).

Dickens, Charles, *Dickens's Dictionary of the Thames, from Its Source to the Nore, 1885: An Unconventional Handbook* (Macmillan & Co., London, 1885).

Dodd, George, *Days of the Factories or the Manufacturing Industry of Great Britain Described and Illustrated by Numerous Engravings of Machines and Processes. Series I – London* (Charles Knight & Co., London, 1843).

Dodd, George, *The Food of London* (Longman, Brown, Green and Longmans, London, 1856).

Dupin, Charles, *The Commercial Power of Great Britain*, Vols. I & II (Charles Knight, London, 1825).

Edwards, Percy J., *History of London Street Improvements 1855–1897* (London County Council, London, 1898).

Evans, David Morier, *The City or the Physiology of London Business with Sketches of 'Change' and the London Coffee Houses* (Baily Brothers, London, 1845).

Farey, John, *A Treatise on the Steam Engine, Historical, Practical and Descriptive* (Longman, Rees, Orme, Brown and Green, London, 1827).

Garland, Thomas C., *Leaves from My Log of Twenty-Five Years of Christian Work among Sailors and Others in the Port of London* (T. Woolmer, London, 1882).

Gast, John, *Calumny Defeated or a Compleat Vindication of the Conduct of the Working Shipwrights, During the Late Disputes with their Employers* (John Gast, London, 1802).

Glover, John 'On the Decline of Shipbuilding on the Thames', *Journal of the Statistical Society of London*, 32 (1869), 288–92.

Gosling, Harry, *Up and Down Stream* (Methuen, London, 1927).

Gould, Nathaniel, *Historical Notice of the Commercial Docks in the Parish of Rotherhithe, County of Surrey* (London, 1844, Reprinted, Rotherhithe Local History Paper No.5), Stuart Rankin (ed.) (Dockside Studio, London, 1998).

Green, Henry and Robert Wigram, *Chronicles of Blackwall Yard, Part I* (Whitehead, Morris and Lowe, London, 1881).

Griffin, Josiah *History of the Surrey Commercial Docks* (Smith & Ebbs, London, 1877).

Hadden, R. H., *An East End Chronicle: St. George's-In-The-East Parish and Parish Church* (Hatchards, London, 1880).

Hall, John, *Observations upon the Warehousing System and Navigation Laws, with a Detailed Account of the Burthens to Which Shipping and Trade Are Subjected, Particularly as Connected with the Port of London* (Richardson, London, 1821).

Hall, John, *Plain Statement of Facts Connected with the Proposed St. Katharine Dock in the Port of London to be Established Upon the Principle of Open and General Competition* (Richardson, J. M., London, 1824).

Hallam, Henry, 'Report of the Council of the Statistical Society of London', *Journal of the Statistical Society of London*, 11 (1848), 193–249.

Harkness, Margaret Elise, *Toilers in London or Inquiries Concerning Female Labour in the Metropolis* (Hodder & Stoughton, London, 1859).

Harrison, Charles, 'The River Thames. Its Port and Conservancy', London Reform Union Pamphlet, (1895).

Holland Sidney, Viscount Knutsford, *In Black and White* (Edward Arnold & Co., London, 1928).

Hollingshed, John, *Ragged London in 1861* (First published 1861. Reprinted Read Books Ltd, London, 2013).

Holt, Alfred, 'Review of the Progress of Steam Shipping During the Last Quarter of a Century', *Minutes of the Proceedings of the Institution of Civil Engineers*, 51 (1878), 2–11.

Hora, W., *Bridge or Tunnel for Improved Communication Across the River Thames Below London Bridge* (City Press, London, 1884), Bristol Selected Pamphlets, University of Bristol Library.

Howarth. Edward G., and Mona Wilson, *West Ham: A Study in Social and Industrial Problems* (J. M. Dent & Co., London, 1907).

Hughes, Thomas, 'Account of the Lock-Out of Engineers 1851–52', *Trades Societies and Strikes. Report of Committee on Trades Societies, National Association for the Promotion of Social Science* (John W. Parker and Son, London. 1860), 169–206.

Hughson, David, *Walks Through London, Volume I* (Sherwood, Neely & Jones, London, 1817).

Humpherus, Henry, *History of the Origin and Progress of the Company of Watermen and Lightermen of the River Thames*, Volume III 1800–1849, Volume IV 1850–1883 (S. Prentice, London, 1887).

Hutcheson, John M., *Notes on the Sugar Industry of the United Kingdom* (James Kelvie, Greenock, 1901).

Ireland, Samuel, *Picturesque Views on the River Thames: From Its Source in Gloucestershire to the Nore; with Observations on the Public Buildings and Other*

Works of Art in Its Vicinity. In Two Volumes, Volume 2 (T. Egerton, London, 1802).

Jones, Harry, *East and West London, Being Notes of Common Life and Pastoral Life in St. James' Westminster and Saint George's-In-The-East* (Smith, Elder, & Co., London, 1875).

Keane, John F. *Three Years of a Wanderer's Life*, Volume I (Ward and Downey, London, 1887).

Knight, Charles, (ed.), *London*, Volume III (Charles Knight & Co., London, 1842).

Lea, Frederic Simcox, *The Royal Hospital and Collegiate Church of Saint Katharine near the Tower in Its Relation to the East of London* (Longmans, London, 1878).

Leighton, Baldwin, *Letters and Other Writings of the Late Edward Denison* (Richard Bentley and Son, London, 1875).

Limbird, John, *Limbird's Handbook, Guide to London: Or What to Observe and Remember* (John Limbird, London, 1851).

London County Council, *Royal Commission on the Port of London, 1900, Statement of Evidence by Clerk of the London County Council* (London County Council, London, 1902).

Longlands, Henry, *A Review of the Warehousing System as Connected with the Port of London* (John Richardson et al., London, 1824).

Low, Sampson, *The Charities of London in 1861* (Sampson Low, London, 1862).

Lowder, C. F., *St. Katharine's Hospital: Its History and Revenues, and Their Application to Missionary Purposes in the East of London* (Rivingtons, London, 1867).

Lowder, C. F., *Ten Years in S. George's Mission Being an Account of Its Origin, Progress and Works of Mercy* (C.J. Palmer, London, 1867).

Lowder, C. F., *Twenty-One Years in S. George's Mission. An Account of Its Origin, Progress and Works of Charity* (Rivingtons, London, 1877).

Mann, Tom, *Tom Mann's Memoirs* (MacGibbon & Kee, London, 1923).

Martindale, B. H., 'Demolition of the North-East Wall of the Gallions Basin, Royal Albert Docks, on the 23rd April, 1886', *Proceedings of the Institution of Civil Engineers*, 86 (1886), 329–35.

Mayhew, Henry, *The Morning Chronicle Survey of London Labour and the Poor, The Metropolitan Districts, Volumes 1–6, Routledge, Library Editions: The History of Social Welfare Volume22* (Routledge, London, 1982).

McCulloch, J. R., *A Dictionary, Practical, Theoretical and Historical, of Commerce and Commercial Navigation* (Longman, Brown, Green and Longman, London, 1844).

Miall, Arthur, *Religion in London. Statistics of Church and Chapel Accommodation in 1865*. An article reprinted from the 'British Quarterly Review', No. 85. With an appendix of tables (Jackson Walford and Hodder, London, 1866).

Morier-Evans, David, *City Men and City Manners: The City; or the Physiology of London Business; with Sketches on 'Change and at the Coffee Houses'* (Groombridge and Sons, London, 1852).

Morton, R. 'The System of Coaling at the Works of the Late London Gaslight Company, Nine Elms', *Proceedings of the Institution of Civil Engineers*, 78 (1884), 357–60.

Mudie-Smith, Richard, (ed.), *The Religious Life of London* (Hodder & Stoughton, London, 1904).

Palmer, C. M., 'On the Construction of Iron Ships', *Report of the Twenty-Third Meeting of the British Association for the Advancement of Science* (John Murray, London, 1864), 696–701.

Pennant, Thomas, *Of London* (Robert Faulder, London, 1790), 281.

Phillips, Watts, *The Wild Tribes of London* (Ward and Lock, London, 1855).

Price-Williams, R., 'The Population of London, 1801–81', *Journal of the Royal Statistical Society*, XLVIII (1885), 349–432.

Priestley, Joseph, *Historical Account of the Navigable Rivers, Canals and Railways of Great Britain* (Longman, Rees, Orme, Brown & Green, London, 1831).

Pulling, Alexander, *The Laws, Customs, Usages and Regulations of the City and Port of London*, 2nd ed. (William Henry Bond and Wildy and Sons, London, 1854).

Purcell, Edmund Sheridan, *Life of Cardinal Manning*, Volume II (Macmillan, London, 1896).

Redfern, Percy, *The Story of the C.W.S.: The Jubilee History of the Co-operative Wholesale Society Ltd 1863–1913* (Co-operative Wholesale Society, Manchester, 1913).

Rennie, Sir John, 'Address to the Institution of Civil Engineers Annual Meeting January 20, 1846', *Minutes of the Proceedings of the Institution of Civil Engineers*, 5 (1846), 19–122.

Ritchie, J. Ewing, *The Night Side of London* (William Tweedie, London, 1858).

Ritchie, J. Ewing, *Famous City Men* (Tinsley Brothers, London, 1884).

Rowe, Richard, *Jack Afloat and Ashore* (Smith, Elder & Co., London, 1875).

Salter, Joseph, *The Asiatic in England. Sketches of Sixteen Years' Work Among Orientals* (Seeley, Jackson and Halliday, London, 1873).

Sharpe, W. R. S., *The Port of Bombay* (Bombay Port Trust, Bombay, 1900).

Simmonds, P. L., 'On the Rise and Progress of Steam Navigation in the Port of London', *Journal of the Royal Society for the Encouragement of Arts, Manufactures and Commerce*, 8 (1860), 153–70.

Sims, George R., *How the Poor Live and Horrible London* (Chatto & Windus, London, 1889).

Sims, George R., *Living London. Its Work and Its Play, Its Humour and Its Pathos. Its Sights and Scenes. Volume I* (Cassel and Co., London, 1902).

Smith, H. Llewellyn, and Vaughan Nash, *The Story of the Dockers' Strike Told by Two East Londoners* (T. Fisher Unwin, London, 1889).

Steadman, W. C., 'Shipbuilding', in Frank W. Galton (ed.), *Workers on Their Industries* (Swan Sonnenschein & Co., London, 1896), 56–66.

Telford, Thomas, *Life of Thomas Telford Written by Himself* (James and Luke G. Hansard and Sons, London, 1838).

Thornbury, Walter, *Old and New London, Vol. II* (Cassell, London, 1878).

Titmarsh, Michelangelo [W. M. Thackeray], 'A Second Lecture on the Fine Arts', *Frasers Magazine*, 19 (1839).

Tomlinson, Charles (ed.), *Cyclopaedia of Useful Arts, Mechanical and Chemical, Manufactures, Mining and Engineering* (George Virtue & Co., London and New York, 1852–54).

Townsend, Francis. *Calendar of Knights; Containing Lists of Knights Bachelors, British Knights of Foreign Orders, Thistle Bath, St Patrick and the Guelphic and Ionian orders from 1760 to the Present Time* (W. Pickering, London, 1828).

Toynbee, Henry, 'On Mercantile Marine Legislation as Affecting the Number and Efficiency of British Seamen), *Journal of the Society of Arts*, 15 (1867), 121–40.

Troubridge Crittell, James and Joseph Raymond, *A History of the Frozen Meat Trade* (Constable & Co., London, 1912).

Tuitt, J. E., *The Tower Bridge, Its History and Construction from the Date of the Earliest Project to the Present Time* ('The Engineer', London, 1894), 32–51.

United States Government, *Reports from the Consuls*, 1889.

Urquhart-Pollard, W., 'Condition of the Irish Labourers in the East of London', *Transactions of the National Association for the Promotion of Social Science* (John W. Parker and Bourne, London, 1862), 744–9.

Vaughan, William, *Treatise on Wet Docks, Quays and Warehouses for the Port of London* (J. Johnson and W. Richardson, London, 1793).

Vaughan, William, *Reasons in Favour of the London Docks* (London, 1795).

Vaughan, William *Memoir of William Vaughan, Esq. F.R.S: With Miscellaneous Pieces Relative to Docks, Commerce, Etc* (Smith, Elder, London, 1839).

Vernon-Harcourt, Leveson Francis, *Harbours and Docks. Their Physical Features, History, Construction, Equipment and Maintenance* (Clarendon Press, Oxford, 1885).

Webb, Sidney, 'The Municipalisation of the London Docks', *Fabian Tract No. 35* (London, 1891).

Webb, Sidney and Harold Cox, *The Eight Hours Day* (Walter Scott, London, 1891).

Webb, Sidney and Beatrice Webb, *Industrial Democracy. New Edition* (Longman's, Green & Co., London, 1902).

Wright, Thomas, *Some Habits and Customs of the Working Classes by a Journeyman Engineer* (Tinsley Brothers, London, 1867).

Xenos, Stephanos, *Depredations; or Overend, Gurney and Co, and the Greek and Oriental Steam Navigation Company* (Stephnos Xenos, London, 1869).

London Directories

Pigot's
Post Office
Robson's

Newspapers and Periodicals

Clerkenwell News
Cork Examiner
Essex Herald
Globe
Hackney and Kingsland Gazette
Hampshire Telegraph
Illustrated London News
Inverness Chronicle
John Bull
Kentish Chronicle

Kentish Independent,
Lloyd's Weekly
Lloyds List & Shipping Gazette
London City Press
London Courier & Evening Gazette
London Evening Standard
Morning Advertiser
Morning Chronicle
New York Times
Pall Mall Gazette
Public Ledger and Daily Advertiser
Reynolds News
Saunders Newsletter
St James' Chronicle
Shipping and Mercantile Gazette
Southend Standard and Essex Weekly Advertiser,
Sussex Advertiser
The Builder
The Economist
The Engineer
The Globe
The Patriot
The Times
Trades Free Press

Secondary Sources

Armstrong, John, 'Climax and Climacteric: The British Coastal Trade, 1870–1930', in David J. Starkey and Alan G. Jamieson (eds.), *Exploiting the Sea: Aspects of Britain's Maritime Economy since 1870* (University of Exeter Press, Exeter, 1998), 37–58.

Armstrong, John, 'Coastal Shipping and the Thames: Its Role in London's Growth and Expansion', in Roger Owen (ed.), *Shipbuilding on the Thames and Thames-Built Ships, Proceedings of a Second Symposium on Shipbuilding on the Thames, 15 February 2003* (Docklands History Group, West Wickham, 2004), 146–56.

Armstrong, John, *The Vital Spark: The British Coastal Trade, 1700–1930.* Research in Maritime History No. 40 (IMEHA, St. John's Newfoundland, 2009).

Armstrong, John and David M. Williams, 'The Thames and Recreation, 1815–1840', *The London Journal*, 30 (2005), 25–39.

Armstrong, John and David M. Williams, 'Steam Shipping and the Beginnings of Overseas Tourism: British Travel to North Western Europe, 1820–1850', *Journal of European Economic History*, 35 (2006), 125–48.

Armstrong, John and David M. Williams, 'British Steam Navigation, 1812 to the 1850s: A Bibliographical and Historiographical Review', in John Armstrong and David M. Williams (eds.), *The Impact of Technological Change: The Early Steamship in Britain.* Research in Maritime History No. 47 (IMEHA, St. John's Newfoundland, 2011), 7–30.

Armstrong, John and David M. Williams, (eds.), 'The Steamship as an Agent of Modernisation, 1812–1840', in *The Impact of Technological Change: The Early Steamship in Britain*. Research in Maritime History No. 47 (IMEHA, St. John's Newfoundland, 2011), 165–81.

Armstrong, John and David M. Williams, 'London's Steamships: Their Functions and Their Owners in the Mid-Nineteenth Century', *The London Journal*, 42 (2017), 1–19.

Arnold, Anthony J., *Iron Shipbuilding on the Thames 1832–1915: An Economic and Business History* (Ashgate, London, 2000).

Ashworth, William J., *Customs and Excise: Trade, Production and Consumption in England, 1650–1845* (Oxford University Press, Oxford, 2003).

Ashworth, William J., 'Labour and the Alternative Economy in Britain, 1660–1842', in Thomas Max Saffley (ed.), *Labor before the Industrial Revolution: Work, Technology and Their Ecologies in the Age of Early Capitalism* (Routledge, London, 2020), 232–52.

Bagwell, Philip S., *The Transport Revolution from 1770* (Batsford, London, 1974).

Baker, Mike, 'The English Timber Cartel in the Napoleonic Wars', *Mariner's Mirror*, 88 (2002), 79–81.

Baker, T. F. T. (ed.) *A History of the County of Middlesex, Volume 11, Stepney, Bethnal Green*, (London, 1998), British History Online www.british-history .ac.uk/vch/middx/vol11/pp7-13

Ballhatchet, Joan, 'The Police and the London Dock Strike', *History Workshop*, 32 (1991), 54–68.

Banbury, Philip, *Shipbuilders of the Thames and Medway* (David & Charles, Newton Abbot, 1971).

Barker, T.C and Michael Robbins, *A History of London Transport. Volume One – The Nineteenth Century* (George Allen & Unwin, London, 1975).

Barnard, Alan *The Australian Wool Market 1840–1900* (Melbourne University Press, Melbourne, 1958).

Barnard, John E., *Building Britain's Wooden Walls, The Barnard Dynasty c. 1697–1851* (Anthony Nelson, Oswestry, 1997).

Barnett, David, *London, Hub of the Industrial Revolution. A Revisionary History 1775–1825* (I. B. Tauris & Co., London, 1998).

Barty King, Hugh, *The Baltic Exchange. The History of a Unique Market* (Hutchinson Benham, London, 1977).

Beaven, B., 'From Jolly Sailor to Proletarian Jack: The Remaking of Sailortown and the Merchant Seaman in Victorian London', in Brad Beaven, Karl Bell and Robert James (eds.), *Port Towns and Urban Cultures. International Histories of the Waterfront, c.1700–2000* (Palgrave Macmillan, London, 2016) 159–78.

Beaven, B. 'Foreign Sailors and Working Class Communities. Race, Crime and Moral Panics in London's Sailortown, 1880–1914', in Christina Reimann and Martin Öman (eds.), *Migrants and the Making of the Urban-Maritime World* (Routledge, London, 2021), 86–106.

Beaven, B. '"One of the Toughest Streets in the World": Exploring Male Violence, Class and Ethnicity in London's Sailortown, c. 1850–1880', *Social History*, 46 (2021), 1–21.

Bédarida, François, 'Urban Growth and Social Structure in Nineteenth-Century Poplar', *The London Journal*, 1 (1975), 159–88.

Berg, Maxine and Pat Hudson, *Slaveru, Capitalism and the Industrial Revolution* (Polity Press, Cambridge, 2023).

Bienefeld, M. A., *Working Hours in British Industry: An Economic History* (Weidenfeld and Nicholson, London, 1972).

Birch, J. G., *Limehouse through Five Centuries* (The Sheldon Press, London, 1930).

Bowen, Frank C., *A Hundred Years of Towage. A History of Messrs. William Watkins Ltd., 1833–1933* (Gravesend and Dartford Reporter, Gravesend, 1933).

Bowen, H. V., *War and British Society 1688–1815* (Cambridge University Press, Cambridge, 1998).

Bowen, H. V. 'So Alarming an Evil: Smuggling, Pilfering and the East India Dock Company, 1750–1810', *International Journal of Maritime History*, 14 (2002), 1–31.

Bowen, H. V. *The Business of Empire. The East India Company and Imperial Britain, 1756–1833* (Cambridge University Press, Cambridge, 2006).

Boyce, Gordon H., *Information, Mediation and Institutional Development. The Rise of Large-Scale Enterprise in British Shipping, 1870–1919* (Manchester University Press, Manchester, 1995).

Brodie, Marc, *The Politics of the Poor. The East End of London 1885–1914* (Clarendon Press, Oxford, 2004).

Broeze, Frank, *Mr Brooks and the Australian Trade. Imperial Business in the Nineteenth Century* (Melbourne University Press, Melbourne, 1993).

Broodbank, Joseph G., *History of the Port of London Volumes 1 and II* (Daniel O'Connor, London, 1921).

Brown, Lucy, *The Board of Trade and the Free Trade Movement 1830–42* (Oxford University Press, Oxford, 1958).

Burgess, Keith, 'Technological Change and the 1852 Lock-Out in the British Engineering Industry', *International Review of Social History*, 14 (1969), 215–36.

Burgess, Keith, 'Trade Union Policy and the 1852 Lock-Out in the British Engineering Industry', *International Review of Social History*, 17 (1972), 645–60.

Burton, V. C., 'A Floating Population: Vessel Enumeration Returns in Censuses, 1851–1821', *Local Population Studies*, 38 (1987), 36–43.

Butlin, Martin and Evelyn Joll, *The Paintings of J.M.W. Turner. Revised Edition. Text* (Yale University Press, New Haven, 1984).

Butt, John, 'The Industries of Glasgow', in W. Hamish Fraser and Irene Maver (eds.), *Glasgow. Volume II: 1830–1912* (Manchester University Press, Manchester, 1996), 96–140.

Carson, Edward, *The Ancient and Rightful Customs* (Faber & Faber, London, 1972).

Chadwick, Owen, *The Victorian City. Part One 1820–1859* (SCM Press, London, 1970).

Chalmin, Philippe, *The Making of a Sugar Giant. Tate and Lyle 1859–1989.* Translated by Eric Long-Michalke (Routledge, London, 1990).

Chapman, Stanley D. 'Fixed Capital Formation in the British Cotton Industry, 1770–1815', *Economic History Review*, 23 (1970), 235–53.

Cherry, Bridget, Charles O'Brien and Nicholas Pevsner, *The Buildings of England, London 5: East* (Yale University Press, New Haven and London, 2005).

Chesterton, Ridley D. and R. S. Fenton, *Gas and Electricity Colliers* (World Ship Society, Kendal, 1984).

Christopher, John, *The London & Blackwall Railway. Docklands' First Railway* (Amberley Publishing, Stroud, 2013).

Clifford, Jim, *West Ham and the River Lea. A Social and Environmental History of London's Industrialized Marshland, 1839–1914* (UBC Press, British Columbia, Canada, 2017).

Clifton, Gloria 'Members and Officers of the LCC, 1889–1965', in Andrew Saint (ed.), *Politics and the People of London. The London County Council 1889–1965* (Hambledon Press, London, 1989), 1–26.

Coad, Jonathan, *Support for the Fleet. Architecture and Engineering of the Royal Navy's Bases 1700–1914* (English Heritage, Swindon, 2013).

Connell, Andrew, "'I feel I am placed at a very great disadvantage". Sir James Whitehead: The Parliamentary Travails of a Liberal Meritocrat', *Journal of Liberal History*, 92 (2016), 25–33.

Cook, Gordon C., *Disease in the Merchant Navy. A History of the Seamen's Hospital Society* (Radcliffe Publishing, Abingdon, 2007).

Cook, Tom 'Accommodating the Outcast: Common Lodging Houses and the Limits of Urban Governance in Victorian and Edwardian London', *Urban History*, 35 (2008), 414–36.

Cookson, Mildred 'The Sun Flour Mills Bromley by Bow', *Milling and Grain*, June 2018, 12–15.

Cookson, Mildred 'City of London Flour Mills, a Millstone Mill', *Milling and Grain*, August 2018, 14–15.

Cookson, Mildred 'The Mills of the Co-operative Wholesale Society', *Milling and Grain*, March 2018, 12–15.

Cookson, Mildred 'Roller Mills of London', https://catalogue.millsarchive.org/roller-flour-mills-of-london

Cooney, E. W., 'The Organisation of Building in England in the 19th Century', *Architectural Research and Teaching*, 1 (1970), 46–52.

Cordery, Simon, *British Friendly Societies 1850–1914* (Palgrave Macmillan, Basingstoke, 2003).

Cox, Alan, 'Bricks to Build a Capital', in Hermione Hobhouse and Anne Saunders (eds.), *Good and Proper Materials: The Fabric of London Since the Great Fire* (London Topographical Society, London, 1989), 3–17.

Cox, Alan, 'A Vital Component: Stock Bricks in Georgian London', *Construction History*, 13 (1997), 57–66.

Cracknell, B. E., 'The Petroleum Industry of the Lower Thames and Medway', *Geography*, 37 (1952), 79–88.

Craig, Robin, 'The African Guano Trade', *Mariner's Mirror*, 50, 1964.

Craig, Robin, *The Ship: Steam Tramps and Cargo Liners 1850–1950* (HMSO, London, 1980).

Craig, Robin, *British Tramp Shipping, 1750–1914* (IMEHA, St. John's Newfoundland, 2003).

Crossick, Geoffrey *An Artisan Elite in Victorian Society. Kentish London 1840–1880* (Croom Helm, London, 1978).

Crouzet, François 'The Impact of the French Wars on the British Economy', in H. T. Dickinson (ed.), *Britain and the French Revolution* (Macmillan, London, 1989), 189–209.

D'Sena, Peter, 'Perquisites and Casual Labour on the London Wharfside in the Eighteenth Century', *The London Journal*, 14 (1989), 130–47.

Darwin, John, *Unlocking the World. Port Cities and Globalization in the Age of Steam 1830–1914* (Allen Lane, London, 2020).

Daunton, M. J., 'London and the World', in Celina Fox (ed.), *London World City 1800–1840* (Yale University Press, New Haven & London, 1992), 21–38.

Daunton, M. J., 'Industry in London: Revisions and Reflections', *The London Journal*, 21 (1996), 1–8.

Daunton, M. J. *Trusting Leviathan. The Politics of Taxation in Britain, 1799–1914* (Cambridge University Press, Cambridge, 2001).

Davies, P. N., *Sir Alfred Jones, Shipping Entrepreneur Par Excellence* (Europa, London, 1978).

Davis, John, *Reforming London: The London Government Problem 1855–1900* (Oxford University Press, Oxford, 1988).

Davis, John, 'The Progressive Council, 1889–1907', in Andrew Saint (ed.), *Politics and the People of London. The London County Council 1889–1965* (Hambledon Press, London, 1989), 27–48.

Davis, John, 'Radical Clubs and London Politics 1870–1900', in David Feldman and Gareth Stedman Jones (eds.), *Metropolis – London. Histories and Representations since 1800* (Routledge, London, 1989), 103–28.

Davis, Ralph, *The Industrial Revolution and British Overseas Trade* (Leicester University Press, Leicester, 1979).

Dixon, Conrad, 'Lascars: The Forgotten Seamen', in Rosemary Ommer and Gerald Panting (eds.), *Working Men Who Got Wet* (Memorial University, St John's Newfoundland, 1980), 265–81.

Dixon, Conrad, 'The Rise and Fall of the Crimp, 1840–1914', in Stephen Fisher (ed.), *British Shipping and Seamen, 1630–1960. Exeter Papers in Economic History* (University of Exeter, Exeter, 1984), 49–67.

Doe, Helen, 'The Thames Merchant Yards in the Napoleonic Wars', in Roger Owen (Ed,) *Shipbuilding and Ships on the Thames. Proceedings of a Third Symposium* (J. R. Owen, West Wickham, 2006), 10–21.

Doe, Helen, *Enterprising Women and Shipping in the Nineteenth Century* (Boydell Press, Woodbridge, 2009).

Donington, Katie, 'Transforming Capital: Slavery, Family, Commerce and the Making of the Hibbert Family', in Catherine Hall et al., *Legacies of British Slave-ownership. Colonial Slavery and the Formation of Victorian Britain* (Cambridge University Press, Cambridge, 2014).

Donovan, P. F., 'Australia and the Great London Dock Strike 1889', *Labour History*, 23 (1972), 17–26.

Draper, N., 'The City of London and Slavery: Evidence from the First Two Dock Companies, 1795–1800', *Economic History Review*, 61 (2008), 432–66.

Draper, N., *The Price of Emancipation. Slave-ownership, Compensation and British Society at the End of Slavery* (Cambridge University Press, Cambridge, 2010).

Duffy, A. E. P., 'New Unionism in Britain, 1889–1890' *Economic History Review*, New Series, 14 (1961), 306–19.

Dunbar-Nasmith, David, *Duncan Dunbar and His Ships* www.danbyrnes.com .au/networks/periods/1800after/1800dunbar.htm

Dyos, H. J., 'The Slums of Victorian London', *Victorian Studies*, 2 (1967), 5–40.

Ehrman, John, *The Younger Pitt. The Consuming Struggle* (Constable, London, 1996).

Ellis, Aytoun, *Three Hundred Years on London River. The Hay's Wharf Story 1651–1951* (Bodley Head, London, 1952).

Ellis, Markman, *The Coffee House: A Cultural History* (Weidenfield and Nicholson, London, 2004).

Ellmers, Chris, (ed.), 'Gordon & Co., Deptford – Discovering a Lost London Shipyard', in *Proceedings of the Fifth Symposium on Shipbuilding on the Thames* (Docklands History Group, London, 2013), 43–72.

Ellmers, Chris, 'Industrial Discontent in the Thames Shipyards 1795–1802' (Docklands History Group, published on-line. November 2016, www .docklandshistorygroup.org.uk/Talk%202016-11.pdf

Ellmers, Chris, 'Deptford Private Shipyards, and Their Relationship to Deptford Dockyard, 1790–1819', in *Five Hundred Years of Deptford and Woolwich Royal Dockyards, Transactions of the Naval Dockyards Society*, 11 (2018), 30–74.

Ellmers, Chris and Alex Werner, *London's Lost Riverscape. A Photographic Panorama* (Viking, London, 1988).

Emsley, Clive, *British Society and the French Wars 1793–1815* (Macmillan, London and Basingstoke, 1979).

Fairlie, Susan, 'The Nineteenth-Century Corn Law Reconsidered', *Economic History Review*, New Series, Vol. 18. 3 (1965), 562–72.

Fairlie, Susan, 'British Statistics of Grain Imports from Canada and the USA, 1791–1900', in David Alexander and Rosemary Ommer (eds.), *Volumes Not Values: Canadian Sailing Ships and World Trade* (Memorial University of Newfoundland, St. John's, 1979), 163–94.

Falkus, M. E., 'The British Gas Industry before 1850', *Economic History Review*, New Series 20 (1967), 494–508.

Farnie, D. A., *East & West of Suez. The Suez Canal in History, 1854–1956* (Oxford University Press, Oxford, 1969).

Farrel, Jerome, 'The German Community in 19th Century East London', *East London Record*, 13 (1990), 2–8.

Faulkner, Alan H., 'The Regent's Canal Dock, Part 1', *Journal of the Railway and Canal Historical Society*, 2 (2002), 70–136.

Fielding, Steven, *Class and Ethnicity. Irish Catholics in England, 1880–1939* (Open University Press, Buckingham, 1993).

Fisher, Michael H., 'Working Across the Seas: Indian Maritime Labourers in India, Britain, and In-Between, 1600–1800', *International Review of Social History*, Supplement 14, 51 (2006), 21–45.

Fishman, William J., *East End 1888. A Year in a London Borough Among the Labouring Poor* (Gerald Duckworth & Co., 1988, Reprinted Five Leaves Publications, Nottingham, 2005).

Fletcher, Max E., 'The Suez Canal and World Shipping, 1869–1914', *Journal of Economic History*, 18 (1958), 556–573.

Fox, Celina (ed.), *London – World City* (Yale University Press, London & New Haven, 1992).

Fraser-Stephen, Elspet, *Two Centuries in the London Coal Trade. The Story of Charringtons* (Charrington, Gardner, Locket & Co., Ltd., London, 1952).

French, Christopher J., '"Crowded with Traders and a Great Commerce": London's Domination of Overseas Trade, 1700–1775', *London Journal*, 17 (1992), 28–35.

Frost, Alan, 'Thomas Rowcroft's Testimony and the 'Botany Bay' Debate', *Labour History*, 37 (1979), 101–7.

Gayer, Arthur D., W. W. Rostow, and Anna Jacobson Schwartz, *The Growth and Fluctuations of the British Economy 1790–1815. An Historical, Statistical and Theoretical Study of Britain's Economic Development 1790–1850. Volume II* (Clarendon Press, Oxford, 1953).

George, Dorothy, M., *London Life in the Eighteenth Century*, 3rd ed. (London School of Economics & Political Science, London, 1951).

Gilbert, Bentley Brinkerhoff, *David Lloyd George: A Political Life. The Architect of Change 1863–1912* (B. T. Batsford Ltd., London, 1987).

Gilding, Bob, *The Journeymen Coopers of East London, Workers' Control in an Old London Trade* (History Workshop Pamphlets, History Workshop, 1971).

Ginn, Geoff, 'Answering the "Bitter Cry": Urban Description and Social Reform in the Late-Victorian East End', *The London Journal* 31 (2006), 179–200.

Gordon, Barry, *Economic Doctrine and Tory Liberalism 1824–1830* (Macmillan, London & Basingstoke, 1979).

Gordon, Lincoln, 'The Port of London Authority', in William A. Robson, (ed.), *Public Enterprise. Developments in Social Ownership and Control in Great Britain* (George Allen & Unwin, London, 1937), 2–57.

Gosden, P. H. J. H., *The Friendly Societies in England, 1815–1875* (Manchester University Press, Manchester, 1961).

Gourvish, T. R. and R. G. Wilson, *The British Brewing Industry* (Cambridge University Press, Cambridge, 1994).

Graham, Gerald S., 'The Ascendancy of the Sailing Ship, 1855–1885', *Economic History Review*, 9 (1956), 134–46.

Green, David R., *From Artisans to Paupers, Economic Change and Poverty in London, 1790–1870* (Scolar Press, Aldershot, 1995).

Green, David R., 'The Nineteenth-Century Metropolitan Economy: A Revisionist Interpretation', *The London Journal*, 21 (1996), 9–26.

Green, David R., *Pauper Capital. London and the Poor Law, 1790–1870* (Ashgate, Farnham, 2010).

Greenhill, Basil, 'Steam Before the Screw', in Robert Gardiner (ed.), *The Advent of Steam. The Merchant Steamship before 1900* (Conway Maritime Press, London, 1993), 11–23.

Greenwood, R. H. and F. J. Hawks, *The Saint George Steam Packet Company 1821–1843*, (World Ship Society, Kendal, 1995).

Greeves, Ivan S., *London Docks 1800–1980. A Civil Engineering History* (Thomas Telford, London, 1980).

Guillery, Peter, 'Building the Millwall Docks', *Construction History*, 6 (1990), 3–21.

Guillery, Peter, 'Warehouses and Sheds: Buildings and Goods Handling in London's Nineteenth Century Docks', in Adrian Jarvis and Kenneth Smith (eds.), *Albert Dock Trade and Technology* (National Museums & Galleries on Merseyside, Liverpool, 1999), 77–87.

Hadfield, Charles, *The Canal Age* (David and Charles, London, 1969).

Hall, Peter H., *The Industries of London Since 1861* (Hutchinson, London, 1962).

Harcourt, Freda, *Flagships of Imperialism. The P&O Company and the Politics of Empire from its Origins to 1867* (Manchester University Press, Manchester, 2006).

Harlaftis, Gelina, *A History of Greek-Owned Shipping. The Making of an International Tramp Fleet, 1830 to the Present Day* (Routledge, London, 1996).

Harley, Charles K., 'The Shift from Sailing Ships to Steamships, 1850–1890'a Study in Technological Change and its Diffusion', in Deidre McCloskey, (ed.), *Essays on a Mature Economy: Britain after 1840* (Methuen, London, 1971), 215–37.

Harley, Charles K., 'Steers Afloat: The North Atlantic Meat Trade, Liner Predominance, and Freight Rates, 1870–1913', *Journal of Economic History*, 68 (2008), 1028–58.

Harrison, Brian, 'Pubs', in H. J. Dyos and Michael Wolff, (eds.), *The Victorian City: Images and Realities, Volume 1* (Routledge and Kegan Paul, London and Boston, 1973), 161–90.

Henderson, Antony and Sarah Palmer, 'The Early Nineteenth-Century Port of London: Management and Labour in Three Dock Companies, 1800–1825', in Simon Ville and David M. Williams (eds.), *Management, Finance and Industrial Relations in Maritime Industries: Essays in International Maritime and Business History*, (IMEHA, St. John's Newfoundland, 1991), 31–50.

Hersh, Mark 'Sailmakers: The Maintenance of the Craft Traditions in the Age of Steam', in Royden Harrison and Jonathan Zeitlin (eds.), *Divisions of Labour. Skilled Workers and Technological Change in Nineteenth Century England* (Harvester Press, Brighton, 1985), 87–113.

Higenbottam, S., *Our Society's History* (Amalgamated Society of Woodworkers, Manchester, 1939).

Higgs, Edward and Amanda Wilkinson, 'Women, Occupations and Work in the Victorian Censuses Revisited', *History Workshop Journal*, 2016, 81, 17–38.

Hilton, Boyd, *Corn, Cash, Commerce. The Economic Policies of Tory Governments 1815–1830* (Oxford University Press, Oxford, 1977).

Hobhouse, Hermione (ed.), *Survey of London: Volumes 43 and 44, Poplar, Blackwall and Isle of Dogs* (Athlone Press, London, 1994).

Hobsbawm, E. J., *Labouring Men. Studies in the History of Labour* (Weidenfield & Nicolson, London, 1964).

Hobsbawm, E. J., 'The Nineteenth-Century London Labour Market', in E. J. Hobsbawm, (ed.), *Worlds of Labour. Further Studies in the History of Labour* (Weidenfeld and Nicolson, London, 1984), 131–51.

Hollen Lees, Lynn, *Exiles of Erin. Irish Migrants in Victorian London* (Cornell University Press, Ithaca, 1979).

Hostettler, Eva, *The Isle of Dogs 1066–1918. A Brief History. Volume I* (Island History Trust, London, 2000).

Hounsell, Peter, *Bricks of Victorian London. A Social and Economic History*, Studies in Regional and Local History, Volume 22 (University of Hertford Press, Hatfield, 2022).

Howe, Anthony, *Free Trade and Liberal England 1846–1946* (Clarendon Press, Oxford, 1997).

Hudson, Pat and Lynette Hunter, 'The Autobiography of William Hart, Cooper, 1776–1857: A Respectable Artisan in the Industrial Revolution. Part I', *London Journal*, 7 (1981), 144–60.

Hudson, Pat and Lynette Hunter, 'The Autobiography of William Hart, Cooper, 1776–1857: A Respectable Artisan in the Industrial Revolution. Part II', *London Journal*, 8 (1982), 63–75.

Hugill, Antony, *Sugar and All That … A History of Tate & Lyle* (Gentry Books, London, 1978).

Hugill, Stan, *Sailortown* (Routledge & Kegan Paul, London, 1967).

Hunt, E. H., *British Labour History 1815–1914* (Weidenfield and Nicolson, 1981), 295–310.

Hyde, Francis, *Liverpool and the Mersey. An Economic History of a Port 1700–1970* (David & Charles, Newton Abbot, 1971).

Ivatt, Ian, 'Lloyd George's Presidency of the Board of Trade', *Journal of Liberal History*, 103 (2019), 22–9.

Jackson, Gordon 'The Importance of Unimportant Ports', *International Journal of Maritime History*, 13 (2001), 1–17.

Jackson, Lee, *Palaces of Pleasure: From Music Halls to the Seaside to Football. How the Victorians Invented Mass Entertainment* (Yale University Press, New Haven and London, 2019).

Jackson, R. V. 'The Decline of the Wool Clippers', *The Great Circle*, 2 (1980), 87–98.

Jarvis, Adrian, *Liverpool Central Docks, 1799–1905. An Illustrated History* (Alan Sutton, Stroud, 1991), 15.

Jefferys, James B., *The Story of the Engineers 1800–1945* (EP Publishing, London, 1945).

Johnson, Paul 'Economic Development and Industrial Dynamism in Victorian London', *The London Journal* 21 (1996), 27–37.

Kaukiainen, Yrjö, 'Shrinking the World: Improvements in the Speed of Information Transmission, c. 1820–1870', in Lars U. Scholl and Merja-Liisa Hinkkanen, (eds.), *Sail and Steam. Selected Maritime Writings of Yrjö Kaukiainen* (IMHA, St. John's Newfoundland, 2004), 231–60.

Kay, Peter, *The London, Tilbury & Southend Railway, Vol. 1* (Peter Kay, Teignmouth, 1996).

Kay, Peter, *The Thames Haven Railway. Essex Branch Line and London Shipping Link 1835–1996* (Peter Kay, Teignmouth, 1999).

Kellett, J. R., *The Impact of Railways on the Victorian City* (Routledge, London, 1969).

Kent, David 'High Church Rituals and Rituals of Protest; the "Riots" at St. George-in-the-East, 1859–1860', *The London Journal*, 32 (2007), 145–66.

Knight, Roger, 'Devil Bolts and Deception? Wartime Naval Shipbuilding in Private Shipyards, 1739–1815', *Journal for Maritime Research*, 5 (2003) 34–51.

Knight, Roger, *Britain Against Napoleon. The Organisation of Victory 1793–1815* (Allen Lane, London, 2013).

Knight, Roger and Martin Wilcox, *Sustaining the Fleet 1793–1815. War, the British Navy and the Contractor State* (Boydell Press, Woodbridge, 2010).

Kverndal, Roald, *Seamen's Missions. Their Origin and Early Growth. A Contribution to the History of the Church Maritime* (William Carey Library, Pasadena California, 1986).

Kynaston, David, 'A Changing Workscape: The City of London Since the 1840s', *The London Journal*, 13 (1987) 99–105.

Kynaston, David, *The City of London. Volume 1. A World of Its Own 1815–1890* (Pimlico., London, 1994).

Lahiri, Shompa, 'Contested Relations: The East India Company and Lascars in London', in H. V. Bowen, Margarette Lincoln and Nigel Rigby (eds.), *The Worlds of the East India Company* (Boydell Press, Woodbridge, 2002), 169–81.

Lee, C. H., 'Some Aspects of the Coastal Shipping Trade: The Aberdeen Steam Navigation Company, 1835–50', *Journal of Transport History*, 2nd Series, 3 (1975) 94–107.

Lee, Robert, 'The Seafarers' Urban World: A Critical Review', *International Journal of Maritime History*, 25 (2013), 23–64.

Lee, Robert, and W. R. Lee, 'The Socio-Economic and Demographic Characteristics of Port Cities: A Typology for Comparative Analysis?', *Urban History*, 25 (1998), 147–72.

Lew, Byron and Bruce Cater, 'The Telegraph, Co-ordination of Tramp Shipping and Growth in World Trade, 1870–1910', *European Review of Economic History*, 10 (2006), 147–73.

Lewis, Frank, *Essex and Sugar*, (Phillimore, London, 1976).

Linebaugh, Peter, *The London Hanged, Crime and Civil Society in the Eighteenth Century*, 2nd ed. (Verso, London, 2003).

Lovell, John, *Stevedore and Dockers. A Study of Trade Unionism in the Port of London, 1870–1914* (Macmillan, London, 1969).

Lubbock, Basil, *The Blackwall Frigates* (Charles E. Lauriat, Boston, 1922).

Luckin, Bill, *Pollution and Control. A Social History of the Thames in the Nineteenth Century* (Adam Hilger, Bristol, 1986).

Lyall, Oliver, *The Plaistow Story* (Tate & Lyall, London, 1960).

Makepeace, Margaret, *The East India Company's London Workers. Management of the Warehouse Labourers, 1800–1858* (Boydell Press, Woodbridge, 2010).

Malchow, H. L., *Gentlemen Capitalists: The Social and Political World of the Victorian Businessman* (Stanford University Press, Stanford, 1992).

Malden, H. E. (ed.) *A History of the County of Surrey: Volume 4* (Archibald Constable: London, 1912), 17–24.

Marden, Dave, *London's Dock Railways, Part 2, The Royal Docks, North Woolwich and Silvertown* (Kestrel Railway Books, Southampton, 2013).

Marriott, John, 'West Ham: London's Industrial Centre and Gateway to the World' I: Industrialisation, 1840–1910', *The London Journal*, 13 (1987), 121–42.

Marriott, John, *Beyond the Tower. A History of East London* (Yale, New Haven & London, 2011).

Martin, J. E., *Greater London. An Industrial Geography* (G. Bell and Sons, London, 1966).

Matthew, W. M., 'Peru and the British Guano Market, 1840–1870', *Economic History Review*, 23 (1970), 112–28.

Matthews, Derek, '1889 and All That. New Views on the New Unionism', *International Review of Social History*, 36 (1991), 24–58.

Matthews, Peter, *London's Bridges* (Shire Publications, Botley, 2008).

Mawer, Bryan, *Sugar Bakers. From Sweat to Sweetness* (Anglo-German History Society, London, 2011).

Mawer, Bryan, Sugar Refiners & Sugarbakers Database, www.mawer.clara.net/intro.html

McClelland, Keith and Alastair Reid, 'Wood, Iron and Steel: Technology, Labour and Trade Union Organisation in the Shipbuilding Industry, 1840–1914', in Royden Harrison and Jonathan Zeitlin, (eds.), *Divisions of Labour.*

Skilled Workers and Technological Change in Nineteenth Century England (Harvester Press, Brighton, 1985), 151–84.

McIlhiney, David, *A Gentleman in Every Slum. Church of England Missions in East London 1837–1914* (Pickwick Publications, Eugene Oregon, 1988).

McLeod, Hugh, *Class and Religion in the Late Victorian City* (Croom Helm, London, 1974).

Michie, R. C., *The City of London. Continuity and Change, 1850–1990* (Macmillan, London, 1992).

Michie, R. C., 'The International Trade in Food and the City of London Since 1850', *Journal of European Economic History*, 25 (1996), 369–406.

Milne, Graeme J., *People, Place and Power on the Nineteenth-Century Waterfront. Sailortown'* (Palgrave Macmillan, London, 2016).

Mommsen, Wolfgang J. and Hans Gerhard Husung, *The Development of Trade Unionism in Great Britain and Germany, 1880–1914* (Routledge, London, 1985).

Morris, Derek and Ken Cozens, *Wapping 1600–1800. A Social History of an Early Modern London Maritime Suburb* (East London History Society, London, 2009).

Morris, Derek and Ken Cozens, *London's Sailortown 1600–1800: A Social History of Shadwell and Ratcliffe, An Early Modern Riverside Suburb* (East London History Society, London, 2014).

Morris, Roger, *The Foundations of British Maritime Ascendancy: Resources, Logistics and the State, 1755–1815* (Cambridge University Press, Cambridge, 2011).

Mortimer, J. E., *History of the Boilermakers, Volume 1, 1834–1906* (George Allen & Unwin, London, 1973).

Munby, D. L., *Industry and Planning in Stepney* (Oxford University Press, London. 1951).

Munro, J. Forbes, *Maritime Enterprise and Empire. Sir William Mackinnon and his Business Network, 1823–1893* (Boydell Press, Woodbridge, 2003).

Murphy, P. J., 'The Origins of the 1852 Lock-Out in the British Engineering Industry Reconsidered', *International Review of Social History*, XXIII (1978), 242–66.

Musson, A. E., 'Industrial Motive Power in the United Kingdom, 1800–70', *Economic History Review*, New Series, 29 (1976), 413–39.

Myers, Norma S., 'The Black Poor of London: Initiatives of Eastern Seamen in the Eighteenth and Nineteenth Centuries', in Diane Frost (ed.), *Ethnic Labour and British Imperial Trade: A History of Ethnic Seafarers in the UK* (Frank Cass, London, 1995), 7–21.

Northcote Parkinson, C., *Trade in the Eastern Seas 1793–1813* (1937, Reprinted Routledge, London, 1966).

Northway, A. M., 'The Tyne Steam Shipping Co: A Late Nineteenth-Century Shipping Line', *Maritime History*, 2 (1972), 69–85.

Norwood, Janice, 'The Performance of Protest: The 1889 Dock Strike On and Off the Stage', in Peter Yeandle, Katherine Newey and Jeffrey Richards (eds.), *Politics, Performance and Popular Culture. Theatre and Society* (Manchester University Press, Manchester, 2016), 250–54.

O'Brien, Patrick K. 'The Political Economy of British Taxation, 1660–1815', *Economic History Review*, 41 (1988), 1–32.

O'Brien, Patrick K. 'The Contributions of Warfare with Revolutionary and Napoleonic France to the Consolidation and Progress of the British Industrial

Revolution', Revised Version of Working Paper 150, LSE, Economic History Working Papers, 264 (2017).

Oliver, Stuart, 'The Thames Embankment and the Disciplining of Nature in Modernity', *The Geographical Journal*, 166 (2000), 227–38.

Owen, David, *The Government of Victorian London 1855–1899. The Metropolitan Board of Works, the Vestries and the City Corporation* (Belknap Press, Cambridge Mass, 1982).

Palmer, Sarah, 'Investors in London Shipping, 1820–50', *Maritime History*, 2 (1972), 46–68.

Palmer, Sarah, 'Seamen Ashore in Late Nineteenth Century London: Protection from the Crimps', in Paul Adam (ed.), *Seamen in Society* (International Commission for Maritime History, 1980), 55–67.

Palmer, Sarah, 'The Most Indefatigable Activity: The General Steam Navigation Company, 1824–50', *Journal of Transport History, Third Series*, 3 (1982), 1–22.

Palmer, Sarah, *Politics, Shipping and the Repeal of the Navigation Laws* (Manchester University Press, Manchester, 1990).

Palmer, Sarah, 'Ship-building in South-east England, 1800–1913', in Simon Ville (ed.), *Shipbuilding in the United Kingdom: A Regional Approach. Research in Maritime History. No 4.* (IMEHA, St John's, Newfoundland, 1992), 45–74.

Palmer, Sarah, 'Ports', in Martin Daunton (ed.), *The Cambridge Urban History of Britain* (Cambridge University Press, Cambridge, 2000), 133–50.

Palmer, Sarah, 'Port Economics in an Historical Context: The Nineteenth-Century Port of London', *International Journal of Maritime History*, 15 (2003), 27–67.

Palmer, Sarah, 'The Labour Process in the 19th Century Port of London Some New Perspectives', in Anne-Lise Piétri-Lévy et al. (eds.), *Environnements Portuaires, Port Environments* (Universités de Rouen et du Havre, Havre, 2003), 318–28.

Pattison, George, 'Shipping and The East India Docks, 1802–38', *Mariner's Mirror*, 49 (1963), 208–12.

Pattison, George, 'The East India Dock Company 1803–1838', *East London Papers*, 7 (1964), 31–40.

Pattison, George, 'Nineteenth-Century Dock Labour in the Port of London', *Mariners Mirror*, 52 (1966), 263–79.

Pattison, George, 'The Cooper's Strike at the West India Docks, 1821', *Mariner's Mirror*, 55 (1969), 163–84.

Paul, Rodman W., 'The Wheat Trade Between California and the United Kingdom', *Mississippi Valley Historical Review*, 45 (1958), 391–412.

Pelling, Henry, *A History of British Trade Unionism*, 4th edition (Penguin Books, London, 1987).

Perren, Richard, *The Meat Trade in Britain 1840–1914* (Routledge & Kegan Paul, London, 1978).

Perren, Richard, 'Structural Change and Market Growth in the Food Industry: Flour Milling in Britain, Europe and America, 1850–1914', *Economic History Review, 2nd Series*, 43 (1990), 420–37.

Phillips, Gordon and Noel Whiteside, *Casual Labour. The Unemployment Question in the Port Transport Industry 1880–1970* (Clarendon Press, Oxford, 1985).

Pollard, Sidney, 'The Decline of Shipbuilding on the Thames', *Economic History Review, Second Series*, 3 (1950), 72–89.

Pollard, Sidney and Paul Robertson, *The British Shipbuilding Industry 1870–1914* (Harvard University Press, Cambridge, 1979).

Porter, Andrew, *Victorian Shipping Business and Imperial Policy* (Boydell, Woodbridge, 1986).

Porter, Dale H., *The Thames Embankment. Environment, Technology and Society in Victorian London* (University of Akron Press, Akron Ohio, 1998).

Porter, Stephen 'All Saints', Poplar: the Making of a Parish, 1650–1817', *The London Journal*, 17 (1992), 103–14.

Powell, L. H., *The Shipping Federation. A History of the First Sixty Years 1890–1950* (Shipping Federation, London, 1950).

Powell, W. R. (ed.), *A History of the County of Essex: Volume VI* (Oxford University Press, Oxford, 1973).

Price, Jacob. M., 'Competition Between Ports in British Long Distance Trade, c.1660–1800', in Agustin Guimera and Dolores Romero (eds.), *Puertos y Systemas Portuarios (Siglos XVI–XX): Actas del Coloquio Internacional, Madrid 19–21 Octubre, 1995* (Madrid, 1996), 19–36.

Prothero, Iowerth, *Artisans and Politics in Early Nineteenth Century London: John Gast and His Times* (Dawson, Folkestone, 1979).

Prouty, Roger, *The Transformation of the Board of Trade 1830–1855; a Study of Administrative Reorganisation in the Heyday of Laissez Faire* (William Heinmann Ltd, London, 1957).

Pudney, John, *London's Docks* (Thames & Hudson, London, 1975).

Quinault, Roland, 'From National to World Metropolis: Governing London, 1750–1850', *The London Journal*, 26 (2001), 38–46.

Quinlan, Michael, 'Precarious Employment, Ill Health and Lessons from History: The Case of Casual (Temporary) Dockworkers 1880–1945', *International Journal of Health Services*, 43 (2013), 724–29.

Rankin, Stuart, *Shipbuilding in Rotherhithe – The Nelson Dockyard, Rotherhithe Local History Paper No.2* (Dockside Studio, London, 1996).

Rankin, Stuart, *Shipbuilding in Rotherhithe – Greenland Dock & Barnard's Wharf, Rotherhithe Local History Paper No. 3* (Dockside Studio, London, 1999).

Rankin, Stuart, *A Short History of the Surrey Commercial Docks, Rotherhithe Local History Paper No. 6* (Dockside Studio, London, 1999).

Rawley, James A., *London, Metropolis of the Slave Trade* (University of Missouri Press, Columbia and London, 2003).

Rawlings P. J., '"Without Feeling and Without Remorse"? Making Sense of Employers' Liability and Insurance in the Nineteenth Century', *British Insurance Law Association Journal*, 126 (2013), 1–16.

Redfern, Percy, *The Story of the C.W.S.: The Jubilee History of the Co-operative Wholesale Society Ltd 1863–1913* (Co-operative Wholesale Society, Manchester, 1913).

Redvalksen, David, 'The Two Kingdoms: The Norwegian Seamen's Church in London 1865–1905', *Journal of Religious History*, 42 (2018), 410–31.

Rees, Graham L., *Britain's Commodity Markets* (Paul Elek Books, London, 1972).

Reynolds, Susan (ed.), *A History of the County of Middlesex: Volume 3* (Oxford University Press, Oxford, 1962).

Rideout, Eric H., 'Development of the Liverpool Warehousing System', *Transactions of the Historical Society of Lancashire and Cheshire*, 82 (1930), 1–41.

Robins, Nick, *Coastal Passenger Steamers of the British Isles* (Seaforth Publishing, Barnsley, 2011).

Rodwell, Jones, *The Geography of London River* (Methuen & Co., London, 1931).

Roseveare, Henry, 'Wiggins' Key' Revisited: Trade and Shipping in the Later Seventeenth-Century Port of London', *The Journal of Transport History*, 16 (1995), 1–20.

Roseveare, Henry, 'The Eighteenth-century Port of London Reconsidered', in Agustin Guimera and Dolores Romero (eds.), *Puertos y Systemas Portuarios (Siglos XVI-XX): Actas del Coloquio Internacional, Madrid 19–21 Octubre, 1995* (Ministerio De Fomento, Madrid, 1996), 37–52.

Rössler, Horst, 'Germans from Hanover in the British Sugar Industry', in Stefan Manz et al. (eds.), *Migration and Transfer from Germany to Britain 1660–1914* (K. G. Saur, Munchen, 2007), 49–63.

Rowan, Alistair J., 'After the Adelphi: Forgotten Years in the Adam Brothers' Practice', *Journal of the Royal Society of Arts*, 122 (1974), 659–710.

Rubinstein, W.D, *Men of Property. The Very Wealthy in Britain Since the Industrial Revolution* (Croom Helm, London, 1981).

Rushen, Elizabeth, *John Marshall. Shipowner, Lloyd's Reformer and Emigration Agent* (Anchor Books, Australia, 2020).

Saini, Raminder K. '"England Failed to do Her Duty Towards Them": The India Office and Pauper Indians in the Metropole, 1857–1914', *Journal of Imperial and Commonwealth History.* 46 (2018), 226–56.

Saluppo, Alessandro, 'Strikebreaking and Anti-Unionism on the Waterfront: The Shipping Federation, 1890–1914', *European History Quarterly*, 49 (2019), 573–80.

Sargent, Edward. 'Frederic Eliot Duckham, M.I.C.E., and the Millwall Docks (1868–1909)', *Transactions of the Newcomen Society*, 60 (1988), 49–71.

Sargent, Edward. 'The Planning and Early Buildings of the West India Docks', *Mariner's Mirror*, 77 (1991), 119–41.

Sargent, Edward. 'Some Steam Warships Supplied to the Spanish Navy in the 19th Century by Thames Shipyards', in Roger Owen (ed.), *Shipbuilding on the Thames and Thames-Built Ships, Proceedings of a Second Symposium* (J. R. Owen, West Wickham, 2004), 87–104.

Schneer, Jonathan, *Ben Tillett. Portrait of a Labour Leader* (Croom Helm, London, 1982).

Schneer, Jonathan, *London 1900. The Imperial Metropolis* (Yale University Press, New Haven & London, 1999).

Schwarz, L. D., *London in the Age of Industrialisation: Entrepreneurs, Labour Force and Living Conditions, 1700–1850* (Cambridge University Press, Cambridge, 1992).

Sejerstesd, Francis, 'Aspects of the Norwegian Timber Trade in the 1840s and '50s', *Scandinavian Economic History Review*, 16 (1968), 139–54.

Shannon, H. A., 'Bricks – A Trade Index, 1785–1849', *Economica, New Series*, 3 (1934), 300–18.

Sharp, Paul, '"1846 and All That": The Rise and Fall of British Wheat Protection in the Nineteenth Century', *Agricultural History Review*, 58 (2010), 76–94.

Shepherd, Francis, *London 1808–1870: The Infernal Wen* (London, Secker & Warburg, 1971).

Sinclair, Peter, 'The Brown Family. Ten Flour Mills in a Hundred Years' (The Mills Archive, Reading, 2017).

Skempton, A. W., 'Engineering in the Port of London, 1789–1808', *Transactions of the Newcomen Society*, 50 (1978–9), 87–108.

Skempton, A. W., 'Engineering in the Port of London, 1808–1834', *Transactions of the Newcomen Society*, 53 (1981–2), 37–88.

Skempton, A. W. et al. (eds.), *A Biographical Dictionary of Civil Engineers in Great Britain and Ireland Volume 1. 1500–1830* (Thomas Telford, London, 2002).

Smith, Crosbie, *Coal, Steam and Ships, Engineering, Enterprise and Empire on the Nineteenth-Century Seas* (Cambridge University Press, Cambridge, 2018).

Smith, Raymond, *Sea-Coal for London. History of the Coal Factors in the London Market* (Longmans, London, 1961).

Smith, Tim, 'Hydraulic Power in the Port of London', *Industrial Archaeology Review*, 14 (1991), 64–88.

Solar, Peter M., 'Shipping and Economic Development in Nineteenth-Century Ireland', *Economic History Review*, New Series, 59 (2006), 717–42.

Stafford, Ann, *A Match to Fire the Thames* (Hodder & Stoughton, London, 1961).

Stedman Jones, Gareth, *Outcast London. A Study in the Relationship Between Classes in Victorian Society* (First Published 1971. Reprinted with a new preface Penguin, London, 1984).

Stein, Richard L., 'Remember the *Téméraire*: Turner's Memorial of 1839', *Representations*, 11 (1985), 165–200.

Stern, Walter M., 'The First London Dock Boom and the Growth of the West India Docks', *Economica*, New Series, 19 (1952), 59–77.

Stern, Walter M., 'The Isle of Dogs Canal. A Study in Early Public Investment' *The Economic History Review*, New Series, 4 (1952), 359–71.

Stern, Walter M., *The Porters of London* (Longmans, London, 1960).

Swann, D., 'The Pace and Progress of Port Investment in England, 1660–1830', *Yorkshire Bulletin of Economic and Social Research*, 12 (1960), 32–44.

Swann, D., 'The Engineers of English Port Improvements 1660–1830: Part 1', *Transport History*, 1 (Reprinted David & Charles, 1969), 153–68.

Sweezy, Paul M., *Monopoly and Competition in the English Coal Trade* (Harvard University Press, Harvard, 1938).

Tann, Jennifer and R. Glyn Jones, 'Technology and Transformation: The Diffusion of the Roller Mill in the British Flour Milling Industry, 1870–1907', *Technology and Culture*, 7 (1996,) 36–69.

Temple, John, *History of the Origin and Progress of the Company of Watermen and Lightermen of the River Thames, Volume 5 1883–1920* (Lavenham Press, London, 2008).

Thacker, Fred. S., *Thames Highway. Volume I: General History* (Published 1914, Reprinted David & Charles, Newton Abbot, 1968).

Thane, Pat, *Old Age in English History. Past Experiences, Present Issues* (Oxford University Press, Oxford, 2000).

Thomas, P. N., *British Steam Tugs* (Waine Research, Wolverhampton, 1983).

Thompson, Paul, *Socialists, Liberals and Labour. The Struggle for London 1885–1914* (Routledge & Kegan Paul, London, 1967).

Tucker, Malcolm, 'St. Katharine Docks', *The Arup Journal*, 5 (1970), 10–19.

Tull, George J. D., *The Port of London Authority 1909–1959* (Unpublished, 1960).

Tully, John, 'A Victorian Ecological Disaster: Imperialism, the Telegraph, and Gutta-Percha', *Journal of World History*, 20 (2009), 559–79.

Vaughan, Adrian, *Samuel Morton Peto. A Victorian Entrepreneur* (Ian Allan Publishing, Hersham Surrey, 2009).

Ville, Simon P., *English Shipowning in the Industrial Revolution. Michael Henley and Son, London Shipowners, 1770–1830* (Manchester University Press, London, 1987).

Visram, Rozina, *Asians in Britain. 400 Years of History* (Pluto Press, London, 2002).

Watson, Bruce, 'The Last Days of Old London Bridge', in Bruce Watson, Trevor Brigham and Tony Dyson (eds.), *London Bridge: 2000 Years of a River Crossing, Museum of London Archaeology Service, Monograph 8* (Museum of London, London, 2001), 156–66.

Watts, Martin, *From Quern to Computer: The History of Flour Milling*, https://new.millsarchive.org/2016/09/06/from-quern-to-computer-the-history-of-flour-milling/

Webster, Anthony, *The Twilight of the East India Company. The Evolution of Anglo-Asian Commerce and Politics 1790–1860* (Boydell Press, Woodbridge, 2009).

White, Jerry, *London in the Nineteenth Century, A Human Awful Wonder of God* (Vintage Books, London, 2008).

White, Jerry, *London in the Eighteenth Century, A Great and Monstrous Thing* (Vintage Books, London, 2012).

Williams, David M., 'Merchanting in the First Half of the Nineteenth Century: The Liverpool Timber Trade', *Business History*, 8 (1968), 103–21.

Williams, David M., '"Advance Notes" and the Recruitment of Maritime Labour in Britain in the Nineteenth Century', in Lars U. Scholl, (ed.), *Merchants and Mariners: Selected Maritime Writings of David M. Williams* (IMEHA, St. John's Newfoundland, 2000), 253–72.

Williams, David M. and John Armstrong. 'An Appraisal of the Progress of the Steamship in the Nineteenth Century', in Gelina Harlaftis, Stig Tenold and Jesús M. Valdaliso, (eds.), *The World's Key Industry. History and Economics of International Shipping* (Palgrave Macmillan, Basingstoke, 2012), 43–63.

Wohl, Anthony S., *The Eternal Slum. Housing and Social Policy in Victorian London* (Edward Arnold, London, 1977).

Woods, Rebecca J. H., 'Breed, Culture and Economy: The New Zealand Frozen Meat Trade, 1880–1914', *Agricultural History Review*, 60 (2012), 288–308.

Wright, Charles and C. Ernest Fayle, *A History of Lloyd's* (Macmillan, London, 1928).

Theses

Channon, G. 'Pooling Agreements Between the Railway Companies Involved in Anglo-Scottish Traffic, 1851–1869', Doctoral Thesis, University of London, 1975.

Cole, Thomas J., 'Life and Labor in the Isle of Dogs: The Origins and Evolution of an East London Working-Class Community, 1800–1980', Doctoral Thesis, University of Oklahoma, 1984.

Dixon, Conrad 'Seamen and the Law: An Examination of the Impact of Legislation on the British Merchant Seaman's Lot, 1588–1918, Doctoral Thesis, University College London, 1981.

Ellmers, Christopher, 'Littoral, River and Sea – Exploring the Maritime History of Deptford, 1700–1850', Doctoral Thesis, University of Portsmouth, 2020.

Forrester, Robert Edward 'The General Steam Navigation Company c.1850–1913: A Business History', Doctoral Thesis, University of Greenwich, 2006.

Franklin, Alexandra 'Enterprise and advantage: The West India Interest in Britain 1774–1840', Doctoral Thesis, University of Pennsylvania, 1992.

Freeman, M. Diane, 'A History of Corn Milling, c.1750–1914, With Special Reference to South Central and South Eastern England', Doctoral Thesis, University of Reading, 1976.

Heaton Page, Reginald A, 'The Dock Companies of London 1796–1864' MA Thesis, University of Sheffield, 1959.

Jones, Graham G., 'Victorian Suburban Society, A Study of Deptford and Lewisham', Doctoral Thesis, Birkbeck College, 1980.

Kennerley, Alston 'British Seamen's Missions and Sailors' Homes 1815–1970, Voluntary Welfare Provision for Serving Seafarers', Doctoral Thesis, Polytechnic South West, 1989.

Marlow, Laurence, 'The Working Men's Club Movement 1862–1912: A Study of the Evolution of a Working Class Institution', Doctoral Thesis, University of Warwick, 1980.

Marriott, John Wesley, 'London Over the Border: A Study of West Ham During Rapid Growth, 1840–1910', Doctoral Thesis, University of Cambridge, 1984.

McIlvenna, Kathleen Francis, 'From the Civil List to Deferred Pay: the British Government, Superannuation and Pensions 1810–1909', Doctoral Thesis, Institute of Historical Research, University of London, 2019.

Moher, James Gerard 'The London Millwrights and Engineers 1775–1825', Doctoral Thesis, Royal Holloway and New Bedford College, 1988.

Palmer, Sarah, 'The Character and Organisation of the Shipping Industry of the Port of London 1815–1849', Doctoral Thesis, London School of Economics & Political Science, 1979.

Sweeting, Spike, 'Capitalism, The State and Things: The Port of London, circa 1730–1800', Doctoral Thesis, University of Warwick, 2014.

Wheble, Cecil Llewellyn, 'The London Lighterage Trade: Its History Organisation and Economics', MSc Thesis, London School of Economics & Political Science, 1939.

Windscheffel, Alex Christian, 'Villa Toryism? The Making of London Conservatism, 1868–1896', Doctoral Thesis, Royal Holloway, University of London, 2000.

Index

Aberdeen, 52, 117
Aberdeen Steam Navigation
    Company, 152
accidents, 49
Acts of Parliament
    Grand Surrey Docks and Canal
        Company, 40
    Labour Exchange (1909), 259
    London Bridge (1823), 100
    Merchant Shipping (1854), 246
    Port of London (1908), 262
    Public Health (1872), 245
    Warehousing (1803), 95
    West India Dock (1799), 103
Adam and Robertson, 51–2
Addington, Henry PM, 59
Admiral Gardner, 59
Admiralty, 52, 103, 126, 128, 130, 217,
    242, 249, 253, 257
Aird and Kelk, 158
Alexander, Daniel, 43–5, 48, 54–5
anchor smiths, 123, 136
Annual Statements of Trade and
    Navigation and subsequent Annual
    Statements of Trade, 165n71
Antwerp, 114, 116, 166, 255–6
Argo, 59
Armstrong, John, 149
Armstrong, William, 182
Askwith, George, 261
Asquith, Herbert MP, 256
Australia, 123, 171, 206, 220
Austrian Lloyd Steam Navigation
    Company, 173
Ayrton, Acton Smee MP, 158

Balfour, Gerald MP, 253–4
ballast, 20, 68, 96, 104, 152, 193, 246
ballast heavers, 138, 193
Baltic Exchange, 111, 122, 125
Bank of England, 41, 55, 63, 107, 253
Barber, Joseph, 114

barges, 16, 21, 75, 110, 119, 128, 154,
    156, 161, 163, 165, 179, 181, 224,
    244, 246–7
Baring, John, 2nd Baron Revelstoke, 250
Baynes, Sir Christopher, 53
Bazalgette, Edward, 175
Beames, Thomas, 136, 234
Bennet & Hunt, 65
Bermondsey, 15, 111, 126n24, 138, 225
Besant, Walter, 239
Betts, Edward Ladd, 155–6, 183
Beveridge, William, 212
Bidder, George, 155–6, 184
Billingsgate, 20
Bird, James, 2–3
Birt, George, 158, 185, 189, 202
Blackwall, 15, 15n10, 29, 36–8, 57, 67,
    92, 120, 120n129, 123, 123n7,
    126–9, 129n41, 132, 156n28, 185,
    214, 216, 227
Blenkarn, John, 106
Board of Trade, 32, 54, 103, 103n40,
    102n41, 156n31, 169n82, 181,
    183n14, 193n52, 201, 202n85,
    236–8, 236n130, 237n134, 242,
    244–5, 247n15, 248, 250, 253,
    255, 256n49, 257–61. *See also*
    British Government
    merchant shipping legislation, 236
    shipping offices, 5, 233, 236–8
Boarding Houses, 15, 121, 139, 142–4,
    233–5. *See also* lodgings
Bolt, Thomas, 21, 97
Bolton & Pixton, 49
Bombay, 247, 250–1, 253
Booth, Charles, 195, 201, 211, 218, 226,
    230–2, 239
Boulogne, 116
Boulton & Watt, 51
Bramah & Sons, 66
Brassey, Thomas, 155–6, 183
Bristol, 5, 13, 25–6, 85, 177n122, 242n5

Printed in the United States
by Baker & Taylor Publisher Services